SPEAKING ABOUT TORTURE

Speaking about Torture

Edited by

JULIE A. CARLSON AND ELISABETH WEBER

FORDHAM UNIVERSITY PRESS

New York 2012

Frontispiece: John Nava, *Signing Statement Law or An Alternate Set of Procedures*, oil on canvas, 41 × 41 inches, from the series "Neo-Icons," 2006. Courtesy of the artist and Sullivan Goss—An American Gallery.

Fordham University Press has no responsibility for the persistence or accuracy of URLs for external or third-party Internet websites referred to in this publication and does not guarantee that any content on such websites is, or will remain, accurate or appropriate.

Fordham University Press also publishes its books in a variety of electronic formats. Some content that appears in print may not be available in electronic books.

Library of Congress Cataloging-in-Publication Data

Speaking about torture / edited by
Julie A. Carlson and Elisabeth Weber. — 1st ed.

p. cm.
Includes bibliographical references (p.   ) and index.
ISBN 978-0-8232-4224-5 (cloth : alk. paper) —
ISBN 978-0-8232-4225-2 (pbk. : alk. paper)

1. Torture in literature. 2. Torture in mass media.
I. Carlson, Julie Ann, 1955– II. Weber, Elisabeth, 1959–

PN56.T62S64 2012

809'.93355—dc23   2012002863

Printed in the United States of America
14 13 12   5 4 3 2 1
First edition

CONTENTS

ACKNOWLEDGMENTS

We thank the College of Letters and Sciences at UC Santa Barbara for selecting "Torture and the Future" for the Critical Issues in America lecture series in 2007, and especially David Marshall, the Dean of Humanities and Fine Arts, for his generous support of this project. We thank co-convener Lisa Hajjar for her initial vision and ongoing counsel, as well as committee members Roman Baratiak, Peter Bloom, Giles Gunn, and Nancy Kawalek. We thank our contributors for making the process of moving from live event to printed text an enlivening experience, and we thank Helen Tartar, the external reviewers, and the editorial staff at Fordham University Press for their endorsement of this volume and of the value of the humanities. We thank Charlotte Becker for her keen eye in helping us prepare the manuscript for publication.

The launching of any book evokes prospects whose structure of hope is embedded in the nature of writing. The prospect associated with ours is deeply imperiled. In that recognition, we mobilize our best things, including words, and dedicate this effort with love to David and Ruben Saatjian.

Speaking about Torture

For the Humanities

Julie A. Carlson and Elisabeth Weber

In his introduction to the collection *Poems from Guantánamo: The Detainees Speak*, published in 2007 by American and British lawyers who represent *pro bono* detainees of the camp, Marc Falkoff makes an observation, the implications of which underlie the impulse for this volume to speak about torture from the perspective of the humanities. Noting that the collection does not offer a "complete portrait of the poetry composed at Guantánamo, largely because many of the detainees' poems were destroyed or confiscated before they could be shared with the authors' lawyers," Falkoff lists as a second inhibiting factor the Pentagon's refusal to allow the publication of most of the existing detainees' poems on the grounds that poetry "presents a special risk" to national security because of its "content and format"—the ostensible fear being that "detainees will try to smuggle coded messages out of the prison camp." In addition, he writes that "most of the poems that *have* been cleared are in English translation only, because the Pentagon believes that their original Arabic or Pashto versions represent an enhanced security risk." As pertains to their translation, then, these poems are rendered in English by linguists whose special competency as translators of poetry resides in their "secret-level security clearances," and thus the translations "cannot do justice to the subtlety and cadence of the originals."[1]

Leaving aside for the moment the question of how words "do justice" to the experiences about which these detainees speak, we wish to pause over the significance of these *Poems from Guantánamo* and the admission by Pentagon officials that they present "a special risk" to national security for the clarity with which they pose the question of the centrality of literature to the sustainability of human rights and their legislation, especially of those "'harder' human rights" such as the right not to be tortured.[2] The fact of their existence is noteworthy, given the paucity of texts written by survivors of torture, especially before full-scale liberation. This is partly because, as Elaine Scarry contends, the experience of pain radically reduces a person's ability and desire to speak, and, as theorists of trauma have shown, traumatic encounters annihilate the capacity to fully represent those encounters.[3] It is also because, as suggested above, these poets are considered highly suspect (non) persons, and thus their writings are subjected to enhanced versions of the techniques of silencing characteristically applied to subversive texts. Such methods include censorship that ranges from the destruction of texts to heavily redacted versions to framing devices that orient the reader in certain ways and translations whose primary task is eradication of the language and culture of origin,[4] as well as claims to the originality, autonomy, and value of its speakers.

Yet these detainees speak, and in a medium—poetry—that accommodates the limits that experiences of torture and trauma foreground. Through figuration, indirection, non-sense-making semiotic and affective processes, poetic discourse has long been said to grant space and even sanctuary to what precisely cannot be captured by *logos*.[5] At the same time, because *these* poems appear in security-grade English translations, they speak most audibly to the kinds of limit that institutional power imposes onto the ontological limits posed by torture. "The military, for instance, confiscated nearly all twenty-five thousand lines of poetry composed by Shaikh Abdurraheem Muslim Dost, returning to him only a handful upon his release from Guantánamo."[6] Assuming that media of transmission are not external to history and its representations, the American authorities, by disappearing the original languages of these poems and by classifying them as an "enhanced security risk," attest to one of the *structural* conditions of witnessing: the fundamental possibility of untranslatability.

The remarkable admission, that the country that has at its disposal arguably the most technically advanced security apparatus sees itself threatened by the medium poem, especially the medium poem that is written in Arabic or Pashto—in other words, in languages whose potential of secret codes is deemed uncontrollable—signals some of what literature and humanistic endeavor bring to the project of legislating against torture: providing modes of witness that, through their powers of insinuation, may not be withstood. Of course, the admission is also remarkable because public discourse on torture as well as on the humanities generally proceeds from the opposite assumption: namely, that hermetic figurations of poetry and poststructural humanistic discourses distract and detract from consideration of urgent, "real world" policy issues such as torture, which is why such issues are best left in the hands of social scientists, political theorists, and military, legal, and government officials. We disagree. The essays in this volume explore how torture and humanist discourses each draw precise attention to the forms and histories of mastery, domination, and misrecognition lodged within concepts of truth. Consequently, we believe that efforts to address the long, though not continuous, history of justifying recourse to torture on the grounds of its capacity to uncover or extract truth from subjects deemed existentially untrustworthy require incorporating into policy discussions on torture the reconceptualizations of subjectivity, opposition, law, and representation that it has been the constant effort of humanist discourse, especially post-1945, to pursue.

One consequence of finding ourselves in the startling situation where we are once again forced to entertain debates regarding the legality of torture is how those debates bring back for discussion long-standing linkages between torture and truth that, one would have thought, have since been discredited. Of course, the terms have changed (from "torture" to "enhanced interrogation techniques" and from "confession" to "actionable intelligence"), as has the absolutism of the endorsement, as evident in the "lesser evil view of torture" affirmed by most consequentialists and some conflicted absolutists. Still, as Lisa Hajjar notes, the post-9/11 response of Bush administration officials to "legaliz[e] practices that constitute torture" is based on claims that bear striking resemblance to the "rationales and legitimizing presumptions for torture in ancient and pre-modern regimes": namely, shared "ideas about the efficacious relationship between torture and truth, and the torturability of certain kinds of people."[7] Debunking the linkage need not proceed on philosophical principles; indeed, one measurable advance over ancient and premodern justifications is the way that heightened awareness of the special relation between torture and marginalized or disenfranchised persons grants cause for skepticism regarding the truth claims ascribed to torture—a point that links social scientific to humanist lines of inquiry.[8] A second approach appears even more pragmatic in posing to consequentialists and conflicted absolutists the question simply of whether torture works. Here Hajjar seconds conclusions reached by Alfred McCoy, Darius Rejali, Mark Danner, and others in stating that "if accurate intelligence is the goal and torture is the means, the record is abysmal"; moreover, "if legal justice is the goal, torture fouls the process and might make it difficult or impossible to prosecute suspects."[9] In sum, abundant new empirical evidence and firsthand accounts from US prisons and black sites affirm that "torture is inefficacious, that its use is not containable, and that its consequences are unremittingly adverse at home and abroad. Torture is not lesser: like gangrene, it can only destroy and spread."[10]

Writers in our volume support the contention that torture does not work, for the above reasons. However, we also enlist many of the philosophical concept words that have been devised to address global atrocities stemming from absolutist or totalizing thought systems, because we contend that such concept words are relevant to the analysis of the current situation, germane to our responsibilities as scholars, and generative of practices of resistance. Thought might be called here to embody "that which is maintained in a certain necessary relationship with the structural limits of mastery"[11]—in other words, to pursue a "hauntology" rather than an "ontology."[12] It is little exaggeration to say that many of the terms created to think conditions of "being" post-1945 remark on the experience of torture: hauntology, the barred subject, the *différend*, bare, precarious, and/or grievable life. As is well known, such terms bespeak the partiality of assertions of wholeness, oneness, universality, integrity, and the sociopsychic dimensions of their strategies of conscious exclusion. They register as well the interconnections between hauntology and social death in regarding categories of subject that the state marks from the start for death and as dead.[13] One of the theoretical models for pursuing the issues at stake can be found in the trauma theory of the last two decades, which is deeply marked by such a "hauntology" and which takes its point of departure in the decision to take seriously the disappearance of the victim—i.e., the elimination of the witness. The recent affective turn in the humanities and social sciences can be seen as struggling to find a language for what remains of this elimination before and beyond language.[14]

According to survivor of Nazi torture death camps Jean Améry, the true purpose of torture is to drive the victim "beyond the border of death into nothingness," which is why for Améry the transgression that torture represents is indelible.[15] On the concrete policy level, this dimension of transgression is clearly marked in the category of "unlawful enemy combatants" used by the US administration in the so-called war on terror—for example, to designate the prisoners in Guantánamo Bay. This category reflects transgression in the sense given above insofar as it is a euphemism for stripping the detainees of any legal existence, a violation that is particularly flagrant for a group of men whose status can only be properly referred to by using a word created during Argentina's "Dirty War": the disappeared. The name given to these highly secret prisoners held in "black sites" whose locations are unknown to anyone but CIA operatives, "ghost detainees," underlines their extra-legal status and echoes Améry's assessment of the true purpose of torture.[16] As a consequence, we need to think "this fearful thing: the *possibility* of annihilation, the *virtual* disappearance of the witness."[17] For Derrida, the acknowledgment of the possibility of such elimination of the witness is the very *condition* for responsible witnessing, even "the only condition for bearing witness, its only condition of possibility as condition of its impossibility—paradoxical and aporetic."[18]

This is essential for a "hauntology": The elimination of the witness, the traumatic interruption of self-presence, of what is commonly called "presence of mind," make the "structural limits of mastery" blatantly visible. But it is precisely this presence of mind that Occidental courts consider to be the condition of possibility of reliable testimony.[19] The discrepancy between the institutional recognition of the so-called eyewitness, whose presence (of mind) at the (crime) scene is given so much significance by the courts on the one hand, and, on the other, the highly problematic status of the victim, whose presence of mind was assaulted, undermined, and possibly destroyed by the trauma he or she suffered, and who frequently suffered her or his ordeal blindfolded, makes the possibility of rendering justice a travesty if courts do not devise different modes of literally representing the victim. The fact that during the Cold War sensory deprivation was developed by leading American and Canadian scientists as the torture method of choice because, as "stealth torture" or "clean torture," it does not leave any visible traces or scars, confirms this discrepancy as one of the very principles of torture.[20] As Darius Rejali, quoting Veena Das, explains, "'in the register of the imaginary, the pain of the other not only asks for a home in language, but also seeks a home in the body.' Stealth torture," Rejali continues, "denies precisely this home in the body, tangling the victims and their communities in doubts, uncertainties, and illusions. . . . The inexpressibility that matters politically is not the gap between the brain and the tongue, but between victims and their communities, a gap that is cynically calculated, a gap that shelters a state's legitimacy."[21] Idelber Avelar makes a similar point in arguing that "torture produces a world in which one can no longer be a witness, since the very act of imagining the other, the very postulation of a 'you' has been cancelled in advance."[22]

Derrida's statement on Paul Celan, that "all responsible witnessing engages in a poetic experience of language,"[23] is thus highly relevant for our context insofar as it marks the potential of one of the areas of humanistic inquiry: the engagement, in literature, with a singular experience of language that is poetic insofar as it *creates* language. Literature responds to the irreducible singularity of the experience of suffering with the creation "de novo" of a language[24] to give it a voice outside of a truth claim that requires generalizability, but also, *at the same time*, outside the reduction to unspeakability—i.e., absolute singularity that would make itself heard only in the cry or the moan in which language is silenced. Literature attempts, in Toni Morrison's formulation, "to shape a silence while breaking it."[25] It strives not to find a compromise or middle way between, on the one hand, the reduction to utter silence, and, on the other, the claim to the "healing" power of words, but rather to assert a faithfulness, aporetic and paradoxical, to both: to acknowledge the always possible reduction to utter silence as the condition of possibility for a language both singular and readable. It does this by crafting words that circumvent the concepts that make the representation and litigation of torture impossible, such as presence and self-presence, truth and fact. It thereby provides precisely those modes of "representation" (now in a different sense than that of "making present") that offer ways to move beyond the arrest and repetitions of trauma, without indulging the fantasy of reconciliation and healing.

Two excerpts from *Poems from Guantánamo*, despite and because of the heavily censored context and form in which they emerge, allow us to suggest how this volume, in shaping a silence without breaking it, understands "poetry" as better bespeaking the "truth" that subordinated subjects speak to "power." They also demarcate opposing representational strategies and belief systems between which essays in our volume range in their various confrontations with the limits that torture sets to both legal and aesthetic representation and to attaining legal or poetic justice. The first example devolves from paratextual information that paradoxically brings into focus Derrida's claim that the feared potential of the "verbal body" is, indeed, fundamental and *structural*, and that the threat posed by the "inexhaustible" reserve of the code extends to the best-known verses of one's mother tongue.[26] The British citizen Moazzam Begg, who was "arrested in Pakistan and detained for three years in Guantánamo," and who is interviewed in the films *The Road to Guantánamo*, *Taxi to the Dark Side*, and *Outside the Law: Stories from Guantánamo*, received one day a "heavily censored letter from his seven-year-old daughter," in which "the only legible line was 'I love you, Dad.'" Never charged with a crime, Begg was released in 2005. "Upon his release, his daughter told him the censored lines were a poem she had copied for him: 'One, two, three, four, five, / Once I caught a fish alive. / Six, seven, eight, nine, ten / Then I let it go again.'"[27] Apparently, a children's verse became here an unbearable security risk for the jailors. The complete text of this counting verse is the following:

> One, two, three, four, five,
> Once I caught a fish alive.
> Six, seven, eight, nine, ten,
> Then I let it go again.
> Why did you let it go?
> Because it bit my finger so.
> Which finger did it bite?
> The little one upon the right.

The medium *counting verse*, through which infants are introduced into language and encounter their bodies as theirs, the medium, then, that contributes to the process through which the infant learns the fictive integration of the stage of the "fragmented body" into the mirror image of the "total form of [the] body," this medium represents an intolerable security risk.[28] Born into an experience of utter fragmentation and lack of control of bodily functions, the infant achieves the fictive integrity of the body with and through the mediation of the other and his or her language.

The medium *counting verse* is exemplary for the medium *language* in the sense of medium defined by Wolf Kittler as a "space to which there is no outside."[29] In this medium the other's face, glance, and encouragement are all integral to the process of learning how to recognize, name, and tell apart what already "belongs" to one's own body—integral, then, to the infant's subject formation. At the same time, belonging is constituted in this medium as "be-longing," as an integration into the community that is constitutively *open* toward the other.[30] It is in this medium of constitutive openness that a fundamental trust in "the world" originates. According to Améry, who survived torture by the Nazis and detention in the Nazi death camp Auschwitz, torture destroys irreversibly this trust in the world—trust without which community founders (for both human and animal). Torture, one could say, undoes the formation of the subject as well as of the community, neither of which comes into being without the other—an entangled formation for which the medium counting verse is emblematic. Torture is the cruel undoing of the subject and, simultaneously, of his or her be-longing to different communities (family, culture, nation, humanity).

This undoing is alluded to in our second example, "Death Poem," by Jumah Al Dossari, who was released in 2007 to Saudi Arabia after having been held in detention for five years, three and a half of which were spent in isolation, without a formal charge ever brought against him.

Death Poem
Take my blood.
Take my death shroud and
The remnants of my body.
Take photographs of my corpse at the grave, lonely.
Send them to the world,
To the judges and
To the people of conscience,
Send them to the principled men and the fair-minded.
And let them bear the guilty burden, before the world,
Of this innocent soul.
Let them bear the burden, before their children and before history,
Of this wasted, sinless soul,
Of this soul which has suffered at the hands of the "protectors of
                                                          peace."[31]

The Arabic original may be under lock and key somewhere in the Washington, D.C., area, but even in English translation the poem attests to the "invincible singularity of the verbal body" and, unreconciled, gives voice in the register of a hauntology to what refuses to be said.

What is left unsaid pertains to the speaking subject of "my blood" and "the remnants of my body." What *is* said concerns the particular media of the torturer and executioner, those so-called "protectors of peace." Precisely these media are turned against their users. Whether the photographs that the poem commissions to be sent "to the world" refer to those sent via the Internet and other electronic media from Abu Ghraib cannot be established for certain. But for us readers, the connection cannot *not* be established, either. The burden of the executioner's guilt and the burden of the innocence of this "wasted soul" are together entrusted to or imposed on these photographs of infamy. In language inspired by the Suras of the Koran, they are said to carry the burden before history and before the children of those who have a conscience—as well as before the children of the perpetrators. Unreconciled, a voice speaks here not even from beyond the grave, but from *before* the grave: from a place in which a proper burial, epitome of a person's be-longing to a community, has not even yet been possible, if not made all but impossible ("take my death shroud"). What in the poem refuses to be said is the shame of the victim of torture: the shame that threatens to exclude him from his very own community, from his be-longing to this community.[32] However, through the photographs, the media of the perpetrators, this shame is brought openly before the entire world. If the poem's language leaves unsaid the shame of the torture victim, the language of the torturers, by contrast, and their self-characterization as the "protectors of peace" are belied—exposed, through their own media, to be absurdity.

Speaking about Torture originated in a series of twelve public events organized at the University of California, Santa Barbara, from January to May 2007 under the rubric "Torture and the Future." Our topic was that year's selection for the "Critical Issues in America" competitive lecture series sponsored by the College of Letters and Science. Designed to confront the facts that torture is a part and consequence of official US policy, that the media entertainment complex is invested in making torture an acceptable form of social containment, and that there is a "surprisingly widespread advocacy of state-sanctioned torture among American academics,"[33] our series sought to investigate, understand, and craft a response from the perspective of the humanities to the "US" and "us" that are complicit in such practices. The series included public lectures, a day-long international conference, art performance pieces, panel discussions, and a collaborating array of undergraduate and graduate courses. Not everyone who participated in the lecture series appears in this volume, and we wish to acknowledge their ongoing presence and influence in this debate, especially lawyers and human rights activists Scott Horton and Gita Gutierrez, former US Army Muslim Chaplain James Yee, and journalist-scholars Mark Danner and Darius Rejali, both also professors. In addition, professors Barbara Harlow and George Hunsinger participated in the day-long conference on "Torture and the Future," poets Alicia Portnoy and Gail Wronsky were keynote speakers at the graduate student-organized conference, and professors Myriam Chancy, Jody Enders, Avery Gordon, Russell Samolsky, Gabriela Schwab, Kaia Stern, and Jack Talbott conducted a discussion with students on strategies for teaching human rights. The essays in our volume by invited series participants (Dayan, Derwin, Eisenman, Falk, McCoy, Nava, Solomon-Godeau) and those commissioned from US and international scholars together present an array of reflections on how the arts and humanities address, redress, resist, and sanction the practice of torture. They indicate that the impulses behind the 2007 "Torture and the Future" series are no less pressing now, despite a US regime change and in light of intensified assaults on the humanities in the United States and around the world.

The essays that comprise *Speaking about Torture* are united in their efforts to up the "anti-" in policies regarding torture at the same time that they employ and evaluate strategies of "being anti-" enlisted by scholars who are skeptical of absolutist forms of thought. The essays share the convictions that torture does not work to elicit truth, secure justice, or maintain security, and that its work is to undermine the existence, sustainability, and grievability of speaking subjects. They engage in various ways with the limits that torture imposes: to language, on subjects and community, by governmental officials. Several essays focus on poems, visual media, and survivor accounts of torture and terrorizing incidents produced since 9/11 in Iraq, Iran, Gaza, and the United States; others enlist textual and visual depictions of past atrocities to mobilize resistance to contemporary torture and/or aesthetic representations of it. Some explore the responsibility of censorship for torture, while others hold saturation by media images and discussions responsible for public indifference in the United States. A couple essays call for an expansion of the judicial definition of torture in light, not only of its widespread practice, but also full-scale assault on the daily lives of subject peoples. As a whole, then, the essays analyze the "us" that is complicit in torture, as well as the "us" whose possibilities for living are radically curtailed through torture's terrorizing mechanisms and legacy, while at the same time working to weaken the us/them, West/East binaries so integral to the history of torture. Among other things, this means that our volume confronts the complicity of artists and humanists in torture, even as our volume also stakes a claim for the special relevance of artistic and humanist practice to a comprehension of torture that better augurs its eradication.[34]

Emphasizing this interaction works in a variety of ways. One approach taken by several essays is to offer analyses of literary texts and visual media critical of torture that are equally critical of certain artistic methods of representation for condoning torture. Given that the US public is hardly ignorant of the facts of torture, certainly after the widespread circulation of photographs from Abu Ghraib in April 2004, anti-torture advocates have to reckon with the various ways that art itself desensitizes people— positions them not to see the bodily and psychic torment of others. Humanist inquiry has long explored how aesthetic representation serves a politics of representation invested in maintaining dominant forms of power. Torture intensifies the stakes of this interconnection because (a) those traditionally silenced by Western culture, whether conceived as external or internal aliens, are frequently the targets of the existential silencing produced by or sought through torture; (b) recourse to aesthetic representation by Western anti-torture advocates is inherently suspect because of its illustrious history of denying voice, agency, or sympathy to such others; and (c) institutional and avant-garde media are as often agents of censorship as subject to it.

Not surprisingly, the realm of visual culture comes in for special scrutiny in these essays, owing to the long-standing philosophical relation of sight to masculinist forms of power and to the compromising merger of cultural and financial capital that undergirds the fine arts, museum culture, and the Hollywood film industry. Essays by Abigail Solomon-Godeau, Hamid Dabashi, Viola Shafik, and Stephen Eisenman variously pursue this charge, evaluating forms and venues of media in relation to their putative distance from repressive aesthetic, religious, and materialist practices. Surveying a range of artistic responses to post-9/11 torture, Solomon-Godeau considers to what extent their form contradicts the political work of these works and promotes the surrealist tactic of *détournement* as one way of seeing *through* what official images and representations seek to affirm. Eisenman effects a similar image exposure by showing how the long history of torture iconography trains viewers to see victims as accepting their own chastisement and destruction, a phenomenon that he suggests helps to explain lack of public outcry over waterboarding owing to its baptismal resonances. The "refusal of the image" finds its motivation in the rejection of the spectacle-like sensationalism of the Abu Ghraib visual archive. Dabashi compares the oversaturation of images of Abu Ghraib in the United States to an underexposure of Iranian responses to abuses at the Kahrizak prison in Tehran in order to showcase how both visual regimes aim at the same effect: erasing events from memory, a cover-up of reality, whether through benumbing or fear. Exploring a similar opposition in the treatment of torture by Hollywood and Middle Eastern films, Shafik finds an underlying consensus in their joint displacement of racial onto gendered antagonisms. The painter John Nava, while employing figural painting, equally avoids the risk of spectacle and voyeurism. His high school- or college-age subjects wear T-shirts recording the language of protest, but also the irresponsible language of the torture architects. They are somber reminders of the grim legacy with which the past (and present?) use of torture and its impunity are burdening particularly the future of today's young generations.[35]

A second approach explores poetic language in its capacity to go beyond representational impasses in two respects: through adherence to the potential untranslatability or singularity of witnessing and by facilitating modes of imaginative sympathy that actually respond to the other's reality or pain through effecting "uncoercive rearrangements of desire" that Gayatri Spivak claims only training in the humanities promises to achieve.[36] Several essays examine texts that shape a silence while breaking it in responding to Abu Ghraib, the Shoah, or the dirty wars in Argentina. Sinan Antoon translates and analyzes two poems by the "only two Iraqi poets" so far to publish poems about Abu Ghraib, in contrast to the "hundreds of articles and essays" published in the Arab world on the topic (not to mention the avalanche of US responses explored by Dabashi). His readings of Saadi Youssef's "The Wretched of the Heavens" and Sargon Bulus's "The Corpse" attend to the strategies they employ at once to affirm and bypass pain's resistance to language. Through close scrutiny of the textual fabric of Améry's *At the Mind's Limits*, Elisabeth Weber develops confirmation of the Derridian account of poetic witnessing by showing how Améry remaps the semantic field of the word *Verfleischlichung* to bespeak the "fleshization" unique to the experience of torture. That is, in contrast to the "Fleischwerdung" (the becoming flesh of God) articulated in the Gospel of John, Améry's poetic intervention depicts an incarnation devoid of any trace of spirit, suited to the living/dead experience of the torture victim. Weber and Susan Derwin, in her account of Primo Levi and Améry, pursue a related implication of torture's *Verfleischlichung*: the desolating solitude of this reduction-to-flesh that leaves the survivor, the ghosted one, no longer at home in the world. Each of these readings testifies to the always possible reduction to utter silence as the condition of possibility for a language both singular and readable.

This possibility, audible in Levi's haunting query, "if this is a man," links the capacity to communicate with an expectation of aid that is necessary for receptivity to alterity, a connection explored in various ways by Derwin, Reinhold Görling, and Colin Dayan. As Derwin and Görling explore, the mother-infant relation positions the mother as witness in ways that allow the child to learn to bear pain and to find him- or herself in a world that is intersubjective, made up by and through others, including through fantasy. For Görling, this "game of recognition," essential for negotiating human vulnerability, underlies the theatricality of culture and the various stagings through which persons are social and become socialized. This theatrical process of recognition is precisely what torture undoes, but also, as Görling demonstrates, what it enlists in designing its deculturalizing intents. Dayan explores one such unholy conflation in her reflection on Operation Cast Lead (late December 2008) in Gaza, whose name invokes a children's poem about a dreidel, one of those games through which language and be-longing are acquired. Peter Szendy and Christian Grüny explore another in their joint attention to the use of loud music, not merely loud noise, as a form of torture new to the post-9/11 scene. They pinpoint the particular devastation of this refinement on non-touch torture, where now the victim's mind, not only body, is turned into a weapon against itself. Owing to the patterned repetitions of music, these sounds come to sound as if they "want something," part of their want being eradication of the bare-minimal distancing available in the capacity to anticipate physical violence.

Such accounts, then, not only explore but also themselves make visible the aporetic stance of poetic witnessing: the creation of words and affective responses that can be said to address survival, even if, and as, they show themselves incapable of addressing survivors or speaking adequately on their behalf. This appeal to, and for, futurity is what Julie Carlson identifies in Percy Bysshe Shelley's defense of poetry, by which poetry's exercise of imagination strengthens not only the capacity but also the desire to expand a person's or culture's range of sympathy, an exercise that entails rigorous resistance to sentiment and sentimental fictions, chief among them the presumed humanity of love for one's biological family. Dayan and Darieck Scott variously deepen this insistence in their accounts of places where extraordinary violence is quotidian and where this fact is what makes such levels of violence seem "reasonable." Dayan asserts that for Palestinians living in Gaza, where the land itself becomes a prison and basic daily activities are designed to foster a "collapse of personality," retaining a strictly judicial definition of torture only perpetuates the terror—as instanced by Israeli and US dismissal of the Goldstone Commission that alleged war crimes against the population of the Gaza Strip in its report on Operation Cast Lead. Instead, Dayan favors Aimé Césaire's definition of torture as "the gigantic rape of everything intimate," a conclusion to which Carlson's reading of Shelley's *The Cenci*, in its linkage of sexual to state violence, also tends.

The validity of Césaire's definition is confirmed toward different ends by Scott's reading of Samuel Delany's violent and sexually explicit *Hogg* and the difficulties that Delany encountered in getting his novel published. "For nothing encourages the practice of political torture and sabotages the pursuit of happiness more"—here Scott quoting Delany—"than blanket restrictions on speaking, in precise, articulate, and graphic terms about either." As Scott and *Hogg* show, assessing the radical homelessness to which survivors are consigned requires recognizing the structural fit between violence and sexual fantasy activity as well as recognizing how societal arrangements foster victimization of its more vulnerable citizens—a lesson often first learned at home because one's vulnerability positions one as prey and because the impregnability of the home from violence is a fantasy. To refuse to acknowledge the appetite for torture is insane, which is why censorship serves its perpetuation. Richard Falk moves censorship closer to the institutional homes of academics in assessing the grounds for possible university sanctions against Professor John Yoo. Objecting to growing encroachments on academic freedom evident in the punitive treatment of professors like Ward Churchill, Falk contends that Yoo's support of the torture policies of the Bush presidency is safeguarded by academic freedom, but actionable on grounds relating to his duties as a professor of international law teaching the next generation of lawyers.

A primary mechanism by which everyday censorship is effected, Scott writes, is euphemism, a signifying capacity with enormous import to humanist responses to torture. As Hajjar's chronology of post-9/11 US torture-related activity makes clear, at every point borderline or outright illegal activities were authorized through changing the name by which they were called: from "torture" to "enhanced interrogation techniques," from "kidnapping" to "extraordinary rendition," from "citizen" to "unlawful enemy combatant," from "human" to "terrorist."[37] The other side of the ramifying, disseminative powers of poetic language, euphemism works to clamp down, lock down possibilities, to avow, by disavowing (and vice versa), the iron hand of the law. This capacity to disavow, facilitated by the public's media-induced amnesia, is how, according to Alfred McCoy, torture debates stay mired in impunity—the situation we are in now under the Obama administration. McCoy offers the "most elemental tool" of the discipline of history, chronology, as an antidote to this oblivion by displaying a pattern of recurrence of CIA torture that is the first step toward preventing future occurrences.

Euphemism is often viewed as a fairly harmless, at times even humane, way of depicting a harsh reality in less offensive terms. However, its use has created a situation in which US national security has been rendered insecure in its very legal foundations and where prosecuting crimes against humanity is now on shakier grounds in the United States than ever. As public defender and law professor David Feige asserted in the debate (in late 2009) around whether admitted 9/11 mastermind Khalid Sheikh Mohammed should be tried in a regular court, the "real price" of trying him in New York City, and not in front of a military commission, is the creation of "bad law." For if the jury convicts on the basis of information at least partially attained through torture, it sets a precedent that in effect endorses the violation of the least derogable law on the books.

[N]o matter how compelling the case for suppressing evidence that would actually effect the trial might be, given the politics at play, there is no judge in the country who will seriously endanger the prosecution. Instead, with the defense motions duly denied, the case will proceed to trial, and then (as no jury in the country is going to acquit KSM) to conviction and a series of appeals. . . . At each stage of the appellate process, a higher court will countenance the cowardly decisions made by the trial judge, ennobling them with the unfortunate force of precedent.[38] As of April 4, 2011, conducting trials of "high-level" detainees in civilian courts is no longer even an option. In sharp contrast to its announced policy to try September 11 suspects in civilian courts, the Obama administration was forced to yield to Congress' 2011 National Defense Authorization Act, which prohibits the use of US Defense Department funds to transfer detainees from Guantánamo Bay to the United States or other countries.[39] Then, on December 31, 2011, President Obama signed into law the National Defense Authorization Act of 2012, which the American Civil Liberties Union characterizes as authorizing "a sweeping worldwide indefinite detention provision" that could be used by sitting and future presidents "to militarily detain people captured far from any battlefield" as well as American citizens captured on American soil. Obama signed the bill "despite having serious reservations with certain provisions that regulate the detention, interrogation, and prosecution of suspected terrorists"; Scott Horton deems the measure "the 'Gitmo Forever' Act."[40]

In light of these rulings and legal setbacks, the harmfulness of indulging in euphemism is placed in stark relief. Whether we can resecure our anti-torture foundations is difficult to say. At a minimum, doing so requires respecting the difficulties of language and truth that are hallmarks of inquiry in the humanities.

PART ONE

America Tortures

CHAPTER I

An Assault on Truth:
A Chronology of Torture,
Deception, and Denial

Lisa Hajjar

"Actionable intelligence" is a euphemism for information that has use-value for the protection of national security interests. At first glance, *actionable intelligence* seems to lack one key characteristic of a euphemism: its elaborated meaning does not refer to something disagreeable or offensive, because gathering information to ensure public safety is a legitimate government function. But the means of eliciting intelligence (actionable or other) is not legitimately unlimited, and this phrase's disagreeable characteristics become apparent in the "war on terror" lexicon, where it has been coupled with the torture and abuse of prisoners, the abuse euphemized as "enhanced interrogation methods."

Officials who seek to push or disregard the limits of legal and legitimate behavior are often inclined to euphemize.[1] On *Meet the Press* on September 16, 2001, five days after the 9/11 terrorist attacks, Vice President Dick Cheney said: "We'll have to work . . . the dark side, if you will. We've got to spend time in the shadows in the intelligence world. A lot of what needs to be done here will have to be done quietly, without any discussion, using sources and methods that are available to our intelligence agencies—if we are going to be successful. . . . [I]t's going to be vital for us to use any means at our disposal . . . to achieve our objectives." Cheney's references to quiet doings and lack of discussion euphemized the secrecy and unaccountability that became hallmarks of the Bush administration.

The following day, September 17, President George W. Bush signed a memorandum of understanding granting the CIA authority to establish a secret detention and interrogation operation overseas. On September 26 Cofer Black, a US counterterrorism expert, testified in Congress that there "was a before 9/11 and an after 9/11, and after 9/11 the gloves came off." The "gloves off" euphemism, along with Cheney's "working the dark side" and using "any means at our disposal" signaled rather succinctly that decision makers were operating on the assumption that violent and dehumanizing interrogation methods would elicit actionable intelligence—in other words, that torture can produce truth, and this truth would keep Americans safe.

By December 2001, Pentagon officials were exploring how to "reverse engineer" SERE (survival, evasion, resistance, extraction) techniques that had been developed during the Cold War to train US soldiers to withstand torture in case they were captured by regimes that don't adhere to the Geneva Conventions. The Clinton-era rendition program (i.e., sending detainees captured abroad to foreign states for trial) was revamped as "extraordinary rendition" to permit the CIA to kidnap people from anywhere in the world and disappear them into secret prisons, euphemized as "black sites," where they could be held as "ghost detainees" (i.e., with no record of their identities or whereabouts and no access to monitors from the International Committee of the Red Cross) or transferred extra-legally to other states for interrogation.

Cheney and his legal counsel David Addington took charge of the Bush administration's interrogation and detention policies,[2] which were varnished with opinions by lawyers in the Justice Department's Office of Legal Counsel (OLC), most prominently Berkeley law professor John Yoo, who served as deputy assistant attorney general from 2001 to 2003. They devised a "new paradigm"[3] based on a radical interpretation of Article 2 of the Constitution, according to which the president, as commander in chief, has unfettered powers to wage war, and therefore efforts to constrain executive discretion in accordance with federal, military or international law would be unconstitutional.

On November 13, 2001, President Bush issued a military order declaring that captured terror suspects were "unlawful combatants," a heretofore nonexistent category[4] conceived to place such prisoners outside of the law by claiming that they are neither combatants nor civilians and thus not privy to the standards of treatment of either. Anyone taken into US custody could be designated an unlawful combatant by presidential fiat rather than on the basis of any status review by a tribunal, and could be held incommunicado indefinitely. Bush also declared that such detainees could be prosecuted in a new kind of military commission whose rules would admit coerced confessions, hearsay, and secret evidence.

On January 11, 2002, the first "unlawful combatants" captured abroad were transported to the detention facility at the US naval base in Guantánamo Bay (GTMO) on the island of Cuba.[5] They were denounced as "the worst of the worst," and trophy photos of them in stress positions (i.e., bound and immobilized in physically straining positions) and sensory deprivation gear (i.e., padded mittens, ear muffs, and goggles) were released for media publication. The plan for GTMO was to interrogate detainees for as long as and in whatever manner was deemed necessary to elicit actionable intelligence. GTMO had been selected because it was far from the hot war zone of Afghanistan and, more importantly, according to the new paradigmers, it was beyond the reach of US courts. But as a military facility holding people captured in what the government itself characterized as a "war," White House counsel Alberto Gonzales advised the president that he should *declare* that the Geneva Conventions do not apply because "[i]t is difficult to predict the motives of prosecutors and independent counsels who may in the future decide to pursue unwarranted [war crimes] charges."

On February 7, 2002, President Bush issued a secret memorandum to his national security team endorsing the claim that the Geneva Conventions are too "quaint" to apply to this novel form of global war against stateless enemies, and asserted that captured terror suspects have no legal rights, but would be treated humanely as "a matter of policy," with the caveat that interrogation and detention policy would prioritize "military necessity." The State Department had sharply criticized the legal flaws and political dangers of disregarding the Geneva Conventions, arguing that this would violate US treaty obligations, contradict military doctrine, damage military discipline and, when exposed, might turn the American public against the war. This criticism was ignored.

Interrogators working in Afghanistan were under intense pressure from Washington for actionable intelligence about al-Qaeda and the Taliban, especially the whereabouts of Osama bin Laden and his top lieutenants, who had eluded military capture during the battle of Tora Bora.[6] Information was elicited from whoever wound up in US custody, which included fighters captured on the battlefields or fleeing military strikes and other men and boys who were picked up in sweeps through villages, sold to the US for bounty, or turned over by allied Afghan warlords or the Pakistani security services. Because most US interrogators lacked the requisite language skills and knowledge about the region to accurately assess the intelligence value of detainees or the veracity of their statements, the tendency was to err on the side of caution in determining who should be shipped off to GTMO for more intensive and protracted interrogation. The suspicions and uncertainties that put prisoners onto planes bound for Cuba became, in flight and by order of the president, an uncontestable presumption of guilt.

At GTMO, intelligence officers were instructed to fill out a one-page form on every detainee certifying the president's "reason to believe" that he was involved in terrorism. Within weeks, the officers began reporting back that interrogations were not producing the information needed to fill out the forms. Pentagon and White House officials assumed the problem was that these hardened terrorists had been trained to resist and dissemble. But when a senior Arabic-speaking CIA analyst was dispatched to GTMO in August 2002 to do an assessment of the detainees, he concluded that at least half and probably a much higher percentage had no ties to or meaningful information about al-Qaeda or the Taliban. He recommended a formal review process to determine who should be released and repatriated, and noted that continued imprisonment and interrogation of innocent people could constitute war crimes. John Bellinger, then serving as the National Security Agency's top lawyer, scheduled a meeting with Gonzales to discuss the analyst's recommendations, but Addington canceled the meeting, declaring: "No, there will be no review. The President has determined that they are ALL enemy combatants. We are not going to revisit it."[7]

In the division of interrogational labor, the CIA was vested with primary responsibility for "high-value detainees" (HVDs)—people assumed to be terrorist leaders or planners of 9/11 or to have knowledge about terrorist operations and plots. On March 28, 2002, the first HVD, Abu Zubaydah (nom du guerre for Zayn al-Abidin Muhammad), was captured in Pakistan and transported to a black site in Thailand. The escalating harshness of Abu Zubaydah's treatment was due to interrogators' frustration that he was not providing the actionable intelligence he was assumed to possess. But contrary to the initial claim that he was a "top al-Qaeda strategist," in fact he was more like a receptionist who had been responsible for moving people in and out of training camps in Afghanistan (which is why he had been named by others under interrogation), and he had not even affiliated himself with al-Qaeda until after the US declared war on Afghanistan (i.e., after 9/11).

The brutal and dehumanizing methods authorized for Abu Zubaydah, which included waterboarding him eighty-three times and placing him in a coffin-like "confinement box," set the stage for the CIA's secret interrogation program. By mid-summer 2002, some agents were growing anxious about their vulnerability to future prosecution under federal laws. In response to the agency's questions about legal liability for torture, the OLC produced two memos dated August 1, 2002. One of these memos interpreted the applicable definition of *physical torture* to exclude anything less than "the pain accompanying serious physical injury, such as organ failure, impairment of bodily function, or even death," and opined that cruel, inhuman, or degrading treatment would not constitute *mental torture* unless it caused effects that lasted "months or even years." The second memo provided legal cover for tactics already in use.

Although these OLC memos were written for the CIA, the White House forwarded them to the Pentagon, which was seeking a solution to military interrogators' frustrated efforts to get actionable intelligence out of GTMO detainees, especially Muhammad al-Qahtani, alleged to be the twentieth 9/11 hijacker. A three-course menu of reverse-engineered SERE tactics was authorized by Secretary of Defense Donald Rumsfeld in December 2002. When top lawyers in the Judge Advocate General (JAG) corps vetted this policy document, they wrote memos to Rumsfeld protesting that the use of tactics that contravene the Uniform Code of Military Justice (which enshrines the Geneva Conventions) would expose soldiers to the risk of court martial. On March 14, 2003, Yoo sent a memo to the Pentagon's general counsel (reproducing the reasoning in the first August 1 memo), which was used to silence the JAGs' dissent.

This confluence of radical legal reasoning and the ideologically driven presumptions that all detainees are terrorists and that torture is effective in obtaining actionable intelligence meant that US military interrogators, CIA agents, and government-hired contractors were, in effect, licensed by the Bush administration to utilize methods that were no longer regulated by the laws of this nation or the world. But the Bush administration never officially authorized "torture." Rather, "torture" became the euphemism for anything that was *not* authorized by the US government. What *was* authorized included stripping prisoners naked; short-shackling them to the floor for protracted periods of time, which forced them to defecate and urinate on themselves; subjecting prisoners to days or weeks of sleep deprivation by bombarding them with constant light and/or excruciatingly loud music or grating sounds and/or extremes in temperature; weeks, months, or even years of isolation; stress positions such as "long-time standing," a euphemism for forcing prisoners to stand for many hours without moving, sometimes with arms extended outward; "wall hanging" prisoners from hooks on the wall or ceiling; "walling," which referred to bashing prisoners into walls; and waterboarding to induce the feeling and fear of death by drowning.

Through the end of 2002, the public knew very little about the Bush administration's interrogation policies or the legal rationales justifying them. The preoccupying issue of public debate was the hypothetical ticking-bomb scenario in which interrogators know with absolute certainty that the person in custody has information needed to defuse a deadly bomb that is set to explode, and the question is what can be done to force this recalcitrant all-knowing terrorist to speak the truth that will save thousands of innocent lives.[8] Harvard law professor Alan Dershowitz made a distinctive contribution to public debate by proposing that American judges be empowered to issue "torture warrants" in order to bring torture "within the law." He also offered a tactical suggestion: sterilized needles under the fingernails in order to achieve "maximal pain, minimum lethality." Dershowitz and other proponents of "torture lite," a euphemism for non-maiming interrogational violence, were not suggesting that the American government should forsake the principle that torture is illegal, but rather that the principle could be suspended in the "war on terror" on the grounds that torture is a "lesser evil" and that terrorists have no right not to be tortured.

The first substantive information about US interrogation practices appeared in a December 26, 2002, *Washington Post* article by Dana Priest and Barton Gellman. Unnamed officials revealed that, in the drive for actionable intelligence, security agents were utilizing "stress and duress" tactics—a euphemism-on-euphemism reference to stress positions, "environmental manipulations," and other means of producing "debility, disorientation and dread." The article also reported that detainees who could not be broken by such methods might be given mind-altering drugs or extraordinarily rendered to the custody of foreign governments, including those with well-established records of torture such as Egypt, Jordan, and Morocco. According to Priest and Gellman, "While the US government publicly denounces the use of torture, each of the current national security officials interviewed for this article defended the use of violence against captives as just and necessary. They expressed confidence that the American public would back their view."

Pentagon and White House officials, having secretly concluded that authorized tactics did not constitute "torture," responded to questions about reports of prisoner abuse with "we don't torture" answers, in a manner that sociologist Stanley Cohen characterized as "interpretive denial."[9]

Another example of interpretative denial appeared in mid-2003: when the number of the attempted suicides at GTMO reached 32, officials reclassified them as "manipulative self-injurious behavior."[10]

The Bush administration's decision to take the "war on terror" to Iraq had to be sold to the American public and skeptical allies. In early 2003 CIA and military interrogators were under intense pressure to produce evidence that the regime of Saddam Hussein had an *active* weapons of mass destruction (WMD) program, and that there was a link between Iraq and 9/11. The "actionable intelligence" that the administration presented to make the case for war included claims about Iraq's attempts to import tons of yellowcake uranium from Niger and a statement by a Libyan prisoner, Ibn al-Shaykh al-Libi, that Iraq had provided training in chemical weapons to members of al-Qaeda. (Al-Libi subsequently recanted the false claim, which he had made to stop the torture, and revelations that the Niger uranium deal was based on falsified documents later devolved into a scandal and the conviction of Cheney's chief of staff, Lewis "Scooter" Libby.)

The invasion of Iraq began on March 20, 2003, with a military campaign featuring "shock and awe," a euphemism for massive aerial bombing to shock the targeted state into confused submission. The strategy succeeded in tumbling the regime. But the Pentagon had no practical contingency for stabilizing the occupied country (aside from the oil-producing facilities), nor did the war makers and cheerleaders anticipate the outbreak of what ultimately proved to be a long and complicated conflict against a shifting array of "insurgents." By the late summer of 2003, the failure to find the (nonexistent) WMD and the escalation of bombings, kidnappings and executions had made a mockery of Bush's claim in May that the Iraq mission had been "accomplished." In August the Pentagon sent GTMO commander Major General Geoffrey Miller to Iraq to provide advice on how to "set the conditions" to get actionable intelligence from the thousands of people—including women and children—who were being taken into custody. Lieutenant General Ricardo Sanchez, commander of the Iraq theater of operations, signed off on a policy to "GTMO-ize" Iraqi prisons, a euphemism for the use of dogs, sexual humiliation, stress positions, protracted sleep deprivation and isolation, and other forms of torture and cruel treatment, despite the fact that up to 90 percent of detainees were picked up in military sweeps or as a result of intra-Iraqi score-settling and had no connection to the insurgency, let alone to al-Qaeda.

On April 28, 2004, shocking photos of naked, abused, humiliated, bloodied, and dead prisoners from the Abu Ghraib prison in Iraq were published on CBS's *60 Minutes II.* The context was provided by the simultaneously published *New Yorker* exposé by Seymour Hersh on the leaked ("not meant for public release") report by Major General Antonio Taguba that concluded that prisoner abuse was "systematic" and "wanton" and that unlawful interrogation tactics linked Iraq to Afghanistan and Guantánamo. The Bush administration's initial reaction to the Abu Ghraib scandal was to blame "bad apples" ostensibly acting autonomously. On May 14, during a surprise visit to Iraq, Rumsfeld told troops at Abu Ghraib, "In recent days there's been a focus on a few that [*sic*] have betrayed our values and sullied the reputation of our country," adding that their actions do not represent "the values of America."[11]

As a parade of officials appeared before Congressional committees to answer questions about how Abu Ghraib had happened, the pressure for information mounted. In June 2004 the first batch of legal memos and policy documents pertaining to military and CIA interrogations was declassified or leaked to the public. These "torture memos" were, in their own way, at least as shocking as the photos, because they exposed a sanctioned and pervasive disregard for the law. The August 1 OLC memo radically narrowing the definition of torture was canceled, but there was no broader renunciation of "the program." On the contrary, top officials asserted the prerogative to continue the use of torture tactics—euphemized as "enhanced interrogation methods"—and defended these practices as necessary and effective means of combating terror.[12]

The Bush administration was handed its first defeat in June 2004 when the Supreme Court rendered its decision in *Rasul v. Bush* that GTMO detainees have habeas corpus rights. This decision, coming on the heels of the Abu Ghraib photos and the torture memos, inspired hundreds of lawyers from all sectors of the profession to sign on to represent prisoners and press their habeas claims in federal court.[13] This influx of lawyers to GTMO (albeit slowed by the glacial process of obtaining security clearances) created a new reservoir of truth about US interrogation and detention operations. However, the reservoir was dammed by overweening gag orders on lawyers to prevent the public from hearing what they were learning about the treatment of their clients.

The administration tried to circumvent *Rasul* by creating Combatant Status Review Tribunals (CSRTs) composed of military officers who *could not be lawyers* to assess the evidence against detainees (including statements elicited through torture) to decide whether they could continue to be imprisoned without trial or be deemed "no longer" unlawful combatants and released. Out of nearly 600 CSRT hearings conducted between August

2004 and January 2005, 95 percent of prisoners were found to be properly classified as enemy combatants. In stark contrast, when the habeas cases finally began making their way before federal judges, the reviews of the evidence resulted in findings that there was no justification for the detention of the vast majority.

The administration also faced some push-back from Congress. Three so-called "Republican dissenters" in the Senate—John McCain, a torture survivor from the Vietnam war, Lindsey Graham, a reservist JAG officer, and John Warner, chair of the Armed Services Committee—were exorcised over the administration's interrogation policy because it exposed soldiers to the risk of court martial and threatened to undermine military discipline. The "McCain amendment," passed by Congress in 2005, (re)prohibited cruel, inhumane, and degrading treatment by military interrogators. But the Republican majority, under pressure from Cheney, conceded to a "CIA exception" allowing agents and contractors to continue using tactics that contravene the law. In December, Congress also passed the Detainee Treatment Act, which contained jurisdiction-stripping language to bar federal courts from hearing GTMO cases.

The torture policy had adverse consequences for US relations with some of its allies. In November 2005 the *Washington Post* reported that the CIA engaged in kidnappings and ran black sites in Europe (subsequently revealed to be in Poland, Romania, and Lithuania).[14] The Council of Europe conducted an investigation into illegal US activities and in 2006 reported that a hundred people had been kidnapped on the continent. The European Parliament's investigative report, released in February 2007 and endorsed by a large majority, exposed extensive collusion by European security services and other government agencies with the CIA's extraordinary rendition program.

In 2005 an Italian court issued indictments for twenty-three CIA agents (along with four Italians) who had kidnapped Hassan Mustafa Osama Nasr (aka Abu Omar) in Milan in February 2003 and transported him to Egypt, where he was brutally tortured. Despite US diplomatic pressure and refusal to cooperate and political opposition by the Italian government, the trial-in-absentia proceeded. (In November 2009 the Italian court handed down guilty verdicts for most of the CIA agents.) In 2007 a German court issued arrest warrants for thirteen CIA agents involved in the December 2003 kidnapping of Khaled El-Masri, a German citizen, from Macedonia. El-Masri was transported to Afghanistan, where he was tortured and held incommunicado for months. When the CIA realized that El-Masri was not who they thought he was and decided to release him, they dumped him in a remote area of Albania, from which he eventually made it back to Germany. In May 2010 Spanish prosecutors issued indictments for the same thirteen CIA agents because they had transited through Spain (using forged documents) on their way to kidnap El-Masri.

Maher Arar, a Canadian citizen, was taken into US custody in September 2002 while transiting through John F. Kennedy International Airport in New York. He was held incommunicado, then extraordinarily rendered via Jordan to Syria, where he was tortured for ten months, confined for most of it in an "underground grave." After Arar was released by the Syrians and returned home, the Canadian government, which had colluded in his rendition, conducted an exhaustive investigation and concluded that there was no evidence that he had been involved in terrorism. He received an official apology and $10 million in compensation from the Canadians. Both Arar and El-Masri brought civil suits against the US officials responsible for their torture. The Bush administration invoked the "state secrets privilege" to shut down their litigation, contending that any response to allegations (despite substantial evidence of both their innocence and their torture) would be harmful to national security and foreign policy. The United States even denied Arar permission to enter the country to testify before Congress; he testified by video link—and remains on the "no fly" list.

Binyam Mohamed, a British national, had been arrested in Pakistan in 2002 and extraordinarily rendered to Afghanistan, then to Morocco, where he was subject to torture-by-proxy for eighteen months (including having his penis sliced with a razor), then back to Afghanistan, where he was held in the "dark prison" (a black site near Kabul), then transferred to GTMO in 2004. After his innocence was conceded and he was returned to Britain in March 2009, public disclosures about British intelligence agents' involvement in his torture sparked a political controversy that led to the first criminal investigation against British agents for their collusion with the CIA.

The use of torture fouled efforts to pursue any modicum of legal justice for 9/11. Salim Hamdan, a Yemeni who had gone to Afghanistan to find work and had been employed as Osama bin Laden's driver, was one of the first GTMO detainees to be charged by the military commissions. His case had gone to the head of the line not because he was a major (or even a minor) terrorist, but because he had agreed, under torture, to a plea bargain; the Pentagon was seeking a quick conviction to boost the image of the beleaguered commissions. The military defense lawyer assigned to represent him, Lieutenant Commander Charles Swift, joined with several civilian lawyers to challenge the legality of the commissions. In June 2006 the Supreme Court ruled in *Hamdan v. Rumsfeld* that the commissions were unconstitutional. The ruling also found that Common Article 3 of the Geneva Conventions—which prohibits torture, cruel treatment, and "outrages upon personal dignity"—applies to "war on terror" prisoners in US custody, and that violations are punishable offenses.

In response to the *Hamdan* decision, on September 6, 2006, Bush publically acknowledged the existence of CIA black sites and the authorization of waterboarding and other "alternative" interrogation tactics, which he characterized as "tough," "safe," "lawful," and "necessary." He announced that fourteen HVDs were being transferred from black sites to GTMO, including self-proclaimed 9/11 planner Khalid Sheik Muhammad (KSM), who had been in CIA custody since 2003 (during which he was waterboarded 183 times). Bush also announced that he was sending draft legislation to Congress to undo restrictions imposed by the *Hamdan* ruling. In October 2006 Congress passed the Military Commissions Act (MCA), which reconstituted the canceled commissions with some slight modifications.[15] The MCA also provided ex post facto immunity (back to 1997) for any US officials and agents who violated the Geneva Conventions in order to block future accountability under the 1996 War Crimes Act.

Although Republicans lost control of the Senate in 2006, the combination of continuing executive secrecy and political partisanship enabled the use of "enhanced interrogation methods" to endure to the end of Bush's second term. The predicament presented by this Orwellian denial-through-euphemism was exemplified during Michael Mukasey's October 2007 Senate Judiciary Committee confirmation hearing to become attorney general. He was asked repeatedly whether waterboarding constitutes torture and thus is a criminal and prohibited practice. The correct answer would have been "of course it is," because, among other reasons, American soldiers and civilians have been convicted in US courts for doing it. But for Mukasey to acknowledge its criminality would have put the nominee at odds with the administration, and would potentially put in legal jeopardy those who had authorized or performed it. He resolved his own predicament by feigning ignorance about the practice and stating blandly that he would enforce the law. A contrasting example was the experience of Acting Assistant Attorney General Daniel Levin, who, when asked to write a memo endorsing the legality of waterboarding, had himself waterboarded to understand firsthand what it involved, decided that it constituted torture, and was subsequently fired.

In an attempt to make the reconstituted military commissions functional, "clean teams" of FBI and military interrogators were sent to "reinterview" prisoners to generate confessions untainted by previous abuse. But six military prosecutors quit because they refused to participate in a system that relies on tortured evidence. In November 2008 the convening authority, Susan J. Crawford, decided that al-Qahtani (the alleged twentieth hijacker) was unprosecutable because he had been tortured; his treatment included forty-nine consecutive days of twenty-hour interrogations, forcible administration of intravenous fluids, drugs, and enemas, sexual and religious humiliations, and death threats. In December KSM and four others charged for their roles in 9/11 said they would plead guilty if they could go straight to sentencing—execution—to "martyr" themselves by military commission, which brought the whole system to a halt. Over the course of the Bush administration, only three GTMO prisoners, including Hamdan, were convicted in the military commissions.[16]

 Thousands of people who were arrested, interrogated, and detained in the "war on terror" were affected by the torture policy.[17] The overwhelming majority were innocent of ties to terror organizations, and many continued to be interrogated harshly long after their innocence or lack of intelligence value was known by officials.[18] The torture policy has affected Americans, too: according to Matthew Alexander (pseudonym), an Air Force major who served as an interrogator in Iraq, the torture and abuse at Abu Ghraib and Guantánamo were the number-one reason that foreign fighters were motivated to go to Iraq. Because many devastating bombings have been carried out by foreign fighters, "at least hundreds but more likely thousands of American lives (not to count Iraqi civilian deaths) are linked directly to the policy decision to introduce the torture and abuse of prisoners as accepted tactics."[19]

The official authorization of torture failed its ostensible purpose to gather human intelligence needed to defeat al-Qaeda and affiliated organizations. By subjecting so many prisoners to violent and dehumanizing treatment, the quest for information and cooperation in critically important communities, let alone the winning of "hearts and minds," was damned. Under torture some people revealed some information about al-Qaeda's structure and operations, but there is abundant evidence that many tortured statements were false. Indeed, the American experience has verified the ageless truism that many people will say anything they believe their interrogators want to hear to make the torture stop; a worst-case example is al-Libi's false claims about a connection between the regime of Saddam Hussein and al-Qaeda that the Bush administration used to advance the cause for war against Iraq, a tortured lie that has cost tens of thousands of lives and a trillion dollars.

The indirect costs of torture include misallocation of resources to follow false leads and, as falsehoods accrete, an increasing incapacity to detect the difference between accurate intelligence and lies. David Rose, an investigative journalist who interviewed numerous counterterrorism officials from the United States and elsewhere, reported that their conclusions were unanimous: "[N]ot only have coercive methods failed to generate significant and actionable intelligence, they have also caused the squandering of resources on a massive scale, . . . chimerical plots, and unnecessary safety alerts."[20] The 2008 report by the bipartisan Senate Armed Services Committee (SASC) rendered its own harsh judgment that the use of aggressive techniques and the redefining of law to create the appearance of their legality "damaged our ability to collect accurate intelligence that could save lives, strengthened the hand of our enemies, and compromised our moral authority."

During the 2008 campaign season, the torture debacle barely registered as an election issue; the nation was consumed by the economic meltdown. But to their credit, both presidential candidates—Republican McCain and Democrat Barack Obama—vaunted their anti-torture credentials on occasion. While Obama promised to end torture, increase governmental transparency, and restore the rule of law, to demonstrate his aspirational post-partisanship he skirted questions about accountability for the authors of the torture policy with the rhetoric of wanting to "look forward, not backward."

Obama's victory provided a hopeful moment for opponents of US torture. On his second day in office, he signed executive orders imposing on the CIA the requirement to adhere to the 2006-revised *Army Field Manual for Human Intelligence Collector Operations* and shuttering their black sites, suspending the discredited military commissions, and promising to close GTMO within one year. But the administration quickly realized that changing the government's course was more complex and daunting than anticipated, not least because every initiative became fodder for partisan attacks that Obama was pandering to "the far left."

Cheney, renowned for his secretive silence, became uncharacteristically voluble after he was out of office. In numerous interviews he defended the Bush administration's record by propounding the message that brutal interrogation tactics (which he described as "tough," but not "torture") had produced excellent intelligence that had kept the nation safe, as "proven" by the fact that there were no "massive-casualty attacks" in the United States (after 9/11, that is), and he admonished the Obama administration for sacrificing security by relinquishing methods that "work." Cheney's fact-free pro-torture offensive found a receptive audience among America's chattering class, who seized the opportunity to engage in woolly speculations about the efficacy of torture and treated partisan historical revisionism as legitimate critique. Because the new administration's consuming priorities were health-care reform and economic recovery, media debate about interrogation policy was dominated by torture advocates. Obama defensively strove to assert a post-partisan posture on the issue by contending that officials who had made the policy decisions and those who had followed orders had acted in "good faith," thus conceding to right-wing arguments that any type of meaningful accountability—even a truth commission—would constitute a "criminalization of policy differences."

Initially, however, the Obama administration imagined that it was possible to reconcile the commitment to unaccountability with the promise of greater transparency. In March 2009 the Justice Department decided to declassify and release more memos produced by the OLC between 2002 and 2005 that described in detail tactics approved for use by the CIA. (The decision might also have been motivated by the publication of a leaked ICRC report based on interviews with HVDs about their treatment in the CIA black sites.[21]) When Michael Hayden, the last CIA director under Bush, learned that these shameful and incriminating memos were about to become public, he rallied former CIA directors to lobby the administration to keep them classified. After entertaining a debate among his cabinet, Obama decided to release the memos on April 16 but, to ameliorate anxieties and subdue criticism, he promised not to criminally investigate anyone except possibly those interrogators who had "deviated" from the torture policy by engaging in practices that were not officially sanctioned (e.g., mock executions). But the fervor of opposition from the intelligence community and critical reporting about the memos' contents had a chilling effect. Later that month Obama defied a court order (and reneged on his own promise) by refusing to release more photos and videos from Abu Ghraib.

The administration learned another hard lesson about the political toll of change when it started devising a plan to close GTMO, despite the fact that Bush and other Republican leaders earlier had attested to the desirability of closure. The team tasked to deal with GTMO, headed by White House counsel Greg Craig, realized that it would be easier to persuade other countries to accept prisoners cleared for release if the United States also accepted some. They proposed bringing in two (of seventeen) Chinese Uighurs who could not be repatriated to their own homeland because

China would imprison them as ethnic dissidents. They also planned to transfer prisoners whom the administration intended to try, a necessity in light of Obama's suspension of the military commission. When word of these plans leaked, critics accused the administration of putting American safety at risk by bringing terrorists into the country, and Congressional leaders from both parties demonstrated their disapproval by refusing to provide funding to close the facility.

On May 21, 2009, Obama delivered a major speech on security and legal issues at the National Archives.[22] He used the occasion to rebut the pro-torture contentions that Cheney and other historic revisionists had been peddling: "[Brutal methods] undermine the rule of law. They alienate us in the world. They serve as a recruitment tool for terrorists, and increase the will of our enemies to fight us, while decreasing the will of others to work with America. They risk the lives of our troops . . . and [make it] more likely that Americans will be mistreated if they are captured. In short, they did not advance our war and counterterrorism efforts—they undermined them[.]" He went on to explain to the nation the "legal mess" he had inherited from the previous administration and the challenges of dealing with GTMO detainees. He said that some would be prosecuted in federal courts and others in the military commissions, thus rescinding his own January suspension (and sending a confused message about why two systems were necessary). But he promised to reform the commissions to exclude evidence elicited through torture or cruel, inhuman, and degrading treatment. (A new MCA was passed in October 2009.) The "toughest" problem, according to Obama, is what to do with detainees who cannot be prosecuted, but who also cannot be released because they might continue to pose a security threat. (He did not address the fact that people in this category—such as al-Qahtani—are unprosecutable *because* they have been tortured.) He suggested that some arrangement for permanent detention without trial was being considered, a disappointment to those counting on him to restore the rule of law. (Several months later the administration decided not to propose new legislation, but rather to follow its predecessor in claiming that Congress had endorsed indefinite detention by passing the Authorization To Use Military Force in the immediate aftermath of 9/11, and this embrace of indefinite detention was further confirmed in the 2010 National Security Strategy.)

On November 13, 2009, Attorney General Eric Holder announced plans to prosecute KSM and four other 9/11 suspects in New York City, explaining that this was the scene of the crime and that federal courts are best equipped to deal with complex capital cases. Within weeks initial support for these trials from New York officials evaporated. White House Chief of Staff Rahm Emanuel, who regarded the whole detention issue as a political minefield for Democrats rather than a matter of grave legal importance, reportedly strived to strike a deal for GTMO with Republican Senator Graham, a strong advocate of military commissions. Political expediency prevailed over legal principle: Holder was increasingly marginalized from White House policy making, and Craig resigned under pressure after clashing with Emanuel.[23]

The ongoing national debate about torture, terror, and the law intensified following the 2009 Christmas Day attempt by Umar Farouk Abdulmutallab, a Nigerian, to detonate a bomb in his underwear while traveling on a transatlantic flight bound for Detroit. Critics excoriated Holder for allowing Abdulmutallab to be read his Miranda rights and for *not* subjecting him to "enhanced" interrogation or shipping him off to GTMO, despite the fact that the Bush administration had followed an identical course of action with Richard Reid, the "shoe bomber," and despite the fact that Abdulmutallab readily provided information to FBI interrogators who used conventional methods when questioning him. In May 2010, following a failed attempt to detonate a bomb in Times Square, Pakistani-born US citizen Faisal Shahzad was captured as he was about to fly out of the country. Again, Holder was challenged about the legitimacy of providing constitutional protections for (non-white) terrorists arrested within the United States. That these events could be treated by so many officials and commentators as evidence of the "need" to subject terror suspects to torture should be unsurprising for a country that has failed to face the truth about the actual record of torture's inefficacy.

The Obama administration's "looking forward" posture functions as a form of denial; the refusal to investigate or acknowledge past crimes has led, inevitably, to a need to rely on heavy-handed classification and other efforts to block public access to information deleterious or embarrassing to the US government. When the CIA's Office of the Inspector General report was finally released in August 2009, excessive redactions made it impossible to glean a clear understanding about how the torture program had grown and spread. The report by the Justice Department's Office of Professional Responsibility (OPR) into the role that OLC lawyers played in formulating the torture policy—which was completed but not released under Bush—was withheld (without explanation) until February 2010. As astute observers had expected, the report contained substantial evidence that OLC lawyers had colluded with the White House to "legalize" unlawful tactics, which, the OPR tentatively concluded, constituted "professional misconduct." But Holder had authorized career bureaucrat David Margolis to make the final determination, and his conclusion was that the lawyers had merely exercised "poor judgment." In another effort to block public access to damaging information, the Obama administration threatened to suspend bilateral counterterrorism cooperation with Britain if documents detailing Binyam Mohamed's torture were entered into evidence as part of his suit against British officials who colluded with the CIA. (In February 2010, the British High Court rejected the Labor government's appeal to keep segments of the documents classified, and they were published.)

The Obama administration emulated its predecessor's strategies to bar judicial oversight of overseas detentions and to stymie legal redress for victims of torture. At a February 2009 hearing of a civil suit by five victims of extraordinary rendition (including Mohamed) against Jeppesen Dataplan, the company whose planes had transported them to torture, the lawyer from the Solicitor General's office refused to take the opportunity to restore the pre-Bush meaning of the states secrets privilege as the government's right to limit specific sensitive pieces of information or evidence. Instead, to the surprise of the judge, he stated that there would be no change in the government's position to invoke state secrets in order to derail the litigation. In a similar vein, in May 2010 the administration filed a motion that opposed Maher Arar's appeal to have the Supreme Court hear his civil suit, and in June the court refused.[24]

Obama replicated the most internationally disdained and legally dubious position of the Bush administration by denying that foreign prisoners held in Afghanistan have habeas corpus rights. In April 2009 a federal judge ruled that *Boumediene v. Bush* (the 2008 Supreme Court decision that *Senator* Obama had praised for its recognition that GTMO prisoners have a *constitutional* right to habeas) applies to detainees who were captured elsewhere and transported—extraordinarily rendered, that is—to Afghanistan and held incommunicado for years at Bagram prison. The Obama administration appealed that decision, arguing that Bagram is unlike GTMO because all of Afghanistan is a "theater of war." In May 2010 the D.C. Circuit Court endorsed the administration's contention that such prisoners have no right to challenge their detention.[25]

And what of the promises to close black sites and end torture? In April 2010 the BBC reported testimonies of nine prisoners who said they had been subjected to beatings, sexual humiliation, sleep deprivation, isolation, and other stress and duress tactics at a facility called the "Tor Jail," which translates as the "black jail" in Pashtu, separate from the main detention facility at Bagram. On May 11 the ICRC confirmed the existence of a secret prison to which it has no access. The facility is run not by the CIA, but by the DIA (the Defense Intelligence Agency), which has secret authorization to use interrogation methods detailed in the classified Appendix M to the *Army Field Manual*. When this news broke, Defense Department officials denied the existence of a secret detention facility. Indeed, in another example of the truth-masking appeal of euphemisms, the Obama administration asserted that the black jail is an "interrogation facility," not a "detention site," and therefore neither does the ICRC have a right to access those held there, nor do the regular rules apply.

In a broader sense, the regular rules that once applied are no longer either "regular" in the taken-for-granted sense, nor are they "rules" in that their binding nature has been undermined. Now, more than ten years into the "war on terror," we are still, in Cheney's words, spending "time in the shadows." The legacy of torture, deception, and denial has changed but not abated; it is not *history* in the sense that this ignominious confluence continues. But it is *our* history, and for citizens of a democracy it is our responsibility. How we reckon with the truth of torture past and present is a burning question. The answer will determine whether torture has a future.

In the Minotaur's Labyrinth: Psychological Torture, Public Forgetting, and Contested History

Alfred W. McCoy

Like Chile after General Pinochet or the Philippines after Ferdinand Marcos, the United States after George W. Bush is trapped in the painful politics of impunity. Despite dozens of official inquiries in the years since the Abu Ghraib photos first exposed abuse in April 2004, the torture scandal has continued to spread like a virus, infecting all who touch it. By embracing a specific methodology of torture, covertly developed by the Central Intelligence Agency (CIA) over decades and graphically revealed in those Iraqi prison photos, Washington has condemned itself to an endless succession of torture scandals. Through every sordid incident in this process of impunity—Dick Cheney's unapologetic claims of torture's efficacy and President Obama's halting retreat from promises to end the abuse—Washington is returning step-by-step to a contradictory policy that had made torture America's secret weapon throughout the Cold War.

This is by no means the first time that a major political controversy over CIA torture has become mired in impunity, thereby failing to punish past abuse or prevent future recurrence. Indeed, on at least five previous occasions over the past forty years, the fusion of psychological torture's elusive character and the CIA's covert application has defeated the country's usual processes of political reform through press exposé, public protest, and congressional action, allowing the practice to persist to the present and perhaps into the future. Concealed from both Congress and the public, the CIA has spent the past half-century developing a sophisticated form of psychological torture meant to defy investigation, prosecution, or prohibition—and so far has been remarkably successful on all those counts.

In contrast to the bureaucratic influence and institutional memory of the US intelligence community, the fluid human rights coalitions that form at each crisis evince a public forgetting about the past, focusing upon the ephemera of the present controversy, unable to probe for the underlying continuities of law, policy, and doctrine that are the genesis of the problem. In this unequal struggle, the critics' main weapons—congressional investigation and media exposé—have proven blunt instruments, capable of stirring up a controversy but incapable of cutting through the complexities of law and bureaucracy to the core of the problem.

In such circumstances history can serve as an antidote to the oblivion that is the prime requisite of impunity. In this unequal struggle between state security with deep institutional memory and the public's media-induced amnesia, history has proven, by default, an effective medium for reconstructing this past and recovering its patterns. Like Penelope unraveling her weaving by night to delay the day of reckoning, state security seeks to tear at the threads of collective memory, making each exposé seem isolated, anecdotal, and ultimately insignificant. But by weaving these threads together into the tapestry of collective memory, history allows the public to discover a larger design, seeing torture as an instrument of state power, impunity as its necessary adjunct, and, in rare circumstances, the past as a path to prevention.

Yet this history is by no means uncontested. Indeed, the past, as we will see below, has many uses. For lawyers in service to the powerful, history provides pretext and precedent for extra-legal action. In the end, when these deeds are done and victims' screams no longer echo, the powerful can reconfigure this history to serve as exculpation and even justification. For critics in the human rights community, recovery of this past is essential for both prosecution and prevention of these crimes. And for historians such as this writer, history's most elemental tool, chronology, provides a trail through clandestine bureaucracies cloaked in layers of secrecy—akin to the thread that guided Theseus through the Minotaur's labyrinth to slay the monster and liberate his victims.

Once the shock of revelation has faded, history, like film or television, can also serve to numb and normalize extra-legal state action among the citizenry of a nation state. But in an age of globalization, such revelations have consequences, informing formal complaints before international bodies and emboldening other states to exercise their universal jurisdiction for human rights violations, thus serving as potent constraint against the usual processes of impunity within national boundaries.

A Short History of Psychological Torture

The roots of the present-day political paralysis over past detainee abuse lies in the hidden history of the CIA's program of psychological torture. Early in the Cold War, panicked that the Soviets had somehow cracked the code of human consciousness, the agency mounted a "Special Interrogation Program" whose working hypothesis was stated in a 1952 memo: "Medical science, particularly psychiatry and psychotherapy, has developed various techniques by means of which some external control can be imposed on the mind or will of an individual, such as drugs, hypnosis, electric shock and neurosurgery."[1]

The CIA tested all of these techniques covertly during the 1950s and 1960s, focusing on a behavioral approach to cracking that code of human consciousness. Starting in 1951 the CIA collaborated with British and Canadian defense scientists to promote academic research into "methods concerned in psychological coercion." Within months the agency defined the aims of its now top-secret program, codenamed Project Artichoke, as the "development of any method by which we can get information from a person against his will and without his knowledge."[2]

This secret research produced two discoveries central to the CIA's emerging psychological paradigm. In classified experiments conducted from 1951 to 1954, famed Canadian psychologist Donald Hebb found that he could induce a state akin to psychosis in just forty-eight hours without drugs, hypnosis, or electrical shock. For two days student volunteers at McGill University simply sat in a comfortable cubicle deprived of sensory stimulation by goggles, gloves, and earmuffs.[3] "It scared the hell out of us," Hebb said later, "to see how completely dependent the mind is on a close connection with the ordinary sensory environment, and how disorganizing to be cut off from that support." This discovery, soon confirmed and elaborated by hundreds of scientific papers, led to the development of a torture technique called "sensory deprivation."[4]

During the 1950s as well, two researchers at Cornell University Medical Center, working under CIA contract, found that the most devastating torture technique of the Soviet secret police, the KGB, was to force a victim to stand for days while the legs swelled, the skin erupted in suppurating lesions, and hallucinations began. Since 2001 US military interrogators have euphemistically called this procedure "stress positions."[5]

After four years of this research, American prisoners in North Korea suffered what was then called "brainwashing," prompting a sudden upsurge of interest in using these mind-control techniques defensively. In August 1955 President Eisenhower ordered that any soldier at risk of capture must be given "specific training and instruction designed to . . . withstand all enemy efforts against him." Consequently the Air Force developed a program it dubbed SERE (Survival, Evasion, Resistance, Escape) to train pilots in resisting psychological torture.[6] Thus two strands of mind-control research became intertwined: aggressive techniques for breaking enemy agents and defensive methods for training Americans to resist enemy inquisitors.

In 1963 the CIA distilled its past decade of research into the "KUBARK Counterintelligence Interrogation" manual, which stated that sensory deprivation was effective because it made "the regressed subject view the interrogator as a father figure . . . strengthening . . . the subject's tendencies toward compliance."[7] Refined through years of practice, the CIA's psychological paradigm came to rely on a mix of sensory overload and sensory deprivation via seemingly banal procedures—extremes of heat and cold, light and dark, noise and silence, feast and famine—meant to attack six basic sensory pathways into the human mind.

After codifying these methods, the CIA spent the next thirty years promoting torture techniques within the US intelligence community and among anticommunist allies worldwide. Along the global arc of anticommunist containment, the CIA trained allied agencies in these coercive counterintelligence techniques, most visibly in Iran, South Vietnam, and Latin America. During the Vietnam War, when the CIA used torture to eliminate top-level Viet Cong cadre, the interrogation effort soon degenerated into the crude physical brutality of the Phoenix program, producing forty thousand extrajudicial executions and little actionable intelligence. From 1966 to 1991 the US Army's military intelligence ran "Project X" to transmit the counterinsurgency lessons from South Vietnam to Latin America via Spanish-language training manuals, an elaborate interrogation curriculum, and field-training programs.[8] In a parallel training program for the Honduran military during the 1980s, the CIA taught local interrogators that they should "manipulate the subject's environment . . . to disrupt patterns of time, space, and sensory perception"—in short, to assault the basic sensory pathways into human consciousness.[9] Significantly, the techniques described in this CIA program's "Human Resources Exploitation Manual—1983" seem quite similar to those outlined twenty years *earlier* in the CIA's KUBARK manual and those used twenty years *later* at Abu Ghraib.

In the half century since its codification in 1963, the CIA's psychological torture paradigm has proved elusive, seductive, and destructive—attributes that merit closer examination. Most important from the perspective of impunity is that psychological torture, unlike its physical counterpart, leaves few clear signs of abuse and easily eludes detection, thereby complicating any attempt at investigation, prosecution, or prohibition. After being trained by British intelligence, which had developed this doctrine in conjunction with the CIA, the Royal Ulster Constabulary applied these psychological methods on IRA suspects at Belfast in 1971. By mixing stress positions and sensory deprivation, the Constabulary tried to break victims by simultaneous application of "five techniques": enforced "wall standing," hooding, blaring music, sleep deprivation, and dietary manipulation. Prompted by articles in the British press and questions in Parliament about these events, an official inquiry headed by Lord Parker of Waddington found that these psychological methods greatly complicated any determination of torture. "Where," Lord Parker asked, "does hardship and discomfort end and for instance humiliating treatment begin, and where does the latter end and torture begin?" The answer, he said with uncommon prescience, turns on "words of definition" and thus "opinions will inevitably differ."[10]

Similarly, when General Randall Schmidt investigated conditions at Guantánamo for the Pentagon in 2005, he found that the standards for physical "torture" were clear, but "anything else beyond that was fairly vague." He added that "something might be degrading but not necessarily torture. And ... it may be humiliating, but it may not be torture." In reviewing treatment of the camp's star prisoner, Muhammad al-Qahtani, the general "felt that the cumulative effect of simultaneous applications of numerous authorized techniques had an abusive and degrading impact on the detainee"—a finding rejected by higher echelons.[11] In both cases, British and American, investigation and any prosecution were frustrated by the elusive quality of these psychological methods.

Congressional and Civil Society Oversight

Over the past forty years, ad hoc civil society coalitions of Congress, the press, and the public have made at least six attempts to check the CIA's use of psychological torture. But they failed time after time to pierce the veil shrouding the psychological torture paradigm's elusive character and covert application. Sometimes these exposés have been sensational, sometimes ephemeral, but all have proved unequal to ending the ethos of impunity surrounding CIA interrogation. In each of these six instances, the official secrecy masking the agency and its methods has succeeded in compromising the usual cycle of US political reform through media investigation, public protest, and legislative action.

The first of these defeats came in 1970-71 after stunning revelations about the CIA's largest interrogation operation, the Phoenix program. In testimony before the Senate Foreign Relations Committee, William Colby, a career CIA officer and chief of pacification in Vietnam, admitted that Phoenix had killed 20,587 Viet Cong suspects since 1968. The Saigon government provided figures attributing 40,994 Viet Cong deaths to the same program.[12] When Representative Ogden Reid (Republican, New York) charged that Phoenix was responsible for "indiscriminate killings," Colby defended his program as "an essential part of the war effort" that was "designed to protect the Vietnamese people from terrorism." In these same hearings, K. Barton Osborn, a military intelligence veteran who had worked with the CIA program in 1967–68, described "the use of electronic gear such as sealed telephones attached to the . . . women's vagina and the men's testicles . . . [to] shock them into submission." During his eighteen months with Phoenix, not a single VC suspect had survived CIA interrogation. All these "extralegal, illegal, and covert" procedures were, Osborn testified, found in the *Defense Collection Intelligence Manual* issued to him during his intelligence training at Fort Holabird, Maryland. Adding to this lethal aura, by 1972 the Phoenix total for enemy "neutralization" had risen to 81,740 Viet Cong eliminated and 26,369 prisoners killed.[13]

In response to these damning allegations, the US Army Intelligence Command conducted a thorough investigation that nitpicked many secondary details of Osborn's testimony, but did not challenge Phoenix's systematic brutality—an assessment later confirmed by both eyewitness accounts and official studies.[14]

Four years later, in the aftermath of America's defeat in Vietnam, a Senate committee, led by Frank Church (Democrat, Idaho), held hearings that probed aggressively for extra-legal CIA programs such as assassination of foreign leaders. But the Senate's investigation of the CIA's drug experiments under the codename MKUltra and subsequent torture training programs did not go beyond the anecdotal.[15] Trying to explain why the agency's "accomplices in torture" had escaped examination, author A. J. Langguth concluded that Senator Church "tried to force some admissions but his witnesses sidestepped his staff's sketchy allegations. Given the willingness of Congress to accept the CIA's alibis about national security, I don't think any other public hearing would fare better."[16]

To correct the Senate's "fragmentary picture . . . of the extent to which the agency was engaged in behavior-control research," the *New York Times* conducted its own investigation into what it called a "secret, 25-year, $25 million effort by the Central Intelligence Agency to learn how to control the human mind." From 1948 to 1973 the agency worked through distinguished scientists to test drugs, hypnosis, and sensory deprivation on unwitting subjects in prisons and psychiatric clinics. Behind a veil of secrecy, the agency "was able to assemble an extensive network of non-government scientists and facilities—apparently without the knowledge of the institutions where the facilities were located." According to a CIA Inspector General's report in 1957, the agency "had added difficulty in obtaining expert services," since some experiments "are considered to be professionally unethical and in some instances border on the illegal."[17] The historical record was now corrected, but the drama of congressional investigation had faded, and this front-page exposé had little lasting impact.

Although the Phoenix program was the largest CIA interrogation effort, it was exposés of its Latin American operations that prompted a Senate attempt to end US torture training altogether. Ironically, the murder of an American police adviser in Uruguay employed by the Office of Public Safety (OPS), a CIA front concealed inside USAID, first exposed this program's involvement in torture training. This story broke in August 1970 when the *New York Times* reported that Tupamaro guerrillas in Montevideo had killed an American police adviser, Dan A. Mitrione. Soon thereafter, a senior Uruguayan police official, Alejandro Otero, told the *Jornal do Brazil* that Mitrione had used "violent techniques of torture and repression"— charges that the US Embassy in Montevideo called "absolutely false."[18] Eight years later, however, Cuban double agent Manuel Hevia Cosculluela, who had joined the CIA and worked with Mitrione in Montevideo, published a book describing how the American tortured four beggars to death with electric shocks at a 1970 seminar to demonstrate his techniques for Uruguayan police trainees.[19]

Just months before Mitrione's death in Uruguay, an unsettling coincidence of US police training in Brazil and evidence of police torture finally raised questions about torture before the US Congress. In May 1971, the Senate Foreign Relations Committee summoned the chief US Public Safety adviser for Brazil, Theodore D. Brown, who attempted to explain away this unsettling coincidence.[20] Four years later, however, congressional investigations led by Senator James Abourezk (Democrat, South Dakota) found substantive allegations that the OPS program was training torturers in the Latin American police.[21] Concerned about these persistent reports, Congress finally eliminated all funds for "training or advice to police, prisons, or other law enforcement," effectively abolishing the OPS by mid-1975.[22]

Though these reforms were well-intentioned, Congress had failed to probe for the source of this torture training. Investigations had exposed some elements of the CIA's mind-control project, but there was no public pressure to restrain the agency's propagation of psychological torture. Moreover, by the time Congress began investigating the OPS, the CIA had already stopped using it as a cover for its foreign operations, shifting its torture training to the US Army's Military Adviser Program (MAP).[23]

During the last decade of the Cold War in the 1980s, media probes and congressional pressure led to surprising revelations about the extent of CIA torture training in Latin America. In 1988 a *New York Times* reporter discovered that while civil war was intensifying in Honduras during the late 1970s, the CIA imported Argentine veterans of that nation's "dirty war" to train local army interrogators and sent Honduran soldiers to the United States for instruction by its own experts. The exposé prompted a congressional inquiry that, though somewhat cursory, revealed for the first time the existence of the agency's torture manuals. When the US Senate's Select Committee on Intelligence, responsible for legislative oversight of the CIA, met in closed session to review the allegations, its chair, Senator David Boren (Democrat, Oklahoma), stated that in the course of the agency's internal review "several interrogation training manuals, including one used to train the Hondurans, had been uncovered." In Boren's view the techniques in these manuals were "completely contrary to the principles and policies of the United States."[24]

Significantly, a fact sheet prepared for the committee showed that US Army Special Forces had conducted at least seven "human resources exploitation" courses in Latin America between 1982 and 1987, confirming that the CIA had shifted its interrogation training from police advisers to army instructors after Congress abolished OPS back in 1975.[25] Although the country's leading newspaper had published a detailed report of CIA torture training, Congress was, as this committee demonstrated, still unwilling to expose the agency's human rights violations. Under the national security pressures of the Cold War, CIA torture training had again eluded serious reform.

Origins of Impunity

When the Cold War came to a close, Washington rescinded its torture training and resumed its advocacy of human rights. In 1991 Congress passed the Protection for Victims of Torture Act to allow civil suits in US courts against foreign perpetrators who enter American jurisdiction.[26] At the 1993 Vienna Human Rights conference, Washington revived its vigorous advocacy of a universal humanitarian standard, opposing the idea of exceptions for "regional peculiarities" advocated by dictatorships of the left and right, China and Indonesia.[27]

Most importantly, in 1994 the Clinton administration ratified the UN Convention Against Torture (CAT) that banned, in equal measure, both physical and psychological methods.[28] On the surface the United States had apparently resolved the tension between its anti-torture principles and its torture practices. Yet when this liberal president sent the Convention to Congress for ratification, he included exculpatory language, drafted six years earlier by the conservative Reagan administration, with a detailed diplomatic "reservation." These clauses defined psychological torture narrowly as "prolonged mental harm caused by . . . (1) the intentional infliction or threatened infliction of severe physical pain or suffering; (2) the administration . . . of mind-altering substances. . . ; (3) the threat of imminent death; or (4) the threat that another person will imminently be subjected to death."[29] All this verbiage, replicated verbatim in the Clinton ratification, was focused on just one word in the twenty-six printed pages of the UN Convention. That word was "mental."

Significantly, the Clinton administration also reproduced this definition verbatim in domestic legislation enacted to give legal force to the Convention Against Torture—first in Section 2340 of the US Federal Code[30] and later in the US War Crimes Act of 1996.[31] Both the reservation and related federal laws complicated any finding of mental torture by requiring an ill-defined "prolonged mental harm" (how long is "prolonged"?), stipulating the perpetrator's specific intent to do harm (with intent lying in the perpetrator's mind), and limiting the causes of harm to four specific acts. Through these slight but significant changes in the UN's language, US laws effected a virtual evisceration of the Convention's ban on mental abuse, opening loopholes for the CIA's later use of psychological torture after September 2001.

Although these contradictions were obscure in the historical moment, the country's dwindling community of peace activists sensed something amiss as they struggled, throughout the 1990s, to correct excesses remaining from the Cold War. Public advocacy of human rights and official secrecy over their violation collided most notably in a long-running controversy over torture instruction at the School of the Americas, a training facility for Latin American officers that the US Army had operated in Panama since 1949.[32] After the school moved to Fort Benning, Georgia, in 1984, critics pressed for its abolition, branding it the "School of Assassins" and mounting an annual demonstration outside the base each November. These swelling protests were led by Catholic activists, Hollywood stars such as Martin Sheen, and Washington liberals such as Representative Joseph P. Kennedy II (Democrat, Massachusetts).[33]

With its ironic mix of celebrity and idealism, this movement served as a catalyst for further disclosures about US torture training. After Representative Robert Torricelli (Democrat, New Jersey) charged that the husband of an American citizen had been murdered by a Guatemalan colonel in the CIA's employ, the executive's Intelligence Oversight Board investigated and, in June 1996, reported that "the School of the Americas and US Southern Command had used improper instruction materials in training Latin American officers, including Guatemalans, from 1982 to 1991." These training materials, the board said, had passages that condoned "executions of guerrillas, extortion, physical abuse, coercion, and false imprisonment."[34]

Just six months later, the explicitness of this CIA torture training was finally exposed to public scrutiny. In January 1997 the *Baltimore Sun*, *Washington Post*, and *New York Times* published extracts from the CIA's Honduran handbook, the "Human Resources Exploitation Manual—1983," describing it as the latest edition of a thousand-page manual distributed to Latin American armies for the previous twenty years.[35] Though these press descriptions of torture were chilling, the public reaction, beyond the small community of activists, was muted indeed.

In effect, public debate complemented the national security bureaucracy's resolution of the torture question in the aftermath of the Cold War—i.e., purging the Phoenix-style physical abuse but preserving the legality of the original CIA psychological paradigm, with its legitimating scientific aura. Through the combined failings of state and civil society, America entered the twenty-first century with a fundamental contradiction in its human rights policy still unresolved.

War on Terror, War of Torture

Right after his public address to a shaken nation on September 11, 2001, President George W. Bush gave his staff secret orders for torture, saying emphatically, "I don't care what the international lawyers say, we are going to kick some ass."[36] After months of recondite legal research, administration attorneys translated the president's eloquent but unlawful orders into US policy through three controversial, neoconservative legal findings: (1) the president is above the law; (2) torture is a legally acceptable exercise of presidential power; and (3) the US Navy base at Guantánamo is not US territory. Drawing on this advice, in February 2002 President Bush ordered that "none of the provisions of Geneva apply to our conflict with al Qaeda in Afghanistan or elsewhere throughout the world," thus removing any requirements for "minimum standards for humane treatment."[37]

Acting on all this legal advice, the White House also allowed the CIA its own global network of prisons and planes to seize suspects anywhere, subject them to "extraordinary rendition," and incarcerate them endlessly inside a supranational gulag of eight secret "black sites" from Thailand to Poland.[38] The Bush administration also approved the CIA's ten "enhanced" interrogation methods designed by agency psychologists, including waterboarding.[39]

In response to White House inquiries about the legality of these techniques, Assistant Attorney General Jay Bybee and his subordinate John Yoo found grounds, in their now notorious August 2002 memo, for exculpating any CIA interrogator who tortured, but later claimed his intention was obtaining information instead of inflicting pain. By parsing the US definition of torture under Section 2340 as "severe" physical or mental pain, Bybee concluded that "physical pain amounting to torture must be equivalent in intensity to the pain accompanying serious physical injury such as organ failure," effectively allowing physical torture to the point of death. "For purely mental pain or suffering to amount to torture," the memo continued, "it must result in significant psychological harm . . . lasting for months or even years"—a permissive standard that reflected the elusive character of psychological torture.[40]

Not only were the Bush Justice Department lawyers aggressive in their advocacy of torture, but they were also meticulous in laying the legal groundwork for later impunity. In a memo for the CIA dated August 2002, Bybee approved all ten of the agency's proposed interrogation techniques, including; "(1) attention grasp, (2) walling, (3) facial hold, (4) facial slap (insult slap), (5) cramped confinement, (6) wall standing, (7) stress positions, (8) sleep deprivation, (9) insects placed in a confinement box, and (10) the waterboard." To exculpate the most severe of these methods, he cited the CIA's contract psychologist at the Thai black site who felt, based on his own use of mild waterboarding in SERE training for ten thousand Air Force recruits, that its long-term psychological effects "are certainly minimal." Even though Bybee himself found that "the use of the waterboard constitutes a threat of imminent death," it could still be considered legal because, first, it did not cause "prolonged mental harm . . . lasting months or years," and, second, "those carrying out these procedures would not have the specific intent to inflict severe physical pain or suffering."[41]

To develop these techniques, psychologists working for both the Pentagon and the CIA "reverse engineered" the military's SERE training, which remained, a decade after the Cold War's end, the sole institutional memory of the early interrogation research. In effect, the agency inverted these defensive methods for offensive use on al Qaeda captives. "They sought to render the detainees vulnerable—to break down all of their senses," one official told *New Yorker* reporter Jane Mayer. Inside CIA headquarters officials felt a "high level of anxiety" about possible prosecution for methods they knew to be internationally defined as torture. The presence of Ph.D. psychologists was considered one "way for CIA officials to skirt measures such as the Convention Against Torture."[42]

In late 2002 Defense Secretary Donald Rumsfeld approved fifteen aggressive interrogation techniques, including harsh stress positions, for the military prison at Guantánamo in Cuba. Significantly, the Defense Department, like other Bush administration agencies, was careful to assure impunity. In a briefing at Guantánamo Bay, the senior counsel at CIA's Counterterrorism Center, Jonathan M. Fredman, advised military interrogators and prison staff that the legal definition of torture was "written vaguely" and "is basically subject to perception" by the perpetrator. Hence, he concluded that US law had no real restraints on interrogation, saying: "If the detainee dies, you're doing it wrong."[43]

Simultaneously, Rumsfeld gave General Geoffrey Miller command of the US military prison at Guantánamo with ample authority to transform it into an ad hoc psychology laboratory. Via a three-phase attack on senses, culture, and individual psyche, Guantánamo's interrogators soon perfected the CIA's psychological paradigm. The older techniques of sensory deprivation and self-inflicted pain remained central to the prison's new interrogation protocol through use of short shackling, strobe lights/darkness, blasting music/silence, and protracted isolation. Moving beyond these sensory pathways universal to all humanity, the general's Behavioral Science Consultation Teams of military psychologists probed detainees for individual phobias such as fear of the dark. Moreover, interrogators strengthened the psychological assault by exploiting what they saw as Arab cultural sensitivities to gender identity, sexuality, and dogs.[44] After regular inspections of this facility, the International Red Cross reported its methods "cannot be considered other than an intentional . . . form of torture."[45]

Torture Advocacy by Professors, Pundits, and Psychologists

Throughout these years of escalating abuse after 9/11, the Bush administration's secret embrace of aggressive methods drew political sustenance from the public advocacy of torture by pundits and professors, both liberal and conservative, who formed a loose advocacy movement for aggressive interrogation. In November 2001 columnist Jonathan Alter wrote in *Newsweek*: "In this autumn of anger, even a liberal can find his thoughts turning to . . . torture." Alter advocated psychological torture or transfer of suspects to "our less squeamish allies."[46] After the Abu Ghraib scandal broke in mid-2004, Harvard Law School faculty members, including Alan Dershowitz, circulated a petition, signed by 481 prominent professors of law and political science at 110 top universities nationwide, calling for serious consideration of "a coercive interrogation policy . . . made within the strict confines of a democratic process." In effect, the country's leading academics were asking Americans to set aside two centuries of Enlightenment principles and think seriously about legalizing torture.[47] Reflecting its long involvement in military research and CIA behavioral experiments, the American Psychological Association (APA) hesitated to bar members from military interrogations outright, saying, simply and vaguely, that they should be "mindful of factors unique to these roles . . . that require special ethical consideration." Moreover, an APA task force refused to recommend that members be bound by "international standards of human rights."[48]

While academics articulated a justification for torture, film and television played a critical, albeit intangible role in fostering mass political support for abuse, gradually translating the hypothetical ticking bomb scenario into an iconic popular belief. First aired just weeks after the 9/11 attacks in November 2001, Fox's *24* soon became the informal signature program of President Bush's War on Terror. Every week, as a large clock ticked menacingly, Agent Jack Bauer of the Counterintelligence Unit used violent torture to save Los Angeles or the nation from the threat of terrorists armed with weapons of mass destruction, often a nuclear bomb. "Jack Bauer saved Los Angeles. . . . He saved hundreds of thousands of lives," Supreme Court Justice Antonin Scalia told a 2007 legal seminar. "Are you going to convict Jack Bauer?" he asked. "I don't think so."[49]

Slow Slide Toward Impunity

This seemingly strong consensus for torture quickly evaporated in the wake of the Abu Ghraib prison scandal. On April 28, 2004, CBS Television broadcast a few of the 1,600 photos that the Army's Criminal Investigation Command had gathered as evidence of abuse at Abu Ghraib prison in Iraq.[50] Within days, Defense Secretary Rumsfeld insisted that the abuses were "perpetrated by a small number of US military," whom the conservative *New York Times* columnist William Safire branded "creeps."[51] With some exceptions, public response to the CBS broadcast was generally muted. With the Iraq war going badly and a burst of color-coded terror warnings fostering a sense of fear across America, the political climate was not conducive to such an exposé.

Ultimately, the upshot of a dozen Pentagon inquiries and several hundred military prosecutions was a reprimand for one female general officer and convictions of low-ranking soldiers like Private Lynndie England. Similarly, in June 2005, over a year after he had buried a CIA report on detainee abuse, Attorney General John Ashcroft announced the indictment of a single CIA contractor, David A. Passaro, for beating an Afghani detainee to death, branding him one of "a small group of individuals" who had betrayed America's most basic values.[52] In this rhetorical strategy of confining the punishment to a few "bad apples," the Bush administration had taken the critical first step toward impunity.

Confronted by public anger over Abu Ghraib, the Bush White House defended harsh interrogation as a presidential prerogative necessary to fight the War on Terror. But in June 2006, in a dramatic rebuke of the president's position, the US Supreme Court ruled in *Hamdan v. Rumsfeld* that Bush's military commissions, convened to try detainees at Guantámano, were illegal because they did not meet the requirement, under Common Article Three of the Geneva Conventions, that Guantánamo detainees be tried with "all the judicial guarantees . . . recognized as indispensable by civilized peoples."[53]

To supersede the Supreme Court and legalize their president's position, Republican partisans drafted compromise legislation on September 21 that sailed through Congress within a week to become the Military Commissions Act of 2006. Significantly, this legislation provided CIA interrogators both legal immunity for past physical abuse and ample latitude for future psychological torture.[54] In presiding over the drafting of this law, Vice President Cheney included clauses, buried deep inside the bill's thirty-eight pages, defining "serious physical pain" as the "significant loss or impairment of the function of a bodily member, organ, or mental faculty"—a paraphrase of John Yoo's infamous August 2002 "torture memo" that the Justice Department had already repudiated.[55] Focusing on the means rather than the end result, this law limits the crime of inflicting "severe mental pain" to the four specific acts written into Section 2340 of the Federal Code back in 1994: i.e., drug injection, death threats, threats against another, and extreme physical pain. Through this narrow, exclusionary language, the law effectively legalized the dozens of CIA psychological torture techniques, including waterboarding, developed over the past five decades.

This legislation sparked a public battle between two groups of lawyers who had been fighting over interrogation policy behind closed doors for the past five years: administration attorneys affiliated with the neo-conservative Federalist Society and military lawyers in the Judge Advocate General (JAG) corps. Over the span of several military generations, these soldier lawyers, known as JAGs, had developed a deep commitment to the rule of law grounded in the Geneva Conventions of 1948, which require "civilized" justice for captives, and to the US Uniform Code of Military Justice of 1950, whose procedures meet that high standard. Their nonmilitary antagonists were members of the Federalist Society, a group whose first chapters were established inside law schools in the early 1980s and slowly built a powerful patronage network of lawyers who came to Washington with the Bush administration in January 2001.

In the House, Republican leaders were determined to pass Bush's bill verbatim, including its revision of Common Article 3 of the Geneva Conventions, but were challenged by the military's senior legal officers. Appearing before a hostile Armed Services Committee on September 7, the four top Judge Advocate Generals were determined that Geneva remain the basis of detainee treatment. The most outspoken, General James C. Walker, drew upon his quarter-century of service as a Marine Corps JAG to criticize Bush's proposed legislation, saying: "I'm not aware of any situation in the world where there is a system of jurisprudence that is recognized by civilized people where an individual can be tried and convicted without seeing the evidence against him."[56] After years of loyal service to the president as secretary of state, Colin Powell broke ranks to write the Senate that any tampering with the Geneva Conventions would cost America "the moral basis of our fight against terrorism."[57] However, this opposition could not block the Republican juggernaut that pushed the legislation through Congress unamended.

Amidst this attempt at preemptive impunity, the historical record provided the most telling critique of the administration's interrogation policy.

In mid-2008, Senate investigators discovered that the CIA's coercive techniques dated back to the 1950s and were derived from North Korean methods used to extract false confessions. This data had originally influenced the design of the SERE training used for decades to harden US servicemen for enemy interrogation in the event of capture. In the aftermath of 9/11, the agency had, the Senate reported, reverse engineered SERE training to create the "enhanced" techniques employed at its black sites worldwide. However, the impact of this finding, which hinted at a half-century history of CIA mind-control research, was blunted when the *New York Times* overlooked the agency's role and attributed this reverse engineering to two contract psychologists—two professional "bad apples."[58]

Impunity

In the transition from Bush to Obama, partisan wrangling over CIA interrogation produced a surprisingly bipartisan move toward impunity for past human rights abuse. Whether in England, France, Indonesia, or America, impunity usually passes through three stages: first, blame the supposed "bad apples"; second, invoke national security ("It protected us"); and, third, appeal to national unity. To these three, we must add an uncommon fourth stage found most visibly in Indonesia and America—a political counterattack by perpetrators and their protectors who condemn human rights reformers for weakening the nation's security. In the years since President Obama took office, the United States has moved, with surprising speed, through all four stages to reach a state of impunity.

Stage one was an unwitting bipartisan effort. In May 2009 President Obama echoed Rumsfeld's original defense of Abu Ghraib, asserting that the abuse "was carried out in the past by a small number of individuals."[59] Next, in early 2009, Republicans took the nation deep into the second stage with former vice president Cheney's statements that the CIA's methods "prevented the violent deaths of thousands, perhaps hundreds of thousands, of people." The Obama administration did not dispute this claim.[60] Then, on April 16, 2009, President Obama brought us to the third stage when he released four Bush-era memos detailing CIA torture techniques while insisting that "Nothing will be gained by spending our time and energy laying blame for the past."[61] Four days later, during a visit to CIA headquarters, Obama promised there would be no prosecutions of its employees. "We've made some mistakes," he admitted. But he urged Americans to "acknowledge them and then move forward." The president's position was in such blatant defiance of international law that the UN's chief official on torture, Manfred Nowak, reminded him that Washington was legally obliged to investigate any violations of the Convention Against Torture.[62]

There were also clear signs that the Obama administration was resuming the policy of outsourcing interrogation, much as Washington had done during the Cold War. Since mid-2008, US intelligence agencies had captured a half-dozen al Qaeda suspects and, instead of shipping them to CIA secret prisons, had them interrogated by allied agencies in the Middle East. Showing that this policy was becoming bipartisan, Obama's new CIA director, Leon Panetta, announced that his agency would continue to engage in the rendition of terror suspects to allies such as Egypt, Jordan, or Pakistan where we could, of course, "rely on diplomatic assurances of good treatment."[63]

By failing to investigate past human rights abuse, President Obama seems to have inadvertently created an opening for that uncommon fourth stage in the process of impunity: a political counterattack from perpetrators seeking not just immunity, but vindication. In this slide toward hyper-impunity, a steady thunder from the Republican right seemed to push the Obama White House toward a compromised position on human rights. After the administration released the Bush torture memos in April 2009, former vice president Dick Cheney and his daughter Liz launched a sustained media counterattack. While his daughter berated Obama for attempting to "libel the brave men and women who conducted this program,"[64] Cheney proclaimed himself "a staunch proponent of our enhanced interrogation program," calling it "the right thing to do."[65] After the abortive bomb attempt on a Northwest Airlines flight to Detroit that December, Liz Cheney formed a patriotic group, "Keep America Safe," whose opening media salvo blasted Obama for "treating terror as a law enforcement matter, refusing to use every tool at his disposal to prevent attacks."[66] A few weeks later her father identified the "tool" in question, insisting that the CIA should have had the option of waterboarding the Detroit bomber.[67]

To publicize his memoirs in mid-2010, ex-president Bush used the media as a megaphone for his view that waterboarding had saved lives. When the London *Times* asked if he had authorized waterboarding, Bush replied: "Damn right! We capture the guy, the chief operating officer of al-Qaida, who kills three thousand people. We felt he had the information about another attack. . . . I believe that decision saved lives."[68] In his memoirs released that November, Bush wrote that these "interrogations helped break up plots to attack American diplomatic facilities abroad, Heathrow Airport and Canary Wharf in London."[69] Amidst a chorus of denials from British leaders, Prime Minister David Cameron asserted that waterboarding was indeed torture, adding "if actually you're getting information from torture, it's very likely to be unreliable information."[70] But the US media did not report this critique, and the ex-president's claims of efficacy generally went unchallenged in the United States.

Standing back from this partisan debate, Obama's first two years in office produced a marked continuity with many of the prior administration's controversial counter-terror policies. Not only did he retain many top Bush security officials, Obama authorized detention without trial for fifty terror suspects, preserved the controversial military commissions, and fought the courts to retain executive counterterror prerogatives. To block civil suits by victims seeking redress for Bush-era abuse, Obama's Justice Department reiterated its predecessor's policy, invoking a "state secrets" doctrine in some cases and in others arguing that the illegality of torture remained an open question. Muting the effect of Obama's original January 2009 ban on the CIA's coercive techniques, the text of this executive order was, according to human rights attorney Scott Horton, "very carefully tailored so that it was only CIA black sites that were closed," thereby allowing the military's Joint Special Operations Command to maintain its secret prisons in Afghanistan, Iraq, and elsewhere. Moreover, the president's own interrogation task force recommended, in August 2009, against any changes to the Army Field Manual, which had been revised under Bush to permit abusive psychological techniques.[71]

By degrees, moreover, Republican conservatives pressed the Obama administration to compromise its initial commitment to human rights. In February 2010 Obama's Justice Department reversed an earlier finding that Bush lawyers Jay Bybee and John Yoo had been "guilty of professional misconduct" in writing those 2002 memos that authorized CIA abuse— just as the Cheneys had demanded.[72] A year later in March 2011, after Congress banned transfer of trials to the United States, the president rescinded a two-year ban on military tribunals at Guantánamo and set procedures for al Qaeda suspects to be held there indefinitely without trial. This "scar on the nation's conscience," rued a *New York Times* editorial, would now remain unhealed for years to come. "This is a step . . . toward institutionalizing a preventive-detention regime," observed the president of Human Rights First.[73] "The Bush administration constructed a legal framework for torture," noted the ACLU's Jameel Jaffer, "but the Obama administration is constructing a legal framework for impunity."[74]

The Obama administration's assassination of Osama bin Laden in May 2011 provided an unexpected political opening for torture advocates to press for the final step to full impunity. Within hours of the news of bin Laden's death, these Bush-era perpetrators formed a media chorus, repeating the refrain that their harsh methods were responsible for this success and demanding an end to the Justice Department investigations of CIA interrogators.

Almost immediately, former Justice official John Yoo called bin Laden's killing "a vindication of the Bush administration's terrorism policies [that] shows that success comes from continuing those policies, not rejecting them as Obama has tried to do for the last two years." Citing speculative, inaccurate news stories that appeared the morning after Navy Seals shot bin Laden, Yoo argued that Bush's harsh interrogation had provided the first clue, the name of bin Laden's courier, by extracting it from Khalid Sheikh Mohammed, the Al Qaeda operations chief who had been waterboarded 183 times.[75] Almost immediately, however, other news outlets reported that Khalid had consistently misled CIA interrogators with fake names and erroneous information.[76] Although the press quickly debunked the claims by Bush-era officials, Yoo published an op-ed in *The Wall Street Journal* insisting that Obama "should end the criminal investigation of CIA agents and restart the interrogation program that helped lead us to bin Laden."[77] Making similar assertions, Jose Rodriguez, chief of the CIA's Counterterrorism Center under Bush from 2002 to 2005, told the media that the use of enhanced interrogation on Khalid Sheikh Mohammed and others had produced key intelligence "about bin Laden's courier . . . that eventually led to the location of [bin Laden's] compound and the operation that led to his death."[78]

Appearing on Fox News after bin Laden's killing, former defense secretary Donald Rumsfeld said: "I think that anyone who suggests that the enhanced techniques—let's be blunt—waterboarding, did not produce an enormous amount of valuable intelligence just isn't facing the truth."[79] Reiterating his belief in the efficacy of harsh methods, Dick Cheney told Fox News: "I would assume that the enhanced interrogation program that we put in place produced some of the results that led to bin Laden's ultimate capture."[80] Five days later, Cheney elaborated, saying: "It was a good program. It was a legal program. It was not torture." In defense of the CIA interrogators, he added: "These men deserve to be decorated. They don't deserve to be prosecuted."[81]

Even though conservative claims for torture's role in bin Laden's death had no factual basis, the Obama administration quickly capitulated and, within weeks, completed the process of impunity. In June 2011 Attorney General Holder announced that his special prosecutor, John Durham, had examined 101 instances of "alleged CIA mistreatment" and found that any further investigation "is not warranted."[82] Although the prosecutor would continue to investigate two deaths in CIA custody, this finding ended any possible prosecution of agency officials for torture during the War on Terror. "I welcome the news," said CIA director Panetta. "We are now about to close this chapter of our agency's history." But an ACLU official, Jameel Jaffer, condemned the decision, saying senior Bush officials had approved CIA interrogation that "subjected prisoners to unimaginable cruelty and violated both international and domestic law."[83] In sum, this process of impunity has led Washington back to a contradictory policy on torture that, during the Cold War, had tacit bipartisan support—i.e., publicly advocating human rights, while covertly outsourcing torture to allied security services and quietly covering up past abuse. In retrospect, the real aberration of the Bush years lay not in torture policies per se, but in the president's order that the CIA operate its own torture prisons and dirty its hands with waterboarding and wall slamming.

International Impunity

In an era of globalization, impunity within the nation state is no longer sufficient, since the prohibition of torture has gained numerous international forums for legal action—the UN, the European Court of Human Rights, and a dozen European national courts. Throughout the last years of Bush and the first years of Obama, Washington applied strong diplomatic pressure on Germany, Italy, and Spain to drop any trials of US principals for illegal rendition under their universal jurisdiction. As early as 2007 the deputy chief of mission in Berlin, John Konig, met with Germany's deputy national security adviser to warn that in the case of Khaled El-Masri, a German citizen rendered to Afghanistan by the CIA, "issuance of international arrest warrants would have a negative impact on our bilateral relationship"—pressures that served to slow any such legal action in Germany.[84] Two years later the Obama administration responded to a Spanish complaint against six senior Bush-era officials for "creating a legal framework that allegedly permitted torture" by warning the Spanish foreign minister "that the prosecutions . . . would have an enormous impact on the bilateral relationship," and were delighted when Madrid's attorney general opposed proceeding with the charges.[85]

Despite these successes, US diplomatic power could slow but not stay the hand of international justice. In May 2009 a Milan court convicted twenty-two CIA agents and a US Air Force colonel for their role in the 2003 kidnapping of Egyptian exile Abu Omar and his illegal rendition to Cairo for torture. Sabrina De Sousa, one of those CIA agents convicted in absentia, told ABC News that the United States "broke the law" with this rendition, "and we are paying for the mistakes right now, whoever authorized and approved this." The victim was eventually found innocent and released to live quietly in Alexandria. "He was the wrong guy," said former CIA agent Robert Baer. "It was not worth putting the reputation of the United States on the line going after somebody like this."[86]

By late 2010 there were numerous torture-related official inquiries and legal cases against US rendition in a half-dozen European nations. Apart from new cases in Germany, Italy, and Spain, there were ongoing investigations in Poland, Lithuania, Romania, Sweden, and Britain. Most significantly, Poland has given a former CIA detainee, Abd al-Rahim al-Nashiri, formal "victim status," while the United Kingdom has announced, in mid-2010, an official "Torture Inquiry" to investigate government complicity in the mistreatment of individuals.[87] Each of these cases has the potential to release more sensitive details about rendition to CIA black sites that operated in Lithuania, Poland, and Romania during the Bush administration.

In marked contrast to the systematic dismissal of every complaint by torture victims from US courts, these European proceedings have evinced a surprising openness to the evidence and a resistance to political pressure. Whatever the outcome of the individual inquiries might be, their persistence indicates that the once-strong *sub rosa* alliance between the CIA and European security services is attenuating, and redress for torture, if it is to come anywhere, will be found in transnational venues remote from the pressures of impunity.

The Price of Impunity

In a half-dozen incidents from 1970 to 2011, the usual US processes of political reform through media exposé and congressional action were stymied when the public's revulsion quickly faded, allowing the CIA to resume its dirty work in the shadows of executive power. As a powerful secret service whose charter permits operations outside the law, the CIA represents an implicit challenge to both due process and democracy. Compounding this problem, the executive itself has an unrivaled ability, through the federal bureaucracy and partisan support, to shape public policy, even when it violates both domestic law and international agreements. Over the past forty years, the capacity of reformers to restrain executive excess through public exposé has been checked by the secrecy shrouding CIA covert action. Whenever this ad hoc human rights coalition of activists, lawyers, media, courts, and Congress has discovered abuse akin to torture, the CIA has retreated behind claims of state secrecy, adapting its covert operations to elude both law and legislative intent.

In retrospect this process of blaming a few rogue soldiers, scientists, or CIA contractors, the first step toward impunity, often assuages public concern about the need for redress, and thus serves as a precondition for public forgetting. Abetted by a sensationalist, often superficial media, the American public has a notoriously short-term memory, quickly absorbing the details of the current controversy, yet unmindful of its antecedents. Meanwhile, the security agencies, with strong institutional continuity of personnel and procedure, can readily revive their abusive methods once the controversy has abated and a new need arises for these same questionable methods.

Against this general grain of public forgetting, historical memory remains the most salient antidote. Through its study of legislative history and legal precedent, the legal profession has an in-built vehicle for memory that is, of course, open to partisan bias or misappropriation. As demonstrated in the half-dozen interrogation memos from the Bush Justice Department, administration attorneys were single-minded in their appropriation of the past to serve present policy—searching US and European precedents for arguments and documenting these tendentious points with elaborate footnotes in long memos. By contrast, military lawyers, through a half-century of codified law and thirty-year careers, seem the state actor with the strongest institutional memory and the most consistent record of observing of human rights.

Outside government, civil society groups—human-rights organizations, media outlets, and congressional committees—are usually staffed with younger workers on short-term, ever-shifting assignments. Their short memories are often abetted by the media. In the six years after the Abu Ghraib scandal broke in April 2004, the *New York Times* provided detailed coverage, but seemed unaware of its own investigative reports from the 1970s that, if recollected, would have revealed strong continuities from the agency's past mind-control efforts through its current interrogation policy.

Indeed, the inclination to overlook any continuity with past CIA involvement in torture in the aftermath of the recent crisis over Abu Ghraib has hampered analysis by journalists, Congress, and human rights groups. Unmindful of the past, these groups often pursued superficial exposés, worked for partial reforms, and left unaddressed the ultimate source of the recourse to torture inside the CIA. In some future foreign policy crisis, the agency or other clandestine service may again have recourse to torture, producing another controversy and extending an ever-lengthening historical procession from the Phoenix program of South Vietnam through the concrete cells of Abu Ghraib to some future prison whose exposé will, no doubt, do further damage to US claims of global leadership.

PART TWO

Singularities of Witness

CHAPTER 3

Torture and Society

Reinhold Görling

No living being is self-contained. We are all involved in a constant process of exchange with something or someone else: we breathe, we drink, we eat, we perceive with our senses and are perceived by the senses of others. Our emotions and thoughts are always already closely connected and interwoven with the world, with the things that impinge upon our senses, the institutions that shape our times and places, and above all with the thoughts and emotions of other living beings. In a very fundamental sense, life takes place in a space shared with other life. This interpersonal space does not first begin beyond our skin; it is just as much within us as without. And above all, it also precedes us in time. Before the subject has a self that relates to others, it is already in relationships. The address precedes the response, as one might say with Emmanuel Lévinas.[1] Research on infants in recent decades, particularly inspired by the work of Daniel Stern,[2] has shown how intense and complex this web of relationships already is in the first months of life. The neurologist Vittorio Gallese, codiscoverer of the so-called "mirror neurons," calls this space a "shared manifold of intersubjectivity."[3] And just as we are already dependent on others before we even exist, we remain dependent on them all our lives. Judith Butler calls this dependency "being beside oneself." Our sexuality is its central expression, which is why it is not merely a dimension of our existence, but is in fact coextensive with it.[4]

The subject is vulnerable precisely because, in its formation, it is fundamentally dependent on the other. Societies can provide us with protection, but they can just as easily threaten us, indeed, they can deliberately and willingly hurt us and cause us pain. Torture is a phenomenon specific to societies. It belongs in all likelihood neither to the basic repertoire of human life nor to that of any other being. Torture is a practice in which the vulnerability of the human being is deliberately used in order to exert control over him or her, a very comprehensive control. It is a technique for making the distinctive characteristic of life, its openness and dependence on others, into the means of its destruction. But since it is just this sociality of the subject that makes society possible and necessary, torture is also a practice that deprives some of its members of what is constitutive of society, denies it to them, excludes them from all protection and provision. Societies thus pervert their own condition of possibility into a threat by acting out and presenting their own unreliability.

The intentional violence to which victims of torture are subjected is a deliberate destruction of subjectivity. The suffering caused to human beings by torture holds them captive for years, perhaps forever. And this suffering is similar in all victims, regardless of what culture, what country, what social group they come from. On the basis of her many years of experience in the therapeutic support of torture victims, Françoise Sironi writes that torture deculturalizes its victims.[5] Torture tears its victims out of the social group, even out of history, and binds them at the same time, like every serious trauma, to history.[6] Rigidity and repetition take the place of dynamism and change.

Torture threatens the anthropological foundations of the human being. But this does not mean that torture belongs to the anthropological character of the human. Torture is not an evil that naturally accompanies our history and can only be held in check with difficulty. But precisely because human beings create their forms of exchange with the world by means of the forms of their cultures and societies, they are able to block these forms and to bring their exchange to a standstill. The deculturalization that affects individual victims of torture passes into the intended destruction of the culture of entire groups, as Sironi shows in her *Psychopathologie des violences collectives*.[7] However people try to legitimize the intended violence, it always possesses a dimension that exceeds the intended relationship between means and ends, as Maurice Merleau-Ponty formulated in

Humanisme et terreur in the late 1940s.[8] Violence is therefore only a means where it is also an end: "necropolitics" is the term that Achille Mbembe suggests for this.[9]

The idea that it is possible to torture another human being also stands in a direct relationship to the consciousness of one's own vulnerability. Torture presupposes a certain degree of empathy, and thus also mental, discursive, and institutional strategies, which turn off or even pervert the effects of empathy on the torturer. Strategies of splitting, projection, reversal, or denial are developed in order to block or at least temporarily reduce the possibility that the intended harm to the helpless other, delivered into the torturer's own power and care, will reflect back upon the perpetrator's concern about his or her own vulnerability. But these mechanisms fail in two respects. Since, on the one hand, the perception of the other always precedes the denial and refusal of his claim to be heard, the neutralization of empathy must always also enact the denial theatrically—by humiliating the other, for example. This quickly results in a spiral of violence and denial, which is why an excess of violence is always inherent in torture. On the other hand, many studies show that in their memories, perpetrators also remain bound to the deculturalization of torture.

To assume that human beings are dependent on others in a very basic sense does not mean that we have to understand the human as a "deficient being," or "*Mangelwesen*," as Arnold Gehlen did.[10] On the contrary: this openness is the condition for our social and cultural wealth; only this openness enables us to desire and to enjoy. Some events, and their institutionalization in rituals (such as the exchange of gifts), exhibit these riches performatively and make possible at the same time the experience of recognition.[11] Recognition is a social protection against vulnerability; the desire for recognition is a part of the care of the self.[12] The care of the self always also includes the experience of one's own vulnerability; humiliation is a form of damage to the psychological construction of this care of the self that can penetrate down to the most basic structures of the *ego*.[13] For this reason the denial of recognition and hurting the other are closely linked. Historically, too, the rise of torture in antiquity seems to have been just as linked with the development and individuation of the care of the self as with the nonrecognition of the respectability of the other—for example, with the definition of his or her social status as a slave.[14]

Recognizing the other as a theatrical or performative act presumably occurs in all cultures, at least symbolically. Such acts also define what a specific recognition entails, or what social and cultural place is being assigned to the other. As a rule, they are connected with the performance and presentation of vulnerability. Societies develop diverse theatrical forms in order to negotiate this, and a large number of a society's institutions re-perform this tension between vulnerability and recognition in constantly new forms. First and foremost, we can think of the rites of passage in which the incorporation of children into the community or the transition from childhood to sexual maturity is performed. They have not vanished from contemporary society, but have rather become everyday events, present in manifold forms of performing humiliation, injury, and recognition and thereby acceptance or rejection: families, schools, sports clubs, and the military are full of them. This continues in factories, courts, and universities. There is no punishment that does not aim at confronting the other with his or her vulnerability. It is for precisely this reason that these institutions do not make life easier for people; rather, they tend to deny people recognition, to humiliate them. Theodor W. Adorno stated this clearly in his argument with Gehlen in 1965 when he pointed to the fact that the institutions demonstrated "the replaceability and dispensibility of every single individual."[15] Humiliation and, in particular, shame, are presumably intensive reactions on the part of the injured subject that also involve consciousness of one's own vulnerability. "In shame, the subject thus has no other content than its own desubjectification; it becomes witness to its own disorder, its own oblivion as a subject," writes Giorgio Agamben, pursuing a thought of Lévinas.[16]

The play of recognition is necessary in order to develop some consciousness of oneself. We do not need to spell this out in terms of the Hegelian dialectics of master and slave, in which this consciousness is connected with the experience of one's own death. One can also describe it in a tradition drawing on the work of Donald W. Winnicott as a "location of cultural experience."[17] This location is certainly not free of experiences of loss and hurt, but what is decisive is that this location constitutes itself by means of a relationship with play, a "pretend mode" of interpersonal communication, as Peter Fonagy and Mary Target call it. This play enables the subject to experience the fact that there is an interpersonal world different from what can be experienced as external reality. Not only empathy, but even the development of a self and a relationship to one's own feelings, already presupposes that a difference between mental and external reality can be perceived and intersubjectively experienced.[18]

In his essay "The structure of evil," Christopher Bollas writes that serial offenders in particular often begin the play of interpersonal communication with a high degree of empathy and can in this way be very seductive. Then, however, from one moment to the next, they refuse the other this empathy, and hurt, abuse, or even kill their victims. These actions seem to be determined by a repetition compulsion. The perpetrator's own traumatic experiences seem to return this way, Bollas suspects.[19] One probably cannot interpret every practice of breaking the empathic bond as the return of a traumatic experience, and certainly not when the offenders do not act as individuals, but rather as groups or at least in institutional contexts. But it does seem plausible that it is first this theatricality of culture, this tendency of culture to perform sociality in theatrical forms and thus to ground them in performances, that makes it possible to reverse just this tendency and to perform the vulnerability and the negation of sociality.

If this is so, then the forms in which sociality is performatively negated are extremely closely and directly related to the social conflicts of a society and to the struggle for wealth, in the many meanings of that word: social, cultural, economic wealth, the wealth of everything a society believes to be particular to a human being, his or her characteristics, peculiarities, and possessions, his or her rights and opportunities. This idea of the human can also be understood as a way in which forms of recognition are preshaped in terms of culture and the collective.

If recognition is thus always also a theatrical act, its denial and the revocation of the basic rights of the other are also theatrical acts, and one can also draw conclusions from the structures of denial about the structures of the social and cultural conflicts that are virulent in a society. Torture is incompatible with the notion of the constitutional state, since the latter is based on the fundamental recognition of the autonomy of the individual.[20] If after its abolition as a source of evidence in legal proceedings, torture is reintroduced in the twentieth century on a large scale in the Soviet Union and in National Socialism, it stands in a modern context. Since then, torture has been a practice of political repression and at the same time an exhibition of the vulnerability of others, directed not only at the individual, but also at a social group or community as a whole. It demonstrates power and arbitrariness; it demonstrates unprotectedness and exploits it; it hurts and humiliates.

To the extent that political power gains its legitimacy by protecting citizens—not just from an "outward" enemy, but also from an alleged "inner" enemy—to the extent that political power bases its legitimacy on the dispositive of safety,[21] to that extent the legitimization of power and the production of its basis enter into a threatening pact. This is the sense in which Michel Foucault spoke of the *raison* of torture.[22] Torture, as the performance of the exclusion of the other as well as the performance of human vulnerability, falls as a possibility within this dispositive. "The object of torture is torture," wrote George Orwell over fifty years ago in his novel *1984*.[23]

As with other forms of deliberate violence—massacre, rape in warfare, forced disappearance—by aiming at the one, an entire group is hit. This is the point of a curious tension between secrecy and revelation peculiar to torture. It takes place in cellars and camps fenced with barbed wire, but it is also exhibited: as rumor, as picture. It thus also puts specific social pressure on those who do not even see themselves as belonging to the social group involved. It demands from them a process of inner split and denial, at least if they accept this procedure without resistance, without mourning. This political act of splitting perception is what the theatre scholar Diana Taylor has called "percepticide."[24] It consists of superpositions: while the act of violence demonstrates how the other can be excluded from empathy and how his or her psychological reality can be split off from the interpersonal relationship, the third party—the witness to this act—is drawn into this relationship. He is required to accept his role as witness and thus to resist the exclusion of the victim from the social bond, or to look away, to close his eyes and to exclude what has been perceived from the realm of possible empathy. But this exclusion always takes place after the perception itself, both on the part of the perpetrator and of the witness. Which is why this exclusion has to be produced performatively. It is not enough merely to close one's eyes. The phrase "to turn a blind eye" better describes the act of exclusion from perception. It is active and restless, because the perception has always already taken place before it can be excluded. It is in memory. And since violence, particularly in extreme forms like torture, is always a dissolution of boundaries and a threat to the most fundamental possibilities of creating a coherent community and subjectivity, there is a continuous, urgent necessity to limit it. Torture, as Elaine Scarry writes, is an "obscene and pathetic drama."[25]

The position of the third party, the spectator—bystander and witness—is probably therefore always implied in the situation of every act of violence. The third party can occupy the position of an authority before whose eyes someone humiliates or kills someone else in order to win his or her approval. The third party can occupy the position of a social representative whose presence is at least the legitimation of the act. But the third party can also occupy the position of the person who is primarily to be hurt by the violence performed. The third party can also play the role of making the perpetrator's own actions appear unreal: by merely watching the event, he helps to make it seem fictional. In the form of monologue, he can also occupy the position of an observation of the self. Aleksandar Tišma's *Die Schule der Gottlosigkeit* ("School of Atheism") provides a haunting example of how that can work.[26] This role can also change in the course of a scene, be cast ambivalently, or even doubled. In any case it constitutes the frame, closes and anchors it; in extreme cases, it can be used as a mechanism of exclusion and inclusion: "Genocide, after all, is an exercise in community building," writes Philip Gourevitch, who spent three years researching the genocide in Rwanda in 1994.[27]

The distribution of images and linguistic information by means of the mass media and the Internet has changed the third party's position for a long time to come. Perhaps if it were still in a village, it would function as a local social, political, or cultural authority; today, however, the third party's position seems to be occupied more and more often by the eye and ear of digital recording devices that produce and distribute a visual and auditory picture of the event. The third party, witness and audience, has thus become a global protagonist, acting also by remaining silent and looking away. If it is the third party who first closes the frame of the picture, then he himself belongs to the picture, even if he remains invisible. That also means that the third party can open this frame and recontextualize it, even change the picture. Judith Butler has insisted on this more than once in her comments on the photographs of the tortures at Abu Ghraib.[28]

This position of the third party, which can be supported by medial techniques, is thus not something that is added to the event. It is always already involved in the event itself. Not seeing something that one sees—denial—is also a relation. Knowledge and ignorance are both medial. But how is one to describe this mediality, particularly if one observes that there is a close connection between an external representation of an action and the mental representation of the event on the part of all the participants? How does looking away and forgetting take place?

This paradoxical mediality of violence is hard to grasp. Violence can on the one hand be defined as a power that intervenes in a social or cultural situation from the outside in order to rob it of its ability to express itself, to make it dumb or destroy it. Violence leaves its mark on its object; it disfigures.[29] Even if other forms of expression replace the destroyed or disfigured one, the fact that violence robs the relation it affects of its forms of expression enables violence to function—in a social, cultural, political sense—as power. Since social and cultural relations create and regulate, hand things down and change them by means of their forms of expression, violence can be understood as an inscription in these forms of expression, as their disruption or even their replacement.

On the other hand, destruction—in a cultural, social, and psychological sense—does not necessarily mean disappearance. There is psychological memory, and certainly cultural and social memory: things, institutions, images, and texts preserve experiences of violence and pass them on, and this all the more permanently the less they are socially bound and worked through in a psychoanalytic sense. And precisely this is what extreme experiences of deliberate violence do not allow, or allow only with great difficulty. These experiences are fixed and remain stubbornly because they are not translatable into any form of social life, because they are isolated, without connections, in our individual, social, and cultural memories.

This isolation and disconnection can extend to the impossibility of expressing experience at all. Trauma research has identified the problem of concretistic language—that is, the restriction of a person's ability to build metaphors.[30] Elisabeth Weber has described this erasure of the capacity for metaphor very precisely as the danger of that persecution to which "the subject of our time" is exposed.[31] Metaphors are fundamentally relational and in motion; their destruction, to return to Sironi's thought, is deculturalization. Freud always understood repetition compulsion ambivalently; on the one hand, it restricts the subject in its possibilities by chaining it to something foreign, but on the other hand, it can be an opportunity to link isolated experiences and to bind them socially. The more radically an experience is split off, the more it feels as if it were emerging from a crypt, the less chance there is of taking it up into the cultural movement of translation.[32]

These processes of isolation, splitting, and denial of experience do not merely concern single individuals; on the contrary, they affect entire societies and their capacity for metaphor. In January 2002, two years before the photographs from Abu Ghraib became known, the US Department of Defense published a photograph taken by a Marine at the American base in Guantánamo Bay, Cuba. It shows a scene from the entrance area of Camp X-Ray. The picture has entered our visual memory: it shows a dozen men dressed in orange overalls kneeling on the rough gravel ground, their hands and feet bound, their beltless trousers scarcely covering their genital areas, ear muffs over their heads, dark ski glasses over their eyes, orange caps drawn down over their heads, respiratory masks over their mouths and noses, thick gloves on their tightly bound hands. Humiliation, sensory deprivation, enforcement of painful positions, restriction of breath: all of this was officially exhibited. The photo was printed in our daily papers and shown in news broadcasts. There were some worried commentaries, but even these avoided for the most part the word "torture." How does it occur that one sees something but does not realize what it is? How is it possible, for many years, to prevent with mere assertions—for example, the assertion that waterboarding is not torture—seeing what one is doing for what it is?

George Orwell asked this question in the 1940s and connected it with the extreme threat to the subject posed by torture. This threat concerns the possibility of creating mental representations of experience—that is, of the other and the self, in a very fundamental sense. Based on these considerations, Peter Fonagy has begun, from a psychoanalytic perspective, to distinguish two kinds of violence. The first kind follows the already discussed schema of projecting threatening parts of the self onto the other and the subsequent displaced and substitutional acting out of the threat in violence toward the other. This projective process presupposes, however, that the subject—or society—really does possess mental or cultural/medial representations of what, in the process of projection, is to be denied in the self and attributed to the other. But many violent acts can no longer be understood adequately by means of this mechanism of representational violence. If it sometimes influences actions, it cannot completely account for them. Fonagy therefore sees a further origin, which is sometimes complementary, but which is also sometimes dominant, in what he calls "violence in the negative." Here, the attempt is to prevent a mental representation from arising at all. What is denied is not something that has already urged someone to accept it as his own; the urge itself is denied. Something is rejected before the subject has actually realized what it is. For this reason, the kind of violence that acts out this rejection is vaguer and less amenable to self-control.[33] This second denial has much to do with the fear of one's own dependence upon the other, of one's own vulnerability. If torture performs our vulnerability as a threat, then perhaps there can only be one answer: to express this exposedness as a witness, as the attempt not to turn a blind eye, to see what is seen, to speak about it, to try to transform splitting, perversion, and exclusion into connection, perception, and acceptance.

Translated from the German by Glenn Patten

CHAPTER 4

What Nazi Crimes Against Humanity Can Tell Us about Torture Today

Susan Derwin

The 1948 Universal Declaration of Human Rights was a direct conse-quence of Nazi crimes against humanity.[1] As chairperson of the human rights commission that crafted the declaration, Eleanor Roosevelt addressed the General Assembly of the United Nations about its significance, stating, "[It] may well become the international Magna Carta of all men every-where. We hope its proclamation by the General Assembly will be an event comparable to the proclamation of the Declaration of the Rights of Man by the French people in 1789, the adoption of the Bill of Rights by the people of the United States, and the adoption of comparable declarations at different times in other countries."[2]

Two years before the Universal Declaration of Human Rights, also in direct response to the Nazi genocide, Primo Levi completed *Survival in Auschwitz*, an account of his ten months in the German death camp. Levi survived deportation; he was stripped of every right, starved, and subjected to the brutal conditions of Auschwitz. He returned to speak and write about what it felt like to live, and survive the experience of having lived, in a universe organized around the principle that "every stranger is an enemy."[3] He wanted people to understand the story of the death camps as "a sinister alarm-signal" that revealed what happens when a nation's social order is predicated upon the principle of enmity.[4]

Investigations have revealed that the "enhanced interrogation techniques" approved by President Bush were the same as, and in some forms even more cruel than, the forms of "intensified interrogation" (*verschärfte Vernehmung*) practiced by the Gestapo.[5] The German term appears to have been coined in 1937 to refer to interrogation methods designed to leave no lasting, detectable marks.[6] President Bush authorized the inducing of hypothermia and the use of the "waterboarding" methods of torture that in 1937 Nazi officials forbade. While the Nazis never authorized "waterboarding," starting in 1943 they approved of the use of "the cold-bath" technique, introduced by a member of the French Gestapo and practiced in France, Norway, and Czechoslovakia.[7] The use of torture practices by the Bush administration identical to those of the National Socialist regime indicates that torture is compatible with both democracy and authoritarianism.[8] In this context, what interests me about Levi's writings is the way in which they make clear that not only the freedoms enjoyed in democratic civil society, but also the very identity of its citizens, depend upon the power of the state to protect and enable, or, as the case may be, jeopardize, the integrity of the physical body, the very integrity that torture violates.

Levi was born in Turin, Italy, in 1919, to a family of assimilated and fairly nonreligious Jews. He studied chemistry, earning his Bachelor of Science degree from the University of Turin in 1941. While the racial laws of 1938 prohibited access to higher education for Jews, Levi pursued his studies nevertheless. After finishing at the university he worked in a pharmaceutical laboratory, which is what he was doing in 1943 when the Germans invaded Northern Italy. Levi joined a partisan group devoted to fighting the German and Italian fascists. He was captured in December of 1943 and interned in a transit camp in Fossoli. Two months later, in the middle of winter, he was deported to the camp of Monowitz-Auschwitz. There he was put to work in one of three I. G. Farben laboratories. Because he was trained as a chemist, he was of use to the German war efforts, and therefore he was not sent to the gas chambers. In January of 1945, when the camp was evacuated in anticipation of advancing Russian forces, Levi was ill. He had contracted scarlet fever, and so the Germans left him behind when they abandoned the camp. After the liberation, Levi made his way back to Milan, where he married and resumed his career as an industrial chemist. In 1977 he retired from his position as manager of a chemical factory in Turin to devote himself exclusively to writing. He became renowned for the first memoir he wrote about his experience in the camps, *Se questo è un uomo*, which in 1960 appeared in the United States under the title *Survival in Auschwitz: The Nazi Assault on Humanity.*⁹ He wrote more non-fiction, as well as fiction and poetry. His nonfictional works include: *The Truce*, 1958; *The Reawakening*, 1958; *Moments of Reprieve*, 1986; and *The Drowned and the Saved*, 1986. Of the 650 people in the railway convoy that had taken Levi to Auschwitz, he was one of only fifteen men and nine women to survive. But on April 11, 1987, he fell into the stairwell of his apartment building, the one where he had lived almost his entire life. He died instantly from the fall. Levi did not leave a suicide note, and thus the question of whether his death was intentional or accidental cannot be answered definitively.

The title of the US translation of Levi's first book is misleading. "*Survival in Auschwitz*" places the emphasis on life in Auschwitz, upon survival. It suggests that however harrowing Levi's camp experience may have been, in the final analysis, it was something he could outlive or overcome. But the literal translation of the Italian title, "If this is a man," has a different tone and emphasis. It unsettles the certainty that, having survived Auschwitz, one returns as a man or unproblematically continues to be a man. In raising the question of whether the survivor has been able to remain human, it suggests that humanness—"our personality," as Levi calls it—is not an inviolable essence, but a "fragile" quality or attribute, "much more in danger than our life."¹⁰ The literal translation of the title of Levi's text therefore asks us to consider how the experience of the camps was one of stripping away, possibly permanently, the qualities associated with humanness.

Levi took the title of his testimony from the poem with which he begins his text. Its opening lines are,

> You who live safe
> In your warm houses,
> You who find, returning in the evening,
> Hot food and friendly faces:
> Consider if this is a man
> Who works in the mud
> Who does not know peace
> Who fights for a scrap of bread
> Who dies because of a yes or a no.
> Consider if this is a woman,
> Without hair and without name
> With no more strength to remember,
> Her eyes empty and her womb cold
> Like a frog in winter.¹¹

The men and women whose humanness Levi asks the reader to consider were referred to in camp slang as the *Muselmänner*, or "Muslims."[12] These men and women were not equipped to survive. They entered the camps and immediately began spiraling downward. They existed in a world apart, only communicating to complain or to talk about food.[13] For those other prisoners who, unlike the *Muselmänner*, did not deteriorate so severely, the stripped-down existence of the *Muselmänner* was a threat; it signified what every other prisoner in the camps could become. Levi writes that all the evil of his time was encapsulated in the image of the *Muselmänner*, "an emaciated man, with head dropped and shoulders curved, on whose face and in whose eyes not a trace of a thought is to be seen."[14]

Aristotle writes that humans and animals are similar in their ability to express pleasure and pain by their cries; but they are different in that only humans can speak, and speaking enables them to make judgments.[15] Levi's description of the *Muselmänner* suggests that although they were alive in a biological sense, they no longer possessed the qualities that Aristotle associates with humanness. Levi writes, "Weeks and months before being snuffed out, they [the *Muselmänner*], had already lost the ability to observe, to remember, to compare, and express themselves."[16] Remembering, comparing, observing, expressing—activities of judgment and speech—are what distinguish the human from animals. It could be said that the threat that the *Muselmänner* posed to the other prisoners was their self-enclosure; they had lost the ability to stay connected to the world through the manifold forms of thought and communication.

In a 1970 interview conducted while he was in prison, Franz Stangl, the former commandant of Treblinka, explained the purpose of the cruelties and deprivations the Nazis inflicted. Stangl stated that they served "to condition those who were to be the material executors of the operations. To make it possible for them to do what they were doing."[17] This conditioning was a process of "dehumanization," the reduction of human identity to the level of mere biological subsistence. Prisoners, and specifically their bodies, were exposed to unbridled state power in a way that intensified their corporeal experience.[18]

Levi does not associate this diminished existence with anything like a return to a state of nature. Rather, he understood the *Muselmänner* as coming into being when "in the face of driving necessity and physical disabilities many social habits and instincts are reduced to silence."[19] He writes in detail about how the prisoners were reduced to barest biological life through assaults that made it impossible for their minds to be filled with anything other than heightened awareness of their suffering bodies. Elaine Scarry's description of the body in pain aptly characterizes the impact of these assaults. According to Scarry, "The person in great pain experiences his own body as the agent of his agony. The ceaseless, self-announcing signal of the body in pain . . . contains not only the feeling 'my body hurts' but the feeling 'my body hurts me.'"[20] When the body is in pain, the person experiences himself as his own aggressor. The container of consciousness becomes filled with the sensations of physical pain. When this happens, the border between outer and inner world collapses and the world seems to fall away. Physical suffering has the potential to fill the mind, to make the body emphatically present, to suspend awareness of everything other than the self's embodiedness. This was the crucial effect of the Nazi abuses of their camp prisoners.

Consider, in this context, the significance of the prisoners' deprivations during their journey to the camps in boxcars. The German authorities did not provide food, water, mats, straw, or "receptacles for bodily needs"; nor did they notify authorities and directors of collection camps to provide these necessities.[21] Of these affronts, Levi writes, a "deep wound inflicted on human dignity" was the necessity of evacuating in public.[22] In the cramped space of Levi's convoy, the prisoners reacted by improvising a screen.[23] Levi writes that this act was "substantially symbolic"; it was an assertion of their humanity, as if to say: "we are not yet animals, we will not be animals as long as we try to resist."[24] One could also understand the improvised screen as the erection of a symbolic psychic shield against the encroachment of the body into the space of consciousness.

The confiscation of belongings from the prisoners hastened the process of their increasing embodiedness. Levi writes,

> But consider what value, what meaning is enclosed even in the smallest of our daily habits, in the hundred possessions which even the poorest beggar owns: a handkerchief, an old letter, the photo of a cherished person. These things are part of us, almost like limbs of our body; nor is it conceivable that we can be deprived of them in our world, for we immediately find others to substitute the old ones, other objects which are ours in their personification and evocation of our memories.[25]

Memory is more integral to the self than limbs of the body, because without memory, there is no self. On the simplest level, if you do not remember your name, you cannot know who you are. At the same time, memory is distinct from body's limbs; it is memory that frees you from the limitations of the body. Through memory, the mind takes flight from the anchoring of the body in present time and immediate space. The objects that personify memory thus derive part of their meaning from the fact that they enable consciousness not to remain bound to the present. When the Nazis forced the prisoners to give up their shoes, clothing, hair, and names, they were consigning them to an immediacy that destroyed these indicators of the mobility of consciousness that characterizes memory.

The enforced nudity, the frequent, harsh stripping, and the weekly total shavings subjected the prisoners to further traumatic embodiedness. Levi writes,

> A naked and barefoot man feels that all his nerves and tendons are severed: he is helpless prey. Clothes, even the foul clothes distributed, even the crude clogs with their wooden soles, are a tenuous but indispensable defense. Anyone who does not have them no longer perceives himself as a human being but rather as a worm: naked, slow, ignoble, prone on the ground. He knows that he can be crushed at any moment.[26]

When Auschwitz was liberated, it was discovered that the SS had warehoused tens of thousands of plastic, aluminum, steel, and silver spoons.[27] And yet, as another means of inflicting violence, the prisoners were deprived of these utensils. Without spoons they were forced to lap up their daily soup like dogs. Hence the word used in the camp for eating: *fressen*, which means "to feed" as animals do. To use a spoon signifies that the conscious self retains control over its instinctual drives. In Judges 7:5 of the Bible, God instructs Gideon to choose as his warriors the men who do not lap the water with their tongues while drinking at the river, as dogs do, or kneel upon their knees to drink, but who lift their hands to their mouths; in other words, to choose the men whose actions bear the mark of mediation and intentionality.[28]

If the intensification of bodily experience through pain and deprivation impairs the mobility of mental life, the most devastating effect of the prisoners' reduction to corporeality through the ongoing subjection to violence concerned the way intensified embodiment subjected prisoners to a desolating solitude. This is the dimension of torture that Auschwitz survivor Jean Améry explored in an essay he published in 1966. The Austrian Améry was born Hans Mayer, but he changed his name after the war in order to disassociate himself from Germanic culture. During the war he had joined the Belgian underground and was captured as a resistor in July of 1943, when he was thirty years old. Before he was deported to Auschwitz, the Gestapo tortured him in Fort Breendonk, a "reception camp" for new prisoners. In Auschwitz, he was part of a forced labor squad that built the I. G. Farben factory where Levi was to work. As the Soviets approached,

Améry was evacuated, first to Buchenwald and then to Bergen-Belsen. After liberation he worked as a journalist and eventually began writing works of philosophy and literature. In 1976 he published an exploration of suicide, and two years later, he took his own life by overdosing on sleeping pills.

Améry's analysis of torture departs from the claim that "the expectation of help is as much a constitutional psychic element as is the struggle for existence."[29] This expectation is an inborn assumption we hold that the other is there to help; that is, in critical situations the self comes to know the other precisely as a provider of relief. We could expand this claim by saying that the self first makes contact with the world as that which offers relief from discomfort. To illustrate this, Améry invokes the situation of a child in pain: "Just a moment, the mother says to her child who is moaning from pain, a hot-water bottle, a cup of tea is coming right away, we won't let you suffer so! . . . In almost all situations in life where there is bodily injury there is also the expectation of help; the former is compensated by the latter."[30]

The child moans, and this moan is not merely a sounding, it is a communication, specifically, an address to the mother. It is the nature of every human moan to be such an address. That is why Améry understands the child's dependency as exemplary of all situations of distress. But what does this moan mean? According to Améry, it communicates the child's expectation of help. This expectation has nothing do with the fact that the mother may or may not be able to alleviate the child's suffering, that there may be no action she can take, no physical remedy she might provide. Rather, the child's compensation for its pain consists of the expectation itself: "where there is bodily injury there is also the expectation of help."[31] The former—the injury—is compensated by the latter—the expectation. The expectation of help *is* the compensation for injury, for when the mother responds to the child's moan as one addressed by it, she serves as witness to her child's pain. This is what constitutes her crucial intervention. In her capacity as witness, she has the power to alter her child's experience of pain, specifically the child's *relation* to its pain. More precisely, her presence creates relation. The child alone in pain is nothing but a body. But with the mother there, perceiving the child in its pain, the child preserves an awareness of itself. It suffers, but it also experiences itself as observed by its mother. The mother's perspective, as one both outside of the pain and yet there with the child, is something that the child adopts as its own. In so doing an internal witness comes into being, a self-consciousness modeled on the mother's awareness. The mother's presence as a witness thus helps the child establish a relation to itself, beyond the immediacy of its own pain. Her presence enables the child to move away, if only for a flicker of a moment, from its burdening physicality.

For the victim of torture, there is no comparable self-distance. The tortured person is all body. Améry's comments help us understand this reduction of self to a body as a result of not having a witness to one's pain to whom suffering would be an implicit appeal for help: "Only in torture does the transformation of the person into flesh become complete. Frail in the face of violence, yelling out in pain, awaiting no help, capable of no resistance, the tortured person is only a body, and nothing else beside that."[32]

The child expects help from the other; the torture victim comes to expect the opposite, that the other is what Améry calls "the antiman," the one who intensifies the bodily being of his victim.[33] We could say that in inflicting pain, the antiman usurps and destroys the place of the witness. To become a body *through the hand of the other* is the closest one can come to nonhuman life. That is why Améry writes that torture "blots out the contradiction of death and allows us to experience it personally."[34]

It was Améry's singular brilliance to have formulated the impact of torture in terms of the primordial anxieties it triggers about human dependency and broken attachments. He understood why, for the survivor of torture, these anxieties are not to be overcome. In his words, "The experience of persecution was, at the very bottom, that of an extreme *loneliness*. At stake for me is the release from the abandonment that has persisted from that time until today."[35] The release from abandonment—this is what is at stake in the aftermath of torture, for it is the memory of having existed in a state of utter aloneness that constitutes the enduring anguish of survival, what Améry describes as a "foreignness in the world" that cannot be compensated by any sort of subsequent human communication.[36]

In light of Améry's formulations about the earliest origins of the individual's need for a sense of security and safety in relation to the other, we can appreciate the profound doubt his text casts upon the likelihood that torture can ever become a memory--that is, a thing of the past. Levi too would have us believe that torture never passes. He writes, "It must be observed, mournfully, that the injury cannot be healed: it extends through time, and the Furies, in whose existence we are forced to believe . . . perpetuate the tormentor's work by denying peace to the tormented."[37] In Scarry's words, "torture . . . announces its own nature as an undoing of civilization."[38]

Even as a prisoner, Levi sensed that his torture would not cease if and when he returned to civilization. He recounts a dream he had while in

Auschwitz that almost all prisoners remember having dreamt in some form. In his dream, Levi has returned home from Auschwitz and is relating his experiences to his sister and some close friends. He describes what it is like to be in the camp barracks, to share a hard bed with a stranger who all but sleeps on top of him. He writes,

> It is an intense pleasure, physical, inexpressible, to be at home, among friendly people and to have so many things to recount: but I cannot help noticing that my listeners do not follow me. In fact, they are completely indifferent. . . . A desolating grief is now born in me, like certain barely remembered pains of one's early infancy. It is pain in its pure state, not tempered by a sense of reality and by the intrusion of extraneous circumstances, a pain like that which makes children cry.[39]

The dream expresses an anguish born of isolation. Levi's loved ones do not recognize him. He has no witness to his experience. In the absence of this recognition, his pain takes him back to a period of early infancy, before the borders of the ego are in place: he associates his inability to make contact with anything beyond himself with a stage of infant development when there is no sense of an autonomous identity.

Forty years later, in his final book, Levi returns to the experience of anguish in the camps. He writes, "[E]veryone suffered from an unceasing discomfort that polluted sleep and was nameless . . . an atavistic anguish whose echo one hears in the second verse of Genesis: the anguish inscribed in everyone of the 'tohu-bohu' of a deserted and empty universe crushed under the spirit of God but from which the spirit of man is absent: not yet born or already extinguished."[40] "Atavastic anguish" must finally be nameless, because the name is the mark of sociality upon the self. In a desolate universe, there can be no name. Without a name, or, in general terms, a system of signs, this anguish cannot be communicated. Without the possibility of communication, there can be no relief. Levi invokes a non-word, a sound that resonates in a universe where no human spirit lives, the "tohu-bohu" that bespeaks only radical exile from language and by extension, from human community. Levi carried this anguish back with him from Auschwitz. He wrote, "The hour of liberation was neither joyful nor light-hearted. . . . Leaving pain behind was a delight for only a few fortunate beings, or only for a few instants, or for very simple souls; almost always it coincided with a phase of anguish."[41]

Even with this anguish, Levi was known as "the Darwin of the death camps," because he wrote about his experience with the lucidity and emotional neutrality of a scientific investigator.[42] In this Levi seemed to deviate from psychiatrist Robert Krell's understanding of the emotional aftermath of survival. Krell, himself a former hidden child who has worked and written about child survivors and their families, notes that their "predominant memories" of the Holocaust often trigger "a rage so great that often the only possible response is silence."[43] Krell relates a personal story about how, during an interview about his history, his interviewer asked him what he was feeling in the moment. Krell writes, "I tried to tell her of my rage, then became mute. I was unable to speak. My silence seemed endless. Words would not form. My mind felt trapped. It was a brush with the darkness within me, a hint of what lies there."[44] Krell's rage stymied his ability to communicate; it blocked him, and his blockage engendered a painful isolation. But agonizing as it was, his silence, for better or worse, also served a purpose: it protected him, and his questioner, from "the darkness within," marking it off as a region where "mental health professionals fear to tread," or as an "arena of unremitting grief and overwhelming rage."[45] Krell writes that "for a long time now survivors and knowledgeable therapists have tacitly agreed to a policy of containment and cooperation in order not to intrude into that realm of protective silence."[46]

Cynthia Ozick believes that Primo Levi's final collection of essays, *The Drowned and the Saved*, reveals emotions that, I would note, are consistent with Krell's observations. According to Ozick, Levi gave voice to his "retaliatory passion."[47] Ozick's point is well taken. In that text, Levi openly expresses his anger; he disputes the perception that he is a "forgiver"; he states that when he heard that *Survival in Auschwitz* was going to be published in Germany, he realized that all along the book had been meant for the Germans. They were "those against whom the book was aimed like a gun."[48]

I think, though, that Levi's volatility was always present, even in his early writing, albeit in a muted and displaced form. In *Survival in Auschwitz*, it lives on the margins, surfacing only in the poem that precedes the main text. When this poem was later included in a collection, it bore the title "*Shemà.*" This Hebrew word indicates that the poem is a rewriting of the central prayer of Jewish faith, which reads: "You shall love the Lord your God with all your heart and with all your soul and with all your might."[49] Levi's invocation of this prayer in his title establishes a parallel between his testimonial writing and obedience to God's law. This parallel continues in the lines of the poem that echo the words that immediately follow those of the *Shemà* in Deuteronomy. The biblical lines read, "Take to heart these instructions with which I charge you this day. Impress them upon your children. Recite them when you stay at home and when you are away, when you lie down and when you get up."[50] Levi's poem echoes this biblical passage. It reads,

> Meditate that this came about:
> I commend these words to you.
> Carve them in your hearts
> At home, in the street,
> Going to bed, rising;
> Repeat them to your children.[51]

But the poem does not end here. Levi departs from the biblical model by appending the following lines:

> Or may your house fall apart,
> May illness impede you,
> May your children turn their faces from you.[52]

The threat here is undisguised. If the poem's addressees do not meditate upon the images of the men and women, the *Muselmänner* depicted in the verse, and how they came to be, a curse will descend, whose precedent is God's wrath. The model for this poetic voice is thus not human, but the accumulating weight of its decree is. It is spoken in the enraged voice of one who stands outside the "warm houses" looking in, fearing, or perhaps knowing, that his message has no place at the table.[53]

We cannot reconcile this poetic voice with that of the narrator who sets out "to furnish documentation for a quiet study of certain aspects of the human mind."[54] This voice speaks through images of bodily fragments—hair, eyes, womb, hearts, faces—which, taken together, comprise bodies in pieces, bodies blown apart by the violence of the speaker's emotion. And yet, insofar as this voice is compressed into one small, prefatory textual space, we might understand the poem as psychically holding or containing that rage. In so doing it clears the way for the measured examination of survival that Levi offers directly after the poem. Viewed in terms of Krell's comments, Levi's expression of rage in a textual space marked off from both the preface and main narrative may have prevented Levi from falling into what Krell described as "the darkness within" that consigns the survivor to silence.[55] It is significant that in Levi's portrait of the *Muselmänner*, to whom he also refers as "the drowned," Levi expresses the decline of these men and women in terms of their relation, or nonrelation, to writing, and he formulates his testimonial charge in terms of the inability of the *Muselmänner* to bear witness, as if to suggest that it is on this basis that he distinguished himself from them. He says, "Even if they had paper and pen, the drowned would not have testified, because their death had begun before that of their body. . . . We speak in their stead, by proxy."[56]

Levi seems to be suggesting that the most vulnerable victims of Nazi persecution, during and after the Holocaust, were those men and women who could not communicate their suffering and whose devastation was signaled by their lapse into silence. In this context it is worth noting that the first person deemed an enemy of the Nazi state was not a Jew, but one who did not have language, a German infant (from the Latin *infans*, "unable to speak"), the so-called "Knauer baby,"[57] who had been born severely disabled and whose father had requested that Hitler allow the child to be euthanized, a request that was granted.[58] Hitler had received a letter from the father of the child in late 1939 requesting that his infant be granted a "mercy death" (*Gnadentod*).[59] Interested in the case, Hitler sent Karl Rudolph Brandt, his personal physician, to Leipzig University Children's Clinic to consult with the infant's doctors and verify the facts of its condition.[60] Hitler also instructed Brandt to assure the physicians that they would not face legal proceedings if the mercy death proved warranted.[61] The doctors who met with Brandt agreed that there were no grounds for the continuation of the baby's life. The secret decree Hitler later issued eventuated in the deaths, between 1939 and 1945, of approximately 5,000 infants, children, and juveniles.[62] These deaths would not have been possible without the cooperation of physicians, nurses, bureaucrats, and parents. Regulations made it mandatory for midwives and doctors to notify authorities whenever a baby was born with birth defects, and panels were vested with the authority to decide which children would be taken into the program.[63] Those deemed "eligible" were in most cases administered a lethal dose of a medication.[64]

In conclusion, I would like to return to the question of the aftermath of rage that torture produces in those who do not return so broken that they cannot speak or who do not die from the abuse. When the photographs of the prisoners of Abu Ghraib came out, Seymour Hersh wrote, "The photographs tell it all."[65] He continued, "As the photographs from Abu Ghraib make clear, these detentions have had enormous consequences: for imprisoned civilian Iraqis, many of whom had nothing to do with the growing insurgency; for the integrity of the Army; and for the United States' reputation in the world."[66]

But the photographs did not, could not, tell it all. They did not, for example, tell how the torture of prisoners, or their detention, was not the beginning of the story. The February 2004 Report of the International Committee of the Red Cross on the Treatment of Prisoners of War includes sections about the abuses of Iraqis *during* their arrest. The report documents "a fairly consistent . . . pattern of brutality by members of the [Coalition Forces] arresting them." It states, for example,

> Arresting authorities entered houses usually after dark, breaking down doors, waking up residents roughly, yelling orders, forcing family members into one room under military guard while searching the rest of the house and further breaking doors, cabinets and other property. They arrested suspects, tying their hands in the back with flexi-cuffs, hooding them, and taking them away. Sometimes they arrested all adult males present in a house, including elderly, handicapped or sick people . . . pushing people around, insulting, taking aim with rifles, punching and kicking and striking with rifles.[67]

The argument made to justify these actions—that the extreme urgency of intelligence gathering necessitated the soldiers' actions—cannot account for another finding included in the report: that the Iraqis were left with no recourse. The arresting authorities did not identify themselves or disclose where their base was, and they rarely told the people they took prisoner or the families of the prisoners why the arrests were being made. The arrestees were taken away, and their families not given news for months. As a result, the families often feared their relatives were dead.[68] For the more than eight thousand Iraqis locked up in Abu Ghraib, between seventy and ninety percent of whom had been mistakenly arrested, the photographs of Abu Ghraib were not a revelation but a confirmation of the ongoing brutality practiced by the occupying forces. This was evident in the responses of Iraqis to journalist Mark Danner, who traveled to Fallujah in November of 2003 to interview the citizens. One young man told Danner: "For Fallujans it is a *shame* to have foreigners break down their doors. It is a *shame* for them to have foreigners stop and search their women. It is a *shame* for the foreigners to put a bag over their heads, to make a man lie on the ground with your shoe on his neck. This is a great *shame*, you understand? It is a great shame for the whole tribe. It is the duty of that man, and of that tribe, to get revenge on this soldier—to kill that man. Their duty is to attack them, to *wash the shame*. The shame is a *stain*, a dirty thing; they have to wash it. No sleep—we cannot sleep until we have revenge."[69]

The young man's words echo these of Améry: "Whoever has succumbed to torture can no longer feel at home in the world. The shame of destruction cannot be erased. Trust in the world . . . will not be regained. . . . It is fear that henceforth reigns over him. Fear—and also what is called resentments. They remain, and have scarcely a chance to concentrate into a seeing, purifying thirst for revenge."[70]

CHAPTER 5

"Torture Was the Essence of National Socialism": Reading Jean Améry Today

Elisabeth Weber

I

Commenting on "a newspaper page with photos that show members of the South Vietnamese army torturing captured Vietcong rebels," Jean Améry, the Austrian-born essayist and survivor of Nazi torture and death camps, wrote in 1966: "The admission of torture, the boldness—but is it still that?—of coming forward with such photos is explicable only if it is assumed that a revolt of public conscience is no longer to be feared. One could think that this conscience has accustomed itself to the practice of torture."[1]

Alfred McCoy, eminent historian of the CIA and US torture, has compellingly argued that TV series like *24* have, more than four decades later, contributed to create a broad consensus on the acceptability of torture.[2] In February 2007 *24*'s executive producer Howard Gordon announced that the show would "have fewer torture scenes in the future," but this decision was not made because of the complaints he had received from several high-level military and FBI officials and interrogators,[3] who had expressed their concerns over the effects *24*'s depictions of torture had on US military personnel in Iraq and elsewhere.

Rather, the reason for the shift was, in Gordon's words, that "torture 'is starting to feel a little trite. . . . The idea of physical coercion or torture is no longer a novelty or surprise.'"[4] The title of Rosa Brooks' February 23, 2007, editorial in the *Los Angeles Times* aptly summarized this state of affairs: "America tortures (yawn)."[5]

As many commentators have noted, and as Giorgio Agamben elaborates in his book *State of Exception*, the military order issued by the US president in November 2001, "which authorized the 'indefinite detention' and trial by 'military commissions' . . . of noncitizens suspected of involvement in terrorist activities," in fact "erase[d] any legal status of the individual, thus producing a legally unnamable and unclassifiable being." The detainees of Guantánamo Bay don't have "the status of POWs as defined by the Geneva Convention, they do not even have the status of persons charged with a crime according to American laws."[6] "They are subject now only to raw power; they have no legal existence."[7] They fit, in other words, the paradigm of the "homo sacer," who finds himself, in Agamben's formulation, as "bare life," subjected to the sovereign's state of exception. The fact that many "enemy combatants" in Guantánamo and elsewhere have been tortured seals their extra-legal status, insofar as the CIA sees them, in Alfred McCoy's words, as "too dangerous for release, [and] too tainted for trial."[8]

Agamben's book *Homo Sacer* is best known for his analysis of another "legally unnamable and unclassifiable being," the *Muselmann* of the Nazi death camps, to whom Agamben dedicated his important book, *Remnants of Auschwitz*.[9] Given the vast differences between the historical and political contexts, it would be devoid of sense to simply juxtapose or compare the victims of US-endorsed torture and those men and women Primo Levi called the "drowned," the "anonymous mass, continually renewed and always identical, of non-men (*non-uomini*) who march and labour in silence, the divine spark dead within them, already too empty to really suffer."[10] However, one of Améry's assertions creates a link between the two contexts. Torture, Améry writes, was "the essence of National-Socialism." To understand this categorical assertion, it is helpful and even necessary to reflect on the absence of legal existence inflicted on *Muselmänner* of the Nazi death camps and on torture victims. The category of "unlawful enemy combatants" used by the US administration in its so-called war on terror, to designate the prisoners in Guantánamo Bay, for example, reflects the legal void analyzed by Agamben. Such absence of legal existence was even more flagrant for a smaller group of men whose status can only be properly referred to by using a word created during Argentina's "Dirty War": the disappeared. These detainees were held in so-called "black sites," secret

US-run prisons whose locations were unknown to anyone but CIA operatives.[11] The name given to those highly secret prisoners points to an ordeal that forms a certain link between *Muselmänner* and torture victims: the men who had been disappeared into CIA black sites were referred to as "ghost detainees."

In Levi's account, the *Muselmänner* are walking dead, "non-men," ghost-like beings,[12] whose overwhelming majority did not survive the camps. The question of why they were called *Muselmänner*—an antiquated word for "Muslim" in German—has been met with different hypotheses, most of which focus on the widespread assumption in early-twentieth-century Europe that Muslims were people "of unconditional fatalism."[13]

In the Nazi camps, not only *Muselmänner* were irrevocably marked by death. Based on his clinical experience, the psychiatrist William Niederland describes the survivors of the death camps as frequently marked by a "deep psychic trace [*psychische Tiefenspur*] that results from the *encounter with death* in the latter's most atrocious forms." Niederland calls this "trace" a "death-engram," using a term from neuropsychology that designates memory traces that, resulting from external stimuli, have triggered biophysical or biochemical changes in the brain or other neural tissue.[14] In Geoffrey Hartman's words, the "Nazi machine" tried to ensure that "even in their afterlife, once out of the camps, [the survivors] would not escape the fate of the *Muselmann*."[15] As a consequence, many survivors' appearance and behavior, in Niederland's words, are "shadow-like" and "ghost-like."[16]

On the side of torture victims, it should be noted that "ghost detainee" was an "official term used by the US administration to designate a person held in a detention center, whose identity has been hidden by keeping them unregistered and therefore anonymous."[17] The term was, for example, used, and the practice condemned, in the courageous report Major General Antonio Taguba wrote in early 2004 to document the now infamous abuses of Abu Ghraib prison.[18] Another neologism was formed in this context: the act of disappearing someone into a secret site was called "ghosting."[19]

These linguistic creations, intended to refer to the victims' invisibility from public witnessing or scrutiny, contain a proposition about torture that is, of course, unintentional, but for that matter all the more telling, and that is central to Améry's reflection: in Améry's text, as well as in other texts on torture, such as Ariel Dorfman's *Death and the Maiden*, the torture survivor is described as dead while still alive, or alive while already dead. In other words, while there is no doubt that "ghosting" is done in order to torture, torture, in other ways, is also a practice, and determined pursuit, of "ghosting."

2

Before approaching the issue of torture, Améry reflects on what he suspects is routine in most police stations in most countries: the beating of people in custody. With the first blow received from an agent of the state, a person's "trust in the world breaks down" irreparably.[20] "The expectation of help, the certainty of help, is indeed one of the fundamental experiences of human beings, and probably also of animals . . . with the first blow from a police-man's fist, against which there can be no defense and which no helping hand will ward off, a part of our life ends and it can never again be revived" (67/29). Already in this first-degree experience of state-sponsored violence, then, one that happens daily in countless places around the world, "a part of our life ends and it can never again be revived."[21] Torture, Améry writes, "con-tains everything" that he "ascertained" in "regard to beating by the police: the border violation of my self by the other, which can be neither neutral-ized by the expectation of help nor rectified through defending oneself [*Gegenwehr*].[22] Torture is all that, but in addition very much more" (74/33).

In formulations that have strongly influenced Agamben's, Améry pro-vides a glance into facets of the psychology of "bare life":

> If from the experience of torture any knowledge at all remains that goes
> beyond the plain nightmarish, it is that of a great amazement [*große
> Verwunderung*] and a foreignness in the world [*Fremdheit in der Welt*]
> that cannot be compensated by any sort of subsequent human
> communication. Amazed [*Staunend*], the tortured person experienced
> that in this world there can be the other as absolute sovereign, and
> sovereignty revealed itself as the power to inflict suffering and to
> destroy [*zu vernichten*; literally: to annihilate]. The dominion of the
> torturer over his victim has nothing in common with the power
> exercised on the basis of social contracts, as we know it. It is not the
> power of the traffic policeman over the pedestrian, of the tax official
> over the taxpayer, of the first lieutenant over the second lieutenant. It is
> also not the sacral sovereignty of past absolute chieftains or kings; for
> even if they stirred fear, they were also objects of trust at the same time.
> The king could be terrible in his wrath, but also kind in his mercy; his
> autocracy was an exercise of authority [*seine Gewalt war ein Walten*].[23]
> But the power of the torturer, under which the tortured moans, is
> nothing other than the triumph of the survivor over the one who is
> plunged from the world into agony and death (84/39–40).

The German is here even more emphatic: The "power of the tormentor [*Peiniger*], . . . is the *limitless* triumph of the survivor over the one who is pushed out of the world into agony and death [*der schrankenlose Triumph des Überlebenden über den, der aus der Welt in Qual und Tod hinausgestossen wird*]" (84/39–40). Améry's qualification of this "triumph" as "limitless" is decisive; omitting it as the English translation does deprives the text of one of its furthest reaching argumentative moves.

In what follows, it will thus be necessary to pay close attention to the formulations chosen by the English translators of Améry's text. The intent is not to criticize an overall excellent translation, but to point out specific word choices that, if not taken literally, or, as in this case, if omitted, substantially alter Améry's argument. In a text on Paul Celan, Jacques Derrida observes that "all responsible witnessing engages a poetic experience of language."[24] In bearing witness to the torture he underwent, Améry engages in this singular experience of language by *creating* language. Since this creation of language enacts, in Dori Laub's formulation, the "creation of knowledge de novo" that can occur during the process of bearing witness to massive trauma,[25] it is the reader's responsibility to listen to the uniqueness of that language, including its rawness in German, even if this comes at the cost of elegance in the English translation. Améry continues:

> Astonishment [*Staunen*] at the existence of the other, as he boundlessly [*grenzenlos*] asserts himself through torture, and astonishment at what one can become oneself: flesh and death. The tortured person never ceases to be amazed that all those things one may, according to inclination, call his soul, or his mind [*seinen Geist*], or his consciousness, or his identity, are destroyed when there is that cracking and splintering in the shoulder joints (85/40).

This is a reference to the torture he suffered: at Breendonk, the main interrogation center in Nazi-occupied Belgium, "torturers suspended victims from a hook-and pulley system" while their hands were tied in the back.[26] Améry concludes: "That life is fragile is a truism that he has always known. . . . But only through torture did he learn that a living person can be transformed so thoroughly into flesh [*verfleischlichen*] and by that, while still alive, be partly made into a prey of death" (85/40).[27]

The most famous line of Améry's text summarizes his analysis: "Whoever has succumbed to torture [*Wer der Folter erlag*] can no longer feel at home in the world. The shame of destruction cannot be erased" (85/40). Again, the German is stronger: "*Die Schmach der Vernichtung läßt sich nicht austilgen,*" which translates literally: "The ignominy (or infamy) of annihilation cannot be erased."[28] The one who has "succumbed" to torture has been annihilated, even though he or she is still among the living.

In perhaps one of the best texts on Améry, G. W. Sebald pointed out the necessity of replacing the "abstract discourse about the victims of national-socialism" with Améry's essays "on his personal past and present" because they provide the "content-heaviest insights into the irreparable state of the victims, out of which alone the true nature of terror can be extrapolated with some precision."[29] Through a patient reading of substantial passages of Améry's text this essay will attempt to listen to it as closely as possible, including to the semantic fields of the original German words, and to thereby amplify the voice of someone who not only underwent torture, but also had the strength to bear witness to it with breathtaking lucidity.

One of the words used by Améry stands out: the word rendered in the English translation as "transformation of the person into flesh." Other than in theological debates about the incarnation of Christ, it is a word used rather rarely in German: *Verfleischlichung* (77/33). In German, the word means, indeed, the utter transformation, through and through, into flesh, and there is, most likely, no alternative to the choice in English. Even though the word is not a neologism, Améry's use of it arguably gives it an entirely new meaning, thereby exemplifying the assertion by Derrida mentioned above, that all responsible witnessing engages in a poetic experience of language.

Among several meanings the German prefix *ver-* can have, one indicates the pursuit of an action to the end, until the fulfillment of a goal (as in *verrichten*). Another meaning is the intensification of an action and the pursuit of something *beyond* a goal, such as *verschlafen* (oversleep) or *versalzen* (oversalt).[30] A third field of meaning is the negation of the verb that follows the prefix *ver-*, such as in *bieten* and *verbieten*: bid/offer and forbid. *Verfleischlichung* is, in a way, an intensified incarnation—but an incarnation out of which any spirit has been driven. The German *Fleisch* can mean both "flesh" and "meat." Christ's incarnation, for example, is usually referred to in German as *Fleischwerdung*, becoming flesh (of God), or, as John puts it in the Gospel, the word become flesh. Grimm's *Deutsches Wörterbuch* has "Verfleischung" for the incarnation of Christ.[31] The "transformation into flesh" of the English translation of Améry's expression would correspond more to such *Fleischwerdung*. By contrast, *Verfleischlichung* in torture drives the word and all spirit out of the flesh. In Améry's redefinition, the expression comes to stand for a boundless intensification of the physical existence of a being to the extent that the torture victim's "flesh becomes a total reality in self-negation."[32]

Améry's German is of exceptional perspicuity and elegance, and he frequently comments on the semantic field of a word or its components.[33]

Listening to a word such as *Verfleischlichung*, whose semantic field he actually remapped, is, thus, not only legitimate, but necessary, because it exemplifies the irreplaceable singularity of testimony. In Améry's usage, *Verfleischlichung*, the "fleshization"—if I may—of the torture victim, his or her utter reduction to flesh in pain, makes her or him experience death while still alive.[34] "Whoever is overcome by pain through torture experiences his body as never before. In self-negation, his flesh becomes a total reality. . . . [O]nly in torture does the transformation of the person into flesh [*Verfleischlichung*] become complete. Frail in the face of violence, howling out in pain, awaiting no help, capable of no resistance [*Notwehr*: legitimate defense], the tortured person is only a body, and nothing else beside that" (74/33).

Verfleischlichung is "fleshization," but can also be "meat-ization," becoming meat. Even though Améry was a fierce critic of French thinkers of the 1960s and '70s, such as Roland Barthes, Gilles Deleuze, and Michel Foucault,[35] one is here reminded of Deleuze's commentary on Francis Bacon's paintings, where Deleuze observes: "such convulsive pain and vulnerability. . . . Bacon does not say 'Pity the beasts,' but rather that every man who suffers is a piece of meat [*de la viande*]. Meat is the common zone of man and the beast, their zone of indiscernibility. . . . The man or woman who suffers is a beast [*une bête*], the beast that suffers is a human being."[36]

In Améry's text, this "zone of indiscernibility" becomes manifest in the scream. Améry describes "my own howling that is strange and uncanny to me [*mein eigenes, mir fremdes und unheimliches Geheul*]." And he continues: "There is howling out under torture. Perhaps in this hour, this second."[37] Améry does *not* say "someone is crying out under torture," as the English translation reads. Again, the choice in English is appropriate, guided as it is by the requirements of idiomatic word usage and elegance. The reason it needs to be changed is that in German, the grammatical structure enacts what is at stake: the sentence is formulated in the impersonal passive voice: "*Es wird aufgeheult unter der Tortur. Vielleicht zu dieser Stunde, in dieser Sekunde.*" ("There is howling-out under torture. Perhaps in this hour, this second.") There is no longer a *some*body. There is a body that is only flesh, and it howls in the "zone of indiscernibility" of becoming meat.

In his novel *Waiting for the Barbarians*, J. M. Coetzee describes the same torture Améry underwent, and here too, the screams are the howling of an animal: "my arms come up behind my back, and as my feet leave the ground I feel a terrible tearing in my shoulders as though whole sheets of muscle are giving way. From my throat comes the first mournful dry bellow. . . . I bellow again and again, there is nothing I can do to stop it, the noise comes out of a body that knows itself damaged perhaps beyond repair and roars its fright."[38]

"Fleshization" is indiscernible from becoming "meat" while still alive. "Flesh" is here what Roberto Esposito calls "an abject material," because "it is intrinsic to the same body from which it seems to escape (and which therefore expels it)." This "flesh . . . does not coincide with the body; it is that part or zone of the body, the body's membrane, that isn't one with the body, that exceeds its boundaries or is subtracted from the body's enclosing."[39] The flesh in Améry's "fleshization" is truly one that, according to Merleau-Ponty, whom Esposito here quotes, "has no name because no philosophy has known how to reach that undifferentiated layer . . . in which the same notion of body, anything but enclosed, is now turned outside [estroflessa] in an irreducible heterogeneity."[40]

The "irreducible heterogeneity" manifests itself as pain of the flesh that breaks the path to an experience of dying that, according to Améry, is, under other circumstances, radically impossible:

> Pain . . . is the most extreme intensification imaginable of our bodily being. But maybe it is even more, that is: death. No road that can be traveled by logic leads us to death, but perhaps the thought is permissible that through pain a path of feeling and premonition [gefühlsahnender Weg] can be paved [or rather, carved out: gebahnt] to it for us. In the end, we would be faced with the equation: Body = Pain = Death, and in our case this could be reduced to the hypothesis that torture, through which we are turned into body by the other, blots out the contradiction of death and allows us to experience our own death.[41]

This is why Améry calls torture "indelible": Once this "path" has been carved out (and the German bahnen does not mean here "to pave," but rather, to carve out),[42] it cannot be undone. For Améry, there is no path back from having experienced death while alive. Torture dissolves the limit between life and death. The tortured one, "while still alive," has been "partly made into a prey of death." Part alive, part dead, neither dead, nor alive, the torture victim occupies a zone in-between in which torture never ends. Three times, Améry returns to the indelible character of torture: "Whoever was tortured, stays tortured. Torture is ineradicably [Unauslöschlich] burned into him, even when no clinically objective traces can be detected."[43] And: "It was over for a while. It still is not over. Twenty-two years later I am still dangling over the ground by dislocated arms, panting, and accusing myself" (79/36).

The torture victim is branded, even if the mark is invisible. He or she is suspended in the arrested time of unending torture in which he or she is forever "a defenseless prisoner of fear. It is *fear* that henceforth brandishes its sceptre above his head [*waffenlos der Angst ausgeliefert. Sie ist es, die fürderhin über ihm das Szepter schwingt*]"[44] (85/40).

The *Verfleischlichung* that, as Améry repeatedly underlines, brutally expulses any spirit, is at the same time an expulsion into death. And because this happens to the living body, it can also be called, albeit now in a different sense, a "ghosting."

In his chapter on Auschwitz, Améry writes that the fear of death is really fear of dying, and that the inmates in Auschwitz did not fear death, but were tormented by the fear of certain ways of dying (49/18). While these ways of dying are dreaded, death is actually wished for. In the torture scene Améry describes, death is wished for at the time of what is self-accusingly referred to as a "betrayal":

> they continued asking me questions, constantly the same ones: accomplices, addresses, meeting places. To come right out with it: I had nothing but luck, because especially in regard to the extorting of information our group was rather well organized. What they wanted to hear from me in Breendonk [the fortress in Belgium where Améry was tortured], I simply did not know myself. If instead of the aliases I had been able to name the real names, perhaps, or probably, a calamity would have occurred, and I would be standing here now as the weakling I most likely am, and as the traitor I potentially already was. Yet it was not at all that I opposed them with the heroically maintained silence that befits a real man in such a situation and about which one may read (almost always, incidentally, in reports by people who were not there themselves). I talked. I accused myself of invented absurd political crimes [*Staatsverbrechen*], and even now I don't know at all how they could have occurred [*einfallen*] to me, dangling bundle that I was. Apparently I had the hope that, after such incriminating disclosures, a well-aimed blow to the head would put an end to my misery and quickly bring on my death, or at least unconsciousness (78–79/36).

Elaine Scarry's book *The Body in Pain* could be described as a long meditation on Améry's above-mentioned assertion that "whoever has succumbed to torture can no longer be at home in the world. The ignominy of annihilation cannot be erased." Without ever mentioning Améry, Scarry describes how intense pain is world-destroying. This destruction engulfs the entire space of the victim's existence: body, shelter, objects, language. The torture victim's body is turned into a weapon against her- or himself. The rooms in which the torture takes place "are often given names that acknowledge . . . the generous, civilizing impulse normally present in the human shelter," such as "'guest rooms' in Greece and 'safe houses' in the Philippines." What has the welcoming name of shelter is "converted into another weapon, into an agent of pain. All aspects of the basic structure—walls, ceiling, windows, doors—undergo this conversion." Equally, "the contents of the room, its furnishings [bathtubs, chairs, beds, etc.], are converted into weapons." Thus, "the objects themselves, and with them the fact of civilization, are annihilated."45

Even though Idelber Avelar's criticism of Scarry's approach is justified when he "take[s] distance" from "her understanding of terms such as 'world,' 'language,' 'representation,' and 'body' as contents already constituted in advance and only subsequently threatened and destroyed by torture;" when he objects to the assumption that "civilization exists precisely because it is *the opposite* of torture," and when he underlines that rather, the histories of concepts such as "civilization," "truth," and "democracy" are "quite indebted to the development of technologies of pain,"46 Scarry's text is a powerful account of the devastating effects of torture on the fundamental trust that characterizes the "pre-ontological" understanding of "being-in-the-world."47

One of the perversities of torture is that this "shredding" or "collapse" of the torture victim's world "earns the person in pain not compassion but contempt."48 This "contempt" becomes obvious in the word choice that calls the so-called confession obtained under torture "betrayal." The implication, that "confessing" torture victims are "traitors," perpetuates their expulsion from the world of the living. Calling the words obtained under torture "confession" and "betrayal" is thus nothing short of becoming complicit with the torturer.49 That the victims too espouse these terms confirms how not only their bodies but also their minds and language have been converted into weapons against them.

The perverted names, including the widespread practice of naming torture methods after everyday objects or practices, such as the "telephone" or the "frequent flyer program," indicate that torture not only "contains" and uses language, but that "it is itself a language." In Scarry's words, interrogation is "internal to the structure of torture, exists there because of its intimate connections to and interactions with the physical pain."50 This is why in French (just as in Latin), as Voltaire noted, torture is sometimes simply called *la question*, just as in German, *peinliche Frage* is synonymous with *Folter.*

Améry's verdict that "[w]hoever has succumbed to torture can no longer feel at home in the world. The ignominy (or infamy) of annihilation cannot be erased,"[51] shows that for him, torture is an irreparable assault on what Heidegger called "being-in-the-world." Following Scarry's analyses, it is also an irreparable assault on the "house of being" that is language.[52]

3

About halfway through his essay on torture, Améry sets out to "substantiate why, according to my firm conviction, torture was the essence of National Socialism—more accurately stated, why it was precisely in torture that the Third Reich materialized in all the density of its being [*Bestandsdichte*]." After listing names of other countries where torture was and is practiced, he continues: "Torture was no invention of National Socialism. But it was its apotheosis. The Hitler vassal did not yet achieve his full identity if he was merely as quick as a weasel, tough as leather, hard as Krupp steel. . . . He had to *torture*, destroy."[53] Again, in German, the word is *vernichten*: annihilate.

The difference between the English "destroy" and the German *vernichten* is decisive. One can destroy without annihilating. What Améry explores here is not the connection between torture and destruction, but between torture and a heightened form of destruction: annihilation. Just as in *Verfleischlichung*, the German prefix *ver-* in *vernichten* indicates an intensification that pursues an action *beyond* the goal. After addressing several possible objections, especially the depiction of communism as prime torturer, Améry writes:

> As a hint, allow me to repeat here in my own name and at the risk of being denounced what Thomas Mann once said in a much attacked interview: namely that no matter how terrible Communism may at times appear, it still symbolizes an idea of man, whereas Hitler-Fascism was not an idea at all, but depravity [*Schlechtigkeit*]. . . . National Socialism . . . was the only political system of this century that up to this point had not only practiced the rule of the antiman [*die Herrschaft des Gegenmenschen*; literally: the regime/sovereignty of the antiman], as had other Red and White terror regimes also, but had expressly established it *as a principle*. . . . The Nazis tortured, as did others, because by means of torture they wanted to obtain information important for national policy. But in addition, they tortured with the good conscience of depravity. They martyred [*marterten*] their prisoners for definite

purposes, which in each instance were exactly specified. Above all, however, they tortured because they were torturers [*Folterknechte*]. They placed torture in their service. But even more fervently they were its servants (70–71/31, my emphasis).

Again, it is useful to listen to the German. The word for "torturers" Améry chooses here is *Folterknechte*, literally "torture-servants" or "torture-slaves." The word indicates that being a *Folterknecht* was considered a lowly profession, but Améry's point lies elsewhere: as he puts it, the torturers are torture's "fervent servants"—*Inbrünstiger aber noch dienten sie ihr*: "Even more burningly they served it." How is this "fervent" or "burning" "service" to be understood? Nazi torture, Améry writes, has to be understood as sadism, not in terms of sexual pathology, but in the terms of the philosophy of the Marquis de Sade, as read by Georges Bataille (76–77/34–35). In other words, Nazi torture has to be understood as sadism in terms of an "existential psychology," as "the radical negation of the other" (77/35).

This is where the difference between destruction and annihilation comes to bear. The Nazi torturer wants to "nullify this world, and by negating his fellow man . . . he wants to realize his own total sovereignty. The fellow man is transformed into flesh [again, literally: fleshisized], and in this fleshization he is already brought to the edge of death; but in the end he is driven *beyond* the border of death into nothingness [*das Nichts*]" (my emphasis). The torturer, with his "control over the other's scream of pain and death" becomes "master over flesh and spirit, life and death" (77/34–35). The true purpose of such "fleshization" is to drive the victim "*beyond* the border of death into nothingness" (my emphasis). Death is not enough.

Agamben quotes Wolfgang Sofsky on the *Muselmann*: "Power abrogates itself in the act of killing. The death of the other puts an end to the social relationship. But by starving the other, it gains time. It erects a third realm, a limbo between life and death."[54] We can add: in torture, power prolongs itself indefinitely, if not infinitely. The torture victim too is suspended between life and death, and that suspension is not over with the torture's ending. Annihilation goes "beyond" death, and it is the limitless power and anticipation of annihilation that transforms a man or a woman into a fervent servant of torture.

The faces of the torturers Améry encountered were not swollen "with sexual-sadistic delight, but concentrated in murderous self-realization. With heart and soul they went about their business, and the name of it was power, dominion over spirit and flesh, orgy of unchecked self-expansion. I also have not forgotten that there were moments when I felt a kind of wretched admiration for the agonizing sovereignty [literally: torturing sovereignty] they exercised over me. For is not the one who can reduce a person so entirely to a body and a whimpering prey of death a god or, at least, a demigod?" (78/36).

What the torturer is pursuing is not just destruction, but annihilation, not just the other's "death," but the other's "nothingness." The difference, again, is decisive: the power to drive another man or woman into nothingness goes further than destruction. This is what the torturer's passion or "fervor" has become, and this is why the figure of God or of a demigod is invoked. Destruction is not enough; in the Marquis de Sade's texts, a destruction that would undo creation is the goal. It is worth noting that some fictional representations of torture also invoke the torturer's godlike powers, such as S. Yizchar's "The Prisoner," Ariel Dorfman's *Death and the Maiden*, and J. M. Coetzee's *Waiting for the Barbarians*.[55]

Thus Améry defines National Socialism as a *system* based on sadism: the sadist wants to "nullify this world, and by negating his fellow man, who also in an entirely specific sense is 'hell' for him, he wants to realize his own total sovereignty" (77/35). But for that, he has to "obliterate/exterminate his feelings of mercy" (70/30).

In another text, "Zur Psychologie des deutschen Volkes" (1945), Améry describes how such "negation" is achieved: namely through the "*Selbsterziehung . . . zur Grausamkeit*" (self-education to cruelty), that can be successful only at the condition of the complete eradication of "human emotion" (*menschliche Regung*), such as pity, mercy, and goodness, an eradication that is then cast as "heroism": for example, in the German writer Rudolf Binding's assertion of 1933, quoted by Améry, "We Germans are heroic in bearing the suffering of others."[56]

This trait is also a crucial part of Bataille's analysis of de Sade: "crimes committed in cold blood are greater than crimes carried out in the ardor of feelings; but the crime 'committed when the sensitive part has been hardened,' that dark and secret crime is the most important of all because it is the act of a soul which having destroyed everything within itself has accumulated immense strength, which identifies itself completely with the movement of total destruction that it is preparing."[57]

Jacques Lacan was one of the French thinkers criticized by Améry,[58] but his analysis of de Sade is helpful in this context. In it, Lacan explores a "border" or "limit" (*limite*) that leads "to the point of apocalypse or of revelation of something called transgression."[59] Lacan shows that the transgression pursued in de Sade is *structurally* limitless. The "limitless triumph" that for Améry characterizes Nazi torture in principle and thus structurally is (especially when taking into account Améry's own mention of the torturer's godlike expansion) structurally apocalyptic.

Again, Georges Bataille: "Transgression is not the negation of the inter-diction, but goes beyond it and completes it [*La transgression n'est pas la négation de l'interdit, mais elle le dépasse et le complète*]."[60] As a consequence, Bataille asserts that "organized transgression forms together with interdiction a whole [*un ensemble*] that defines social life."[61] While Bataille proposes this analysis in the context of his reflection on war and certain religious rituals, it is equally valid for National Socialism as the apotheosis of torture: organized, generalized torture.

Ariel Dorfman's play *Death and the Maiden* gives a precise account of the intensifying dynamics of transgression in the mind and actions of a torturer. The play stages Doctor Roberto Miranda's forced confession of his involvement in torture during a military dictatorship that could be Chile's. The reader or spectator never learns for sure whether Miranda was, indeed, Paulina Salas' torturer, but she asserts she recognizes enough of him, his voice, "the way he laughs, certain phrases he uses," to subject him to forms of torture in return, a forced confession among others.[62] Without engaging in the debate over whether Miranda is, in fact, Paulina Salas' torturer, his "confession" illuminates Bataille's theses. Miranda starts his "confession" with an attempt at an exculpating explanation: he was first called to monitor the torture with electricity, and he told himself that his participation "was a way of saving people's lives." But then,

> bit by bit, the virtue I was feeling turned into excitement—the mask of virtue fell off it, and it, the excitement, it hid, it hid, it hid from me what I was doing, the swamp of what—By the time Paulina Salas was brought in it was already too late. Too late . . . too late. A kind of brutalization took over my life, I began to really truly like what I was doing. It became a game. My curiosity was partly morbid, partly scientific. How much can this woman take? More than the other one? How's her sex? Does her sex dry up when you put the current through her? Can she have an orgasm under those circumstances? She is entirely in your power, you can carry out all your fantasies, you can do what you want with her.[63]

In the next sentence Miranda makes it clear that, to quote Bataille's sentence again, "transgression is not the negation of the interdiction, but goes beyond it and completes it": "She is entirely in your power, you can carry out all your fantasies, you can do what you want with her. . . . Everything they have forbidden you since ever, whatever your mother ever urgently whispered you were never to do."[64]

If one wants to exclude the possibility that the mother actually verbalized, in her whispering, the concrete possibilities of transgression and thus insinuated them, one is left with the option that what this sentence suggests is an original prohibition, a prohibition at the origin, in other words that what Jacques Lacan described in his discussion of the ten commandments. For Lacan, the ten commandments, even though they are violated every day, have an "indestructible character," because they are "the very laws of speech" (*les lois mêmes de la parole*),[65] insofar as they spell out (*explicitent*) "that without which there is no speech" (*parole*), not discourse, but speech.[66] Lacan's reading of the ten commandments enacts a series of "disruptions," to quote Carol Jacobs from a different context: "disruptions" that are "not the failure of the ethical but rather the beginnings of a redefinition of it as responsibility . . . a nontyrannical ethical no longer irrevocably bound by a must."[67] In another context, Lacan described speech as "a symbolic gift . . . ripe with a secret pact."[68] Speech, *la parole*, is in this context the given word, in the sense of whenever I address myself to you, whenever I speak to you, I already, even prior to any spoken word, give my word, that "I give you my word." This promise, this promise of keeping a promise, as Derrida has shown so eloquently in numerous instances, is the condition of possibility of any contract, any community, any society. It is the surplus beyond any contract that makes every contract possible.[69] It is thus the most delicate fabric of society.

In this perspective, the torturer's perversion of language confirms and underscores the apocalyptic totality of annihilation: The laws without which there is no speech are obliterated in torture.

Torture, to quote another text by Dorfman, "corrupts the whole social fabric."[70] As Jane Kramer, Alfred McCoy, Darius Rejali, and others have noted (including some of the interrogators interviewed for Rory Kennedy's film *Ghosts of Abu Ghraib*), whenever torture is used, it is impossible to control its ever-widening reach or the ever-intensifying torture methods used. Furthermore, as Britta Jenkins has observed in her work with trauma survivors, "the ramifications of torture are like the ever-widening circles made by tossing a stone into water."[71]

Torture is the "essence" of National Socialism. Améry specifies while using Aristotelian concepts that torture is not just an "accidental quality" (*Akzidens*)—an unnecessary, secondary trait of National Socialism—but its "essence" (*Essenz*), its core. Other regimes—many other regimes—torture. For Améry, the uniqueness of National Socialism is the apotheosis of torture as the *principle* of a state. Torture as the "essence" of National Socialism is the totalization of the transgression onto the other's physical and mental/psychic boundaries. The floodgates of transgression were opened, openly, deliberately, systematically, and as a principle.

This does not mean that the effects of torture are less severe on victims when used by governments that have not systematized, generalized, the rule of torture. Améry's famous sentence is categorical: "Whoever has succumbed to torture can no longer feel at home in the world. The infamy of annihilation cannot be erased." As such, even if used on an individual, and not generalized, basis, torture as transgression is *structurally* limitless, and structurally it pursues not destruction, but annihilation.[72]

This may be one of the reasons why, at least since the Geneva Conventions, the prohibition against torture is stronger than the prohibition against killing; while it is possible to legally kill, it is never possible to legally torture[73]—except in a society in which, to quote Améry once again, the social world has been "totally turned inside out" (*totalen Umstülpung der Sozialwelt*).[74]

CHAPTER 6

"What Did the Corpse Want?" Torture in Poetry

Sinan Antoon

When the torture at Abu Ghraib finally came to the attention of the global media in April of 2004, there was considerable outrage throughout the world. In the Arab world, where the images had a more devastating impact, hundreds of articles and essays were written in response to the scandal. In contrast to the "West," the cultural milieu of the Arab world is one in which poetry still retains immense symbolic power and capital.[1] This was quite evident during the recent revolutions in Tunisia and Egypt, as well as the ongoing revolts in other Arab countries. The rallying chant for the revolutionaries in Tunisia and Egypt was a line of poetry by the famous Tunisian poet Abu 'l-Qasim al-Shabbi (1909–1934): "If, one day, the people want life, fate must yield."[2] The line comes from a well-known poem in the canon and is one that every literate Arab knows by heart. It was echoed in protests and written on placards and walls in Tunisia, Egypt, and other Arab countries where protests in solidarity with the revolutions took place. Unlike most poets in the Western world, many Arab poets are politically engaged and active in the politics of their societies. In Egypt, for example, the vernacular poet, Ahmad Fu'ad Nigm (1929–), who was imprisoned under Nasser and Sadat for his scathing political satire and oppositional politics, was a vocal critic of the Mubarak regime and used his poetry and persona to rally protesters, especially during the last few years, by recording YouTube messages urging citizens to be politically active.[3]

It might be surprising, therefore, that in a region where poetry still functions as a potent and vibrant medium for social and political critique and where satellite channels feature shows on poetry, the number of poems written in formal Arabic about Abu Ghraib was and remains quite low. Only a few poets took up the challenge of writing about such a monumental event. However, if one considers the difficulty of representing bodily pain, then it shouldn't be surprising that only two Iraqi poets published poems about Abu Ghraib. Elaine Scarry reminds us of "the rarity with which physical pain is represented in literature."[4] Furthermore, perhaps the relative silence on the part of so many Arab poets reflects the traumatic effects of the event itself. The spectacle of Abu Ghraib not only disciplined and tortured the bodies of the prisoners themselves, but reenacted, in its deployment of cultural assumptions and tropes and racially motivated techniques, a ritual of collective domination and assault. Its effects extended to the audience of the visual event and were traumatic for those who identified with the naked and assaulted bodies of the victims.[5] Thus, one may suggest that the collective Arab cultural body itself was in pain and thus at pains to find the adequate verbal response to its trauma. Silence becomes less baffling. But even when this silence is broken, there are other complications and considerations. The political and ethical complications that result from attempting to represent torture are another important consideration that could further discourage writing or make it more difficult.

How did the two Iraqi poets who published poems on Abu Ghraib confront what Scarry calls the "unsharability" of pain and its resistance to language?[6] What textual strategies did they employ to speak on behalf of the victims of torture and what political claims, if any, were they making, consciously or unconsciously, in the process of speaking *of* and *on behalf of* the victims of torture? These and other related questions will be explored by reading two poems by two major Iraqi poets, Saadi Youssef (b. 1934) and Sargon Bulus (1944–2007).

The Wretched of the Heavens[7]

Saadi Youssef
We will go to God
naked
our shroud is our blood
our camphor

the teeth of dogs
turned wolves
The closed cell suddenly swung open
for the female soldier to come
our swollen eyes could not make her out
perhaps because she comes from a mysterious world
she did not say a thing
she was dragging my brother's bloody body behind her
like a worn-out mat
We will walk to God
barefoot
our feet lacerated
our limbs wounded
Are Americans Christians?
We have nothing in the cell to wipe the lying body
only our blood
congealing in our blood
and this smell coming from the continent of slaughterhouses
Angels will not come here
The air is perturbed
These are the wings of hell's bats
The air is motionless
We have been waiting for you O Lord
Our cells were open yesterday
We were lifeless on their floor
and you did not come O Lord

But we are on the way to you. We will remain on the way even if you let us down. We are your dead sons and have declared our resurrection. Tell your prophets to open the gates of cells and paradises! Tell them that we are coming! We have wiped our faces and hands with clean earth. The angels know us one by one.

The title of the poem points to Fanon's "The Wretched of the Earth."[8] The reading is already oriented by a reference to the colonial archive and its practices. It is important to note that *mu'adhdhabun* means both "wretched" and "tortured," so the title could also be translated "The Tortured of the Heavens." The space of the poem allows the muted and silenced victims of torture to speak. The first-person plural voice is theirs: "We." But this voice is not the voice of life or a voice *in* life. It is the voice of those who are dead or almost dead and on their way to God; somewhere between the earth and the heavens. However, something is amiss in the circumstances surrounding their death. They have been stripped of everything and cannot even have a proper burial. Instead of a proper shroud, as is customary, they only have their own blood. Instead of the camphor usually mixed with the pure water with which the dead are washed before a proper Islamic burial, they are treated to the teeth of dogs turned into wolves. The figure of the dogs performs a dual role here. First, it compounds the sense of abandonment; for not only one's own species, but another one, usually friendly, is conscripted to inflict pain and humiliation. Second, considering the references to Islamic rituals of shrouding and cleanliness, canines are considered a source of uncleanliness and would thus further violate a proper burial, perpetuate impurity, and subject one to more torture in the grave.[9] With the appearance of the dogs in the first section and the "female soldier" in the second, the images from Abu Ghraib are summoned, and the poem's political and historical anchoring moment, Abu Ghraib, is evident. The poem was written in May of 2004, right after the Abu Ghraib torture became widely known and reported in the media.

In the second stanza the cell opens, not for God to come, but for the torturer to bring back another body from a torture session. The third stanza opens with a variation on the first line of the poem, repeating "we will" as if to salvage a sense of lost agency. The nudity and physical damage inflicted on the body are reiterated. In the fourth stanza the poetic voice wonders, rhetorically, if the Americans are Christians. At this point there is a shift toward Christian motifs. The lying body (*musajja* in Arabic) is reminiscent of the body of Jesus, but the religious exit is not functional. The cell is a condemned space: torture has transformed it into a hell on earth and the "angels will not come here"; the only motion is that of hell's bats. The prisoners are already dead and await God, but he comes not. In the fifth stanza the appropriation of biblical discourse is more explicit: *"We have been waiting for you, O Lord."*[10] The powerful biblical vocative is repeated twice, but still, God does not come to the lifeless bodies. The poem could have ended at this point, but the agency the poet is at pains to restore or reconstruct would have been lost. In the final stanza the collective plural voice affirms the will to go to God even if he lets them down. The tone and the mode of address are reversed; it is not God who is instructing humans and making demands, but rather the other way around. As if gaining more momentum and reclaiming agency, the plural voice tells God to relay the message to his prophets. The penultimate line is crucial: "We have wiped our faces and hands with clean earth." Youssef uses a particular verb, *tayammamna*, with important resonance. In the Islamic tradition, *tayammum* is using clean earth for ablutions and purifications if and when water is not available. The sentence appears in the Qur'an a few times, but as a form of a command: "[If] . . . you do not find water, then use some clean earth and wipe your faces and hands."[11] In the poem it is an answer of sorts: we have done our part and are ready. Perhaps what is being reiterated is also that "we must save ourselves and cannot keep waiting for a savior." Hence, the resurrection is declared. What are all these Qur'anic and biblical motifs doing in Youssef's poem, and what is their potential effect? The coupling of biblical imagery with Qur'anic references in the poem inscribes the Abu Ghraib event in a more universal narrative and distances itself from narratives of civilizational and cultural clashes. What is fascinating is that Youssef uses religious motifs, but in order to disable their traditional telos as I will show below. The rhetorical question about Americans being Christians in the fourth stanza, the representation of tortured bodies in line with Christian iconography, and the biblical vocative all blur the lines, making it difficult to categorize or read these bodies as solely Muslim. The same goes for the God to whom they are going.

Youssef is one of Iraq's most famous communist intellectuals, and has continued to pledge allegiance to communism. One of his most recent collections was entitled *The Last Communist Enters Heaven*.[12] The predominant poetic persona in most of the poems is an unattached communist who rejects the institutional compromise or peace struck between an unnamed party and the capitalist status quo and reaffirms his belief in the validity of communist ideals. Youssef has also been vociferous in his rejection of the US occupation and the regime it has produced.[13]

The poem is powerful and effective in bespeaking the voices of the tortured, but it simultaneously performs another political act. The very title of the poem alludes, as mentioned earlier, to Fanon's *Wretched of the Earth*, which is taken from the first line of "The Internationale": "Arise, wretched of the earth!" Looking at the second stanza of "The Internationale," one finds that Youssef's entire poem seems to crystallize its message:

> There are no supreme saviors
> Neither God, nor Caesar, nor tribune
> Producers, let us save ourselves
> Decree the common welfare
> So that the thief expires,
> So that the spirit be pulled from its prison
> Let us fan the forge ourselves. . . .[14]

If one of torture's ends is to "systematically prevent the prisoner from being the agent of anything,"[15] the tortured prisoners in Youssef's poem reclaim their agency and their voices, but the latter are then appropriated for a larger political project. This is not to belittle Youssef's poem or to take issue with the ideology it points to, but to stress the challenge of writing about torture and the inevitable ethical and political traps involved. This leads to the question of whether it is at all possible for a poet to write a poem about torture and restore or attempt to restore the voice of the victims, yet still guard it against any ideological appropriation. Perhaps this also partly accounts for the rarity of poems on torture. Youssef's friend and fellow exile, Sargon Bulus, has written a unique poem entitled "The Corpse,"[16] in which the poetic narrative does not point to a specific ideology, or at least does not lend itself to explicit appropriation as I will show.

The Corpse
Sargon Bulus
They tortured the corpse
until the day broke
worn out
and the rooster stood up and protested.
They thrust hooks in its flesh
whipped it with electric cables
and hung it from the ceiling fan.
When the torturers were a bit tired
they took a break.
The corpse wiggled its little finger
It opened its wounded eyes
and muttered something.
Was it asking for water?
Did it perhaps want bread?
Was it cursing them or asking for more?
What did the corpse want?

Bulus' poem obviously presents a different approach to the subject. There is no reference in this poem to Abu Ghraib, but it was included in the poet's last collection, posthumously published in 2008. Most of its poems deal with the carnage in Iraq, as well as its tortured past, but what separates Bulus from most other Iraqi poets is his ability to inhabit a unique space vis-à-vis the various ideological narratives competing for Iraq's history and its viability and future as a nation-state. These narratives, of course, range from the denial that any sense of an imagined Iraq or Iraqiness existed before British colonialism and that Iraq is merely a hodgepodge, to its very antithesis, increasingly internalized and adopted by many Iraqis for obvious reasons: Iraqi nationalism, which, deploying the land's rich history and civilizational past, projects its existence back millennia (this is the narrative many artists and writers are espousing). Such imagined pasts tend to come with a usual heavy cargo of triumphalism and a false promise of a glorious future, built solely on the past and not necessarily with a critical and conscious deployment of it that takes into consideration recent developments in material reality. Betwixt and between these two poles of Iraq as a postcolonial construction and Iraq as a transhistorical entity, there are a variety of ethno-sectarian ideologies, whether Islamist or non-Islamist, Ba'thist, Arab nationalist, or other much more exclusive nationalist narratives that are dominating the sociopolitical and cultural arena. A constant thread in many of the collection's poems embeds Iraq's political tragedies and horrors within a universal history of violence. The tone is elegiac, and the poetic narrative resists closure of any type.

"The Corpse" is striking in its simplicity and its eloquent silences, rather than in what it says. The title merits a pause; not unlike Youssef's poem, the subject of the poem is the dead body of a tortured prisoner. However, unlike Youssef's poem, there are no hints whatsoever as to the identity of the torturers. Their institutional or national affiliations are not specified. They are simply "they." The victim's humanity and identity have been erased, and what is left is a corpse; a dead body whose only means of communication is gestures or undecipherable signs. The isolation of the prison cell is mirrored in the poem itself. Aside from a worn-out dawn and the sound of the rooster protesting, there is no outside to the torture chamber. The cell is the universe, and it is dominated by the torturers and their instruments. The narrative of their sovereign power erases the body's narrative and detaches it from its history and prior affiliations. Throughout the first stanza the torturers perform their task using a variety of techniques, but the corpse does not move or respond. Even the day was worn out after such an arduous night, as "world, self, and voice are lost, or nearly lost, through the intense pain of torture and not through confession."[17] Although Bulus is not one to shy away from employing religious and mythological symbols in his poetry, especially his last collection, there are none here. Unlike Youssef's poem, there are no angels or prophets to invoke. The corpse's only solidarity comes from the member of another species: the rooster who stood and protested. The imagery of hooks thrust in flesh hanging from the ceiling is akin to a slaughterhouse. Although the acts of torture are described vividly, there is no expression or description of the pain the body itself might have experienced. Is it already dead?

No, because in the second stanza it gestures and mutters, but it does not say anything coherent or comprehensible. It is impossible to accurately translate what it might be saying. According to Scarry, "physical pain does not simply resist language but actively destroys it, bringing about an immediate reversion to a state anterior to language, to the sounds and cries a human being makes before language is learned."[18] The third stanza is composed of three haunting questions about the possible content or meaning of the corpse's gesture and what it might have demanded. Perhaps the extent to which the subjectivity of the victim has been eroded and the immensity of the gap between it and the world is driven home by the fact that it is no longer possible to even know whether it is completely defeated and is merely asking for nourishment to survive, or if it is in fact still defiant and has yet to give in. Here torture makes its own ends impossible to verify, as it erases the rational faculties of the victim and destroys the possibility of communicating its subjugation.[19] The very last line of the poem does not answer these questions, but rather reinforces them with the central question of the poem: "What did the corpse want?"

Unlike Youssef's poem, where the collective voice is present, audible and decodable, there is no longer a voice in Bulus' poem. Nor is there any recourse to religious or even secular symbols or narratives and trajectories of salvation and redemption. Torture has succeeded in destroying the voice of the self, and all that remains is what Scarry calls the "self-announcing signal of the body in pain."[20] It would be a mistake to read Bulus' poem as defeatist or to translate the absence of explicit political affiliations or appeals to emancipatory narratives as any less political or timely than Youssef's poem. "The Corpse" crystallizes the essential condition of politics. It gazes at the body that is stripped bare and taken outside of biopolitical life by sovereign power, to use Agamben's terms.

Ending the poem with the haunting question "What did the corpse want?" is disquieting on many levels. The corpse remains fixed inside the cell and the torture scene, as if waiting there for us to keep on repeating the question. The ending also reiterates the harrowing effects of torture and the silencing and elimination of voice and of self, so much so that it becomes impossible to communicate. The body is a corpse robbed of self-expression. Moreover, the poem, and the ending in particular, remind us in a way of the challenge and difficulty of attempting to speak *for*, or *on behalf of*, victims of torture.

How to "attempt to lift the interior facts of bodily sentience out of the inarticulate pre-language of 'cries and whispers' into the realm of shared objectification"?[21] How can one do so, but without appropriating the suffering or memory of the victims of torture for this or that political agenda, whether explicitly or subtly? Perhaps this poem is one of those that succeed in doing so. The brutality of torture and its harrowing effects are represented, but the haunting question takes us back to the heart of the poem and to the moment of torture itself, when "The corpse wiggled its little finger / It opened its wounded eyes / and muttered something." That fixed gaze of the corpse is directed at the torturers, and by extension, at us. We know, for sure, that the corpse did not want to be there.

PART THREE

Graphic Assaults, Sensory Overload

CHAPTER 7

Painting Against Torture

John Nava

In the wake of 9/11, not only did America come together—the whole world stood with us. "Today," it was repeated everywhere, "we are all Americans." With breathtaking arrogance, exceeded only by stunning incompetence, the Bush/Cheney administration destroyed that unity in a matter of months.

The disastrous failures of the administration have come at a tragic cost both at home and abroad. And the aftermath of its tactics have unfairly saddled the young people in these images with a shameful legacy. How could their parents' generation have gone along with a trumped-up and irrelevant "preemptive war"? How could they have accepted a gulag of secret prisons, tacitly approved of torture, tolerated illegal domestic spying and all the rest? How is it that at each critical juncture, the media and the Democrats were cowed into acquiescence? Could the administration's flag-waving and fear-mongering really have been so intimidating?

In fact, during the headlong rush to war, millions of people both in America and across the world took to the streets in opposition to the reckless hubris of the president and his men. Some of the pictures here record the language of those protests. But their voices were glibly dismissed by the smirking ideologues in charge. Instead, they blundered on with upside-down strategies that unified and multiplied our enemies even as they divided and alienated our friends. They eroded American justice and devastated our nation's moral standing in the world.

And so today our vulnerabilities have hardly diminished. A new attack would, as we saw on 9/11, bring out America's best, just as surely as it would fail to defeat us. On the contrary, we are defeated only when the enormous tragedy of such a crime is played on to license illegitimate war and the corruption of a free society.

John Nava
September 6, 2006

That short essay was written for the catalog of an exhibition of paintings and tapestries held at Sullivan Goss Gallery in Santa Barbara, California, in October 2006. By the time of Barack Obama's arrival four years later it had become commonplace to view the invasion of Iraq and, indeed, the entire George W. Bush reign, as a disaster.

But back in the nightmare days of Bush it was often asked, "Where is the outrage?" The frustration over that question was the impetus, I imagine, for a lot of works of dissent by artists of all sorts during the long winter of "W."

It is hard now to believe the wrath that followed in serene Santa Barbara when the exhibition announcement arrived in the mail with an image on the cover of a teenager wearing a T-shirt inscribed with the words "America Tortures." Despite years of news stories from Abu Ghraib to "Gitmo," the simple statement of this illusion-shattering fact was indigestible. There followed the bizarre spectacle of an art gallery enduring weeks of threats, editorial attack, and police involvement.

Beyond being confronted with the unvarnished statement of a shameful reality, there was, I think, a vehement "how dare you" anger at art for speaking out of turn. By and large it is the role of the popular arts in America to provide "relaxation products." This isn't necessarily a condemnation. Matisse famously said that a painting should be like a comfortable chair to a tired businessman at the end of a hard day. Beyond décor and escapist fantasy, art's provision of consolation, poetic revelation, and spiritual renewal is not unimportant. But even in the extremely marginalized and self-referential world of modern art, the inhumanity of the Bush era reignited a moral voice that responded to the national somnambulance.

The soul-destroying legacy of the habituation to torture should not be underestimated. With Obama's presidency the entire planet hoped that the American low point had passed. The recovery of our ideals seemed a thrilling possibility. But Bush's poisonous gifts have kept on giving, confounding the new president. In 2006, saying that America tortures unleashed deeply offended outcry. But now it's no longer un-American. "W." himself proudly confirms this perverse new patriotism in his book *Decision Points*. When CIA director George Tenet asked the president if waterboarding was now permitted, Bush blustered, "Damn right."[1]

March 2011

John Nava, *Our Torture Is Better Than Their Torture*, 2008.
48 × 36 inches, oil on canvas. Image courtesy of the artist.

John Nava, *Neo-Icons*. Installation shot of exhibition at Jenkins Johnson Gallery, New York, New York, 2008.

CHAPTER 8

Torture and Representation: The Art of *Détournement*

Abigail Solomon-Godeau

Because various forms of torture have been routinely practiced throughout recorded history, there exists a substantial visual archive illustrating certain of its techniques. A sixteenth-century woodcut illustrating the practice of what is now called waterboarding is one such example, taken from a legal codex.

Whether represented in the form of monumental sculpture celebrating victory and conquest (for example, the massive carvings from ancient Mesopotamia) or in the grisly martyrdoms of Christian art, the imagery of torture is part of the West's visual history. Employed in the service of obtaining information or, as has been the case for much longer, to provoke confession or attest to the truth of the utterance, torture has long been a juridical technology wielded by state or religious powers.[1] Its prohibition in the United Nations' *Universal Declaration of Human Rights* of 1948 was predicated on the signatories' acceptance of universal principles of law, justice, and human rights, and is thus of historically recent vintage.[2]

In his provocative discussion of the artistic prototypes that either illustrate acts of torture or, more generally, depict relations of domination and subjugation, Stephen F. Eisenman has argued that the imagery of torture

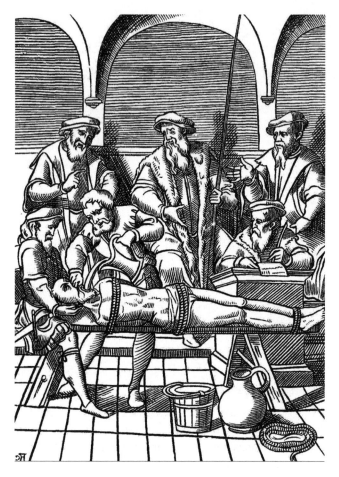

The Water Torture. Facsimile of a woodcut, Antwerp, 1556.

grounds the discourse of Western art history itself.[3] He takes as one of his principal examples the Hellenistic sculpture of Laokoon and his sons, a canonical work in Western art history celebrated by J.-J. Winckelmann, art history's "founder."[4] Eisenman argues that, as one of the most venerable and lauded works in this figurative tradition, the Laokoon, along with comparable representations throughout art history, contains visual representations of cruelty and violence that operate to naturalize them within political and social life. For Eisenman, even the depiction of animals to be sacrificed or scenes of the hunt operate to affirm man's godlike dominion over all living things. But whatever the significance or effects of the representations of violence in premodern Western culture, in our own epoch, its representations have been increasingly assimilated into the domain of leisure and entertainment.

Where torture-as-spectacle may historically have intersected with daily civic life—for example, in gladiatorial combat or public executions—contemporary simulations of torture require a different interpretive frame. Various acts of torture are not only frequent in movies and television, but are now a trope in fashion photography. Moreover, in contrast to the spectacle of torture in premodern cultures, the imagery of torture is now often consumed privately. And because the psychic elements of the act of torture are also shaped by sadistic and masochistic components of the human psyche, torture both real and simulated may be eroticized or focused on the sexual organs. Rape of both women and men is, as we know, frequent in wartime—it is indeed a weapon of war, and is commonly committed in prisons. (Although generally considered as an act distinct from torture, rape might well be considered as co-substantial with it).

How the imagery of torture in its mass media simulations is received and what might be its effects have long been subject to debate, but there exists little hard evidence that censorship either reduces violence or produces more virtuous citizens.

As Eisenman has also observed, until quite recently (certainly not before the eighteenth century), depictions of torture did not manifest any identifiable critique of its practice or, for that matter, sympathy for its victims.[5] Even when the image operates rhetorically to express pathos or tragedy, it is not the extremity (or perversity) of the infliction of pain that is subject to question. On the contrary, the spectator of Poussin's *Martyrdom of Saint Erasmus* was not expected to reflect on the procedure of disemboweling, or to regard it as "cruel and unusual punishment." Judging from the extant visual record, it appears that image-maker, spectator, or commissioning entity accepted the legitimacy of torture as such, as well as the power relations it affirmed, enacted, and commemorated. The serene Apollo implacably flaying Marsyas, the heretics dismembered, the witches burned, the torments suffered by the damned—in all cases, the meaning of the representation served to confirm the just and natural order of the world in both its secular and religious organization.

Where the spectator was prompted to feelings of compassionate and empathetic identification viewing the agony of the victim (as in representations of Christ's flagellation, the *Ecce Homo*, or the sufferings of the saints), these were not a denunciation of the inhumanity of the act of torture per se. Such a perspective became possible only when torture as part of the juridical process was open to question, and this occurred in the broad context of the Enlightenment.[6] It is in fact difficult to find any earlier prototypes of a work such as Francisco Goya's pen and brush drawing, ca. 1810–1814, "The Custody of a Criminal Does Not Call for Torture" ("La seguidad de un reo no exige tormento"). Even so, Goya's *Disasters of War*, his eighty-odd copperplate engravings depicting the horrors of the Peninsular War, were only published in 1863, more than forty years after Goya produced them. But it seems fair to say that they inaugurated an artistic practice whose legacies can be identified today in the work of many politically engaged artists active throughout the world.

It goes without saying that physical pain is internal to the body and incommunicable, and that the experience of torture, like trauma of any type, exceeds representation. As Elaine Scarry writes, "physical pain does not simply resist language but actively destroys it, bringing about an immediate reversion to a state anterior to language, to the sounds and cries a human being makes before language is learned."[7] Moreover, many forms of torture are literally unrepresentable in visual forms (e.g., sleep deprivation, isolation, sound assaults). When we confront the actual photographic representation of acts of torture that emerged from Abu Ghraib prison, there is obviously an unbridgeable gulf between our reception of these fifteen hundred–odd images as spectators and those acts as they were experienced by the victims, or for that matter, by the perpetrators. We, as spectators, can look at them; we can be ashamed, appalled, or horrified, or perhaps, like Rush Limbaugh, find them equivalent to fraternity hazing ("animal house on the night shift," as the Schlesinger report had it).[8] But in no case is what Elaine Scarry describes as the victim's "world shattering" experience of torture communicable or representable as such.

This leads me to the central issue I want to address, which is focused on the possibilities and limitations of what is considered as "political art" in the wake of what Abu Ghraib prison has given us to see. In the larger context of an investigation of torture and the arts, one issue to explore concerns what kinds of cultural production are most effective in prompting dissent or contestation. We need to consider what tactics can mobilize spectators, bystanders, and audiences (these are all quite distinct collectivities), to reflect, to take heed, to pause, to consider, to confront the evidence of torture so as to make its deployment both present and visible, to work against its continuing practice being either ignored or repressed. Reacting to the revelations of the torture of detainees and prisoners by the United States, a number of contemporary artists have made it a subject of their work; however, many of these well-intentioned practices raise complex issues about the politics and ethics of representation. These issues have been on the table, so to speak, since the 1970s, and have been especially prominent with respect to representations of the Holocaust, ranging from debates around the reproduction of archival imagery to reenactments, such as those staged in various movies.

I want to consider certain of the forms used by artists who have chosen the practice of torture by the US military and civilian personnel at Abu Ghraib prison as their subject. In terms of artistic practice, these approaches range from those of the well-known Colombian painter Fernando Botero, who, as of 2006, has produced eighty-eight large-scale works; Clinton Fein, a photographer who has elaborately restaged scenes of torture derived from the Abu Ghraib archive; Jenny Holzer's large scale installation work *Protect Protect*; and finally, to work by anonymous artist/activist groups such as the Los Angeles-based collective Forkscrew.

First exhibited in several venues in Europe, Botero's paintings based on the Abu Ghraib archive were also exhibited in January 2006 at the Marlborough Gallery in New York City. The headline of art critic Roberta Smith's *New York Times* review of the exhibit—"Botero Restores the Dignity of Prisoners at Abu Ghraib"—might be queried.[9] The sentence from which the headline derives reads as follows: "These paintings do something that the harrowing photographs taken at Abu Ghraib do not. They restore the prisoners' dignity and humanity without diminishing their agony or the injustice of their situation. Mr. Botero does this, as painters always have, through manipulations of scale, color, and form. He has also made surprisingly astute adjustments to his own daffy style."[10]

Putting aside the question as to what could possibly be meant by the claim for the restoration of dignity to former or current prisoners, who were probably unaware of the paintings' existence, one might question the adequacy of this practice as a form of political protest and contestation. Does the historical form of the easel painting—itself subject to critique within artistic/political criticism at least since dada and Productivism—constitute a meaningful or effective act of political dissent? And if it does, what are those conditions and properties that might give it this charge and thus make it operate effectively on its viewer, whether heuristically, affectively, or formally? Is the form of the work in contradiction with the work of the work? How is such a work received by its spectators, who may or may not share the artist's own outrage, and what are its conditions of visibility? Does the pictorial representation of acts of torture in and of itself provide an adequate framework with which to discredit either the political, carceral, or military regimes that are responsible for its use? For if a work

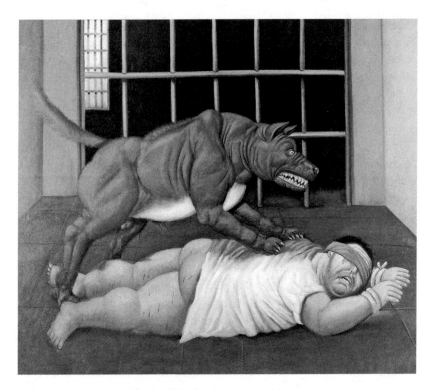

Fernando Botero, *Abu Ghraib 45*. © Fernando Botero. Courtesy
Marlborough Gallery, New York.

is perceived as generally denunciative of what is widely considered abhor-
rent and, in the case of torture at Abu Ghraib, illegal, does this in and of
itself serve any political ends?

Insofar as these questions are applicable to practices of artistic dissent in
its many forms, we might contrast a work such as Hans Haacke's *U.S.
Isolation Box* of 1983 with any of the Botero paintings or the series itself.
Responding at the time to the exposé of the treatment of prisoners by the
US military, Haacke produced an exact replica of the eight-foot-square
isolation boxes used to imprison Grenadans in the wake of Reagan's invasion of that year.[11]

The presence of Haacke's *Isolation Box* on 42nd Street was itself a
scandal—more so, it seemed at the time, than the actual military practice
itself. At some point, and in response to political pressure, the box was
moved to a less conspicuous place further back from the mall entrance and
thus easily overlooked by passersby. Observing the box, walking around it
(one could not enter it), and reading the information about the physical

Hans Haacke, *U.S. Isolation Box, Grenada, 1983, 1984*. Wood, hinges,
padlock, spray-painted stencil lettering, 244 × 244 × 244cm,
© Hans Haacke/Artists Rights Society, New York/VG Bild-Kunst,
Bonn. Courtesy Paula Cooper Gallery, New York.

conditions experienced by the prisoner made palpable, visceral, and immediate how such a confinement would be experienced. With little ventilation
(this was supplied by small holes bored into the wood), no view to the outside (the small windows placed near the top were above viewing level), no
bed, no toilet, claustrophobic scale, made even more terrible by the island's
tropical heat, it required little imagination to understand the physical suffering produced by such imprisonment. Refusing to depict an actual prisoner, *Isolation Box* presented the nature of prisoners' treatment as factually,
as coolly and clinically, as self-evidently as possible. But the brute presence
of the box was itself an inescapable statement: *This is how the US military
treats detainees and prisoners.*

With respect to Haacke's practice overall, and in contrast to Botero's
paintings, it is significant that Haacke has never had what is so identifiable
in Botero's work—that is, a signature style. Haacke's artistic practice, in all
its diverse media and scale, has always been determined according to the

subject of the work, and only in rare instances were oil paintings produced as elements within larger individual installations (e.g., Haacke's academically painted portraits of Margaret Thatcher and Ronald Reagan as specific and discrete elements within them).[12]

Without doubting the political and moral outrage that Botero wishes to express through his art, the problem is to do with the contradictions that arise when artists attempt to confront an immediate political and ethical catastrophe. As works by Botero (either in the form of individual canvases or as a series of them), the paintings' contents may summon up the reality to which they allude, but they remain, nevertheless, "Boteros." This, however, is but one of the difficulties confronting artists, especially painters, when they seek to fashion artworks intended to be politically, ideologically, or heuristically mobilizing. For the educated consumer of art, a work of art is not "about" its content or, at least, not in a defining way. Therefore, whether a painting represents a landscape or a massacre, it is aesthetic criteria that determine its reception rather than its ostensible subject matter.

In the case of Clinton Fein, a web-based artist who lives and works in San Francisco, the medium of photography is used to literally restage the nightmarish scenes from Abu Ghraib.[13] Absent the knowledge that these are elaborate simulations made with hired models, and viewed on the Internet, the viewer might well mistake them for the actual images. Closer inspection, however, reveals that the men's bodies are toned and beautiful, the details more grisly, the qualities of the image far superior to the digital originals.

If the actual pictures from Abu Ghraib are often disturbingly close to web-based amateur pornography, Fein's reconstructions might be considered the professional equivalent: well-made, sharply focused, attentive to color values, composition, and framing.[14]

Given the accessibility of so many of the Abu Ghraib images, including the now-iconic photograph of the hooded man on his box, we must ask what such artistically rendered simulations accomplish. How does such an imitation avoid titillation and prurience, voyeurism and sadism—motives and attributes that haunt, and indeed prompted, the making of the original pictures? These questions of spectatorial address and reception, as well as these images' potential for exploitation and sensationalism, are of primary concern. Exhibited in galleries and other art venues or accessed on the web, Fein's pictures provide neither additional information nor insight nor any framework that might resignify these images. Moreover, their deliberate aestheticism, manifest in Fein's choice of models, compositional strategies, and other formal elements, accentuates the obscenity of the torture itself.

Clinton Fein, *Rank and Defile 1*, 2007. Chromogenic digital print, 96 × 126 inches. Courtesy Toomey Tourell Gallery, San Francisco.

And because of his photographs' status as simulations, the viewer is absolved of any guilt evoked by pleasurable looking, indemnifying him or her from responsibility. From this perspective it is the solicitation of a (potentially) prurient gaze, the allure of an unconstrained voyeurism that constitutes the most problematic element of such a project—which is simply to say that if the ethics and politics of representation turn on the responsibility of the imagemaker to resist the lure of spectacle as well as that of aestheticism, this requires some form of reckoning with the complex attributes of the spectatorial gaze, its elements of eroticism, mastery, projection, and fantasy.

Jenny Holzer's recent work on the Iraq war, of which the torture of Iraqi detainees is only one component, provides a significant example of alternative practices within the institutional space of art. In pointed contrast to the work of Botero or Fein, Holzer rejects both figuration and iconization. In her 2009 exhibition *Protect Protect* at the Whitney Museum of American Art, Holzer orchestrated a vast multimedia installation that included her familiar LED scrolling texts, as well as maps and paintings derived from

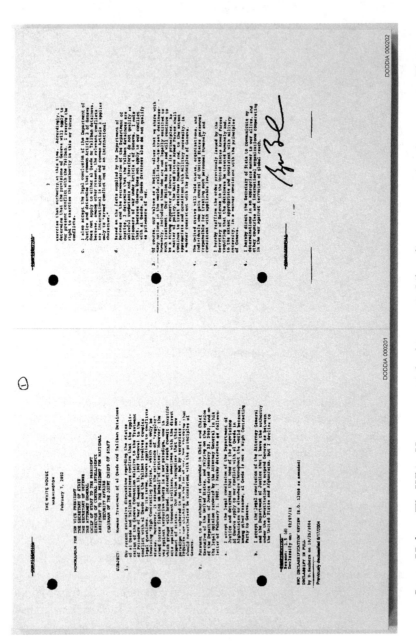

Jenny Holzer, *The White House 2002 pink white*, 2006. Oil on linen, 33 × 51 in.; 83 × 129 cm. Text: U.S. government document. © 2006 Jenny Holzer, member Artists Rights Society (ARS), New York.

declassified but redacted official documents obtained through the Freedom of Information Act by organizations such as the ACLU.

Among the works mounted on the walls are enlarged handprints of Iraqi detainees who have died in captivity, as well as military memos, policy statements, autopsy reports, maps, and other relevant materials. These are, in fact, *paintings* (of texts, redacted official documents, handprints, etc., but executed by other hands) and, as such, establish their own discourse about the space of museum, challenging conventional assumptions about its role and ideologies even as they conscript (and subvert) the concept of painting as such.

Floor spaces in several rooms were dominated by LED installations consisting of phrases and sentences also derived from existing documents. Thus, in the tradition of critical art practices such as those of Hans Haacke and Krzysztof Wodiczko, the project is conceived in relation to a dense network of information and documentation, whose discrete elements are all drawn from the specific data (or propaganda) of the current wars waged by the United States, including the so-called war against terrorism and the war against Iraq and the US occupation; the military and

Exhibition view: Jenny Holzer, *Protect Protect*. Whitney Museum of American Art, New York, 2009, © 2011 Jenny Holzer, member Artists Rights Society (ARS), New York. Photo: Lili Holzer-Glier.

geopolitical determinations of the US presence in the Middle East; and the issues of detainee abuse and torture.[15]

It is significant that even when addressing the use of torture, Holzer uses no figurative or representational imagery, as is consistent with her artistic practice. This refusal of the image avoids the risk of reiterating either the sensationalism or the spectacle-like aspect of the Abu Ghraib visual archive, and it includes the sorts of information, history, and context that images alone cannot provide. Moreover, and in contrast to her earlier work, none of the textual material is written by her; words, phrases, sentences, and documents were selected by Holzer, but the chilling bureaucratic language of government officials and military personnel is itself one subject within the larger ensemble. The torture inflicted at Abu Ghraib began, after all, not with the actions of a dozen or so reservists, but with memos, legal opinions, and directives originating from the Bush White House, many of them predating the war on Iraq and relating to the treatment of prisoners at Guantánamo. As James Glisson has observed, "the blots, blotches, and telltale marks from repeated Xeroxing along with the crude redactions . . . are indicators of the distance between the originals and the public version. . . . These marks are indices of the various hands and bureaucratic processes the documents go through before they are released. . . . These passages reiterate the idea that the documents are also the product of human actions: someone crafted these policies, typed this letter, initialed this memo."[16]

While these paintings are only one component of *Protect Protect*, they exemplify what the French Situationists meant by the notion of *détournement*—appropriating images, texts, advertisements, and so forth, to subvert, alter, derail, or transfigure their original meaning. The new meanings unleashed or enabled thus function as tactical unveilings of what the image or text in its official guise operates to mystify, occlude, disavow. *Détournement* is thus conducive to the conscious and focused activity of decoding and decrypting, of reading between the lines, of seeing behind the signs. Ideally, this helps to construct an active viewer, just as the inclusion of documents, chronologies, and other textual materials provides necessary information for an informed reading of the historical context.

This brings me to my final example: the posters designed and distributed by an anonymous group of artist/activists based in Los Angeles who produce their work under the collective name Forkscrew. Among their graphic works is a set of posters mimicking the Apple iPod advertisements one sees on billboards and in other public spaces; those Forkscrew adaptations, such as the one illustrated here, appeared in Los Angeles and San Francisco on walls, billboards, and kiosks.

iRaq [Abu Ghraib prisoner], Forkscrew Graphics, Silkscreen, 2004, Los Angeles, California.

The "iRaq" posters, which are offered as free downloads to all users on the group's website, circulate both virtually and materially, and can be possessed by anyone.[17] In public space, the iRaq images seamlessly blend into the urban landscape and, if not really looked at, can pass undetected. But when they are noticed, it is in the split second between the viewer's automatic—i.e., distracted—perception of the poster *as* poster, and the shocked recognition of the identity of the silhouetted figures, that the possibility of reflection rather than visual consumption is enabled. The mobilization of shock effects has been and remains a tactic of oppositional or dissident cultural production, but what is important here is the *kind* of shock the iRaq posters mobilize. First, there is the shock of recognition: the instant when one recognizes the hooded detainee from Abu Ghraib or any of the posters' other icons of resistance as the sources for the silhouettes.[18] Then there is the shock of dissonance—the desirable commodity transformed into confrontational emblems of warfare or torture. In this respect, the use of the iPod—a technology not only of solitary entertainment and distraction, but also a globalized commodity that "everyone" recognizes—is significant. Sequestering the user in his or her hermetic aural world, the iPod is thus likened to the indifference or disregard that has, among other things, prevented any serious consequences for those in the Bush administration who sanctioned and indeed prescribed the use of torture. However, in its broadest implications, what the Forkscrew project suggests is that an artistic/political response to any given political imperative need not be limited (or contained) within the aesthetic sphere. As critics like Douglas Crimp have long argued, there is no reason to suppose that a public work, placed in public space, produced anonymously or collectively, is in its essence any less a work of art than one that is painted in the studio, exhibited in the gallery, and purchased by a collector or institution.[19] Although there is no way to calculate the political effects of any given artistic practice, at the very least, street art, posters in public places, agitprop, and other such interventions have the merit and advantage of operating in the public sphere—which, in the final analysis, is the only space—discursive, civic, political, ethical—that can ultimately determine the future of torture, or, at the very least, the United States' own future of torture.

CHAPTER 9

Waterboarding: Political and Sacred Torture

Stephen F. Eisenman

The Scene of Politics

After the release of photographs of tortured prisoners at Abu Ghraib prison in Iraq in May 2003, a Gallup Poll indicated that 54 percent of Americans were "bothered a great deal" by the revelations. A year later the number had declined to 40 percent. In December 2005 an AP/IPSOS poll revealed that 61 percent of Americans agreed that torture was justified, at least on some occasions.[1] A May 2006 report by the UN High Commission for Human Rights about US torture at Guantánamo Bay was widely reported in newspapers, radio, and television, but produced no major outcries, public protests, or congressional investigations. Soon thereafter, President Bush—invoking the fictional "ticking bomb" scenario—successfully argued to Congress that the CIA should be allowed to use so-called "alternative interrogation procedures" and be given immunity from criminal prosecution for prisoner abuse and war crimes. Despite the efforts of a few senators, notably Patrick Leahy of Vermont, Sheldon Whitehouse of Rhode Island, and Joe Biden of Delaware, that immunity was granted. The US public and its representatives, it would seem, were not bothered by the fact that the US government permitted and even encouraged its agents to torture people held in their custody.

Admittedly there has been more discussion and controversy about torture in the last four years than previously. The legal protection granted by Congress to CIA agents does not extend to the destruction of evidence in criminal, civil, or legislative proceedings, and the CIA's admission in December 2007 that it erased videotapes showing its agents employing waterboarding in the questioning of two presumed al-Qaeda members raised a brief hue and cry in the press and among some Congressional Democrats and put some operatives in legal jeopardy. But the criminal investigation, announced by Attorney General Michael Mukasey on January 2, 2008, should not in fact be taken as evidence that public or political sentiment turned decisively against torture. To begin with, the *prima facie* criminality recorded in the videotapes, namely waterboarding, was not the subject of the inquiry, only the destruction of evidence. In addition, the prosecutor put in charge of the case, John Durham, a deputy US attorney from Connecticut, was not independent. He initially reported to Deputy Attorney General Mark Filip, who, like his boss Mukasey, refused during confirmation testimony to state that waterboarding was a form of torture. Durham was, in fact, recommended for his job in Connecticut by the previous US attorney, Kevin J. O'Connor, who left his post to become chief of staff for Alberto Gonzalez, who oversaw the preparation of the infamous 2003 memo that underlay the entire executive branch's legitimation of torture. In other words, the deputy to the torture czar hired the man charged to investigate the destruction of the torture videotapes. The appointment of Eric Holder to the post of US Attorney General did not change the dynamics of the investigation, and President Obama indicated from almost his first day in office that he was not inclined to prosecute CIA agents or other government officials for human rights abuses. And in fact, in November 2010 John Durham allowed the statute of limitations to lapse in the destruction of evidence case.

Support for torture in the United States is not hidden in a web of professional loyalties and secret agendas; it is open and available for all to see. The 2008 Republican Party presidential candidates argued in public debates in favor of more latitude for Army and CIA interrogators—that is, for more torture, not less. Rudolph Giuliani, whose police practiced torture under his mayoral watch in New York City, was particularly unabashed. (Recall here that the police who tortured and sodomized Abner Louima in a Brooklyn police station in 1997 were said to have shouted, "This is Giuliani-time." That is how his administration is now largely remembered.)

Even the eventual Republican nominee, John McCain, who co-sponsored a law banning torture, agreed to a loophole permitting the CIA, FBI, and other agencies to continue to use whatever interrogation measures they saw fit, including waterboarding. The very law designed to curb torture thus actually provides its first *de jure* legitimation. The two major Democratic candidates for president, Clinton and Obama—while denouncing torture on the few occasions the press asked them their opinion—did not make Republican support for it a major campaign issue. And given that a more pandering, poll-driven political process can hardly be imagined, it is highly unlikely that the Republicans and Democrats completely misjudged US public opinion. In his recent autobiography, George W. Bush declared himself torturer-in-chief by admitting to having personally approved the use of waterboarding. "No doubt, the procedure was tough," he coolly wrote.[2] Therefore the question remains: can so many Americans have truly come to accept torture as necessary and appropriate in the struggle against terrorism?

Pictures of Torture

What if there were something about the pictures of torture from Abu Ghraib, or the pictures, descriptions, and even demonstrations of waterboarding—now widespread on television and on YouTube—that blunted outrage? What if the US public, with the connivance of interested sectors of government and mainstream media, share a kind of moral and visual blindness—I have called it elsewhere the "Abu Ghraib Effect"—that allows them to ignore, overlook, or even justify, however partially or provisionally, the facts of degradation and brutality manifest in the pictures? And finally—and more hopefully—what if the "Abu Ghraib Effect" can, in some small measure at least, be made alien by means of its exposure, analysis, and public discussion?

I will not, in the limited space I have here, recapitulate the thesis of my 2007 book. Suffice it to say that I argued that many critics and observers misunderstood the nature of the brutal images from Abu Ghraib prison. Far from being exceptional pictures that reveal the existence in the United States of what the philosopher Giorgio Agamben, following the political theorist Carl Schmitt, called a state of emergency or state of exception— "pure, de facto sovereignty . . . outside of the law"—they are images of normative practices in US history, as in the history of Western politics and representation. The Abu Ghraib photographs, I argued in addition, expose a longstanding pathos formula whereby torture victims are shown accepting and even participating in their own chastisement and destruction. That formula, a protean expression of the barbarism of civilization, may be traced from the Hellenistic *Pergamon Altar* to Michelangelo's *Bound Slave* to Sodoma's *St. Sebastian* and beyond. It is an important basis for late Renaissance fresco cycles of capture and enslavement, and veritably ubiquitous in Baroque imagery of martyrdom. By the end of the nineteenth century, the motif of the captive or the victim who seems to welcome, participate in, or even take pleasure in his own abjection or subjugation—or where that subjugation is made erotic—had migrated from the realm of high art to commercial and mass media—and most frequently, in the twentieth century, in movies and TV, such as *The Thief of Baghdad*, (1940), *The Ten Commandments* (1956), and *Star Trek* (1968).

In television programs such as *24*, films such *Missing in Action III* (1978), other Chuck Norris vehicles, and *Casino Royale* (2006), starring Daniel Craig, torture has come to seem both gratifying and comfortingly domestic; in one episode of *24*, a father tortures his own son; in the Chuck Norris feature, a father is tortured in front of his son; and in the Daniel Craig movie, a man suffers excruciating pain and yet asks for his torture to continue. After the diabolical Le Chiffre strikes two terrible blows with a knotted rope against James Bond's testicles, 007 says to his nemesis, "I've got an itch down there—do you mind?" After still another blow, he says "to the right," and then finally, "now the whole world is gonna know you've scratched my balls." In *Missing in Action III*—in a scene that strangely anticipates the iconic image from Abu Ghraib—Chuck Norris is tortured with electrical charges attached to his chest while standing naked on a box; if he moves more than a few centimeters, a gun will automatically discharge, killing his son. He is thereby made responsible for his own suffering and the life or death of his child.

The treatment of physical torture as a kind of contract—an entente between torturer and victim—is in fact basic to its mise-en-scène, as it is to psychologically coercive interrogation. The latest US Army Field Manual (FM 34-52, 2006), entitled "Human Intelligence Collector Operations," extends to its logical conclusion the central premise of previous interrogation manuals—the necessity of establishing a rapport between interrogator and potential source. It contains a section called "Emotional Love Approach" (sec. 8-29) that begins, poetically enough, "Love in its many forms (friendship, comradeship, patriotism, love of family) is a dominant emotion for most people. The HUMINT collector focuses on the anxiety felt by the source about the circumstances in which he finds himself, his isolation from those he loves, and his feelings of helplessness." It continues: "Sincerity and conviction are critical in a successful attempt at an emotional love approach as the HUMINT collector must show genuine concern for the source, and for the object at which the HUMINT collector is directing the source's emotion." Observe here that the phrases "sincerity and conviction" and "genuine concern for the source," if they are to be taken seriously—and they surely must—mean that a real bond of affection is to be established between the HUMINT and the source, or the torturer and the victim. In the notorious 1963 CIA KUBARK manual (KUBARK is a cryptonym for the CIA headquarters at Langley, Virginia), under the section entitled "Coercive Counterintelligence Interrogations of Resistant Sources," section B, we read:

> One subjective reaction often evoked by coercion is a feeling of guilt. [Dr. Malcolm L.] Meltzer observes, "In some lengthy interrogations, the interrogator may, by virtue of his role as the sole supplier of satisfaction and punishment, assume the stature and importance of a parental figure in the prisoner's feeling and thinking. Although there may be intense hatred for the interrogator, it is not unusual for warm feelings also to develop. This ambivalence is the basis for guilt reactions, and if the interrogator nourishes these feelings, the guilt may be strong enough to influence the prisoner's behavior. . . . Guilt makes compliance more likely."[3]

The creation of an affective bond between interrogator and source, and between torturer and victim, serves more than just practical aims. It serves at least two essential ideological functions: (1) assuring those who hold the whip that they are as not as bestial as their acts would make them seem; and (2) salving the consciences of the citizens of empire: when victims are rendered abject, or in the case of detainees at Abu Ghraib or Guantánamo Bay, represented as debased or sexually degenerate, the public is encouraged to believe that they are deserving of chastisement, conquest, or destruction. According to the perfect tautology of torture, the victim deserves his fate simply because he *is* a victim. As Agamben writes in *State of Exception*: "in the detainee at Guantánamo, bare life reaches its maximum indeterminacy."[4] The coerced homoeroticism in the Abu Ghraib images was specifically staged both to conform to Western stereotypes of Islamic (or Oriental) sexuality, and to especially offend Muslim sensibilities by violating the doctrine of "halal" or "religious purity." The digital photographs may thus be placed within the tradition that Said defined as "Orientalism."

Waterboarding

But what about images—extant and erased—of waterboarding? Does the relatively mild US public response to revelations about waterboarding have anything to do with the nature of this practice and the character of these pictures? May public reactions to them too be subsumed under the rubric of the "Abu Ghraib Effect"? Do the US military and CIA employ waterboarding precisely because it can be made to seem benign and even consensual—because it too can be assimilated to the "emotional love approach"?

The practice of waterboarding, sometimes called with intentional irony "the water cure," has been documented in the United States since the mid-nineteenth century, and has always been considered a form of torture. US Army soldiers stationed in the Philippines in 1900 employed the water cure against Filipino soldiers and were court-martialed two years later for the offense. Theodore Roosevelt stated that though he believed "nobody was seriously damaged . . . torture is not a thing we can tolerate." At the Tokyo War Crimes Trial convened in Tokyo in May 1946, several Japanese prison commanders and guards were convicted of so-called Class B and C offenses—War Crimes and Crimes against Humanity—for having overseen or conducted interrogations of US prisoners employing waterboarding. Two victims testified about the practice: "They would lash me to a stretcher then prop me up against a table with my head down. They would then pour about two gallons of water from a pitcher into my nose and mouth until I lost consciousness." The second stated: "They laid me out on a stretcher and strapped me on. The stretcher was then stood on end with my head almost touching the floor and my feet in the air. . . . They then began pouring water over my face and at times it was almost impossible for me to breathe without sucking in water."[5] (It should be noted that US soldiers also waterboarded Japanese.)

Waterboarding was used by North Korea and China during the Korean War, by the Soviet Union under Stalin, and by the French in Algeria. In the journalist Henri Alleg's book from 1957, *La Question*, which became a rallying cry for French intellectuals opposed to the colonial war, the author described his own water torture. An interrogator tied the naked Alleg to a plank, wrapped a rag around his head, and forced his mouth open with a wooden wedge. Then, a rubber tube attached to a spigot was suspended over his face. Alleg writes:

> When everything was ready, he said to me: "When you want to talk, all you have to do is move your fingers." And he turned on the tap. The rag

was soaked rapidly. Water flowed everywhere: in my mouth, in my nose, all over my face. But for a while, I could still breathe in small gulps of air. I tried, by contracting my throat, to take in as little water as possible and to resist suffocation by keeping air in my lungs for as long as I could. But I couldn't hold on for more than a few moments. I had the impression of drowning, and a terrible agony, that of death itself, took possession of me. In spite of myself, all the muscles of my body struggled uselessly to save me from suffocation. In spite of myself, the fingers of both hands shook uncontrollably. "That's it! He's going to talk," said a voice.[6]

Waterboarding was also practiced by US soldiers in Vietnam and by Pol Pot's Khmer Rouge in Cambodia, and there are recent reports of water-boarding in Ethiopia (approved by the United States) and elsewhere in the horn of Africa.

The main purpose of waterboarding, like most forms of torture, is not the extraction of truthful testimony—the victim will say anything to stop the ordeal—but the eliciting of confession: confession of error, apostasy, or moral responsibility. (The mere fact that torture so rarely obtains truth, and yet intelligent and highly trained people do it again and again, is an obvious indication that it serves another purpose.) However, there is something special about the practice of waterboarding, which, since its inception in the late Middle Ages, has allowed its adepts to believe they are engaged not in an act of physical torture, but of moral suasion, and even religious sanctification. At the time of the Inquisition in Spain at the end of the fifteenth century, water torture and death by drowning—*tortura del agua* or *tormenta de toca*—were seen as particularly suitable punishments for Anabaptists (those who withheld baptism during childhood, in preference for adult anointing) and indeed for anyone (especially Jews and Gentiles) who denied the purifying waters of Catholic baptism. In a sort of inversion of this actuality, the artist Albrecht Altdorfer in 1520 in his St. Florian altarpiece (Ufizzi Museum) represented the imminent drowning of the fourth-century St. Florian—a Roman soldier who refused direct orders to torture and kill Christians. He will be sanctified as a martyr by his water cure. Similarly, the fourteenth-century St. John Nepomuk, the national saint of Bohemia, received his water cure—drowning in the Vtlava (Moldau) River—for having refused to divulge the secrets of the confessional. (A painting by Syzmon Czechowicz from 1750 in the National Museum of Poland shows the saint being ushered off the side of the bridge by a contingent of polite soldiers and a chorus of cherubim.) One sacrament, baptism, was inverted to punish the saint for his rigid observance of another, confession.

The frontispiece illustration to the anonymously written *A Memento for Holland* (1652), an account of the tortures perpetrated by men from the Dutch East India Company against some Englishmen accused of conspiracy, recalls an image of crucifixion, and the text speaks of the barbarism of Christians and Muslims:

> Now comes *John Clerk*. . . . First, they twined him up by the hands with a cord on a large door, where they made him fast to two staples of iron, fixt on both sides on the top of the door-posts, stretching his hands asunder as wide as they could: and being thus made fast, his feet hung about two foot from the ground, which also they extended as far as they could, and so made them fast unto the bottom of the door. They bound a cloth about his neck and face, so close, that little or no water could go by. When they had done this, they poured the water softly upon his head, until the cloth was full up to his mouth and nostrils, so that he could not draw breath, but he must suck in water; which being still continued to be poured in softly, forced his intrails to come out at his eyes, ears, and nose, almost to strangling. Never were there such horrid cruelties exercised among the Turks and Barbarians, as among those that pretend Christianity. They were so cruel to him, that they tormented him until his breath was gone, so that he fainted: then they took him quickly down, and made him vomit up the water; and being a little recovered, they pull'd him up again, and charged him with the water again, till they had stifled him as before: and this was exercised on this poor wretch three or four several times, till his body was swoln twice as big as ordinary, his cheeks puft up like a pair of bladders, and his eyes starting and strutting out beyond his forehead.[7]

The practice of today's waterboarding is largely unchanged since the practice was first described. In a videotaped demonstration of waterboarding given by a group of ex–Navy Seals, produced for CNN and widely available on YouTube and elsewhere, the practice is made to seem almost sacred—a forced baptism—and in the end, the victim is almost giddy. Perhaps the apparent general comfort with waterboarding—on the parts of the 2008 Republican candidates (avowed baptizers all, including one Baptist minister), the born-again president, and the broadly Christian public—was connected to their inevitable faith in the cleansing and sanctifying character of water. Perhaps waterboarding, invariably called "simulated drowning" or "feigned drowning" in the media instead of simply "drowning" or "water torture," is perceived to be no more threatening than full-immersion adult baptism?

Countereffects

Let me just conclude by saying that images may be used to buttress imperial and other forms of violence, or they may be used to contest them. Certain artists, writers, and filmmakers in the modern tradition—Hogarth, Goya, Picasso, Sartre, Benjamin, Pontecorvo, and others—have challenged this regime of imperial images in the name of emancipation, autonomy, and democracy. They have represented torture as it really is—the unmitigated and wanton imposition of violence and cruelty by those with power upon those with none, and have even roused public opinion against violence and war. For example, the late American painter Leon Golub's *Mercenary, Interrogation* and *White Squad* series from the late 1970s and '80s are life-size figure paintings of leering, hyper-masculine men of uncertain nationality or race, shown taunting or abusing seated, kneeling, bound, hooded or otherwise subordinate men or women. These works, including Golub's *Interrogation II*, were derived from news photographs and journalistic accounts of actual torture scenarios in South Africa, Guatemala, El Salvador, and elsewhere. Scab-colored, scraped raw, unstretched, unframed, and hung from grommets, the paintings themselves appear to have been beaten and abused, the physical evidence of prior acts of debasement and torture. Golub lived to see the photos from Abu Ghraib, and told his friend, the critic David Levi Strauss, that

> the techniques pictured—hooding, forced nakedness, sexual
> humiliation, stress positions, dogs, etc.—were all common torture
> techniques, right out of the book. "Walling up" with hoods or
> blindfolds increases the sense of isolation and defenselessness. Essential
> to torture is the sense that your interrogators control everything: food,
> clothing, dignity, light, even life itself. Everything is designed to make it
> clear that you are at the mercy of those whose job it is not to have any
> mercy. Hooding victims dehumanizes them, making them anonymous
> and thing-like. They become just bodies. You can do anything you want
> to them.[8]

The thing-like character of the seated, bound, hooded body in *Interrogation II* is contrasted with the angular athleticism of the standing torturers; they gaze at the spectators insolently, daring them even to reprove, much less stop them. The physically raw and emotionally extremist theatre depicted in *Interrogation II*—unlike the artifacts of recent mass culture cited earlier—precludes erotic pleasure. The painting instead describes the emotional insensibility of the torturers and the complete physical vulnerability of

Sue Coe, *We Do Not Torture*. © Sue Coe, image courtesy
of the artist.

the victim. They draw upon an ancient pathos formula in order to expose its artifice and viciousness, turn it upside-down, and render it useless as a weapon in the war of the powerful against the vulnerable.

Sue Coe's recent lithograph *We Do Not Torture* reprises the history of the pathos formula, thereby engaging both in critique and metacritique. Three men hold a wooden board upon which is strapped an emaciated victim. They tip it backwards at a forty-five-degree angle so that water from a spigot may be forced into the torture victim's mouth. The faces of the tortures are difficult to interpret—pitiless, but also matter-of-fact; grotesque, but also ordinary. A barred window at the upper left is the source for the triangle of light that illuminates the scene. At the upper right, a limp figure dangles from a rope. Holbein, Caravaggio, Goya, and Blake are touchstones for Coe. She says she uses their works because they are shortcuts for her—fast and easy ways to move the spectator to an understanding of the history of violence, the complicity of artists in programs of coercive violence, and the sometimes ambiguous line between images that eroticize pain and images that challenge the assertion that torture is ever the free choice of victims. Torture bears no resemblance to truth, pleasure or cooperation; it is oppression, violence, frequently death, and nothing more.

CHAPTER 10

Damnatio Memoriae

Hamid Dabashi

There is not in the world one single poor lynched bastard, one poor tortured man, in whom I am not also murdered and humiliated.

—Aimé Césaire, *Et les chiens se taisaient*
(And the Dogs Were Silent), 1946

The publication of Mehdi Karrubi's letter to Akbar Hashemi Rafsanjani shook the already wobbly Islamic Republic to its foundations.[1] Nobody had ever dared to speak so openly about the most notorious public secret of the theocratic state—something that everyone knew and no one ever spoke of—that the Islamic (no less) Republic kidnaps, incarcerates, savagely beats up, rapes, tortures, murders, and then secretly buries in mass graves its young citizens, men and women; that the prisons of the Islamic Republic are evidently a cut from Pier Paolo Pasolini's *Salò o le 120 giornate di Sodoma* (*Salò, or the 120 Days of Sodom*) (1975). Though the film, a troubling cinematic rendition of Fascist Italy, was never officially screened in Iran, it was part of the underground lore at the wake of the Islamic Revolution (1977–1979). As self-flagellating as Karrubi's letter was, it

140

exuded a narrative reluctance, an emotive reticence, a discursive dissonance, that defied its own prose and politics, as if the letter wrote itself
despite its author. The horrors that Karrubi was about to reveal publicly
had stirred the old man to the marrow of his bones, shaken him to the
foundations of his faith. He did not quite know how to start, how to write,
how to divulge the secret on which he had sat for a while, and then how to
end. The aging revolutionary was troubled.

Dated 7 Mordad 1388 (July 29, 2009), and released ten days later on
17 Mordad 1388 (August 8, 2009), Karrubi's letter was pointedly addressed
to Ali Akbar Hashemi Rafsanjani, former Iranian president (1989–1997)
and current head of the Expediency Council, rather than to Ali Khamenei,
the *Vali Faqih*, thus implicitly incriminating the Supreme Leader in the
atrocities he was about to reveal. Karrubi begins his letter to Rafsanjani
with a litany of wrongdoings that the heavily militarized security apparatus
of the Islamic Republic had perpetrated against peaceful demonstrators in
the aftermath of the June 2009 presidential election, including kidnapping,
beating, verbal abuse, illegal incarcerations, torture, and outright murder.[2]
Though the letter begins quite matter-of-factly, there is a sense of frightful
drama in its verbal casuistry, a narrative anxiety bespeaking a bearing witness for victims who are otherwise blinded, silenced, by their own fearful
insights—victims and witnesses that they are, at one and the same time.

There is something uncanny about Karrubi, an aging cleric, a committed revolutionary, so openly writing against the atrocities of a regime he
has been instrumental in building after a lifetime of conviction and struggle. *Havades-e talkh* (bitter incidents) is the expression that he uses for the
atrocities that the security apparatus of the Islamic Republic committed in
the aftermath of the presidential election. "Even women," he emphasizes,
have been the target of what he calls *raftar-ha-ye shena'at-amiz* (ghastly
behavior). Karrubi further describes how the security forces broke their
clubs and batons on people's heads, injuring them so severely that for weeks
they were unconscious, with pains and bruises of injury marking their
bodies days after they were beaten up. Karrubi writes as if he is opening the
oozing bandage of a self-inflicted wound, the depth of which is unfathomable to him—with every turn of the gauze he is gazing at an ulcerous lesion
that he cannot conceive has grown on his own body. There is something
Kafkaesque about the politics of Karrubi's prose—as if Gregor Samsa were
writing about the metamorphosis of Iranian body-politic.

Karrubi finally opens a new paragraph and dares to look: "But I have
heard something else that even still, thinking of it makes me shiver. I have
not been able to sleep the last two days since I heard this. I went to bed

at 2 a.m. but, and I am not exaggerating, I could not fall asleep, until I finally got up at 4 a.m., read from the Koran for a while and took a shower so that water might calm me down a little. I even did my morning prayers but still was not able to sleep."[3] He digresses again, turns his face away, takes some time to assure Mr. Hashemi of the reliability of his sources for what he is about to write, that they are high-ranking officials, that even if one of these reports is true, "it is a catastrophe for the Islamic Republic of Iran which has turned the bright, shining history of Shia clerics into an atrocious, shameful fate and has outdone many dictatorial regimes, including that of the tyrannical Shah." He still cannot completely bring himself to write what he wants to write, goes into yet another excursion about Islam, the Revolution, the Imam.

There is a little-known Iranian film called *K* (2002) by the exquisitely talented multimedia artist Shoja Azari, based on three short stories of Franz Kafka—"The Married Couple," "In the Penal Colony," and "A Fratricide." By far the most successful of Azari's adaptations is "In the Penal Colony," done in a silvery black-and-white that captures the eerie vacuity of the original story. I remember when I first read "In der Strafkolonie" ("In the Penal Colony"), in a seminar with Philip Rieff at the University of Pennsylvania, where I did my doctoral work in the late 1970s, I was completely lost in the blankness of Kafka's prose, which kept pulling the reader in toward a central terror that was always in the offing but never in complete view. By the time we actually get to the core of what the blasted Machine does, it is so late in the protracted narrative that it is as if we have become deaf, dumb, and blind to its violence and terror, having almost no sympathy for the wretched Condemned Man; happy, almost, that we are as much invested in the Machine and its ghastly tasks as the Visitor, whose aloof narrative remains always on the verge of leaving us behind. It is precisely this vacuous distance between what one fears and what one feels that Shoja Azari manages best to capture in his version of the story, not as much in depicting the actual plot, but in portraying the emotive desolation of the environment, that gives a sense of the Freudian uncanny to his *K*. The same is true about Karrubi's letter, written against the prosaic banality of an Islamic Republic that for thirty years has sustained its warring posture in order to hide the terror that it inflicts upon its own citizens, condemned to and by their own place of birth. Karrubi writes this letter very much in the way that the Condemned Man in Kafka's "In the Penal Colony" looks at the Machine that is about to torture and murder him—unaware, bewildered, innocent, guilty, determined, condemned, walking to the slaughterhouse of his own convictions. He is losing faith as he is exercising it, consuming it. Toward the end of the letter, Karrubi finally collects his courage and writes:

> Mr. Hashemi, this is what I have been informed about: Some of the detainees have reported that certain individuals have so severely raped some of the girls in custody that the attacks have caused excruciating damage and injury to their reproductive organs. At the same time, they report that others have raped the young boys so violently that upon their release, they have had to endure great physical and mental pain and have been lying in a corner of their homes since.

He then pleads with Rafsanjani to do something about this, and concludes by saying that "I have prepared two copies of this letter, one of which I have signed and sealed and will send to you, and will keep the other." He then sends his salutations, signs his name, and dates it. A weight is lifted off the old man's chest. He can breathe now, perhaps even take a nap. The mental picture of innocent children born barely after the Islamic revolution he helped bring about being raped in the prisons of the Islamic Republic was just too daunting for his aging nerves to take. Perhaps he could now take a short nap after the letter was off his chest.

The publication of Karrubi's letter dropped a napalm bomb on the presumed legitimacy (even a certain air of sanctity) of the Islamic Republic, whose custodians were furious with the old man; some even said that he ought be put on trial and lashed eighty times. Karrubi was unrepentant and promised he would reveal more—and he did.

On 2 Shahrivar 1388 (August 24, 2009), Karrubi proceeded to publish his first evidence in the form of a testimony by one of the victims of rape while in custody.[4] In this testimony, the person (whose name and gender were withheld) begins by reporting how it took days of conversation with Karrubi finally to come to terms with what had happened to him (later it was revealed that the victim was a young man) and get rid of his false sense of shame and start talking. He then reports how three official investigators sent by the government began interrogating him with an accusatory tone of voice and with a language that he says confused him as to whether he was the plaintiff or the accused. Most of the investigators' questions had to do with his connections with Karrubi, how he had come to him, why he trusted him, and why he agreed to do a videotaping of his story with him. The investigators asked him against whom is he lodging a complaint, to which he responds, "I don't know, you tell me"—meaning anyone from the person who raped him to Mahmoud Ahmadinejad to the Supreme Leader. When he objects to their lines of questioning, the interrogators tell him that he is raising some serious charges, challenging "the sacred regime," so they have to make sure. He answers back that they seem to have forgotten what the issue is, to which they respond by asking him, "how deep did they penetrate, and did they ejaculate?" They finally take him to the Surgeon General for examination, and on their way intimidate him and accuse him of having received money to make these accusations. At the Surgeon General, the presiding physician says that he has to consult with the initial physician who had examined the victim, at which point the security officials begin to accuse the plaintiff of lying and tell him that if he was indeed raped the physician would have been able to tell "even the size of it" (using the word "size" in English.) They subsequently go to his home and do a local investigation, thereby further intimidating him and damaging his name and reputation in the neighborhood. Soon after his interview was published, the victim disappeared.[5]

From Abu Ghraib to Kahrizak

Soon after these two reports, first Ayatollah Ali Khamenei, the Supreme Leader of Iran, and then-President Mahmoud Ahmadinejad explicitly acknowledged that there were criminal atrocities that took place in Kahrizak prison. Khamenei promised there would be investigations, but dismissed the incidents as unimportant compared to "the dignity of the regime," which had been sullied.[6] Ahmadinejad, meanwhile, completely reversed his own Supreme Leader and said that these abuses were planned and carried out by those who wanted to topple the regime—meaning the security apparatus of his own government were "the enemies of the state."[7] There was a common denominator to the incriminating statements of the custodians of the Islamic Republic: something was rotten in the theocratic state, and someone had to read the mullahs and their henchmen their Miranda rights.

The principal features of the Kahrizak atrocities were the reticence and reluctance with which Karrubi initially broke the news and the evident outrage of the regime over hearing it. The narrative anxiety (an anxiety of revelation) at the heart of the matter remained unrelenting. Those who cared were hesitant to reveal the atrocities; those in charge angry to hear or admit them; those who had perpetrated the crimes were nowhere to be seen. If the revelation about the US military atrocities in Abu Ghraib prison in Iraq glutinously indulged in overexposure, in visual fetishism, in narrative overkill, whereby the factual documentation and the outrage about what had happened were buried under overwhelming evidence, news reports, investigative journalism, detailed analysis, photography exhibitions, artistic productions, and aesthetic theorization, the news of Kahrizak emerged in exactly the opposite fashion, one of underexposure, of reluctance to reveal, of fear and loathing at the sight and suggestion of what had actually taken place. There were no pictures in the case of Kahrizak— nothing like the way Lynndie England and her comrades-in-arms posed for the camera, with heaps of their victims piled up in front of them. One of the interrogators of the victim/witness that Karrubi was able to persuade to talk was horrified by the news that Karrubi had evidently videotaped his testimony.

In the case of Abu Ghraib people saw more than they wanted or needed— they had to turn away in shame, or else remain and watch and soon be numbed by too much exposure to something no one should ever watch, something that should never happen to put people in a position to watch or not to watch. There was a massive visual orgy at work in and about Abu Ghraib. The torturers themselves took pleasure in taking pictures of their victims, posed in front of or behind them in happy and triumphant gestures, and sent them as souvenirs to their friends and families. They did not intend them for journalists, photography curators, art critics, or scholars. The US soldiers posed in front of their victims very much the same way that Southern racist vigilantes did when lynching black people. There was a visual performance to the cruelty—or perhaps more accurately, the cruelty was in the visual performance. These people tortured for the camera— for if the camera were not there to capture it there would be no point to torturing. They tortured for posterity, for aftertaste, for others to see—a pornographic deferral was at work in these torturing pictures. Lynndie England and her company took evident pleasure in imagining themselves watched by others peeping at them doing what they were doing. The exhibitionism was integral, definitive even, to the cruel act.

The flaunted exhibitionism of the torturing performance at Abu Ghraib set the stage for what was to follow. When the atrocities in Abu Ghraib were revealed, there was in fact a public exhibition of these pictures in New York from mid-September to late November 2004, curated by Brian Wallis at the International Center of Photography, and by Jessica Gogan and Thomas Sokolowski at the Andy Warhol Museum, with a text written by the prominent investigative journalist Seymour M. Hersh.[8] Here was Specialist Sabrina Harman and Specialist Charles Graner posing behind a pile of naked Iraqis. Here was Private First Class Lynndie England, with the face and demeanor of a young suburban housewife on a Sunday stroll at a local mall with her beloved dog, holding, in this case, a leash to an Iraqi prisoner. This photography exhibition of the visual orgy at work in Abu Ghraib upped the ante, put on stage what was already staged—there was a *double entendre* in even entering that exhibition, for on exhibition was exhibitionism. As the curators framed the pictures, the pictures staged the curators—like two opposite mirrors reflecting a single *objet de curiosité* ad infinitum. Who was staging and who was staged—and what were the New Yorkers doing in that exhibition, having just walked out off of a street into the simulacrum of a torture chamber? They would soon walk out, unharmed, off to a luncheon meeting perhaps, over sushi and sake, probably. What was consumed in that exhibition?

The overexposure of Abu Ghraib was not limited to such exhibitions of their exhibitionism. The visual effects of Americans torturing Iraqis were assuming a reality *sui generis*, living a life of their own. Within a year after the revelations, and on the trail of these pictures mushrooming around the globe on myriad websites, Seymour Hersh had published his bulky volume *Chain of Command: The Road from 9/11 to Abu Ghraib* (2004), detailing the excruciating minutiae of the atrocities at the torture chambers.[9] Soon Fernando Botero, the prominent Colombian figurative artist, followed suit and did a series of paintings based on the snapshots of Abu Ghraib, put on exhibition in Washington, D.C., at the American University Museum at the Katzen Art Center (November–December 2007),[10] as did before him the American artist Susan Crile at the Leubsdorf Art Gallery of Hunter College in New York (October 2006). As Andrea K. Scott put it in her review of Susan Crile's work, "a sanctimonious air permeates the show, heightened by allusions to classical Western art. . . . Ms. Crile's sincere desire to elicit empathy for her subjects is laudable, but none of her drawings have the gut-wrenching impact of the shameful photos themselves."[11] Be that as it may, Susan Crile's rendition of the "shameful photos themselves" plunged them even further into oblivion, as did Andrea Scott's review. The paradox had become so thick by now that one furthered its self-negating tenacity if one learned more about Abu Ghraib or else wished no longer to hear about it anymore.

The crescendo, though, continued. The amassing of the visual cloning and analytical literature on the fact and fantasy of Abu Ghraib reached an apex when the distinguished American art critic Arthur Danto reflected positively on the exhibition of Botero's work in New York:

> When it was announced not long ago that Botero had made a series of paintings and drawings inspired by the notorious photographs showing

Iraqi captives, naked, degraded, tortured and humiliated by American soldiers at Iraq's Abu Ghraib prison, it was easy to feel skeptical—wouldn't Botero's signature style humorize and cheapen this horror? And it was hard to imagine that paintings by anyone could convey the horrors of Abu Ghraib as well as—much less better than—the photographs themselves. These ghastly images of violence and humiliation, circulated on the Internet, on television and in newspapers throughout the world, were hardly in need of artistic amplification. . . . As it turns out, his images of torture . . . are masterpieces of what I have called disturbatory art—art whose point and purpose is to make vivid and objective our most frightening subjective thoughts. Botero's astonishing works make us realize this: We knew that Abu Ghraib's prisoners were suffering, but we did not feel that suffering as ours. When the photographs were released, the moral indignation of the West was focused on the grinning soldiers, for whom this appalling spectacle was a form of entertainment. But the photographs did not bring us closer to the agonies of the victims.[12]

Danto's take on Botero is exactly the opposite of Scott's on Crile—he thinks Botero brings "us" closer to the pain of Iraqis; she thought Crile's distanced "us" from that pain. Common to both Scott and Danto, however, remains the centrality of "us" (Americans, that is, or that chimerical construct called "the West") as the *locus classicus* of pain, of feeling the pain of others, the pain of the Iraqis.

Through the process of their successive abstractions—from fact to photography to art to aesthetic theory—even the Iraqis' bodily pains were not allowed to be theirs, for now that too was made "ours"—*ours* meaning Americans', their art theorists, and their liberal readership, following on the heels of their army as liberators. The same pronominal subterfuges for who is torturing and who is being tortured was invoked by Susan Sontag's famous essay, aptly called "Regarding the Torture of Others." She too thought these pictures were "us"—meaning Americans.

To have the American effort in Iraq summed up by these images must seem, to those who saw some justification in a war that did overthrow one of the monster tyrants of modern times, "unfair." A war, an occupation, is inevitably a huge tapestry of actions. . . . Considered in this light, the photographs are us. That is, they are representative of the fundamental corruptions of any foreign occupation together with the Bush administration's distinctive policies. The Belgians in the Congo, the French in Algeria, practiced torture and sexual humiliation on despised recalcitrant natives.[13]

Iraqis were tortured bodily so Americans could discover themselves analytically. Here the "progressive" politics of Susan Sontag and Arthur Danto and the opposing politics of Alan Dershowitz and Michael Ignatieff had become entirely irrelevant. What mattered was who was "us" and who "them"—on one side of the political divide, Iraqis were dehumanized and allowed to be tortured, and on the other dehumanized and allowed to reveal who "we" are. Terrorizing at Abu Ghraib and theorizing in New York now collided.

Abu Ghraib was thus incessantly etherized into theoretical nullity as it dropped from a site into a citation—not from absence of evidence, but in fact from excessive evidence, evidence so overwhelming that the whole event had to be alienated from reality via a bizarre case of *Verfremdung*, so that Americans could vicariously feel it as "theirs"—purchase, buy, own, consume, and discard it. The fact and phenomenon of Abu Ghraib—as moral insolubility that had to remain that way in order to register its horrors—had to be incessantly deciphered, coded and decoded, sold and purchased, curated and watched, for Americans to pack and tuck away and "consider it done." It made no difference if Alan Dershowitz and Michael Ignatieff legally and even morally justified torture, or Arthur Danto and Susan Sontag visually theorized, analyzed, and implicitly or explicitly denounced torture. What remained constant among them all was the sublation of visual evidence into theoretical speculation, of one sort or another, the aggressive transmutation of unfathomable horror into comprehensible analytical tropes.

The case of Kahrizak poses exactly the opposite phenomenon, but to the same effect: its hesitant, taboo-breaking underexposure effectively erases the memory before it is even allowed to form and then to bother. In the Kahrizak case, the absence of visuality, evidence, and testimony was geared to disallow the memory, to abort it, at the moment of its conception. It is of course true that upon assuming office, President Barack Obama prevented further exposure of incriminating Abu Ghraib pictures for reasons of national security.[14] But by then the visual, narrative, aesthetic, and theoretical oversaturation had overwhelmed the scene, numbed the senses, and buried the facts—bought, sold, consumed, and discarded the evidence. It is also reported that some of the torturers and rapists in Basij detention camps in Iran took sadistic pleasure in taking pictures with their mobile phones of their naked victims. According to one victim who spoke with *The Times*, "they [the security forces raping young people they had arrested] also liked to take several of us out at the same time and forced us to ride each other, doggy-style, whilst naked. They laughed and took pictures with their mobile phones. They would watch this for ten minutes and then proceed to rape."[15] To this evident copycatting of Abu Ghraib pictures, we also need to add the fact that at the writing of this essay we are only months into reports of Kahrizak atrocities, but years into Abu Ghraib's. Reports and multiple and varied coverage of the atrocities in Kahrizak and other detention camps in Iran may indeed snowball and develop in unforeseen directions. But my central argument—that in Iran facts are buried under absence of evidence, while in the United States these facts are overexposed—speaks to a different concern. The effect of both practices, underexposure of Kahrizak in Iran and the overexposure of Abu Ghraib in the United States, is the same: *Damnatio Memoriae*, damnation of memory, removal from remembrance. The difference, though, speaks to two diametrically opposed visual regimes, one that works through an aesthetic minimalism of the sort that is perhaps best evident in Abbas Kiarostami's cinema, and the other via a cinematic gluttony perhaps best on display in Quentin Tarantino.

Two Visual Regimes

What the comparison of Abu Ghraib and Kahrizak reveals, as two complementary sites and citations, is the working of two divergent visual regimes affecting the same result: covering up reality, one by overexposure and the other by underexposure, one by overwhelming the visual market, the other by underwhelming it. What the overexposure of Abu Ghraib reveals is not the open-minded democratic nature of empire—it actually reveals precisely the opposite. It helps conceal the terrorizing fact under the avalanche of its evidence, fueling an imperial visual regime that is, *ipso facto*, the globalization of the society of spectacle that sustains and informs it, and as such overwhelms all other (and "othered") visual cultures, where the varied artistic forms from around the world are effectively museumized in film festivals, or else over-aestheticized and theorized, or, even worse, anthropologized by the continuing operations of ethnographic power-basing between primitivized *image* and privileged *theory*.

What overwhelms and covers up the atrocities in Iran is not just the absence of visual evidence, but the effective erasure of whatever evidence is produced in the context of the aggressive reduction of the world at large (Iran included) into an "empire of camps," as Nicholas Mirzoeff, and before him Giorgio Agamben, have diagnosed the epidemic.[16] These "camps," as Mirzoeff and Agamben understand them, are not just the repetitions and cloning of Guantánamo Bay. They are the result of the transmutation of nation-states into functional simulacra of camps, where their facts become invisible, and even when they are made visible, they are subsequently overtly aestheticized, museumized, and made into *objet de curiosité* in art-house movies in order to be subsequently depleted of their terror and theorized into learned cinema-studies projects. This over-aestheticization is (paradoxically) exactly the opposite side of an equally dominant propensity toward the primitivization of visual evidence of the "camps" via disciplinary regimens of ethnographic exercises at the service of vacuous anthropological projects. In other words, even if produced, the visual evidence on the sites of nation-states cum camps are ab/used for two diametrically opposed, but effectively identical, projects: excessive aestheticization in visual theories on one hand, and systematic primitivization by ethnographic projects of visual anthropology on the other.

Mirzoeff laser-beams on the second Persian Gulf War (2003–present), where this visual fetishism at the heart of the imperial imagining came to a crescendo, for it is during this war that "more images were created to less effect than at any other period in human history,"[17] a "saturation of images" that continues to null, numb, and make their audiences care less by the passage of time and the piling of more visual evidence of carnage. Mirzoeff's diagnosis of this development picks up where Guy Debord left off in the 1960s. As Mirzoeff puts it:

> In 1967 in response to the first wave of such image-commodification, Guy Debord argued that modern life had become a society of spectacle that eliminated all sense of history. . . . Debord was extending Marx's argument about [commodity fetishization]. . . . Debord argued that the next stage of development was for capital to abstract itself entirely from the process of production and become an image. . . . [Now] the image has undergone a further stage of capitalist development and accumulation. If in the 1960s capital had become an image, by 2003 the image has become a smart weapon. Following Ernest Mandel's analysis of late capitalism, such a development might have been expected because it is precisely the existence of a "permanent arms economy" that has prevented capitalism from falling into crisis caused by the tendency of the rate of profit to decline. . . . Mandel argued that the armaments economy continually intervenes in this process and changes its dynamics, accelerating the rate of technological change. It is therefore not surprising that the intense pace of change in visual technologies during the 1990s, produced in part by military research, also generated a militarized form of image.[18]

These days Hollywood precisely corroborates Mirzoeff's diagnosis by oversaturating viewers with torture scenes, as, for example, in Gavin Hood's *Rendition* (2007), where the Chicago-based chemical engineer Anwar El-Ibrahimi (Omar Metwally) is suspected of links to terrorism, kidnapped by CIA from a US airport and sent off to a "Middle Eastern" country to be interrogated and tortured. The scenes of an Arab official torturing Anwar El-Ibrahimi are vicarious—evincing things that can (presumably) happen only in an Arab/Muslim world, but can only (certainly) be seen in an American film.

Beyond their evident differences, both these diametrically opposite visual regimes concur in burying the evidence—in one way or another corroborating what Jean Baudrillard diagnosed as "the perfect crime" against reality. "What we have forgotten, by dint of constantly accumulating," he said, diagnosing our condition, "is that force comes from subtraction, power from absence. Because we are no longer capable today of coping with the symbolic mastery of absence, we are immersed in the opposite illusion, the disenchanted illusion of the proliferation of screens and images."[19] That accumulation is of course now the *conditio sine qua non* of globalized capitalism running amok on consumption. But that sense of subtraction, to be sure, cannot be preached to a culture that has produced an Abbas Kiarostami in its cinematic culture—the very *cinema of subtraction* if there ever was any. But, again, the *bête noire* of that cinema is when it is burned on a DVD and put on a shelf at the closest Blockbuster to a university campus to be rented by the local anthropologist and fed into the next issue of *Visual Anthropology* or the next season's catalogue of one university press or another. Left to its own devices, and before it is neutered by anthropology, that sense of abstraction is not lost on the world at the receiving end of capitalist modernity, which remains the principal site of Baudrillard's investigation. That site produces the oversaturation of Hollywood imagery and overexposure of Abu Ghraib at one and the same time—from Charles Graner and Lynndie England, who perpetrate the crime on *others* to Arthur Danto and Susan Sontag, who theorize it as *ours*.

Iranian cinema, otherwise perfectly capable of registering the lived experience of the people who produce it (as does any other "Third World Cinema"), is instead vastly anthropologized, mystified, codified, and symbolized for useless theoretical speculations, precisely at a time when Hollywood has a monopoly over what Mirzoeff aptly calls "the saturation of images."[20] Consider a book like Michael Fischer's *Mute Dreams, Blind Owls, and Dispersed Knowledges: Persian Poesis in the Transnational*

Circuitry (2004),[21] in which the ethnographic curiosities of a seasoned anthropologist of Iran get the better of him, and send him off-tangent on futile speculations (about everything from ancient Zoroastrian rituals to what he takes as postmodern fictional casuistry) to produce a massive tome of unreadable prose about nonexistent phenomena. When one reads Fischer's book, the legitimate suspicion arises that it is vaguely related to aspects of Iranian visual culture, and yet in an entirely vacuous and deboned prose that could have been about marine biology in the Pacific Ocean. One reads from one end to the other of this anthropological prying into a people's artwork aghast at how the literary and visual art of an entire people— entangled as it is in matters of life and death—could be so categorically denied a caring intellect. Iran is not a site of visual desolation. It has its share of visual culture, produced on a sizeable cosmopolitan canvas that can mean a lot to those who care to watch. But the ethnographic gaze that reduces that visual culture to mere conjectural "fieldwork" destroys the evidence by reducing it to primitivized "raw data" for spurious theorization. Some aspects of "cinema studies" do a similar thing by over-aestheticizing the evidence in entirely vacuous terms. In these terms, the anthropological project has found a new way of serving the imperial imagining by reducing the visual sites of alternative cultures to raw material for their power-basing theorization.[22]

Of Empires and Camps

The visual imperialism that enables US militarism and facilitates American indulgence in overexposure to the point of "regarding" and thus claiming "the pain of others" is precisely the *modus operandi* that makes the camps that comprise it invisible. The Israeli occupation of Palestine is perhaps the best example of how a military garrison state prohibits the visibility of Palestinians as a people and literally (not figuratively) reduces them to "camps." As Edward Said once elaborated on Amira Hass's comment about the invisibility of Palestinians in their own homeland, invisibility is the principal aspect of the predicament of the Palestinians ever since their Nakba ("day of the catastrophe") in 1948.[23]

The Palestinian refugee camps, in and out of their homeland, are the factual prototypes of the transmutation of nation-states into stateless camps, and its citizens into enemy combatants, stripped of their civil rights and reduced to their condition as *zoë* and bereft of their *bios*.[24] As Mirzoeff understands them, "these camps are not the exception to democratic society. Rather they are the exemplary institutions of a system of global capitalism that supports the West in its high-consumption, low-price consumer lifestyle. I call this regime the empire of camps."[25] Prior to Mirzoeff and Agamben's theorization, by a distance of more than half a century, Palestinian refugee camps became the historic documentations of the phenomenon, though for both Mirzoeff and Agamben the Nazi concentration camps have provided ample evidence from Europe. Invisibility is definitive to these camps. "For all its religious overtones," Mirzoeff points out, "the empire of camps has no scruples, no moral agenda and no desire to be seen or to make its prisoners visible, although surveillance is everywhere."[26] In our more contemporary terms, Guantánamo and Kahrizak are two sides of the same coin, and Christian fundamentalism and militant Islamism (as in fact messianic Zionism and Hindu fundamentalism), have no moral scruples against torturing or raping people. The only thing that the empire of camps needs is an effective Enemy, which for George W. Bush was a fictive Muslim terrorist he suspected lurking in every Muslim he imagined, and for Ahmadinejad is an agent of "the West" lurking under the skin of any defiant soul that said no to the banality of his evil. In this respect, the identical banality of Bush and Ahmadinejad (two cogent examples of Hannah Arendt's diagnosis) is copycatting the Nazi political theorist Carl Schmitt, who stated that without an Enemy there would be no concept of the political. "The specific political distinction to which political actions and motives can be reduced," Schmitt wrote, "is that between friend and enemy."[27]

That constitution of "the Enemy" in the Islamic Republic is now entering a cul de sac in which the political apparatus seems set to undo itself. As the presumption of an Enemy that is dead-set on destroying the regime has become central to its endemic anxiety of legitimacy, the very binary of "friend and foe" has lost its cogency in the aftermath of the presidential election of June 2009. Kidnapping, torture, rape, murder, and nocturnal burial in mass unidentified graves—all done by Iranians to Iranians, by Muslims to Muslims—have finally broken the fictive binary particularly poignant in the age of tribal warfare between "Islam and the West" and opened a whole new vista onto the globalized carnage of capital and its evolving culture of domination. Much of the animus of Abu Ghraib revelations was centered on Americans torturing Iraqis, Americans torturing Afghans, both predicated on Israelis torturing Palestinians—or, put in a different register, Christians torturing Muslims, Jews torturing Christians and Muslims. The case of Kahrizak seriously compromises all such binaries, for it is the case of Iranians torturing Iranians, Muslims torturing

Muslims—so, the central trope of *othering* is categorically overcome, and the naked life (Agamben's diagnosis), stripped of its strategic distancing via cultural registers, has been completely exposed. What is happening here is the dissolution of *Potenza* as "legitimate authority" into *Potere* as "naked force," and, *a fortiori*, the transmutation of *civic life* into *naked life*, of *civil rights* into *human rights*. The exposure of the *naked life*, stripped of all its protective binaries, reduces the colonial body to a *homo sacer* precisely at the moment when the visual regimes that have reduced it to an ethnographic oddity cover and conceal it either by over- or underexposure.

Hyperrealizing Reality

The underexposure of the facts of Kahrizak in Iran is coterminous with the overexposure of evidence of Abu Ghraib in the United States. Talking and writing about torture or picturing torture in an overexposed visual culture—even or particularly by way of remembering, reminding, or condemning it—*hyperrealizes* it (Jean Baudrillard's term) to the point of rendering viewers numb and its horrors nil. Writing about torture becomes a subterfuge that allows for the camouflaging of the desire to forget it, wipe it out of memory, through a palimpsestic palette or prose that by drawing or writing (on) torture wipes out the terror of torture—becomes a therapeutic confessional that exonerates the confessor, perhaps, but, *ipso facto*, covers up the evidence by indulging in it. The hyperrealization of Abu Ghraib in America covers torture also by way of covering up the plight of millions of other Iraqis who may not have been tortured in Abu Ghraib, but are victims of a malignant warmongering that Susan Sontag does not own up to so long as she has owned up to the "pictures" of torturing always "other" people. The scandal that emerged over Abu Ghraib eventually became a ruse to cover over the much more horrid fact, the torturing of the body politic of Iraq—Abu Ghraib was categorically condemned as an aberration, and it most probably was, but precisely as an aberration it summoned a diversionary tactic to coagulate the pain of a people, a nation, a country, raped and burned (just like Abeer Qassim Hamza al-Janabi), and is getting away with it.

Hyperrealization overkills. Discussion of torture thus emerged as a cover-up for torture—its normative narrativization, robbing it of its barbarity by bringing it into the domain of liberal analytic, and of course eventually scholarly disciplines of the humanities. Visual and literary discourses discuss torture and in doing so alienate the subject from the predicate of talking "about" torture. Perhaps painting torture has been therapeutic for Fernando Botero and Susan Crile, Arthur Danto and Susan Sontag, but certainly not for those who have been tortured, and those who never get to see themselves (or their tormented nation) painted, portrayed, analyzed, theorized, and terrorized at one and the same time. It is not just the Iraqis who for generations will not be able to talk about what Americans talk about as "the Second Gulf War." More than sixty years after they have been robbed of their homeland, Palestinians can still scarcely talk or write or film *about* their Nakba. The only feature-length film that exists on Nakba, *Gates to the Sun* (2004), is by an Egyptian filmmaker, Yousry Nasrallah, based on an epic by a Lebanese novelist, Elias Khouri.[28]

Hyperrealization often lives through good intentions. There is no narrating torture, analyzing it, theorizing it, packaging or publishing it. Those who have been tortured do not talk about torture. It is torturous for them. I have known people (all of them Iranians and Arabs)—close friends, scholars, filmmakers, photographers, poets—who have been tortured. They never talk about torture—except in jest, except in indirection, in their art, in their punctuated silences, in their cinema, their photography, their painting, their poetry, their dreamlike memoirs, from a distance, a safe (perhaps therapeutic) distance.[29] *Indirection* is how torture speaks—when the speaker has been tortured. Writing "about" torture is writing about, if anything, silence, and about darkness, about the decency of being silent in face of torture, for not facing, not looking at, scenes of torture, of turning the lights off, of darkness—of shame. Only people who have never been tortured talk *about* torture.

In the hidden light of that genteel darkness, and the screams of pain hidden in that explosive silence, writing *about* torture is *not* writing about Guantánamo Bay, *not* painting Abu Ghraib—for to read, write, paint, perform, or in any other way portray torture is to kill the messenger of the unseen and the unseemly, to destroy the revelatory evidence of the unknowable, and thus speaking the unspeakable act, making an obscene spectacle of the despicable deed. Hyperrealization does not allow for emancipatory mystery, for moments of the unknown. Those pictures of Abu Ghraib are the very last vestiges of a sign that cannot and must not be seen, cited, or read. The temptation to look at and read them is one liberal guilt that must never be allowed to be allayed. There are certain scenes from which one must turn away, and not look at evil. In Geneva once Mohsen Makhmalbaf told me the story of a script he had just written about a young boy who was sworn never to cast a glance at any evil act. Years later he turned that story into a movie, *Silence* (1998), the central character of which is a blind boy.

Hyperrealization intensifies with border-crossing. Writing on torture of colonized people in English is erasing it. Translating from an underexposed reality into an overexposed language will lose the "torture" in the translation. There is something terrifying about *shekanjeh* in Persian that is lost in English *torture*. Translating from camp to cosmopolis, from the peripheries into the centralized, resonates with gaps of gasps in not being able to speak. Here, a shaky camera is infinitely better than sharply focused pictures, for memory is more effective than overriding evidence—for that is the reason that Karrubi could not sleep, and that is precisely how memory of torture and rape ought to be kept, so it keeps you awake. For if Lynndie England tortured and Susan Sontag wrote about Lynndie England, then Lynndie England subsumes Susan Sontag: For those snapshots of Abu Ghraib are the very last vestiges of a sign that cannot and must not be read, left indecipherable as they must—they must remain haunting, unnarrated, just there. Writing (about) torture is enacting a *Damnatio Memoriae*, "damnation of memory," removing the evidence from the act of remembrance, as it was a form of dishonor passed by the Roman Senate upon those it thought traitorous to the Roman Empire.[30]

Hyperrealization transgresses from fact to phenomenon. Writing *about* Abu Ghraib is writing Abu Ghraib, authoring it, authorizing it, just like George W. Bush, Dick Cheney, and Donald Rumsfeld—and thus unwriting those responsible for it, from the US president, to the US vice president, to the US secretary of defense, to the US attorney general, down all the way to Alan Dershowitz, who thought it was necessary to torture people, and Michael Ignatieff, who seconded him.[31] In defiance of torturers and in negation of the native-informers-turned-anthropologists of Iraq, Afghanistan, Lebanon, or Palestine, the only way to write *about* torture is to write about the defiant dignity of silence—when in the indirection of art, the distancing *Verfremdung* of laughter, the sinuous un/certainty of poetry, tortured people refuse to be interviewed in any "field trip," or to be removed from memory.

From the secretary of defense to the (embedded) anthropologist,[32] through the art and aesthetic theory of torturing people, hyperrealization is hard at work, where the visual has taken over the real—and precisely for that reason, Baudrillard saw Abu Ghraib coming, and saw the erasure of Abu Ghraib coming, years before it came. "Now," he said in 1995, almost a decade before the Abu Ghraib revelations,

Now, the image can no longer imagine the real, because it is the real. . . .
It is as though things had swallowed their own mirrors and had become

transparent to themselves, entirely present to themselves in a ruthless transcription, full in the light and in real time. . . . The reality has been driven out of reality. . . . The only suspense which remains is that of knowing how far the world can de-realize itself before succumbing to its reality deficit or, conversely, how far it can hyperrealize itself before succumbing to an excess of reality (the point when, having become perfectly real, truer than true, it will fall into the clutches of total simulation).[33]

Body as Evidence

The absence of the body of evidence on the colonial corner of corporeal modernity—and thus Karrubi's sleeplessness—has an archeological site that is yet to be unearthed. Because colonial conquest was aterritorial (people came out of nowhere and conquered your land) it was conducive to the production of an *aterritorial body*, where the colonized became alienated from their own bodies (not just selves) and began inhabiting always already disembodied bodies.

The absented, disembodied body of the colonial person is thus made corporeally invisible and, *a fortiori*, incapable of pain or pleasure, for the body has self-metamorphosed into the very last visible site of state violence. Up until Abu Ghraib, representation of torture and its signs on the deterritorialized and disembodied colonial body was impossible—the snapshots of Abu Ghraib brought that impossibility full circle, that body was made visible, put on a pedestal as a tortured body, sexually molested and physically abused. This tortured body had hitherto been in the unconscious of the colonized subject, and Abu Ghraib was the return of the colonized repressed, making visible the otherwise invisible ferocity of torture, the absence of a verbal or visual language to articulate it. After Abu Ghraib, the *Muselmann* of the Nazi concentration camps has finally come full circle and become what she or he was—a Muslim.

The disembodied Muslim in Abu Ghraib—the updated *Muselmann* of the concentration camps—refuses to be read. Ahmadinejad, denying the Muslim youth he has tortured, blames the Enemy, as did his counterparts Dershowitz and Ignatieff on the opposite side of the fence—thus doing away with the fictive fence. Karrubi, with the stroke of his pen one sleepless night, breaks the binary, and on the following morning the self-othering of "Islam and the West" has, if not entirely collapsed, been bracketed. The Enemy is now within—which is why the custodians of the Islamic (no less) Republic insist it is outside. They protest too much. The collapse (or bracketing) of the binary strips the naked life of its presumption of clothing, for now the sacrosanct "Islam Itself" is implicated. The political predicament points to a moral crisis—to a metaphysical implosion—from which the Shi'i meltdown occurs. From there the naked lives East and West come together and the twain meet, as the naked life is corroborated by the extension of "human rights" that are lent to it momentarily to protect it, as opposed to the "civil rights" that it permanently needs in order to live a politically plausible life. Look at the Iranian kangaroo courts that replicate Guantánamo military courts and the idea of "preemptive, indefinite incarceration" that was legalized in Bush's White House, upheld in Obama's, and practiced in the Islamic Republic. The cycle of naked life is now complete—and the human body is reduced to its organs, ready for sale to the highest bidders.

Futile academic exercises to prove that the presidential election of June 2009 was perfectly fine—that the Green Movement is part of an imperialist design—and that do so with a straight face as if people's young children had not been kidnapped off the streets by the security apparatus of the Islamic Republic, tortured, raped, murdered, and buried secretly in mass graves, amount to diversionary tactics that can only reveal the darker densities of what is surfacing in Iran. In *Homo Sacer*, Agamben notes the publication of Karl Binding and Alfred Hoche's *Authorization for the Annihilation of Life Unworthy of Being Lived* (1920) by the prestigious German publisher Felix Meiner and the correspondences between a certain Dr. Roscher and Heinrich Himmler in 1941 concerning a number of VPs (*Versuchspersonen*, human guinea pigs) that the doctor wished to use in his medical experiments, for he believed using animals in such experiments would be useless.[34] As Agamben discusses these two sets of documents, what above all is terrifying is the straight face with which these German scientists talk about killing what they believe to be useless human beings, or else subjecting them to experiments that will result in their torturous death in the interest of safeguarding Nazi Germany.

A similar disregard for the most basic conceptions of human decency is now evident among those who come to the defense of Ahmadinejad's "presidency" and unequivocally denounce the civil rights movement as a product of imperialist design. To declare, without an iota of moral discomfort and even with a self-righteous assumption of the upper hand,[35] that what we are witnessing in Iran is an imperialist-instigated plot to oppose the "social justice" projects of Ahmadinejad on behalf of the "economic liberalism" of Mir Hossein Mousavi, simply betrays a depth of moral corruption that defies reason and borders on obscenity. To be able to argue that the commencement of the civil rights movement in Iran is in fact a rich people's resentment against a poor people's president[36] reveals a depth of moral depravity that begins and ends with a total disregard for either the masses of millions who have put their lives on the line or been tortured, raped, or cold-bloodedly murdered by the security apparatus of the selfsame "popular" president. These people blame the victims in precisely the way that their counterparts did in Nazi Germany, with a mendacious matter-of-factness one cannot fathom, read, or write in any ordinary language; in fact, in academic language it is reminiscent of the doctors that Agamben unearthed, writing with straight faces about mass murder.

The End of Hegemony

The hegemony of imperial visuality is precarious, like any other culture the promiscuous capital has created and discarded at whim. The mobile phone images dispatched from Iranian rallies and consumed by globalized media (BBC, CNN, Aljazeera, et al.) changed, forever, the very architecture of mass media and gave currency to the notion of "citizen journalist." Facebook did not save the Iranian civil rights movement; the Iranian civil rights movement saved Facebook by extending its architecture to a vast social uprising. The avalanche of Persian blogs did not just force Google to expedite its Persian-English translation software; it put the assumption of any global ("Western") control of both narrativity and visuality on the defensive. Consider Neil Blomkamp's *District 9* (2009), in which Agamben's notion of "the camp" is turned upside down, when a very large alien spaceship stops above Johannesburg in South Africa and a band of aliens ("prawns") are incarcerated in a camp-cum-slum called "District 9." Forces of Multinational United (MNU)—a private military contractor not unlike Blackwater—are sent to evacuate the aliens and relocate them, and one of the MNU employees, Wikus van de Merwe (Sharlto Copley), is infected by the aliens and is turning into one of them over the course of the film. The superior technological machinery that is embedded in the aliens' presence dwarfs the Earthlings not just in military, but also, it turns out, in moral terms. Compare the Abu Ghraib snapshots taken on digital cameras and sent from Iraq to the United States for entertainment of family and friends with what the very same technology did in Iran—conveying to the whole world the groundwork of a massive civil rights movement. In the course of the postelectoral crisis of June 2009, Iranian demonstrators were dictating the terms of their own visual presence and representation in the globe and were no longer the victims of globalized visual regimes beyond their control.

The end of visual hegemony is the end of distancing sympathy and an invitation to equalizing empathy. The power-basing self-othering of the victims and their victimizers has now collapsed, and claiming the pain of "others" (always "others") has become quite untenable. Even Aimé Césaire's humanism, that he feels tortured by the news of anyone else being tortured, amounts to a claim that affective sympathy can lead to the annihilation of the Self by the Other. The Self must remain the same, so that the pain of others remains theirs, rather than being imperially appropriated. Vicarious sympathy wipes out the site of the Other by annihilating the site of the Self—thus denying the overriding immutability of the real. The tortured body is the bared body, the body that is stripped of all its civil rights and left naked and at the mercy of one human rights organization or another to save it by (paradoxically) concurring with the denial of its civil rights. We must leave the *human* behind in order to reach for the rights of the citizen.

Iranian (or Palestinian) cinema, as one among many other non-Hollywood cinemas, is the model and the precursor of visual revolts that refuse to be regimented and thus keep one awake at night, and it is precisely that cinema that will scandalize tyrannies that seek to censure and regiment it. Consider, for example, Hana Makhmalbaf's work, presented at the Venice Film festival of 2009. Her *Green Days* (2009) narrates the defiant streets of Tehran for the whole world to see. "Twenty-one-year-old Iranian director Hana Makhmalbaf," reports Reuters, "brings the bloody street protests that followed June's presidential vote to the big screen in a film looking at the hopes and frustrations of the country's youth."[37] This is what will bring the Islamic Republic down. Watch Shirin Neshat's *Women without Men* (2009), the winner of the Silver Lion Award for the Best Director category in the same festival. "At the movie's Venice premiere," wrote the *Los Angeles Times*, "Neshat walked the red carpet with her creative team, all of them dressed in green (the unofficial color of the Iranian protest movement following the recent elections). If anyone knows how to make a bold visual statement, it's Neshat, whose video art work has been shown in prominent museums around the world."[38] Yes, this *is* the plunging of the spectacle into the spectacle—where Hana Makhmalbaf and Shirin Neshat become the spectacle that frames and forms the bespectacled reality. But this is also what it takes to defeat and scandalize the otherwise hidden rapists and torturers of the Islamic Republic. The Islamic Republic will fall not by a military strike by the US or Israeli army—acts of folly that will in fact sustain and prolong it. It will fall by the weight of its own insoluble invisibilities, made visible by a visual minimalism that eludes the world's widest screens. Like the insomniac nights of one aging revolutionary, the silenced screams and hidden horrors of innocent boys and girls raped and tortured in invisible sites of a murderous Islamic Republic are filled with visions of many bright and early dawns.

CHAPTER II

Rituals of Hegemonic Masculinity: Cinema, Torture, and the Middle East

Viola Shafik

In echoing Stuart Hall's theory on popular culture,[1] Patrick Fuery wrote: "The cinematic body as discourse . . . operates as a site in which these distinctions and connections between force and power are played out."[2] Indeed, the representation of the human body on film is not just a matter of narrative necessity or pictorial symbolism, but is rooted in the often contradictory and polarized realm of the social and political apparatus. Consequently, the cinematic depiction of torture or, in other words, the infliction of pain on people's bodies, should be seen as tied to a struggle over political sovereignty. Through this struggle, in which the politics of difference plays a constitutive role—this is my main thesis—a hegemonic white masculinity seeks to impose itself.

Convinced that it is impossible to separate real-life conditions from representational practices, in this essay I sketch out the meandering of on- and off-screen physical torture in relation to the Muslim East. For torture is not just an important means of political and cultural subordination; it is also governed by seemingly archaic cultural practices such as mimesis and ritual, which in turn permit its transition into the realm of cultural representation. This essay relates mass-mediated abuses against Arabs and Muslims in Afghanistan, Iraq, and Guantánamo to some relevant American movie productions since the 1980s and some Middle Eastern films to show how such cultural representations are tied to the international power structure and what kind of ideological premises underpin them. For even though abuses of the body occur in both sets of fiction films, and both demonstrate a strong interdependence in their use of cross-references, the works differ substantially in their choice of film genres and modes of representation.

My survey also yields a more important point: whatever particular discourse is being voiced through the depiction of the body in relation to torture, it draws on codes of ethnic and sexual difference for that purpose. Here we find an interesting bifurcation. While characterizations of ethnic difference vary according to the particular political and racialized agenda being espoused, those relating to sexual difference follow a more uniform and consistent set of codifications. Emphasis on physical traits, such as weakness, passivity, and penetrability, are crucial to delivering a gendered political message that links recourse to torture to a drive for absolute power and gender domination.

Cinematic Torture and the Availability of the Body

There is nothing surprising in suggesting that torture and corporal violence are favored in action-oriented films, and such films can thus be made instrumental in narratives that depict the nation and its Others. This is because "the action scenario is not simply a narrative of empowerment, in which we identify with a heroic figure who triumphs over all obstacles, but is also a dramatization of the social limits of power." And—I might add— the action scenario can be considered an interactive performative fantasy about attaining and falling prey to sovereign power.[3]

On the formal level, action films tend to "sacrifice the chain of character-centered causality, foregrounding artistic motivation" in favor of spectacular action scenes, simulated visions, and the like; in other words, they sacrifice narrative consistency to a "disruptive force that creates gaps in the narrative" and highlights the mere bodily performance.[4] A similar narrative fragmentation characterizes pornography and splatter films that depend almost entirely on an accumulation of "set pieces," on fragments of action that are only loosely connected to the main action and in which the most brutal and graphic torturing and dismembering of bodies form the primary content of cinematic spectacle. This structure emphasizes torture as such and its ritualistic repetitive aspects by representing "specific filmic rituals which are supposed to provoke the wanted emotional reactions by means of strictly codified surrogate actions and simulations."[5]

Germane for our purposes is Marcus Stieglegger's further contention that the curiosity regarding the interior of the Other's body displayed in exploitative cinematic representation yields to a "seduction to sovereignty" that is equivalent to a total and arbitrary domination over the Other's body, exerted through sadistic torture (*Verführung zur Souveränität*).[6] The idea of acquiring sovereignty through sadism is drawn from Bataille's analysis of the Marquis de Sade's writings, which Pier Paolo Pasolini, in his *Salò o le 120 giornate di Sodoma* (*Salò, or the 120 Days of Sodom*) (1975), interprets as the basis of totalitarianism. Pasolini's film implies—and here it anticipates Giorgio Agamben's articulation of the *homo sacer*—that the so-called sacred and inalienable rights of man prove to be completely unprotected at the very moment that total sovereignty gets installed, and that they thus cease to be equal to the rights of the citizens of a state.

However, the desired subordination of the body in action films does not stop at the simple representational or symbolical level. It reaches out to include the body of the spectator, passively and actively. Richard Dyer, for example, underlines the genre's "reproduction of a masculine structure of feeling" in the sensational experience of movement. Here action "is represented as experienced not within the body but in the body's contact with the world, its rush, its expansiveness, its physical stress and challenge."[7] This sensational experience of movement is linked to the "delicious paradox" that Dyer associates with that genre: For action adventure movies "promote an active engagement with the world, going out into it, doing to the environment; yet the enjoyment of them means allowing them to come to you, take you over, do you," an experience of passivity that Dyer equates with sexual fellatio.[8]

Yet, the body's involvement can also enter a much more active phase. Recent film theories show how mainstream action films employ similar mechanisms like the stigmatized splatter films. In mobilizing cinema's general ability to "make the body do things"—that is, make us scream, weep, cry—they expose the interaction between filmmakers and their viewers as sadomasochistic.[9] In a similar vein, Paul Gormley considers the arbitrary cinematic assaults on the body to be a key element in what he calls the postmodern "new brutality films," using as a prominent example Quentin Tarantino's *Reservoir Dogs* (1992), with its sadistic torturing scene of the policeman (which seems popular enough to circulate independently of the whole and in different versions on the Internet).

Gormley perceives perpetrator and victim in this scene as stand-in for the director and his viewers, who are glued to their seats in the theatre, watching a tethered policeman as he is at once fascinated and paralyzed while he watches his torturer, Mr. Blonde, dance around him, "changing rhythm mid-step, cracking a joke here, slicing off a bit of flesh there."[10] Thus, what Gormley believes to be most pivotal to action blockbusters, as well as to new brutality films, such as Tarantino's *Reservoir Dogs* and *Pulp Fiction* (1994), is "concentration on the vulnerability of the body—any body."[11] If so, then one of the primary aspects of cinematic pleasure in torture, involving the viewer either in a passive or more active way, verges on a sadomasochistic game of alternating sovereignty and subordination, a subordination that—and this should be underlined—runs along ethnic and national lines.

True, Gormley downplays the violence in earlier US action films by characterizing them, especially the 1980s *Rambo* series, as Tom and Jerry cartoons. Yet he perceives that the cathartic moments of new brutality films reside in deep-seated American responses to blackness. In contrast to prior forms of action film, and "due to the mimetic engagement with 1990s Afro-American culture and film," the new brutality films of the third millennium "attempt to produce an affective shock by imitating the immediate and bodily response provoked in white viewers by images of black bodies" without actually using black bodies as a direct reference.[12]

If new brutality films choose to suppress direct visual allusions to black bodies, the same applies to mainstream action films concerned with the Muslim and Arab world. The latter, likewise, draw on internalized assumptions regarding African Americans, but project the affective shock caused by the African American black body onto so-called Orientals and Arabs. It is no secret that Arabs, just like African Americans, have been subjected to a long history of representation in Hollywood inspired by xenophobia and racism. Jack Shaheen's anthology *Reel Bad Arabs* discusses some nine hundred full-length fiction films featuring stereotypical Arab characters, all produced or distributed in the United States.[13] These include degenerate Arab sheikhs; hook-nosed, darkly robed blood-lusting villains; wily, evil Egyptians often juxtaposed with fantastic mummy-stories; and Palestinians obsessed with the use of force and violence. At first, the lustful sheikhs of the first half of the twentieth century are satisfied with the abduction of occidental beauties (to be rescued later). After World War II, they turn into ultra-rich, conniving sheikhs floating on a sea of oil and weapons. Finally, they are replaced by Arab terrorists, "carrier[s] of the new primitivism," to use Shaheen's words.

The American-Israeli production house with the telling name "Cannon" run by Menechem Golan and Yoram Globus is responsible for some twenty-six of the most extreme "hate-and-terminate-the-Arabs" movies, as Shaheen terms them, including *Hell Squad* (1985), *The Delta Force* (1986), and *Killing Streets* (1991). These are all action films that use Arab terrorism as a pretext for killing the highest possible number of Arabs. Cannon, however, is not the only producer of this category. Films like Robert Zemecki's *Back to the Future* (1985) and James Cameron's *True Lies* (1994) introduce Arabs as the new nuclear threat to the West, thus replacing the Soviets. Tellingly, even though Hollywood had in the meantime been working hard to portray in a more positive light the two largest nonwhite communities of the United States, African Americans and Latinos, Arabs remain largely excluded from this progress in racial consciousness, except in a very limited number of works, such as *The Siege* (1998), *The 13th Warrior* (1999), *The Three Kings* (1999), Stephen Gaghan's *Syriana* (2005), and Gavin Hood's *Rendition* (2007). However, even these more Arab-friendly films still tend to pit the experiences of African Americans against those of Arab Americans to the benefit of white supremacy.

Starring Denzel Washington as an FBI agent and Bruce Willis as an over-ambitious general, *The Siege* (1998) by Edward Zwick, for example, anticipates some of the apocalyptic 9/11 scenes. It pictures huge explosions with heavy casualties initiated by Arab terrorists that lead to such chaotic conditions in New York that the army is called in after the matter seems to have exceeded the capabilities of the FBI, represented by the African American special agent Hubbard, or "Hub" (Washington). The arrival of General Devereaux (Willis) forces the events to another climax. He proclaims a state of emergency, hunts Arab suspects, opens internment camps for Arab Americans, and, in anticipation of the excesses of Guantánamo and Abu Ghraib, allows one detainee to be tortured to death. This suspension of civil rights is what motivates agent Hubbard not only to confront Devereaux, but also to seek means to dethrone him.

At the same time, white racism gets tackled in a side story concerning Hub's assistant, Frank Haddad, who is Arab American. After his own son is deported to a camp, Haddad feels so alienated that he quits his job, informing Hub that he will stop being the FBI's "sand nigger." Hub tries to get Haddad's son released and storms Devereaux' office. In response, the latter's assistant asks Hub to leave "or I might consider you an Ethiopian." The agent hits back: "You are stupid enough to think this is an insult." With exchanges like these, the film seeks to foreground its racial consciousness, neutralizing accusations of anti-Arab bias with its general climate of respect for equal rights. At the same time, the African American character is made to internalize a racialized social hierarchy in which he serves as mediator between the "abject" Arab and the white "sovereign," while—in a redemptive dramatic twist—stylized as the one who safeguards democracy and civil rights (in striking parallel to Barack Obama's current role as the first black president of the United States).

This, however, does not prevent *The Siege* from insisting on the Arab terrorist threat that is, according to the film's narrative, both made instrumental for and only possible by white power games. Hence the scenes described above belong to the conscious and unconscious discursive negotiations that govern narratives and their style, a dynamic that Stuart Hall defines as a struggle of discourses over textual domination.[14] Here the film's style plays a crucial role. Quite in contrast to a much less political work, to name only James Cameron's quasi-comic *True Lies* (1994), in which Arnold Schwarzenegger fights a nuclear threat from an Arab country, but where the Arab threat motif is downplayed through the use of highly exaggerated spectacle, the realist mise-en-scène in *The Siege* makes it more difficult for an audience to suspend its disbelief in Arab perfidy, given the general absence of balanced information in the United States regarding the Middle East and the Muslim world.

For, as Edward Said points out in *Covering Islam*, aggressive Islam is the master default explanation for all social and political phenomena, particularly unrest, in the Middle East, an explanation that disregards the West's actual involvement in them: "[the] media often represents aggression as coming from Islam because that is what 'Islam' is. Local and concrete circumstances are thus obliterated. In other words covering Islam is a one-sided activity that obscures what we [the West] 'do,' and highlights instead what Muslims and Arabs by their very flawed nature 'are'"[15] To just what extent narratives of terrorism and Islam dominate the US media in combination with complete ignorance of the realities of the region can be sensed in the incidents of Arab-bashing after 9/11, whose first victims were non-Muslim and non-Arab "Orientals," an Egyptian Copt and an Indian Sikh.

Torture and Ideological Catharsis

The Siege is not the only work to display a semi-enlightened racial consciousness *and* a vision of the Arab as threatening cruelty and aggression. David Russell's *The Three Kings* (1999), a war and action movie starring George Clooney, is another. In this film, it is precisely the vulnerability of the white male American body, made evident in a moment of quasi-ritualistic torture, that overturns all the good political intentions of its makers—despite the fact that media analyst Jack Shaheen was hired as a consultant to the production. Shaheen reported later that the film's producers were serious about presenting a balanced representation of Arabs in narration and style, and that they had indeed complied with many of his suggestions.

The film's plot, briefly summarized, concerns a treasure hunt undertaken by four American soldiers who are sent to Iraq during the first Gulf War and who desert their troops after receiving a tip regarding the location of Saddam's hidden gold. On their way they not only put their own lives in danger, but also find themselves caught between different Iraqi parties: both Saddam's supporters and local rebels. The American GIs are portrayed as motivated by greed and selfishness, even though they too have their heroic moments. Moreover, the narrative makes a considerable effort to move the focus away from male warriors and toward regular people—namely to picture Arabs also as human beings who have families, love their children, may be victimized, and who are able to "speak" for themselves—an effort that offers the opportunity to confront American racism and imperialism in its dealings with the Arab world.

One of the four treasure hunters, a sergeant played by Mark Wahlberg, is captured by some former Iraqi soldiers and is subsequently subjected to a painful and arbitrary interrogation. After connecting his victim to electric wires, the Arab interrogator (Said Taghmaoui), pointedly contrasted to the fair blond American through his black hair, dark eyes, mustache, and rough physique, starts questioning the sergeant about Michael Jackson in broken English and why his "country making chop off his face?"

The sergeant does not understand the question at first, but then replies: "Bullshit, he did it for himself."

The interrogator hits him for this:

> "It is so obvious! A black man made the skin white and his hair straight and you know why?"
> "No. "
> "Your sick fucking country made the black man hate himself, just like you hate the Arab and the children you bomb over here."
> "I don't hate children."

And indeed the sergeant was earlier introduced as the father of a little baby and shown to treat Iraqi hostages more humanely than his colleagues. The interrogator continues talking about how his own family was bombarded and his son killed, something the sergeant regrets. This doesn't prevent the

Said Taghmaoui as Iraqi torturer in *The Three Kings*.

infuriated Iraqi from beating and electrocuting his hostage, though. In a final climax, the Arab identifies the United States' real interest in the region, namely oil, then opens his victim's mouth and pours petrol into his throat.

Mark Wahlberg being tortured.

Quite strikingly, then, the ostensibly transformative and cathartic nature of this scene plays a pivotal role in reaffirming Arab aggression. Unlike in real-life torture, here it is not the victim who breaks down and confesses, but the aggressor, the torturer himself, who reveals his monstrous face, his hidden identity, in a moment of unexpected "truth." Yet, this truth-telling ironically implicates the producers of the film through the quasi-archaic performance of Arab cruelty, which subverts their conscious attempt to present a balanced depiction of Arab and American motivations.

And, similarly to what Susan Jeffords attests about Sylvester Stallone's character in *Rambo*, the evident vulnerability of the American male body provides the justification for the putative American need for self-defense in Iraq, Afghanistan, and elsewhere. Even though *The Three Kings* does not employ the sadistic and graphic brutality of splatter films, the torturing and wounding of sympathetic American protagonists represents in its essence a struggle over and a reaffirmation of sovereignty (national and ethnic). Gender plays a pivotal role in this representational process, whose main concern is with a male body that has come to be identified with the national body per se.

The Advent of the Hard Male Body in US Politics

In her analysis of Hollywood masculinity during the 1980s, Susan Jeffords associates the appearance of the symbolical hard (and hegemonic) male body in politics with the Reagan era (1981–1989), a period whose set of priorities depends on a valorization of the hard body. For Jeffords, the hard male body becomes emblematic of Reagan-era philosophies, politics, and economies. "In this system of thought marked by race and gender, the soft body invariably belonged to a female and/or a person of color, whereas the hard body was, like Reagan's own, male and white"—and of course in power.[16]

The *Rambo* trilogy (1982–1988), featuring Sylvester Stallone's muscular body as the most popular icon of the era, epitomizes her argument. A victimized body, at first seemingly rejected and socially marginalized because of his negative wartime experience in Vietnam, this body then becomes, once its inhabitant turns against the inefficient and egocentric representative of law and order at home, the almost invincible rescuer of the Afghani people against the evil Soviet intruder. It is no accident that Rambo is a Vietnam veteran, for his ascent from a devastated wreck into a physically strong defender of the nation's interests against its major political and military adversary of the time, the Soviet Union, is easily read as a rescue narrative. Moreover, his military affiliation throughout the sequels is apparent in terms both of the story line and his bodily performance and mastery of weapons.

In her analysis Jeffords juxtaposes relevant Hollywood blockbuster films and sequels, such as *Rambo*, *Terminator*, *Back to the Future*, and *Unforgiven* (1992), to the respective political rhetoric of the ruling elite and proposes a clear chronology for the development of the hard body. Starting in the early 1980s, the hard body appears as "a resuscitated body" of the Vietnam War era; in the mid-1980s it becomes a remasculinized foreign policy heroic; in the late 1980s it softens to "reveal" a more sensitive and emotional interior; in the early 1990s, it gets reconfigured as a "family" value, often as an "aging but still powerful foreign and domestic masculine and national model."[17]

As Jeffords observes, the repeated wounding of Rambo's body and his simultaneous insensitivity to pain send out contradictory signals. In particular, she refers to a scene in Ted Kotcheff's *First Blood* (1982), where the protagonist stitches himself up after his skin has been ripped open, and to another in Peter MacDonald's *Rambo III* (1988), where he cauterizes a wound in his side by pouring gunpowder in it and lighting it with a stick he had taken from a fire. This is a masculinity to be admired, if not copied, but at the same time a masculinity understood as vulnerable, which serves to underline that the national body can be wounded, as well, and has to be protected.[18] In the George W. Bush era, this urge to protect extends not only to sending out soldiers to foreign war zones but, more importantly, to chasing terrorists and banishing (or perhaps even exorcizing) their danger by mutilating and exterminating their bodies altogether.

Not everyone interprets muscular stars of Stallone's stature, such as bodybuilder Arnold Schwarzenegger, who ascended to stardom during the same period, in a politically motivated manner. Yvonne Tasker describes them as instead engaged in a "parodic performance of masculinity" through overstatement.[19] By dubbing this type of body performance "musculinity" (i.e., muscular masculinity), Tasker links it to the machismo of a "failed masculinity."[20] Yet the reality of this sort of masculinity, as William Gibson shows in his *Warrior Dreams* (1994), is not confined to the screen. On the contrary, a decided "cult of weapons in the hypermasculine 'paramilitary culture' . . . grew after the US defeat in Vietnam," thus reflecting on and replicating the masculinity displayed in cinema.[21]

Rambo: Sylvester Stallone's hard but
vulnerable body.

Torture as Mimesis and the Assertion of Gendered Sovereignty

Interestingly, this Reagan-era logic of the strong male body as an asser-
tion of sovereignty is fully at work in the torture procedures developed for
Arab and Muslim detainees after 9/11 and the subsequent invasion of
Afghanistan and Iraq. In his 2007 documentary, *Taxi to the Dark Side*, Alex
Gibney shows the abusive practices of the US military police in Bagram,
Aghanistan, that were soon exported, with some additional refinements
such as waterboarding, sensatory deprivation, drugging, and sexual moles-
tation, to Guantánamo Bay and eventually Abu Ghraib.

Particularly in Bagram, male interrogators qualify for their job precisely
because of their strong, tall, and stout bodies. Such bodies portray the
hegemonic masculinity of their homeland not only on a symbolic, but also
physical level. Witness accounts of the practices used during detention

highlight the quasi-ritualistic, almost surreal, and completely performative character of the procedures, particularly the so-called "shock of capture" explored in *Taxi to the Dark Side*: The moment detainees enter the prison they are confronted with the loudest, biggest, and scariest-looking personnel. They are hooded, exposed to a combination of loud speakers, flashlights, barking dogs, spitting, and yelling; they are insulted, undressed, shackled, subjected to body searches (including cavity searches); they are questioned, chained with their arms up to the ceiling, deprived of sleep for twenty-four hours, after which it is decided whether or not they will be locked up in isolation and deprived of even more sleep or not—and every time they resist, cry, or weep they are kicked in the legs or beaten.

In general, ritual structures certain actions into a defined order with fixed, repeatable rules that in turn possess strong transformative potential. This transformative power is fundamentally based on mimesis. Michael Taussig has described the mimetic faculty as "the nature that culture uses to create second nature, the faculty to copy, imitate, make models, explore difference, yield into, and become Other. The wonder of mimesis lies in the copy drawing on the character and power of the original, to the point where the representation may even assume that character and that power."[22] In the case of torture, mimesis is manifested in the shift from a relation of equality to sovereignty by which two humans, or, more accurately, two citizens get divided into torturer on the one side and tortured on the other. While the torturer, by virtue of this act, sacrifices his own personal individuality to become the representative of someone or something else—namely the military, the state, or the sovereign—the abused, through this dehumanization, is in the position of Giorgio Agamben's *homo sacer*.[23]

Yet Agamben's notion has to be qualified in one important aspect: the rituals of selection and abjection that pertain to today's *homo sacer*-cum-terrorist rely essentially on the operations of gender, ethnicity, and culture, both on the symbolic and practical levels. Returning to the concrete events that occurred at Bagram, Guantánamo, and Abu Ghraib, we need to underline that the majority of both interrogators and victims, at least in Bagram and Guantánamo, were men. In contrast, Abu Ghraib hosted female detainees as well, yet their fates are rarely discussed, and no imagery of them circulated, even though some of them were also subjected to sexual harassment, culminating in some cases in rape and impregnation.[24] This occlusion transforms discourses on and visual representation of torture into a male domain.

The Abu Ghraib photographs in particular, by picturing a multitude of primarily sexual assaults on prisoners, betray the gendered nature of torture and the construction of the subordinate Muslim male *homo sacer*. Officials considered the dissemination of these images to be a deplorable lapse, yet it served a decided purpose. Drawing a parallel between the Abu Ghraib photographs and American lynching photos, Dora Apel notes that the latter were thought to help heighten the "sense of community sanction" as well as deepen a spirit of fellow-feeling among the perpetrators, "reaffirming a gendered and racial hierarchy."[25] In this way the mass-mediated Abu Ghraib abuses can be said to stand in the tradition of earlier male-dominant Rambo narratives.

Of course one can counter that it was pictures not of male soldiers humiliating Iraqi prisoners, but of one specific female US soldier, Private First Class Lynndie England, that gained the most media attention, obtaining an iconic status in the Abu Ghraib scandal. However, with her short hair cut, her uniform, and her aggressive gesture of pointing her hands gun-like toward the genitals of hooded, naked Iraqis lined up before her, England's femininity seems completely submerged into a staged masculinity that, even when represented by a woman, still appears superior to the stripped and deprived masculinity of these objectified and faceless Arab bodies.

Although England was later tried as an individual, representing one of those allegedly few "bad apples" singled out by Donald Rumsfeld, the widely circulated images of her reinforce R. W. Connell's observations regarding modern states, including the United States, that "the centres of state power, the top decision-making units, are heavily masculine," and that this institutional masculinization extends from the lowest to the highest rank.[26] He states that "the masculinization of the state . . . is principally a relationship between state institutions and hegemonic masculinity," which excludes other, more subordinated masculinities.[27]

Masquerading Impotency

The hegemonic masculinity represented by the "hard bodies" of US cinema did not go unnoticed in the Arab world. It was watched with awe and admiration by at least a certain strata of local audiences. Egyptian producers even copied such films, though quite unsuccessfully, hoping to stylize Egyptian bodybuilder Shahat Mabruk into just such a hero. However, contrary to less-muscled stars, Mabruk never made it to the upper reaches of box office blockbusters, for good reasons, of course. If we accept the assumption that nationalism and politics migrate into film narratives, we might question whether such a politically subordinated nation like Egypt could develop a cinematic hard body at all. Despite its success in the October or Yom Kippur War, didn't Egypt accept the hegemonic presence of the United States in the region, as well as its Israeli ally, by giving up its lead position in the Non-Aligned Movement founded in 1955 during the Cold War? And by declining to continue as the leader of pan-Arabism as it had been during the years of decolonization?

Indeed, it has to be stressed that the Egyptian film industry (active since the 1930s and popular throughout the Arab world) did not develop genres heavily dependent on sadism and graphic violence, such as splatter films or "body machine" action films. The absence of the latter I have discussed elsewhere, placing it in the context of a symbolic as well as economic "underdevelopment" that made Egyptian action heroes adopt a parodic, carnivalesque masculinity rather than the hegemonic type of masculinity embodied by the effective body machine.[28] Thus, apart from a few exploitative espionage films featuring female vamp Nadia al-Gindi and involving Israeli secret agents torturing the heroine, the use of torture and the masochistic infliction of pain on men typical of the examples that Jeffords discusses, as well as the overall emphasis on speed, expansiveness, and male physicality, have remained largely foreign to the Egyptian action film. (A recent exception is Marwan Hamid's 2009 *Ibrahim Labyad*.)

I have argued that the deficiencies of the genre, besides reflecting Egypt's relative lack of technological advancement, expressed the general disillusionment and sense of powerlessness that followed the de facto political appeasement of the post–Camp David Accords (1978) era and remaining difficulties surrounding the Palestinian question on the political level. Thus the inability to produce a perfect "body machine" on a symbolical level runs parallel to the lack of access to high-cost technology (also true for genres like the horror film, science fiction, and even the historical narrative). This phenomenon is especially visible in the personae the stars of the action film have developed over the last three decades of the twentieth century. It applies in particular to top star Adel Imam ('Adil Imam), who started his career as a comic underdog and ended up as Egypt's king of comedy, whose preferred genre is, tellingly, the local action that, all aspirations to the contrary, always remains close to parody. No wonder that, in the course of his long career, Imam's persona even offers some anthropophagic responses to the American terror-phobia being displayed on its silver screen. A good example is his appearance in Nadir Galal's comedy *Halu Amrika* (*Hello America*) (2000). With its cinematic quotations of American political thrillers, such as scenes on airplanes, along with a CIA investigation, its political intrigue, and humorous style, the film clearly employs the cannibalistic and carnivalesque strategies of cultural resistance sketched out by Robert Stam and Ella Shohat.[29] Produced before 9/11 and the Iraqi invasion, the film is characterized by a partial association of the "white" Egyptian with American hegemonic white masculinity.

The film features Bakhit (Imam) and his fiancée 'Adila, who undergo a financial crisis and decide to try their luck with Bakhit's cousin in New York. The cousin and his family, however, no longer adhere to traditional Egyptian values of family loyalty, generosity, and hospitality. Instead they abuse Bakhit and 'Adila, using them as cheap labor and eventually abandoning them to the streets, where the couple experiences the most severe ups and downs of American life. The spatial representation of the Egyptian immigrants' adoption of so-called Western attitudes, their prosperity and egotism, is embodied by their vast villa and garden, which are pointedly contrasted to the densely populated lower-class neighborhood from which Bakhit originates, with its full cafes and alleys, and the intimacy between neighbors and friends that we view in scenes prior to Bakhit's departure, where friends gather to bid him a cheerful farewell.

More importantly, American preoccupation with Arab terrorism is debunked as mere hysteria in one of the film's most hilarious scenes, in which American special agents mistake a glass of stinky old Egyptian cheese (*mish*) in Bakhit's possession for a biological weapon. The scene progresses in a way similar to American plane-hijacking films. Yet in this case the putative assault on the United States is treated in an extremely funny way. Taken away for questioning, Bakhit resolves the matter quite simply: he swallows the whole salty cheese at once. At the same time, it is telling that *Hello America* expresses no ambivalence over US expansionism; on the contrary, the narrative explicitly aligns the Egyptian hero with white America in its racist representations of African Americans. For example, in one episode Bakhit is offered the hand of an American woman as a solution to his visa problem. Bakhit waits expectantly with a bouquet for his bride in front of the registry office, but when she arrives, Bakhit is shocked. His future wife turns out to be a huge, stout, and coarse-looking black woman, much bigger than himself, who crudely and immediately asks for material compensation. Later, in the home of this same woman, male and female roles are further confounded as she forces him to share the bed with her and finally rolls over to lie on top of him as if raping him. In every scene the African American, portrayed as a corpulent, ugly, muscular (therefore masculine), and sexually aggressive woman, is equated with a quasi-animalistic sexuality. Her features are totally opposite to the milky-white complexion, blond hair, and petite fragility of Bakhit's fiancée. Thus the character of the African American helps the film align the Egyptian characters with white, and hence hegemonic, rather than black, subordinated America.

Sexual Penetration as Initiation into the New World Order

Real angst over political domination and colonial "penetration" in light of US expansionism is something that appears for the first time on the Egyptian screen after the invasion of Iraq in 2003. The comedy *Laylat suqut Baghdad* (*The Night Baghdad Fell*) (2006), directed by Muhammad Amin (who also authored the script), presents the "American threat" entirely as a matter of sexuality. The story concerns a schoolmaster who believes that, after the fall of Baghdad, Egypt is under immediate threat of occupation by US forces. Since his country's leadership is obviously either unwilling to act or incapable of acting, he decides to invest his own money in the development of an effective defensive weapon being devised by a genius student, Tariq. Ugly, unfocused, and with meager resources, Tariq swears to sacrifice everything, even his own "desires," to the mission. Yet despite being provided with new, comfortable accommodations and all the necessary equipment, his drug addiction and sexual deprivation prevent him from making headway, a matter that seems to get resolved through his marriage to the schoolmaster's patriotic daughter (she agrees only for the sake of Egypt!). But it turns out that he is unable to perform in bed. When Tariq goes to the doctor for help, he learns that his impotency is linked to his fear of the coming invasion. His pretty young wife eventually finds the cure by disguising herself as a GI, thus inciting his sexual aggression and sparking his creativity. At this point the CIA intervenes and tries to bribe the schoolmaster and his protégé. When the two refuse to cooperate they are declared insane and hospitalized. The film ends with the American invasion, during which Tariq and the schoolmaster are able to escape, join their family, and use Tariq's weapon of resistance against the invaders.

By means of its highly comic mise-en-scène, innumerable sexual allusions, and constant wordplay, the film exposes Egyptian "backwardness" on the one hand, while calling for patriotic resistance on the other. Its encoding of US military aggression as sexual assault is achieved by nothing less than the conjuring of photographic images of the naked Abu Ghraib prisoners and by a redeployment of one of the most widely circulated iconic stills picturing Lynndie England aiming at prisoners. The film's version, though, includes one important difference: the schoolmaster's wife and daughter are also present at the scene, wearing the same red clothes as the male prisoners. The situation eventually culminates in the girl's—not the men's—sexual abuse at the hands of a soldier, who picks her out and begins to rip off her clothes, at which point we discover that this is all merely the nightmare of her father. The sexualized interpretation of military invasion is reinforced on the verbal level, too: when Tariq activates his invention for the first time, the experiment fails, and the schoolmaster as well as present family and friends start whimpering in full view of a cardboard GI they use for shooting practice, begging in English: "Please, don't fuck me, please don't fuck me!"

In view of its main motif, penetration, the film's turning point uncovers an even deeper paradox. For Tariq's sexual potency is revived not via seduction by his wife's feminine qualities, but rather through her appearance in *male* disguise, dressed in uniform—that is, in drag, so to speak. This iconic cross-dressing is further underlined and echoed in subsequent scenes when all the other women in the house copy the formula and dress up as soldiers, with the emblematic American flag serving as a tool to incite sexual arousal. For example, when it is attached to the military attire of the schoolmaster's wife it causes her husband to undress immediately. Yet, even though these depictions seem to be situated in the heterosexual arena, they display a strong homoerotic subtext. For women incite their male partner's capacity for penetration only in male disguise, thus rescripting feminine desirability and construing penetration as an act of male-to-male aggression and desire.

This twist recalls Richard Dyer's account of the psychological complexity of penetration, which attempts to counter the dominant Freudian explanation: "It is . . . more probable that it is the taboo of male anal eroticism that causes masculine-defined men to construct penetration as frightening . . . an act of violence."[30] That an allusion to the taboo of (frightening) male anal eroticism surfaces in an Egyptian film after the circulation of the images of Abu Ghraib is telling. For exactly this taboo is incorporated into the repertory of abusive US American interrogation practices, an enlistment that turns on the assumption, sanctioned by Raphael Patai's *The Arab Mind* of 1978, that Arab and Muslim men are particularly vulnerable to sexual humiliation.[31]

One major underlying (and essentialist) assumption is that this vulnerability is part of the Arab's supposedly strong attachment to heterosexual masculinity. However, Georg Klauda argues quite convincingly that current polarizations of hetero- and homosexuality and the increasing criminalization and pathologization of homosexuality in the Arab and Muslim world are a result of the East-West encounter and not an essential part of traditional Muslim culture.[32] Apel too emphasizes this forced acculturation

Cross-dressing in *The Night Baghdad Fell.*

in quoting cultural theorist Slavoj Žižek: "The torture at Abu Ghraib was thus not simply a case of American arrogance toward a Third World People. In being submitted to humiliating torture the Iraqi prisoners were effectively *initiated into American culture*"[33]—a culture governed by hegemonic (white) masculinity.

Arab Cinema and the Hetero-Normative Rules of Torture

No wonder the female presence essentially vanishes from the typical American Rambo narratives and even in more sophisticated political films,

The headmaster's Abu Ghraib nightmare in *The Night Baghdad Fell*.

such as *Syriana*, while a film like *The Night Baghdad Fell* evidently struggles with the presence of the female and what it is thought to represent. Yet to the extent women in Egyptian films are made to represent the endangered nation, they are implicitly relegated to the realm of nationalist romanticism. The imagined rape of the patriotic daughter, along with the young man's impotency, betray the hetero-normative and gendered rhetoric of Egyptian nationalism, which mirrors exactly the conservative American belief that the successful nation can only be imagined as strong, dominant, and masculine; in moments of colonization the image of the nation turns into either an impotent man or a raped woman. Indeed, as is the case for many other nations, the predominantly female coding of the Egyptian nation was particularly prevalent before and in the immediate aftermath of national independence.[34]

Thus, since their appearance in the 1930s in Alexandria's and Cairo's film studios and their subsequent spread to other Arab countries during the era of decolonization, accounts of colonialism and the struggle against it are shaped into entirely gendered narratives, with rape becoming a pivotal motif. This is the case even in films relating to Palestine, like the Syrian film *Al-sikkin* (*The Knife*) (1972), and to Algeria, where, for example, Youssef Chahine's *Jamila al-Jaza'iriyya* (*Jamila the Algerian*) (Egypt, 1958) explores the persecution and torture of the *mujahida* (female freedom fighter) Djamila Bouhired by the French military. Even Guilio Pontecorvo's sober anti-colonial Algerian co-production, *The Battle of Algiers* (1966), released four years after the country's independence, does not completely escape a gendered iconography: the last shots of the film show an Algerian woman dancing and waving a flag celebrating independence and the birth of her nation.[35]

At the same time, none of these films, from the anti-colonial Egyptian allegory, Bahiga Hafiz's *Layla al-badawiyya* (*Layla the Bedouin*) (produced in 1937 and released in 1944), up to the films of the 1970s, never picture rape or any other form of abuse in a graphic manner. Films rely instead on dramatic means of moral antagonism. The details of physical torture are often only alluded to through the course of the narrative, sparing spectators its visual depiction. This applies to *Jamila the Algerian*, too, even though it was made at the height of Egypt's pan-Arab Nasserist phase, a period characterized by strongly nationalist and anti-colonial rhetoric, during which the country signed the nonalignment pact in 1955, nationalized the Suez Canal in 1956, and saw itself attacked by Israel, France, and Great Britain. Given this context, the film that contributed to the Third-Worldist anti-colonial rhetoric can be seen to show its solidarity with fellow Arab country Algeria, caught up at that time in a ferocious war for national liberation (1954–1962). By casting Egyptian film star Magda, known for her performances in melodramatic love stories, in the role of Algeria's famous *mujahidda*, the film pays more than full tribute to that genre's requirements by representing an oppressed female heroine. At the same time the heroine's plight does not offer the disturbing realism of Jean-Luc Godard's *Le Petit Soldat* (*The Little Soldier*) (France, 1960), for example, produced during the same period and depicting the waterboarding and electrocution of a French secret agent by—surprisingly—Algerian agents.

In fact, *The Battle of Algiers*, just like the subsequent *Décembre* (1972) by Algerian Mohamed Lakhdar Hamina, does not display overt interest in the emotional and rhetorical mobilization of the viewer typical of other anti-colonial Arab films. Rather, both films are concerned with rationally dissecting the oppressive system of colonialism that employs torture to uphold power relations. Particularly in *The Battle of Algiers*, torture is presented as a key element in the French strategy to uncover the FLN members operating within Algiers' Kasbah. Here the waterboarding of a detainee is depicted at length and serves as a prelude to the tragic climax of the film, where the last remaining freedom fighters, among them a child, are seen waiting in hiding, only to be blown up by the French troops.

In popular Egyptian cinema the earliest and most graphic (though still comparatively moderate) torture scenes are presented in the context of religious films of the 1950s dealing with the persecution of the Prophet's first followers, which include archaic practices like the chaining, whipping, blinding, and burning of victims. Such depictions have continued in a very limited number of political and social films that criticize internal Egyptian affairs, and have been presented in a few cases in the context of exploitative cinema, such as espionage films. Outright political films too have occasionally resorted to overt depictions of physical abuse as a means of discrediting the national leadership's oppressive practices, without, however, achieving at any point the same sadomasochistic entanglements of the above-described American action films.

One frequently discussed example of political film in Egypt is 'Ali Badrakhan's *al-Karnak* (1975). Badrakhan's work goes so far as to associate the past Nasserist regime with torture and rape by telling the story of a politically active student couple who is seized by state security forces. The pair is subjected to brainwashing attempts and, as the film culminates in its depiction of the regime's worst abuses, the female student is raped by the officers. A more recent example is Marwan Hamid's *'Imarat Ya'qubian* (*The Jacoubian Building*) (2006), in which one of the characters, a disillusioned but educated son of a poor doorkeeper, joins the Muslim fundamentalists, gets caught by state security, is tortured, and eventually takes a bloody revenge that ends his life and that of his torturer. In both cases victim and torturer are pictured as opponents, both morally and in degrees of power, and thus the films maintain the structure of classical drama and its penchant for staging existential battles between good and evil.

Dramatic polarization is also a characteristic of espionage films starring Nadia al-Gindi, an actress of modest acting capabilities associated primarily with trivial, sexually permissive films (moderate, of course, in comparison to the West), who had reached the peak of her popularity in the 1990s. By deploying the genre's characteristic violent conflicts and showing herself successful at countering physical threats despite her female body, al-Gindi has challenged some of the premises of a nationalist deployment of gender. Asked about her preference for the espionage theme, the actress commented: "These kinds of movies address the national sentiment and raise the degree of national affiliation. I consider this a patriotic task as it presents Egyptian heroism that any Egyptian may be proud of."[36] The figure of the kamikaze for the national cause who withstands seduction, terror, and physical torture recurs in her espionage films, whether in *Malaf Samya Sha'rawi* (*The Samya Sha'rawi File*) (1988), *Muhimma fi Tall Abib* (*Mission in Tel Aviv*) (1992), or *Imra'a hazzat' arsh Misr* (*A Woman Shook the Egyptian Throne*) (1995).

One of the most graphically depicted abuses of al-Gindi occurs in a scene in Nadir Galal's *48 sa'atun fi Isra'il* (*48 Hours in Israel*) (1998) and involves the highly symbolical penetration of her fingers with a knife-like phallic object, causing the actress to issue horrified screams. The film tells the story of a woman searching for her younger brother, who had been captured by the Israeli Mossad before the 1973 October or Yom Kippur War. In all al-Gindi films the heroine's moral strength and stamina compensate for her submission to physical abuse and implied sexual humiliation; under no circumstances does she give in to her oppressors, and she always finally succeeds in outwitting them by means of her intelligence. These films, then, may be interpreted as female empowerment narratives, with torture serving as a pivotal climatic moment in the plot and character development, a catharsis that admits her finally into the (male) realm of the nation's defenders without completely negating her feminine qualities, such as physical weakness and vulnerability to penetration.

Torturous Cinema

Produced and distributed outside the commercial networks of the Egyptian film industry, non-Egyptian *auteur* films have largely refrained from any allegorical or rhetorical use of torture that directly implicates any particular political actor. Tunisian productions, such as *Safa'ih min dhahab* (*Golden Horseshoes*) (1989), by Nouri Bouzid, *Sultan al-madina* (*Sultan of the Medina*) (1992), by Mouncef Dhouib, and '*Urs al-dib* (*Tender is the Wolf*) (2006), by Jilani Saadi, or those from Syria, including *Al-kumbars* (*The Extras*) (1993), by Nabil Maleh, Muhammad Malas' *Al-layl* (*The Night*) (1991), Ussama Muhammad's *Sunduq al-dunya* (*Sacrifices*) (2002) and *Kharij al-taghtiya* (*Out of Coverage*) (2007) by 'Abd al-Latif 'Abd al-Hamid, have certainly also been shaped by the system of state and self-censorship imposed by the autocratic and authoritarian regimes in which they are made. These films transmit the experience of pain and torture by means of a non-illustrative, yet still highly mimetic mise-en-scène that succeeds primarily via its rhythm to make the viewer's "body do things"; in other words, the viewer is made to share the pain on a physical level. However, its narratives are organized along similarly gender-polarized lines, like the above-mentioned American and Egyptian films.

In his feature film *Golden Horseshoes*, Tunisian scriptwriter and director Nouri Bouzid tells the story of an intellectual, newly released from political imprisonment and torture, who alienates family and friends in various encounters that expose his inability to reconnect with them after the experiences of his confinement. In a pivotal scene the protagonist roams the dark and deserted rooms of his former house and is haunted by memories of his physical abuse at the hands of the secret police. Bouzid, who uses this film to convey his own experience as a leftist political prisoner in his homeland, also wrote the script for Mouncef Dhouib's *Sultan of the Medina*, which narrates in a much more allegorically encrypted way a similar story of entrapment featuring a young bride who gets abused the moment she escapes from her enforced seclusion.

The quasi-mythical storyline and its stylized premodern setting provide in essence a double imprisonment. It is not only the young girl who is kept in the house to be delivered over to the holder of absolute power, but also Fraj, the young brother of her absent bridegroom. While Fraj enjoys the freedom to climb the terraces and mark the walls, he is nonetheless without the power to leave the suffocating Medina and live in a different, more just, and more friendly environment. Shot predominantly at night, the myriad terraces, old walls, dark alleys, and cramped state of Bab's house all serve to elicit a strong feeling of enclosure.

In contrast, the action of the Syrian film *Out of Coverage* by 'Abd al-Latif 'Abd al-Hamid is dominated by an almost breathless mise-en-scène that conveys a similar sense of suffocating entrapment. It presents the unsettling story of a middle-aged man who spends much of the film oscillating madly between two jobs, two women, and two sets of children, his own and those of his friend, a political prisoner whose family he agrees to care for. These double duties persist until he falls desperately in love with his friend's wife. His feeling for her is so strong that, at least for a moment, he is willing to denounce his friend in order to prevent him from being released and returning to his family.

The film's pace, as it chronicles the man's frantic attempts to satisfy the needs of two families, his profuse sweating, his relentless running from one place to another, and the growing sexual tension between him and his friend's wife, mounts to a painful level. This sense of physical uneasiness is further emphasized through the only sexual encounter between the hero and his friend's wife. What is supposed to be a joyful moment is rather depicted as a tour-de-force of two sweating, struggling people, who at the point of orgasm break out in tears and turn away from each other, overwhelmed by shame and the knowledge that they have betrayed the jailed husband and friend.

Ironically, films like *Out of Coverage* and Ussama Muhammad's *Sacrifices*, which radiates with the same sense of breathlessness, are, despite their critical potential, state-produced films. For since the mid-1970s, Syria has abandoned commercial production (which was partly shared with Lebanon), turning its film industry into an entirely state-run enterprise. This enterprise is known for its "cave films," hundreds of film rolls that have been either locked away by censors, not good enough to find an audience, or are simply too difficult and cryptic to be understood. In fact, the dark and violent symbolism that characterizes some of the most accomplished Syrian works is certainly related to the experience of oppression and isolationism that have been forced on Syrian cinema by state censorship, which does not so much interfere directly as simply drain away all film resources and distribution outlets, leaving the number of movie theatres greatly reduced.

Films being produced in countries with a long record of human rights abuses and torture, such as some Syrian films as well as the above-described Tunisian film, entertain a difficult relationship with their audiences, not least because they expect viewers to share their pain by exposing them to an experience of physical unease coupled with thwarted wish-fulfillment. Torture has become the subtext of their narratives in their attempt to create mimetic moments that require the viewer to actually experience abuse through his or her senses without necessarily seeing it depicted thematically. This occurs in both Tunisian and Syrian films, particularly through the repetition of painful and constantly obstructed heterosexual encounters that epitomize the sense of a ferocious state oppression and omnipresent, but hidden violence.

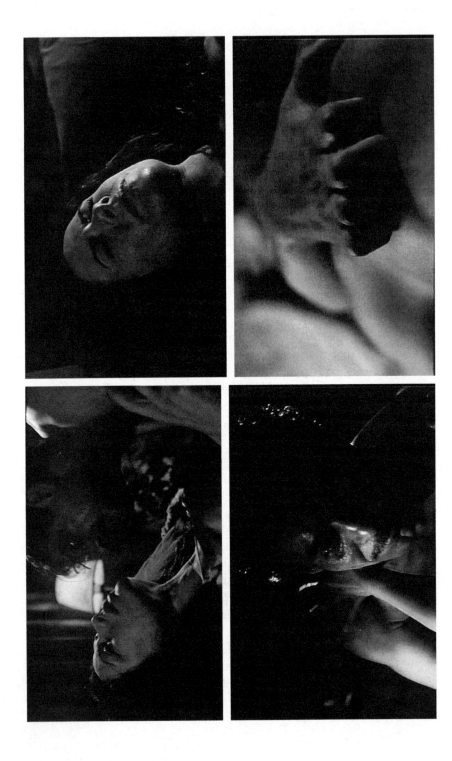

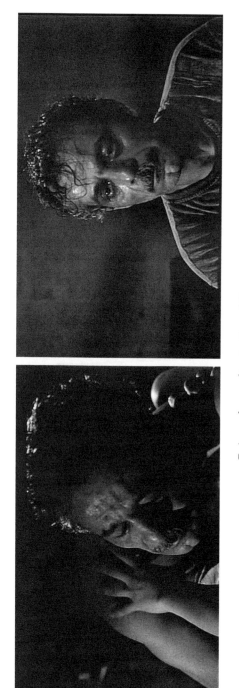

Pain and sexuality in *Out of Coverage*.

Aimed at tackling systematic oppression by demonstrating its sadistic effects on the films' characters, these narratives fail to deconstruct the hetero-normativity of the system as a whole. For women are made first of all to occupy the place of home and desire, object rather than subject, while approaches to or acquisition of them are both threatened and eventually thwarted due to a male-defined system of oppression that exercises its humiliating power specifically over men. The humiliation of men based on the exclusion of women from the system of political signification is the common denominator of these narratives, something that, ironically enough, brings them close to the Abu Ghraib imagery and its total saturation in masculinity.

Of course, one must distinguish the hegemonic masculinity that shores up new American brutality and exploitation films from that which underlies intentionally critical cinematic practice. Instead of transgressively heightening the viewer's morally ambiguous participation in a physical assault on self or other, Arab torturous cinema confirms men's masochistic experience of male powerlessness and subordination to the state's hegemonic masculinity, a masculinity whose silent and passive bystanders are necessarily women. It is women who are shown as confirming men's sense of degradation, their psychic and moral mutilation.

Thus, both subversive and affirmative cinematic forms that deal with torture and reproduce some of its ritualistic and mimetic aspects tend to portray physical abuse as a primarily male domain. In the American case, torture confirms a white hegemonic masculinity that is based on the total or partial exclusion of an abject non-white femininity, on whomever that is inscribed. In the Arab case, torture subverts white hegemonic masculinity for the sake of a subordinated masculinity. The latter objectifies and silences the excluded female through politicized symbolic codings, governed primarily by male fear of anal penetration and the inability to imagine a pleasurable, nonaggressive sexual encounter that could successfully circumvent hetero-normative polarization and exclusion.

CHAPTER 12

Music and Torture: The Stigmata of Sound and Sense

Peter Szendy

It is a fact now proven by many testimonies: in US prisons, in Guantánamo, and in Iraq, *music is used for torture.*[1] Not only is the sound of the music used as accompaniment or as a sonic mask to cover the cries, but indeed it is torture *by means of music.* This arguably novel practice must be denounced and cannot be denounced enough. But we must also think about it, we must analyze it, to attempt to understand that which was able to render possible this collusion or unheard-of conjunction: music and torture.

"A cruelty consecrated by use" (*una crudeltà consacrata dall' uso*):[2] these are the first words of the chapter on torture (*Della tortura*) in the work of Enlightenment-era Italian lawyer and man of letters Cesare Beccaria. Regarded as the first great abolitionist speech, to which today's adversaries of capital punishment continue to refer, Beccaria's *Dei delitti e delle pene* (*On Crimes and Punishments*) was published in 1764, translated soon after by the encyclopedists, and then published in the United States in 1777. Beccaria's argument against torture is clear from the start:

> Either he is guilty or not guilty [*o il delitto è certo o incerto*]; if guilty, no other punishment suits him but that established by law, and the torture is useless, for the confession of the culprit is useless [*se certo, non gli*

*conviene altra pena che la stabilita dalle leggi, ed inutili sono i tormenti, perché
inutile è la confessione del reo*]; if not guilty, one tortures an innocent, for
he is, according to the law, a man whose offenses have not been proven
[*se è incerto, non devesi tormentare un innocente, perché tale è secondo le leggi
un uomo i di cui delitti non sono provati*].[3]

Torture would nullify itself in this way, juridically, in a sort of paradox:
where it could be justified as punishment, it is useless; where it could be
useful, it is against the law. And "this dilemma," says Beccaria, "is not a
novelty" (*non è nuovo questo dilemma*).

Yet to this argument, which he clearly considers well-known, Beccaria
seeks to *add* something novel. *Ma io aggiungo di più*, he says, in advancing
this distinctive new consideration:

> But, as for me, I add that it confuses all relationships to demand that a
> man be both accuser and accused [*Ma io aggiungo di più, ch'egli è un voler
> confondere tutt'i rapporti l'esigere che un uomo sia nello stesso tempo accusatore
> ed accusato*] . . . and that the criteria (of truth) reside in the muscles and
> fibres of a wretch [*nei muscoli e nelle fibre di un miserabile*]. It's the surest
> way to absolve sturdy villains and condemn weak innocents [*Questo è il
> mezzo sicuro di assolvere i robusti scellerati e di condannare i deboli innocenti*].[4]

If the second stage of this supplementary consideration is perfectly clear,
that pain cannot possibly be the touchstone of truth without risking infliction of the gravest injustice on the least resistant, its first stage is somewhat
elliptical. Torture, Beccaria seems to say, places the victim in the position of
accused and accuser at once. Accuser of whom? This is what one comes to
understand in reading the striking prosopopoeia by which, toward the end
of this same chapter, Beccaria gives voice to torture itself, in person:

> Men . . . if Nature has given you an inextinguishable self-love [*uno
> inestinguibile amor proprio*], if it has given you an inalienable right to
> self-preservation [*se vi ha dato un inalienabile diritto alla vostra difesa*],
> I create in you a completely contrary affect, namely a heroic hatred of
> yourselves, and I command you to accuse yourselves [*io creo in voi un
> affetto tutto contrario, cioè un eroico odio di voi stessi, e vi comando di accusare
> voi medesimi*].[5]

The accused, while he is tortured, cannot thus limit himself to assuring his
defense, as he may justly do through the proceedings of his trial: he is also
forced, at the same time, to *accuse himself*, to carry out his *autoaccusation*.

Whether the notion of torture, such as Beccaria defines and characterizes it here, has changed or not since the Age of Enlightenment, whether it

was or was not maintained intact until the most recent abuses of which we now know, is difficult to establish. It seems, however, that certain modern torture practices, hypocritically presented as "no-touch torture," push the perversion of this confusion of roles (of the "rapports" between accused and accuser, as Beccaria says) so far as to pursue the identification of the torturer with the victim himself: it is the latter who, without being touched, is supposed to inflict the pain upon himself. Contemporary with other operations of linguistic whitewashing (like the too-famous "surgical strikes" with their "collateral damage"), this torture for which the torturer need not dirty his hands, not only hides itself behind banal expressions (one speaks thus, in the military or police lexicon, of "additional psychological strategies"), but above all places the victim, in pushing him to auto-mutilation or suicide, in the position of self-executioner.

However, this self-torment, as Beccaria's text already suggested between the lines, has its principal model in the Christian tradition, at the intersection between the lineage of confession and that of stigmatization. Beccaria writes,

> Another motive of torture, just as ridiculous, is the purging of infamy [*un altro ridicolo motivo della tortura è la purgazione dell'infamia*]. . . . This usage seems to be borrowed from religious and spiritual ideas, by which mankind, in all nations and in all ages, is so greatly influenced [*Sembra quest'uso preso dalle idee religiose e spirituali, che hanno tanta influenza su i pensieri degli uomini, su le nazioni e su i secoli*]. . . . [I]n the same way that pain and fire erase the bodily and spiritual stains, why would not the agony of torture erase the civil stain that is infamy [*come il dolore ed il fuoco tolgono le macchie spirituali ed incorporee, perché gli spasimi della tortura non toglieranno la macchia civile che è l'infamia*]? I believe the confession of the accused, considered essential to prosecution in some courts, has a similar origin, for with the mysterious tribunal of penitence the confession of the sins is an essential part of the sacrament [*Io credo che la confessione del reo, che in alcuni tribunali si esige come essenziale alla condanna, abbia una origine non dissimile, perché nel misterioso tribunale di penitenza la confessione dei peccati è parte essenziale del sagramento*].[6]

In summary, for Beccaria, torture is readily conceived as the erasure of a trace, of a defamatory mark, like purification that would wash away the stain of sin with pain. By torture, which would thus ultimately have to be conceived and accepted as self-punishment, the victim—victim above all of the evil working in him and through him—would have, so to speak, the chance to produce on himself the redemptive *countermark*. In this sense, torture would become the sacrificial passion of a body marked by the *stigmata* of its future redemption.

In fact, torture leaves traces, wounds, scars. The body subjected to torture carries its marks. It recounts, from now on in a voiceless, but cruelly painful manner, the violence inflicted upon it. It is, so to speak, the silent archive of this violence: *the evidence*, as one says in English, the proof. Now that which is evident is that which is *seen*. The Latin etymology attests to this: the evidence comes from, it issues from (*ex-*, out of) the visible (*videns*, present participle of *videre*, to see).

And what about the audible?

I will not speak of the sound and the fury, of the cries and protests at the instant the body finds itself subjected to pain.[7] I will not speak of this intolerable soundtrack that accompanies cruelty. My question, in my preparation to investigate the suffering caused by music, will rather be this: do the sonorous instruments of torture leave, if not traces, at least a remnant? In other words, would there be sound marks, sound stigmata? And if so, what would be their nature?

The history of the use of music in torture remains to be written, and its field delimited. For pain—whether deliberately inflicted or not—is at work everywhere in the musical experience, also and especially where music is supposed to bring comfort or reconciliation.

Szymon Laks, who was conductor of the orchestra at Auschwitz, recounts a particularly disturbing memory:

> On Christmas Eve 1943, I took a small group of Dutchmen to the women's hospital where at the instructions of Commander Schwarzhuber we were supposed to play a few carols to console the sick. . . . I would rather not describe the sight that spread out before our eyes or the stink that blew on us when we crossed the threshold. It was unbelievable that this was a hospital whose calling was the treatment and care of weak, emaciated women who were near death. I chased away gloomy thoughts. We had come here to play. . . . We started with the traditional German carol "Silent Night, Holy Night" . . . which the audience listened to attentively. We also had Polish Christmas carols in our repertoire. We began with "Sleep, Little Jesus."[8] After a few bars quiet weeping began to be heard from all sides, which became louder and louder as we played and finally burst out in general uncontrolled sobbing. . . . I didn't know what to do; the musicians looked at me in embarrassment. To play on? Louder? . . . From all sides spasmodic cries, ever more numerous, ever shriller—in Polish . . . "Enough of this! Stop!" . . . What could we do? We cleared out. I did not know that a carol could give so much pain. [9]

That a Christmas carol can give pain in Auschwitz: one is tempted to hear in this case the reversal, the inversion of the alleviating virtue traditionally attributed to music. One is brought to believe that, in inhuman conditions, music's capacity for consolation resounds like a painful reminder of a lost humanity. And thenceforth, in spite of appearances, it would not be responsible, it would not be an accomplice to the suffering it causes: on the contrary, in the middle of the barbarity, music would simply be *too horribly good*.

However, I insist, the pain—deliberately inflicted or not—is at work everywhere in the musical experience. It is even conceived in certain contexts as necessary, as a passage of initiation, like a kind of sacrificial trial in preparation for the construction of musical beauty, one that will be disembodied. It suffices to recall here a testimony among so many others on the apprenticeship of the piano that pianist and composer George Antheil describes in his autobiography (*Bad Boy of Music*, 1945): the propitiatory suffering on the path toward virtuosity:

> A pianist's fingers are both his ammunition and his machine guns. By the time you are ready to be a concert pianist, they must have been tempered into steel. . . . You practice slow trills until it almost kills you, until your two forearms are like sore throbbing hams, twice, three times their normal size, or so they seem. Then you wait until the soreness gets out of them. Then you start all over again. Finally, after weeks, you commence playing on an octave scale. . . . Up and down, up and down, until, at last, your forearms seem as if they will burst again. Moreover, by this time, the pain creeps up to your shoulders, spreads over your back. You keep on. You must never stop. And so technique comes to you.[10]

One can always think that it's a matter of contingent effect, of a collateral damage brought on by the means necessary for the development of a virtuoso technique worthy of this name. Once acquired, it is forgotten, disappeared in the bodiless beauty that it makes possible.

There is, on the other hand, an experience that we all have, I believe, to differing degrees, and thanks to which we should be able at least to glimpse, from very far off, what those detainees lived through, who, according to many recent testimonies that I will shortly cite, were subjected by the military or the police to a systematic use of torture by music.

I mean the experience of *melodic obsession*, as it has been described notably by Theodor Reik in his fascinating essay entitled *The Haunting Melody*. I will not recount here the pages that I devoted to this phenomenon elsewhere;[11] suffice it to say that the melody or the most beautiful song, the most moving or the most pleasant, can become detestable when it haunts your mind from morning to night, sometimes for days, preventing you from thinking, torturing you with its unwelcome, yet insistent presence.

It's no accident if, to name what one calls a *tube* in French or a "hit" in English, namely, a huge success that not only repeats itself on the market of musical merchandise, but also especially ends up invading the economy of the psyche, if in Italian, then, one calls it *tormentone*: i.e., in the language of Beccaria, a *great torture*.

If music thus implies suffering induced or endured, if the musical experience is so often indistinguishable from pain, it seems difficult to circumscribe its torturing dimension. Certainly it exposes itself in a privileged way on the battlefields of war against what is called terrorism or during interrogations led in Iraq and Guantánamo, as we will soon see. However, starting with certain myths of ancient Greece (like that of Apollo having Marsyas flayed at the outcome of their flute contest) up to certain bellicose episodes in the Bible (like the famous walls of Jericho, which collapse under the force of the clamor triggered by the sounding of trumpets),[12] the art of sounds has long been linked to the art of inflicting pain or defeat.

But let us for the moment assume that the use of music for torture can be limited to its *intentional* application in order to produce suffering with the goal of obtaining strategically important information.[13] In maintaining this provisional characterization, in pretending to believe that musical violence is specifically a military or police affair, we can follow the remarkable study of Suzanne Cusick, the first to my knowledge to retrace the recent history of sound torture.

In "Music as Torture / Music as Weapon,"[14] she shows how the idea to use music as a weapon of war or as an interrogation technique goes back to the notion of *no-touch torture*,[15] born of US military research after World War II, in collaboration with the Canadian and British secret services. In fact, as early as 1978, the European Court of Human Rights deemed the thunderous noises that the English used against their Irish prisoners "inhuman and degrading." And in December 1989, when the United States invaded Panama, Manuel Noriega, who had taken refuge at the Apostolic Nunciature, surrendered after having been bombarded without respite by hard rock.

One could certainly question this supposedly US American or Anglo-Saxon origin of the tactic of nontactile torture, in particular if one thinks of the technique falsely described as Chinese, whose invention is attributed, rather, to an Italian jurist of the sixteenth century, Hyppolitus de Marsiliis, and which consists of letting fall, in a regular or irregular fashion, drops of water on a part of the victim's body, in particular the face. This "Chinese Water Torture," as it is called in English, is thus also a manner of causing suffering that requires no contact whatsoever between the torturer and his victim: its terrible efficiency resides, it seems, in the devastating psychic effects, because the victim *awaits* the drop. It would also be advisable, no doubt, to consider here other methods of inflicting injuries without contact, from a distance. The long and complex history of stigmata and the stigmatized, to which I have already alluded and to which I will return, would be a remarkable example, beginning with the tradition initiated by St. Francis of Assisi, when, in 1224, in the solitude of a hermitage, he received his stigmatic wounds from the simple, remote vision of a seraph who presented the image of the crucifixion to him.

But it remains that concerning the explicit use of music for torture the phenomenon seems to be essentially US American and recent. For, as Cusick recalls, it was at the end of the 1990s that the United States signed contracts with companies who in turn applied for patents for technological devices like the Acoustic Blaster, produced by Primex Physics International, which generates repetitive impulse waveforms at a volume of 165 decibels, which can be aimed precisely for "antipersonnel" use. However, the product that ended up dominating the sinister market of the nonlethal arms races is the Long Range Acoustic Device (LRAD), developed by the American Technology Corporation beginning in 2000, capable of projecting at high volume, at a distance of up to a kilometer, a "strip of sound" about a half-meter in breadth. In March 2006, according to sources cited by Cusick, 350 LRADs had been sold to the US Navy and US Army and to the Boston, New York, and Los Angeles police departments, who use it primarily for "clearing streets" or for "drawing out enemy snipers." The intense acoustic energy that is thus "fired" from a distance causes the target to be spatially disoriented. According to other testimonies concerning similar weapons used by Israel in Lebanon or the Gaza Strip, one feels "hit by a wall of air that is painful on the ears"; one sometimes has "nosebleeds" and is "shaking inside."

This bellicose use of acoustic projection is not necessarily musical, but it can be. According to US Army spokesperson Ben Abel, the privates engaged in operations of psychological warfare (PsyOps) are generally responsible for deciding which music is blasted by connecting, for example, an MP3 player to the LRAD: "our guys have been getting really creative in finding sounds they think would make the enemy upset. . . . These guys have their own mini disc players, with their own music, plus hundreds of downloaded sounds. It's kind of a personal preference how they choose the songs."[16]

If the music is thus, in the acoustic war, a simple option left to the discretion of the combatants who fight it, this is not the case for its torturous use, according to testimonies that have filtered out of US American prisons. In May 2003 the BBC's website reported the remarks of a sergeant at PsyOps, Mark Hadsell, who in regard to the prisoners in Iraq declared, "These people haven't heard heavy metal. They can't take it. If you play it for 24 hours, your brain and body functions start to slide, your train of thought slows down and your will is broken. That's when we come in and talk to them."[17]

According to other sources, children's melodies, notably the *Sesame Street* theme and the theme song from *Barney and Friends*, "I Love You," are used as instruments of torture.[18] In addition, in a detailed report published by *The Nation* (December 26, 2005) we learn that the space reserved for the exercise of musical violence is readily nicknamed "The Disco" by US soldiers. It is generally a dark room, even a shipping crate, where the prisoners are inundated with sounds of Eminem or Bruce Springsteen ("Born in the USA"), exactly as they might be submerged in ice water. Sometimes the artists themselves gave their blessing *post factum*, such as James Hetfield of Metallica, who expressed "pride" that his music is "culturally offensive" to Iraqis.[19] A good part of public opinion also gave its blessing, as evidenced by the flourishing number of "torture playlists" on the Internet, each one making its small suggestion as to the best "mood music for jolting your jihadi."[20]

In short, the fact that music can be conceived as an instrument of torture also says much about the use and representation that *we* have of it *for ourselves*. As Cusick very accurately writes: "the blogosphere responses [which she analyzes in detail] document an important aspect of the current wars' *home* front."[21] And she goes further still in questioning the "eerie resonances" between, on the one hand, the ideology that underlies the practice of *no-touch torture* by means of sound,[22] and on the other hand, "the aesthetics shared by a wide range of music cultures since the 1960s." "Both," she says, "blur the distinction between sound and music"; and, she adds, both rest on the idea that "listening to music can dissolve subjectivity."

This history of torture *by* music, of which I have recalled a few brief recent episodes, would need to be accompanied by a history of torture *in* music itself. Otherwise said: it would be necessary to dwell at length on the way in which musical works have described, staged, and represented torture. I am thinking in particular of *Il Prigioniero*, by Luigi Dallapiccola, in 1949, or *Bluebeard's Castle*, by Béla Bartók, in 1918.

In the prologue and first act of *Il Prigioniero*, it is the jailor who, with his song, gives hope to the prisoner, detained and tortured by the Spanish Inquisition in the sixteenth century; his air, "The Song of the Beggars," resembles a popular song of uprising. The prisoner tries to sing it, too, but he does not succeed: like the agonizing patients at Auschwitz in the account of Szymon Laks, he bursts into tears; he doesn't have the strength to bear the hope the music embodies. However, when he realizes that the jailor has voluntarily left the door of his cell open, he escapes; he wanders in the subterranean labyrinths of the prison; and when he finds what he thinks is the exit, he realizes that he has only thrown himself into the arms of the Grand Inquisitor himself: he has thus succumbed to the ultimate torture, that which music as such embodies best, that of *hope*.

If, as Adorno wrote at the beginning of his *Mahler*, "all music, with its first note, promises that which is different," this promise inherent in music is here figured by three notes (those that the jailor introduces when he sings the word *fratello*, "brother") that form an omnipresent motif in the dodecaphonic texture of the opera.[23] In *Il Prigioniero*, the music is in a way rolled up into itself; it notices and designates in itself the core of hope that it carries, which is also the heart of the suffering it causes.

As for Act One of *Bluebeard's Castle* by Bartók—its libretto was written by Béla Balázs, inspired by Charles Perrault's *Bluebeard*—the torture rooms of the castle are musically painted, just as Judit discovers them one by one, by mixing the tones of the xylophone and the woodwinds in high pitch, as well as with scales rapidly traversing the interval of tritone: all musical attributes traditionally associated with the devil or sorcery, with supernatural forces of evil. But if the musical figuration of cruelty is thus most conventional (while being orchestrated in a remarkable way), it inscribes itself in a dramatic argument that blurs the distinction of roles between the torturer and the victim: it is Judit who quite often appears to be the inquisitor, with her insatiable curiosity, with her desire to know everything about Bluebeard's secrets.

As *Il Prigioniero* lets us hear it, music would thus carry at its heart a sort of enclave of hope, a kernel of promise always ready to turn into a cyst of pain. Consequently one understands that music does not really admit stability in the distribution of roles between the torturer and his victim. Musical joy (*jouissance*) is as if *beyond pleasure*: such is perhaps the encrypted secret that Judit searches for in the vaults.

But I'll interrupt here this very brief overview of the history of torture *by* or *in* music, to return to my initial question: what would be acoustic stigmata of musical torture, if there is such a thing? What would be the remainder, the mark or the trace left by the torture that music inflicts?

Such is, I believe, the motif around which Stanley Kubrick's *A Clockwork Orange* (1971) turns. And the answer consists in a reply by a certain doctor Brodksy. This reply—which perhaps says nothing, that is to say nothing other than that which *remains of music*—we will approach step by step, scene by scene.

Accompanied by a soundtrack of music that Purcell composed for the funeral of the Queen Mary (interpreted in the film on synthesizer), a red-orange screen serves as background to the short opening credits. This image is very quickly replaced by a close-up of Alex (Malcolm McDowell). His right eye is surrounded by false lashes; he has cufflinks in the shape of torn and blood-stained eyeballs. While the camera moves slowly away, revealing little by little the scene of the bar where Alex is sitting with his acolytes, his fixed gaze, in the center of the image, seems to oscillate in place, in a vibrant immobility, between these two allegorical attributes of sight that he wears: the ornament of the makeup, as if to say in advance the perverse pleasure (*jouissance*) of the surplus of vision; and the cadaver-like rigidity of a dead eye, having become simple vitreous matter.

"There was me," says Alex in the voice-over. This is, after the credits, the lead-in of the film, which gives it its tone, that of an autobiographical account. But, before these first words, before an "I" or "me" can be enunci-ated, there will thus have been the music and the image. A funeral music that seems to express mourning, perhaps the mourning of itself, since it presents itself already as differing from itself in its arrangement or syn-thetic derangement owed to Walter Carlos.[24] And an apparently stable image, that of a look in which the fixedness seems to already tremble, how-ever, between the vitrified indifference of a pure projection screen and the ornamental proliferation of the artificial supplement.

"There was me," says Alex, as if this "me," this "I," was in some way the *product* of the disturbing superposition, of the slow slide where, on the one hand, a music estranged from itself passes by, and on the other hand, an eye pulled between insensitivity and the desire of the image. It is, we will see, in the movement of this reciprocal gliding that the question of the remainder or of Alex's sonic stigmata resides.

But we must first follow the narrative of the stations of his passion after his first phrase, which marks the threshold of the world of ultraviolence in which we prepare ourselves to enter with him. "A bit of the old ultravio-lence," says Alex, according to a formula that rhymes in advance with so many others: "the old in-out, in-out," Alex's expression for coitus, as well as "the old Ludwig van." One of the most common terms in Alex's language, in this strange mélange of archaic or slang English and Russian, one of the recurring adjectives in this futurist jargon borrowed from the eponymous novel of Anthony Burgess, is indeed *old*.[25]

The association of the "good old" Beethoven with this "good old" ultra-violence is announced, is signaled for the first time by the ring of the door-bell, preparing "the old surprise visit" of Alex and his acolytes to the calm countryside residence of the Alexanders, near London. At the threshold of this scene, which will conclude with the rape of Mrs. Alexander, choreo-graphed to the tune of "Singin' in the Rain," we hear in the ringing the abbreviated form, transformed into a sort of jingle, of the first measures of Beethoven's *Fifth Symphony*, with its famous rhythmic motif: three short, one long.[26]

But the real soundtrack accompanying the sadistic dreams of Alex will be Beethoven's *Ninth Symphony*. One hears for the first time the "Ode to Joy" in the bar where the four young men return after their nocturnal jaunt. They are exhausted, sitting and sipping their milk enriched with drugs ("milk-plus"), when an elegant woman surrounded by "sophistos from the TV studios" (as Alex says in his idiom) begins to sing the famous line: "*Freude, schöner Götterfunken. . . .*"

Alex, whose musical idiosyncrasies were evoked in the first scene of aggression,[27] is jubilant as innumerable ecstatic images come to decorate his already flourished language: "And it was like for a moment, O my brothers, some great bird had flown into the milkbar and I felt all the malenky little hairs on my plott standing endwise, and the shivers crawling up like slow malenky lizards and then down again. Because I knew what she sang. It was a bit from the glorious *Ninth*, by Ludwig van."[28]

But it is only when Alex gets home, after this long and memorable night, that the "glorious *Ninth*" will produce a whole gushing of images. Seated in front of his stereo equipment, Alex thinks, "It had been a wonder-ful evening and what I needed now to give it the perfect ending was a bit of the old Ludwig van." In fact, when the second movement of the symphony starts, the camera first pans across the icons that cover Alex's room: the portrait of Beethoven, printed on the drawn blind in front of the window; a large poster of a naked woman, legs spread, in front of which the domes-tic snake belonging to the young man darts his head phallically; and four statuettes of Christ, whose detailed stigmata in close-up are soon choreo-graphed in a tight montage, to the rhythm of the music. "Oh, bliss!" exclaims Alex, "bliss and heaven! Oh, it was gorgeousness and georgeosity made flesh. It was like a bird of rarest-spun heaven metal or like silvery wine flowing in a spaceship, gravity all nonsense now. As I slooshied, I knew such lovely pictures."[29]

On these words, the camera leaves the room and enters directly into Alex's *imagination*: it penetrates on the set where he shoots over and over in himself his own oneiric images, it situates itself in the place of the producing agency of the young man's paradisiacal visions: a trap door that opens to let fall the hanged body of a woman; Alex himself with a vampire's blood-dripping teeth; explosions; an old film showing a landslide and crushed bodies.

Happiness, splendor, pure pleasure: Alex seems here to be his true self, Alex is Alex, it is this "me" that enjoys itself (*jouit de lui-même*)—that is to say, a certain audiovisual production of himself.

But the values of these dreamlike visions produced by "the *Ninth*" in Alex's sadistic psyche will be, little by little, inverted, starting from the moment he finds himself in prison for the murder of a certain Mrs. Weathers. Now another Alex will be produced by the montage, or rather by the incessant reciprocal slippage of music and imagery.

The first indication of this transvaluation of values and of this metamorphosis is the name of the experimental treatment for which Alex volunteers himself: *The Ludovico Treatment Technique*—Ludovico, like Ludwig van, like the one whose bust and portrait still adorn the table and shelves of Alex's cell, where the Minister of the Interior observes them during his visit in the prison, before making his speech on penal theory.

Alex, along with the other detainees, listens to this piece of anthology on the supposed difference between surveillance and punishment:[30]

> *Minister:* Cram criminals together and what do you get—concentrated criminality . . . crime in the midst of punishment.
> *Governor of the Prison:* I agree, sir. What we need are larger prisons. More money.
> *Minister:* Not a chance, my dear fellow. The Government can't be concerned any longer with outmoded penological theories. Soon we may be needing all of our prison space for political offenders. Common criminals like these are best dealt with on a purely curative basis. Kill the criminal reflex, that's all. Full implementation in a year's time. Punishment means nothing to them, you can see that . . . they enjoy their so-called punishment.

On these words, Alex, unable to hold back, cries: "You're absolutely right, sir!" He is quickly transferred to the Ludovico Medical Center. And there, while he receives an injection of an experimental serum, he asks Dr. Branom about the exact nature of the treatment:

> *Dr. Branom:* It's quite simple really. We're just going to show you
>   some films.
> *Alex:* You mean like going to the pictures?
> *Dr. Branom:* Something like that.
> *Alex:* Well, that's good. I like to viddy the old films now and again.
> *Alex (voice-over):* And viddy films I would. Where I was taken to,
>   brothers, was like no cine I'd been in before."

So Alex goes to the movies. And in following him, to the cinema in the cinema, we will witness his metamorphosis, that is to say his new *audiovisual montage*. This will be a different *punctuation*, a different way to stop, to *nail* the images to the music, which will produce a totally new Alex: a new way for Alex to say "I," to pronounce "there was me."

Held by a straitjacket, his head surrounded by electrodes and his eyelids held open by clamps, Alex initially enjoys this constraint, which relentlessly imposes upon him the audiovisual of "a very good professional piece of cine [that] looked like it was done in Hollywood." Listening to the cries of a fight scene, watching blood flow, Alex exclaims: "It was beautiful!"[31] But over the course of the next projection, during which he must witness a scene of gang rape, Alex begins to feel bad. He suffers from violent nausea and, as he says himself: "I could not shut me glazzies." While Alex, immobilized in front of the images from which he cannot escape, cries for help, Dr. Brodsky comments, in a coldly scientific tone, on the transformation in progress, before Dr. Branom herself offers the explanation to Alex:

> *Dr. Brodsky:* Very soon now the drug will cause the subject to experience
>   a death-like paralysis together with deep feelings of terror and
>   helplessness. One of our earlier test subjects described it as being
>   like death, a sense of stifling and drowning, and it is during this
>   period we have found the subject will make his most rewarding
>   associations between his catastrophic experience and environment
>   and the violence he sees.
> *Dr. Branom (to Alex):* Dr. Brodsky's pleased with you. Violence is a very
>   horrible thing. That's what you're learning now. Your body is
>   learning it. You felt ill this afternoon because you're getting better.
>   You see, when we're healthy we respond to the presence of the
>   hateful with fear and nausea. You're becoming healthy, that's all. By
>   this time tomorrow you'll be healthier still.

The next day's session begins with images of Nazi military processions and air raids, accompanied by a soundtrack that Alex ends up recognizing: "Ludwig van, *Ninth Symphony*, fourth movement" (again, a synthesized version). With his eyes wide open and his head covered in wires, like Jesus wearing his crown of thorns, Alex screams in pain and horror:

> *Alex:* Stop it . . . stop it, please! I beg of you! It's a sin! It's a sin! It's a sin, please!
> *Dr. Brodsky:* What's all this about sin?
> *Alex:* That! . . . Using Ludwig van like that! He did no harm to anyone. Beethoven just wrote music.
> *Dr. Branom:* Are you referring to the background score?
> *Alex:* Yes!
> *Dr. Branom:* You've heard Beethoven before?
> *Alex:* Yes!
> *Dr. Brodsky:* You're keen on music?
> *Alex:* Yes!
> *Dr. Brodsky (to Dr. Branom):* It can't be helped. Here's your punishment element perhaps.

This irreducible punitive element resounds like a cruel and ironic echo that reveals the biopolitical phantasm lodged in the heart of the smiling and banal adage "music soothes the savage breast" (*la musique adoucit les moeurs*). For behind the mask of the good will to power, there exists the shadow of a training or breaking down (*dressage*) of which certain contemporary politicians dream, facilitated by the work of behavioral science.[32]

Still, here the *Ninth Symphony* changes painfully in value and function: in its synthesized version, these are no longer pleasant sadistic visions that gush out before Alex's eyes, but sinister archival footage in black and white. In place of the fake decorative lashes connoting his scopic pleasure (*jouissance scopique*), Alex is from now on adorned with metal clamps, which make his eye a kind of pane or screen: such is the ongoing reconfiguration of the link that ties the visible to the procession of the musical flow.

Leaving the cinema in the cinema, at the outcome of this operation of audiovisual reorganization, something, then, remains. It is the *Ninth*, yes, the glorious *Ninth* of Ludwig van that appears as this remainder, ineffaceable, impossible to suppress, of a penalty based on punishment. Within the same experiment, which aims, rather than punishment or atonement, at a medicalized readaptation of Alex, the *Ninth* seems to embody that which escapes the therapy without pain, redemption without suffering. It is this trace or this mark by which Alex, even though cured or purified—that is to say, having incorporated the values imposed upon him—will be able to continue to suffer and endure.

By the way, later in the film, the *Ninth*'s second movement, blasted by speakers as big as totem poles, is used as an instrument of torture by Mr. Alexander for his revenge in order to push Alex to a suicide attempt that could be exploited by the adversaries of the Minister and of his bio-politic against delinquency.[33] Finally, during the Minister's last visit to Alex, still recovering in his hospital bed, it is again the *Ninth* that he is offered, by the politician seeking to regain popularity, as "a symbol of new under-standing . . . an understanding between two friends." With bouquets of flowers and the press gathered for the occasion, immense loudspeakers are again pushed toward Alex's bed. He smiles and shakes the Minister's hand before rolling his eyes in his head, losing himself finally, again, in the remembered visions sparked in him by the good old *Ninth*: he dreams of making love in the snow to the applause of a distinguished public, while the final orchestra bursts out. "I was cured all right," he says—and these are the last words of the film before the credits.

Thus, in *A Clockwork Orange*, the *Ninth* appears as a kind of *pharmakon* of behavioral therapy that seeks to associate violence with nausea in Alex's mind. It is at the same time the curative supplement that intensifies the effects of the cure and that remainder that holds in reserve other inversions of value, new gushes of images to come.

As this *punitive remnant*, the *Ninth* has in some ways become Alex's sonic stigma. In the manner of the Christ figures that he collects and displays in his room, resembling the points (*stigmata*, in Greek) that the nails of the crucifixion have engraved in the palms and on the feet of the Savior, the *Ninth* is each time that which nails, that which rivets Alex to a meaning. This music, which in itself is however nothing but a pure flow referring to nothing else than its own differential organization, this music capable of producing or giving rise to all possible images, without discrimination, endowed with the most contradictory and varied signifiers,[34] this music, as soon as it is stopped, *fixed* on one set of images rather than another, is also that which attaches, that which binds Alex to a system of values. It immo-bilizes him; it fastens him to an ethic, to a moral code.

The connection between music and images, in Kubrick's film and beyond, could undoubtedly be compared to that of the signifier and the signified according to Lacan: the musical flow, the procession of sound signs slip infinitely on or under the sparkling images that it births.[35] And that which temporarily stops this procession, this sliding of the music and of the image one over the other, is the punctuation of a point (which

Lacan named the "button tie" [*le point de capiton*]).³⁶ It is the *stigmatic* stop of a *coup de force*, it is a punctuating violence done to the music that makes it mean this rather than that—that *pins* it, Lacan would again say, to sing the sadistic pleasure (*jouissance*) rather than stir up self-righteous humanist nausea. And this violence, which *nails*, which *rivets* the music to a meaning, this violence which is in a way its signifying stigma or its internal stigmatology, is what music in turn imprints, from a distance, on those who are the victims of its "no-touch torture."

The phantasm that accompanies or supports the acoustic machine-gunning of musical torture is indeed the mastery of this stigmatization. It is a question of pushing in the nail, from afar and without seeming to touch, in order to signify: thus it is, period.

The violence of musical torture could well be, in the end, the reflection of the violence one inflicts *on* music, when one stops it in the slippage where it defers itself and differs from itself (*se diffère*), to rivet it onto the stigmatizing punctuation of a meaning.

And to nail there the subject of its passion.

Translated from the French
by Allison Schifani and Zeke Sikelianos

CHAPTER 13

The Language of Feeling Made into a Weapon: Music as an Instrument of Torture

Christian Grüny

Anyone who first hears about music being used as an instrument of torture will probably react ambivalently: on the one hand, he or she will be surprised that such a sophisticated and ubiquitous cultural practice can indeed be used for torturing people; on the other hand, this will immediately coincide with certain everyday experiences—isn't the hip-hop that the neighbors' son keeps blasting through the house or, alternatively, the awful dissonances of contemporary music a form of torture? This attitude is reflected in the reaction of a member of the American Musicological Society to a resolution of his organization condemning the use of music as an instrument of torture: "American students now have a precedent to decry 20th-century music surveys—with their compulsory exposure to headache-inducing cacophony and traumatic collisions of sonic debris—as academic torture."[1]

Apparently it is precisely these everyday experiences that lead most people to ridicule and trivialize reports on music torture. Blogs and commentaries are full of more or less aggressive reactions making fun of this phenomenon, and there are plenty of personal torture playlists containing names like Barry Manilow. The attitude behind all this seems to me to be the following: being annoyed by the neighbors' listening habits or by being exposed to the band one hates most may be called torture in everyday conversation, but of course that's not what it is. It may prevent sleep and work and cause aggression, but this certainly cannot be compared with a real torture victim's anguish. Consequently, this attitude claims, it can't be all that bad, and even if the euphemistic strategies of legitimation employed by the previous US government for practices like waterboarding are repulsive, to consider music as torture is clearly taking things too far.

When we turn to actual victims' reports, the impression is altogether different. Binyam Mohamed and Ruhal Ahmed, whose statements have been widely quoted, were both subjected to a combination of different forms of torture, physical as well as psychological. Both maintain that they found it less difficult to deal with physical violence than with the use of music—they considered the former more predictable and consequently less disturbing. These strategies apparently did not work with music, and both victims talk about their fear of going insane. While the unbearable pain in physical torture is always also directed against the psyche, music seems to take a shortcut, directly attacking the victim's sanity. Being subjected to this form of torture seems to amount to having to watch one's mind fall apart.

My questions in this context are how this drastic encroachment works and what this means for the future of torture: what is it about music that has such an effect? To answer this question, I first describe the context and the situation of its use and then try to outline a conception of music that is consistent with both our everyday understanding and the possibility of its use as an instrument of torture. My premises are that music is indeed used as music, not as a kind of arbitrary noise that is resorted to for the simple reason that it is readily available, and that what is being done really is a form of torture and not a comparably harmless discomfort without any long-term effects.[2]

Music torture is usually subsumed under the category of "psychological" torture. In an obvious way, this makes some sense, but I find it unconvincing in several respects. The methods so termed were devised by the CIA under the impression of the apparent efficacy of the Stalinist show trials. Years of research activity were spent in developing and testing methods that substituted for physical violence, gaining direct access to the victims' psyches.[3] Aiming directly at regression and trauma, these techniques are more openly "psychological" than simple blows. On the other hand, however, it is always the body that is subjected to extreme cold or heat and to sensory deprivation, forced into unbearable positions, and deprived of any chance to recover. Is the need to sleep psychological or physical? It is obvious that this alternative makes little sense. As we shall see, music poses similar difficulties.

For this reason I find the expression "no-touch torture" more appropriate, a phrase that was apparently coined by the CIA itself: a form of torture where the perpetrators don't dirty their hands or leave visible traces. In most cases these techniques are attractive for very simple pragmatic reasons. A security officer in Zaire (today's Democratic Republic of Congo) who, unlike his colleagues in many other countries, probably had to get by without CIA training, explained his reluctance to subject prisoners to a simple and effective beating as follows: "There will be scars, and then we'll get complaints from Amnesty International."[4] This matter-of-fact statement may sound cynical, but it seems to give a more realistic account of the background of music torture than the CIA's ambitious aims to psychologically reprogram prisoners.

Besides, direct physical violence seems to be as attractive as ever. In this light, Gustav Keller's assessment from his 1981 book on the psychology of torture appears erroneous: "Purely physical torture is losing importance. Psychological and psychiatric findings and methods are taking its place, planned and sometimes administered by white-collar torturers."[5] Even though the techniques that are usually termed psychological have indeed gained importance, there is hardly a substantial decrease in physical torture—Amnesty's complaints don't seem to be that effective, after all. Furthermore, it seems unlikely that most torturers who have added new methods to their repertoire of terror have really drawn on scientific research. The intuitive application of roughly described methods by lay personnel—rank-and-file soldiers in most cases—may do just as well. In the US army, however, even these have experienced a kind of basic torture training—as victims. The so-called Survival, Evasion, Resistance, and Escape Training (SERE) administered by the Joint Personnel Recovery Agency, an institution of the Department of Defense, trains soldiers to resist torture, giving them some firsthand experience. When the Secretary of Defense inquired of the agency in 2008 to what extent the techniques used in training could actively be employed, his question may have been highly unusual, but the ground was well-prepared.[6] Reports of actual incidents of torture in Iraq and Afghanistan show that in some cases CIA members—Keller's white-collar torturers—were involved, but not always. Responsibilities seem to blur among CIA, army, military intelligence, and military police, especially when seemingly harmless instruments like music are employed.

Unlike acoustic bombardment in general, music torture doesn't seem to be part of the CIA experiments and is missing from the "five techniques" that were used in the 1970s against members of the IRA.[7] Nor can it be found in the torture handbooks compiled by the CIA since the 1960s. In US practice it makes its first appearance in a memorandum issued by the commander of the US forces in Iraq, Ricardo S. Sanchez, in 2003.[8] Music now seems to come into play as an instrument that is readily available, whose employment is easy to realize, and which is considered so commonplace that it appears to be relatively harmless.

The contexts in which it was and is employed, however, are far from harmless. In the "black site" in Afghanistan, Binyam Mohamed was detained for months in a dark, dirty cell full of cement dust, where he was repeatedly handcuffed to the walls or the ceiling. Donald Vance, an employee of a security company in Iraq, was held in a cell cooled down to an extremely low temperature. Both report on being subjected to incessant music. If I focus on the role of music, this should not be understood as minimizing the impact of all these circumstances—in the case of Binyam Mohamed they probably would have been enough to drive him to the limits of sanity. Still, the particularly disturbing effect of music that the victims describe demands closer investigation.

The actual or supposed effect of music has several aspects I will consider individually. In some cases music really seems to be a simple instance of noise: the "five techniques" mentioned above include sensory overload by constant exposure to extreme noise, which the Royal Ulster Constabulary practiced successfully for years. In this context all kinds of sounds were used, as long as they were loud and annoying enough. From this point of view, the recent use of music may be attributed to the simple fact that it is nearly universally available: most soldiers are able to contribute suitable CDs and MP3s.[9]

In other cases, torturers rely on one aspect of particular types of music, namely metal and rap: the acoustic representation of Western male aggression and violence. Metallica, Rage against the Machine, and Eminem, artists in whose music this second aspect is particularly prominent, all found themselves on top positions in the torture playlists circulating in the media—irrespective of their political orientations.

The third aspect is a genuinely musical quality: its repetitive organization. This feature can be found in such a broad spectrum of music that the actual choice of music is probably fairly arbitrary. Still, if repetitiveness is indeed responsible for some of the most terrifying effects of music torture, it needs some explanation. In fact, to me it appears to be the most decisive aspect of music's torturous effect.

A fourth aspect relates to the cultural associations of specific types of music. This may explain why country music was repeatedly used to push Muslim detainees to their limits.

Lastly, there is the dimension of explicit meaning. In my opinion, this dimension figures primarily in the perpetrators' imagination, but is relatively insignificant for the victims: it may well be that Bruce Springsteen's "Born in the USA," with its seemingly blatant patriotism—the critical attitudes it expresses will hardly be perceived in this context—is particularly insulting to some people, but I doubt very much that its disturbing effect lasts very long. Moreover, using David Gray's song "Babylon" in Iraq because of geographic associations makes no sense at all. Rather, it seems to point to the unprofessional character of this type of torture, which needs no scientific support to be highly effective. I will omit the aspect of explicit meaning in my discussion because of its relative irrelevance.

It is as commonly known as it is significant that we can close our eyes, but not our ears. We can use our hands to block our ears, but even so we cannot entirely shut out the acoustic world. We say that sounds penetrate our ears, an expression we wouldn't use for the optical realm. More than the visible, the audible is organized around degrees of intensity, and it seems to imply a rather different relation between activity and passivity. Accordingly, Hans Jonas writes in his essay on the "nobility of vision," "In hearing, the percipient is at the mercy of environmental action, which intrudes upon his sensibility without his asking and by mere intensity decides for him which of several qualities distinguishable at the moment is to be the dominant impression."[10]

I note that his formulation is not entirely true: even though we cannot move our ears like our eyes, we can make choices among the audible. Were we not able to block out louder sounds in favor of quieter ones, we couldn't possibly have a conversation in a noisy place. This ability has something to do with the organization of the audible: in focusing on the specific quality of something that is acoustically perceptible, we *comprehend* it in a very basic sense. To isolate a particular sound from the mass of what is audible at a given moment, we have to recognize its quality, and if we want to draw someone's attention to a specific sound, we can't just point to it—we have to describe or imitate it. Language and music, as very distinctly organized, intended acoustic events, facilitate this kind of selective attention and add a whole new layer of meaning to the audible. To be sure, all of this is true only up to a certain threshold, beyond which we are completely at the mercy of the penetrating force of sound.

These features of the audible make music the only form of art that readily lends itself to be used as torture; it is hard to imagine literature, theater, or dance as instruments of torture. Film has a pervasive quality similar to that of music, but is not as effective in overcoming every possible perceptual barrier. The example of Alex's reconditioning in Anthony Burgess' *A Clockwork Orange*—and in Stanley Kubrick's movie—clearly shows this: in order to secure his exposure to the films he is being required to see, his head needs to be clamped into a vise and his eyes held open. Even so it's hardly possible to achieve the inescapable lack of distance that music imposes.

Besides this, the audible has another specific quality that probably stems from our phylogenetic heritage: what is heard is affectively charged, a quality that is largely independent of its actual volume. Undefined low sounds alert us immediately, and we can only relax when we've identified them as harmless. In this they are similar to something seen out of the corner of one's eye; the periphery of the retina is particularly sensitive to movement. Loud noises appearing unexpectedly cause a strong physical reaction that momentarily blocks out all other sensations. If a noise continues over a long period of time, it leads to lasting physical stress or even psychophysical illness, even if its volume is well below the pain threshold.

When people are exposed to sounds of extreme intensity and long duration, their ability to discern structures decreases. What remains is the impression that the sounds want something, that they make a vague demand to which we need to react, be it by directing our attention toward them and keeping them at bay cognitively or by resorting to flight. The testimony of one victim, Ruhal Ahmed, points exactly in this direction: "It makes you feel like you are going mad. You lose the plot and it's very scary to think that you might go crazy because of all the music, because of the loud noise, and because after a while you don't hear the lyrics at all, all you hear is heavy banging."[11] This "heavy banging" is not an event that can be apprehended in a neutral way, but is an assault calling for a reaction that can't be carried out. Still, it wasn't arbitrary noise that was used, but sounds of very specific kinds. Whereas in Northern Ireland high-pitched whistles or crying babies were used, where the sound's demand is not purely acoustic,[12] now torturers employ music. There are types of music that seem to embody this "heavy banging" particularly well, which brings me to my second point.

The title of my essay refers to eighteenth- and nineteenth-century music philosophy, with its depiction of music as a "language of feeling." Theorists and composers of the time assumed a natural correspondence between music and emotions that they tended to emancipate from the more strongly codified signification that formed the basis of the baroque *Affektenlehre* (doctrine of affects). This correspondence was supposed to be immediate and graspable without any background knowledge or formal training—a conception that is still familiar to us today. Music expresses feelings, or so it seems, and makes them comprehensible in all their subtle detail.

Richard Wagner's text on Beethoven gives a good example of this theory: "The Object of the tone perceived is brought into immediate rapport with the Subject of the tone emitted: without any reasoning go-between we understand the cry for help, the wail, the shout of joy, and straightaway answer in its own tongue."[13] The acrimonious discussion between supporters of this aesthetic and those of formal approaches like Hanslick's, with its polemical thrust against the "rotten aesthetics of feeling" (*verrottete Gefühlsästhetik*),[14] need not concern us here. Significantly, even Hanslick does not deny a close connection between music and affectivity (such a denial would not be very convincing), but limits the correspondence to the temporal shapes, the dynamic aspects of affectivity, excluding specific emotions like anger, love, or sorrow in favor of affective gestures like vehemence, tenderness, or subduedness.[15] For the time being, suffice it to note some general agreement over the "natural" connection between music and the emotions.

Positing this natural connection is immediately convincing in the case of Western popular music, where so much of today's music appears little more than a subtle (or not-so-subtle) manipulation of the listeners' emotions. Next to the blurry sentimentality of pop ballads there is another affect that figures prominently in several genres of popular music like Heavy Metal: aggressiveness often bordering on physical violence. This has little to do with the lyrical content, where Rage Against the Machine, with its coarse political stance, works just as well as Metallica (although I should mention that Rage Against the Machine was outraged that its music was being used for torture, while Metallica welcomed it, at least in some interviews).

Music like "Enter Sandman," a popular song by Metallica that was used by US torturers, allows for two fundamentally different attitudes: one can move into it, go along with it, and enjoy being moved by its force—which makes it a song suitable for being played in sports arenas—or one can remain outside it and experience it as a violent assault. Either way force is the central feature; for Jonathan Pieslak, this is the basic principle of Heavy Metal in general. The dedicated fan identifies with this force: "The music operates not as a dominating force over the fan, but as an empowering agent."[16] Seen from the outside, the violence of the music (and the often extreme brutality of the lyrics) remains just this: a dominating force.

Suzanne G. Cusick describes the experience as "being utterly at the mercy of a merciless, ubiquitous power."[17] Also, the fan's identification has some prerequisites: an affinity for this kind of music and an environment that is not in itself threatening or dangerous. Even so it must remain an intermittent activity, as even James Hetfield, Metallica's lead singer, admits.[18] None of this is the case when the music is used in torture contexts.

Keeping up a detached attitude toward this kind of music is hard enough for the casual listener, and it is completely impossible for the detainee in Iraq or Afghanistan. The effects of the sheer loudness of the music are aggravated by its gesture, its affective dynamics. The prisoner feels exposed to a violent, destructive assault that he or she has no way of evading. It seems appropriate to say that the violent force of the music is understood, even though this does not refer to a purely cognitive process. But there is continuity between cognitive understanding and physical reactions like acceleration of the heartbeat or surges of adrenaline. These reactions are aimed for, *meant* by the music. It reaches its goal not by its structures, but rather by its specific sonority: hammering drums, heavily distorted guitars, and a voice that is always on the verge of screaming.[19]

This kind of music, not surprisingly, is well represented on soldiers' iPods and in their CD collections. Testimonies from the second Iraq war show that soldiers use it, as Pieslak aptly formulates it, as an "inspiration for combat."[20] Obviously, leaving the base to face an unclear and often incomprehensible situation where they are likely to be attacked and might have to kill is not easy, and music by Slayer, Drowning Pool, and Eminem help overcome this anxiety. Discerning the difference between the emotional state of the musician, the expressivity of the music, and the emotional reaction of the hearer, which plays a prominent role in the philosophical debate, is hardly relevant here. As one soldier puts it: "When I needed to get aggressive, I'd put some aggressive music on."[21] One and the same music fulfills a double function: whereas the soldier uses it as a preparation for committing acts of violence, the prisoner experiences it as immediate violence directed against him.[22]

One might assume that music associated with Western male aggression is the only kind employed in this context, but this is not the case. On the torture playlists circulating on the Internet we find the Bee Gees, David Gray, and Sesame Street next to Metallica and Eminem, which I find extremely disconcerting. But before attempting to explain this phenomenon, I want to return to Eduard Hanslick and his arguments against Wagner's aesthetics of feeling. As I mentioned, Hanslick is not arguing against the connection between music and emotion. Rather, he categorically rejects an aesthetics that considers emotions to be the one and only content of music. According to him, the content of music can only be described as "tonally moving forms" (*tönend bewegte Formen*).[23] Obviously, this raises plenty of questions, but for him it created the possibility of a genuinely musical examination that doesn't rely on nonmusical references at every step. For Hanslick, music is "spirit giving shape to itself from within" (*sich von innen heraus gestaltender Geist*),[24] an organization within the sensible that in itself has mental character.

When he does concede that there are analogies between music and dynamic shapes of emotions, he focuses on the latter. These draw on the affective and bodily dimensions of hearing and the affinity of musical organization to our emotional life, which often endows musical pieces with existential significance. To understand this, we can turn to a concept that developmental psychologist and psychoanalyst Daniel Stern proposed. Stern assumes that the first weeks in the cognitive, emotional, and social development of the infant are dominated by the perception of dynamic shapes that are at once affective and kinetic. He calls them "vitality affects"[25] or, in a later text, "temporal feeling shapes."[26] These dynamic gestures, which seem to me to be exactly what Hanslick has in mind, structure the experiential world of the small infant. At this stage there is no distinction among the cognitive, the affective, and the kinetic, nor between the self and the other (even though the latter differentiation is, according to Stern, a product of these dynamic structures). In this sense, vitality affects are not perceived as objects at a distance, but rather as performed, and the gestural shapes of the parents' movements cause immediate resonances in the child. My thesis is that music functions primarily on this level, as well, and no matter how sophisticated its structures may be, they retain the affective and kinetic field of resonance of their origin.[27]

These affectively charged forms play a central role in Western tonal music: the cadence as the basic principle can be described as a taking off from and returning to an energetic center, a play of expectation and disappointment, tension and relaxation, and it is experienced intellectually, cognitively, affectively, and physically at the same time. Repetition functions as a kind of anchor facilitating orientation.[28]

This is true even for very simple music, where the basic principles lie on the very surface. How much complexity one is willing and able to deal with in music depends on practice and personal preferences. Music that is too complex for us sometimes completely bypasses us, but when we are confronted with music that we consider too simple, we don't just feel under-challenged—we can find it a nerve-racking experience. This kind of reaction would not be possible if we weren't involved on all receptive levels at once, from kinetic movement and affective involvement to intellectual comprehension, with the forms and structures that we hear. Our freedom to decide if we want to follow these basic structures or not is limited: the affective dimension of hearing and the organized form of music—provided that it is sufficiently familiar—join forces and constitute acoustic events that make demands so insistent that evading them becomes nearly impossible. The simpler and more repetitive the music is, the more insidious it is in this respect.

Turning to the "torture playlists," we find a song that is of such simplicity and manipulates the listeners' emotions so crudely that even among songs for small children it appears particularly imbecile: the theme song from the TV program *Barney and Friends*. Most likely, adults who hear this song will try to avoid having to listen to it again. Paying attention to one's own reactions, one might observe the response I described at the beginning: we might say that it would be torture to be forced to listen to this song ten times in a row, but of course it wouldn't be *real* torture. Those who live or work with children and thus have some experience in listening to children's music know how these songs force their way into one's mind, but comparing this nuisance with waterboarding or having one's fingernails extracted seems extreme. The composer of this song displays exactly this reaction: "It's absolutely ludicrous. A song that was designed to make little children feel safe and loved was somehow going to threaten the mental state of adults and drive them to the emotional breaking point?"[29] Yes, indeed.

Once again this is a very obvious case, and even though it leads in a different direction than metal and hip-hop, it is immediately plausible. Precisely the fact that the movement we find ourselves subjected to has a mental, intellectual dimension is what makes the song so nerve-racking. But still, this is not all. We still need to ponder the disturbing fact that some of the music that was used in torture was neither violent and aggressive nor as simple as this famous product of the culture industry's "children's department."

Take David Gray's "Babylon" as an example: there is nothing in this song that points to the possibility of its being used to torture someone. Apparently it was selected not because of any musical properties, but because of the superficial association of the title—in other words, its choice was completely arbitrary. It is a light, friendly, fairly interesting song that nonetheless works just as well as the previous examples. The question then is: are there any musical properties that warrant this kind of use?

Apparently these would have to be qualities it shares with countless other pop songs: it has a continuous, rather simple rhythm, it is catchy, even inviting, and it has a structure that is not too complex without being tedious. What's so terrible about all this?

Binyam Mohamed describes the use of music during his torture as follows: "There was loud music, Slim Shady and Dr. Dre for 20 days. I heard this non-stop over and over, I memorized the music, all of it."[30] The mechanism behind music torture lies hidden in these last words. For lack of a better description, Binyam associates the fact that the music has been burned into his brain with an activity he himself performed. This is very close to the truth. The mere fact that the music is playing over and over again would not be a problem if the mental-emotional activity of going along with it could simply be stopped, leaving just a harmless kind of background noise. However, extreme loudness, context, and the music itself all work together to make sure that this is impossible to achieve. At first the conscious effort to memorize the songs may have been an attempt to deal with them by appropriating them, as it were. By and by this activity is overcome by an inescapable force coercing the victim into reenacting the structures of the music, leaving him no room for anything else and making it impossible to keep it at a distance. Songs like David Gray's will not dissolve into "heavy banging," even after one thousand repetitions. They will remain organized, structured sensibility, and repetition will forge precisely this structure into a weapon.

This form of violence is exceedingly subtle. While the music of Metallica could be turned into the acoustic equivalent of physical violence, here it is the victim's own mental activity that becomes a means of torture. In a way this is a variation of the "victim's fight against himself,"[31] an expression Keller coined to describe passive methods of torture like hanging victims from their hands or forcing them to stand for hours on end—only here it is not the body's weight that becomes a cause of anguish, but the insatiable activity of the mind that is unable to fight off the incessant demand arising from the music, and to prevent the seemingly endless repetitions from being burned into one's memory.

The long-term effects of this no-touch violence appear to be exactly the same as those of physical torture. When the journalist Donovan Webster played David Gray's song to Haj Ali, who had been tortured with precisely this song in Abu Ghraib, to confirm that this is indeed the right piece of music, Ali collapsed. Moustafa Bayoumi reports in *The Nation*: "Ali ripped the earphones off his head and started crying. 'He didn't just well up with tears,' Webster later told me. 'He broke down sobbing.'"[32] The extreme loudness may have been what nearly made his head burst initially. But now the cause of his reaction is the music itself.

The whole repertoire of music torture is made up of pop songs with their continuous, repetitive structures. Considering this, then, it is hard to imagine a pop song that could not be used, while it is equally hard to imagine the use of a classical sonata with its complex structure and long dramatic curves. If contemporary classical music had been utilized, it probably would have been perceived as a mass of dissociated sounds, i.e., as noise, not primarily as music. But what was also missing completely is any kind of non-European music. Would music torture in Guantánamo, in Iraq, and in Afghanistan have worked if the music of the Egyptian singer Umm Kulthum, *the* musical icon of the Arab world, had been employed? If what I have argued above about the mechanisms at work is correct, the answer would have to be "yes." The fact that it *wasn't* used brings me to my fourth point, the cultural dimension.

Again, there is a very pragmatic reason for its lack of use: availability. While Metallica and David Gray were on most soldiers' iPods, Umm Kulthum most likely wasn't. Besides this, perpetrators place some importance on the cultural component, thus making country music the third genre besides Metal and hip-hop that played an important role in torture sessions. Like David Gray's song, country music is usually neither particularly aggressive nor exceedingly repetitive—its obvious association with US culture is what counts. This will hardly have made the torture more effective—if David Gray, Metallica, and the *Barney* theme song can be used, country won't make that much of a difference, but it does add another dimension. Even though almost any type of music will do, the victim remembers very well to what kind of music he was subjected. American pop or country music may be perceived as a symbol of worldwide cultural imperialism and hegemony, and as such be a target of hatred. In being used as an instrument of torture, its imperialist and forceful character is not denied, but, on the contrary, made explicit. Compared to this, the political stance of the respective musicians who may be highly critical of all this—like Rage Against the Machine—is of little importance. For someone who does not recognize these internal differences, the impression remains the same, and even the Dixie Chicks remain a symbol of American culture.

One aspect of a lot of pop music that was directed specifically at Muslim detainees is its blatant sexualization. Playing them songs by Christina Aguilera seems to follow a similar logic to draping women's underwear over the heads of detainees at Abu Ghraib or forcing them to masturbate in front of female army personnel. However, I have my doubts about the analogy. My guess is that, after prompting a reaction of disgust and resistance, the sexual content of the music has little specific effect.

More likely, the cultural component is hard for US intellectuals to bear (it should be recalled that I am writing from a German perspective). In the article quoted above, Bayoumi writes: "With torture music, our culture is no longer primarily a means of individual expression or an avenue to social criticism. Instead, it is an actual weapon, one that represents and projects American military might. Cultural differences are exploited, and multiculturalism becomes a strategy for domination."[33] It's not just that torture practices utilizing music discourage victims and others in their social and cultural surroundings from adopting a friendly attitude toward US culture (and Western culture in general). The fact that arbitrary examples of Western popular music can easily be turned into instruments of torture, regardless of the musicians' political attitudes and the internal differences so cherished by musicians and listeners, is in itself highly worrying.

This kind of torture in general might be called cultural torture. Elaine Scarry has shown that, in a way, torture always has this dimension, and the use of everyday objects amounts to a kind of recoding of the world of objects in its cultural familiarity: "The room, both in its structure and its content, is converted into a weapon, deconverted, undone. Made to participate in the annihilation of the prisoners, made to demonstrate that everything is a weapon, the objects themselves, and with them the fact of civilization, are annihilated: there is no wall, no window, no door, no bathtub, no refrigerator, no chair, no bed."[34] Now art as a mental-affective formation of sensibility is included in this recoding. It may well be that the victims will not be able to tolerate any kind of music after they have been subjected to this treatment, be it country music or the folk music of their home countries. Consequently, triggers for traumatic flashbacks are omnipresent in a world such as ours, which is pervaded by popular music. The more these triggers are generalized, from specific songs to certain genres or even to music in general, the harder it will be for victims to escape them. It makes sense that musicians take a stand against this form of torture (the initiative *zero dB* is an important example).[35]

In the end music torture is alarming because it is so easy to realize, because it points to the fact that there is little in the cultural world that cannot be utilized as an instrument of torture, because it seems to be hard to recognize it as torture and much easier to justify it as comparably harmless. What is particularly alarming is that for all these reasons, we are likely to hear more of it in the future.

PART FOUR

Declassifying Writing

CHAPTER 14

Romantic Poet Legislators:
An End of Torture

Julie A. Carlson

Worse than a bloody hand is a hard heart?

—Percy Bysshe Shelley, *The Cenci*

Percy Bysshe Shelley's concluding statement in *A Defence of Poetry* (1821), that "poets are the unacknowledged legislators of the World," affirms the centrality of the arts to social policy legislation for reasons that remain indispensable to the prohibition of torture in his day and ours.[1] Indeed, Shelley's formulation and the reasoning that undergirds it are unsurpassed in positioning the arts and humanities at the heart of a just society and suggesting how they are and why they must remain so. At the core of his defense, as is well known, is the primacy of imagination understood in both its aesthetic and moral dimensions as the faculty of approximation to the beautiful, a definition that receives fuller elaboration below. But I begin with his rousing statement also because it foregrounds what remains unfinished in his and subsequent efforts to achieve through the arts a more humane world: that one day the legislative authority of poets become acknowledged. Key to Shelley's view that poets should take the lead in social and political reform is the power of poetry to expose injustice, envision more perfectible states, and inspire humans to bring them into fruition by thinking beyond the "petty sphere" of self—understanding under the category "poet" not only all forms of artist, but also teachers, prophets, and spiritual leaders, enacting the root sense of *poiein* as cultural making.[2] The visionary nature of this project necessitates an impassioned defense of the efficacy of poetry at the same time that it directs attention to the defensiveness that often accompanies efforts by humanists to assert their usefulness and purchase on events of the "real" world.

The reality or realism attending Shelley's promotion of this faculty of approximation to the beautiful is not simply a debate within, or about, British romanticism. A major defense of imaginative practices as inaugurating the concept and fledgling reality of human rights has recently been remade by historian Lynn Hunt in *Inventing Human Rights* (2007). Portraying the 1948 United Nations Universal Declaration of Human Rights, 1949 Geneva Conventions, and 1984 United Nations Convention Against Torture as the outcome of late-eighteenth-century Anglo-European declarations of rights, Hunt argues that this entire history could not have been envisioned or effected without a redefinition and expansion of imaginative literary and visual culture in late-eighteenth-century Britain and Europe.[3] For the first time, the argument goes, imaginative practices enabled large groups of people to identify—and to *want* to begin to identify—with others who were unknown, and until then envisioned as profoundly foreign or hostile, to them, an aesthetic-ethical position usually termed sympathy or sympathetic identification that is attributed to Adam Smith's *Theory of Moral Sentiments* (1757) and brought to a final elaboration in Shelley's *A Defence of Poetry*. Part of a broader "cultural revolution" in ethical thinking occurring between 1750 and 1820 that, in James Chandler's description, "installed imaginative sympathy at the center of moral life," its emphasis on sympathy addresses moral questions no longer through a process of religious casuistry, but according to a logic of sentimental probability or what Chandler, invoking Smith, terms the "case of the heart."[4] Deeply aware of the highly circumscribed nature of the "all men" that these practices actually only included, Hunt nonetheless starts her investigation from what she considers a less self-congratulatory, present-oriented position. "How did these men," she asks, "living in societies built on slavery, subordination, and seemingly natural subservience, ever come to imagine men not at all like them and, in some cases, women too, as equals? How did equality of rights become a 'self-evident' truth in such unlikely places?"[5]

My desire ultimately to endorse the spirit of Hunt's argument requires that my defense of poet legislators confront more directly two sets of objection often leveled against the universalist promise of imagination by both contemporary romanticists and anti-torture advocates. One set asserts that the severe restrictions that attend romantic-era notions of "human" or the "sympathy" directed toward it severely qualify, if they do not invalidate, the humanism associated with promoting imagination. From romanticists, this objection finds its basis in the equivocal legacy of the abolition of slavery, a signal accomplishment of the period that nonetheless failed to grant full rights or humanity to the subjects it allegedly freed.[6] Contemporary anti-torture advocates object that this era is at best a prehistory to universal human rights on the grounds that, because such formulations were "neither global in their jurisdiction nor universal in their reach"—indeed, because they excluded the "vast majority of humans even within their own jurisdictions"—there was "no such thing as 'human rights' prior to 1948."[7] Another set of objections uses debates about romanticism to launch policy-oriented critiques of the idealist, impractical, and/or insubstantial tendencies of humanist, and especially literary, discourse. Here objections of left-leaning romanticists that the reign of imagination only shored up hegemonic power meet arguments by anti-torture advocates that eliciting sympathy is a pitiful substitute for the reality and force of law.[8] In what world *are* hard hearts worse than bloody hands? Or, even if they are in an abstract fashion, how would one litigate against them?

Such polarizing responses (ideal/real, theory/practice) are epitomized in the reception history of Shelley, which has oscillated wildly, but also period-predictably, between depictions of a red Shelley or a colorless, because ethereal, even angelic, Shelley, a poet whose works are too radical, too juvenile, or too incomprehensible to publish.[9] Revisiting the case of Shelley in contemporary discussions of torture is useful, then, for investigating why claims for the political efficacy of poetry provoke binary and defensive thinking (why "defences" of poetry? Vindications of rights?), a mechanism also highly visible within the Shelleyan texts (*Adonais, A Defence of Poetry*) and pairings of text (*Prometheus Unbound* and *The Cenci, A Philosophical View of Reform* and *A Defence of Poetry*) that have made him so deservedly famous and such a case. At the same time, the case of Shelley offers a poetic blueprint for safeguarding physical and psychological nonviolence that highlights what remains relevant and yet-unrealized about the capacity of Shelleyan sympathy to transform a cruel and inhumane world. To explore this, the second section of this essay focuses on his family tragedy, *The Cenci* (1819), the best literary treatment of torture in the period and one that is itself inspired by a "true story" of domestic, state, and papal violence in late-sixteenth-century Italy. One of Shelley's few avowedly popular works, literally framed by his most ideal and abstract work (the lyrical drama of *Prometheus Unbound* that, true to the myth, is also about torture), *The Cenci*, I ultimately argue, stages the inhumanity of torture by placing on trial the efficacy of sympathy to redress the most atrocious acts.

My point of entry, however, is the anarchist philosopher, political theorist, and novelist William Godwin (1756–1836), whose *Enquiry Concerning Political Justice* (1793) and novel *Things as They Are; or, The Adventures of Caleb Williams* (1794) for a time made him the most lionized radical thinker in Britain, the most famous of the New Philosophers, whose platform of rationalism, sincerity, and private judgment upended every social piety and provided a vehement critique of things as they are. Godwin also happens to be Shelley's primary mentor and eventual father-in-law, the man whose life/writings set the course and conditions of Shelley's lifelong confrontation with torture, injustice, and the adequacy of poetry to overturn them. My first section, then, explores Godwin's engagement in book 7 of *Enquiry Concerning Political Justice* (*PJ*) with Cesare Beccaria's *On Crimes and Punishments* (*CP*, 1764), the book long credited with galvanizing the movement to abolish torture in Enlightenment Europe. Doing so illuminates Godwin's indictment not only of torture, but also of the criminal justice system for itself perpetrating crimes against humanity that then occasion his ensuing defense of fiction and Shelley's defense of poetry.

Godwin v. Beccaria: The Justice System as a Crime Against Humanity

> Depend upon it that, wherever there are laws at all, there will be laws
> against such people as you and I.
>
> —William Godwin, *Caleb Williams*

Italian writer Cesare Beccaria has long been credited with galvanizing public opinion against torture and leading to its abolition throughout enlightened Europe. His *On Crimes and Punishment*, published in Italian in 1764, in French in 1765, and in English in 1767, is said to have been instrumental in achieving the revocation of provisions for torture in the criminal codes of Europe such that, by 1800, as Edward Peters states, they were barely visible.[10] Beccaria's impact on England is no less important, however one construes the claim that torture in Britain has never been legal; Beccaria is credited with having sparked the penal reform ascribed to John Howard

and the judicial critiques and innovations of Jeremy Bentham.[11] My interest in Godwin's debates with Beccaria is how it establishes the linkage
between anti-torture advocacy and the priority of courts of literature over
law in the achievement of justice. It also shows how Godwinian rationalism
is intimately tied, not opposed, to imagination and why perceiving this
close alliance is crucial to understanding each author's "heart."

Godwin references Beccaria's work on three occasions in book 7, itself
entitled "Of Crimes and Punishments."[12] The beginning of chapter 4
hails "the humane and benevolent Beccaria," the only time that this nine-
chapter investigation names a specific legal or social reformer in the body
of the text. Godwin's first reference (in chapter 3) approves the reasoning
behind Beccaria's objections to the least tenable of the three "objects" of
punishment, that of making an "example" of the criminal (the other two
being restraint and reformation), the object most often instanced when
justifying judicial torture.[13] The second begins with praise for the "humane
and benevolent Beccaria," but then demurs from Beccaria's claim that the
"true measure of criminality" is the "damage" or "harm" done to society
and that the "malefactor's intention" can form no measure of that harm.
Godwin objects on the grounds that demarcations between external action
and intention are not all that clear, as even "imperfect" legal terms sanctioned by "the most odious tyrannies" suggest (terms like "chance medley,
manslaughter and malice prepense" [*PJ*, 384]). More importantly, he states
that consideration of the consequences alone, by conflating situations that
are vastly diversified in terms of motive or intent, subverts the very foundations of ethical decision-making. "Shall we inflict on the man who, in
endeavouring to save the life of a drowning fellow creature, oversets a boat
and occasions the death of a second, the same suffering, as on him who
from gloomy and vicious habits is incited to the murder of his benefactor?"
(ibid.) To confound the two "subvert[s] the very nature of right and wrong"
and exposes "the Hall of Justice" as a sham (*PJ*, 385). Given this, Godwin
contends that ascertaining the "antisocial dispositions" of the offender
must form part of deliberations over the proper infliction of punishment
but, for reasons that Godwin ascribes with approval to Beccaria, determining the offender's intentions, or the intention of any person, is a near-
impossible undertaking. Even "moderate men perpetually quote upon us
the impenetrableness of the human heart" (*PJ*, 386).[14]

Both men being harsh critics of contemporary legal systems, the core of
their differences consists of varying evaluations of the adequacy of law in
general, and the criminal justice system in particular, to amend human
hearts. While Beccaria laments that the laws of any given nation lag "a

hundred years" behind its corresponding "stage of enlightenment and goodness" and devotes much of *On Crimes and Punishments* to exposing the corruption and class bias inherent in current legal practice, he does so in order to support the ideal of law and thus advocates reform of existing laws to bring them into accord with reason—laws should be "clear," "simple," consistent, impartial, and equitable (*CP*, 74, 104). In addition, in determining the principles on which any valid theorizing about crime and punishment is based, Beccaria contends that legislators must "consult the human heart." For "it is vain to hope that any lasting advantage will accrue from public morality if it be not founded on ineradicable human sentiments. Any law which differs from them will always meet with a resistance that will overcome it in the end" (*CP*, 10).

Godwin, by contrast but for some of the same reasons, advocates abolishing legal systems altogether. Precisely the desired results of uniformity, generalizability, and consistency that motivate Beccaria's proposed reforms produce a legal system that, according to Godwin, undermines the rationality that law is meant to safeguard and serve. An "enlightened and reasonable judicature," in ruling on the case before them, should have recourse to "no code but the code of reason. They would feel the absurdity of other men's teaching them what they should think, and pretending to understand the case before it happened, better than they who had all the circumstances of the case under their inspection" (*PJ*, 385). For "[t]here is no maxim more clear than this: Every case is a rule to itself. No action of any man was ever the same as any other action, had ever the same degree of utility or injury. It should seem to be the business of justice, to distinguish the qualities of men, and not, which has hitherto been the practice, to confound them" (*PJ*, 411).[15] Though Godwin too recognizes the synergy between support for law and public opinion, his insight into the insinuations of power makes him profoundly skeptical of the justice accorded to those deemed criminal on the evidence of ineradicable human sentiments. But the true fighting words come in the apparently self-evident verdict that Beccaria gleans from his consult with the human heart: "No man has made a gift of part of his freedom with the common good in mind; that kind of fantasy exists only in novels. If it were possible, each one of us would wish that the contracts which bind others did not bind us. Every man makes himself the centre of all the world's affairs" (ibid.).

Invalidating each of these assertions *is* the heart of Godwinian justice. Over the years Godwin's positions alter on several of the tenets affirmed in *Political Justice* concerning the transparency of truth, the relation of attachment to autonomy, the factuality inherent in fancy and imagination, and the kind of progress heralded in reform. Yet Godwin never adopts the position that humans are governed solely by appeals to self-interest or that psychological realism, not to speak of idealism, is served by allowing anyone—even a child—to feel justified in considering himself the center of the world's affairs. Put a different way, Godwin's unwavering commitment to the exercise of private judgment for every individual does not entail sanctioning the usual accompanying features of possessive individualism (private property, bourgeois family values, laissez-faire economics). One can even argue that it rejects most of the features that, according to George Lipsitz, undergird possessive investments in whiteness.[16]

The specific counter to Beccaria's dismissive view of fiction entails strengthening the ideal that Godwin increasingly sees as the precise work of fiction and the "philosophical work of fancy": crafting individuals who make decisions with the common good in mind.[17] Striving better to realize this ideal motivates Godwin's many socio-literary innovations, including his reformulation of character, attacks on domestic affection, strictures on mourning, and commitment to pedagogy, including running the business of the Juvenile Library and M. J. Godwin Bookstore. All of these projects have as their goal exorcising the "magic" of "the pronoun 'my'" by redesigning the fantasy lives of individuals so that they are less self-involved, more desirous, precisely within their sphere of discretion, of connecting to a larger whole (*PJ*, 50).

This general project relates to anti-torture advocacy through Godwin's emphasis on the special capacity of fiction to alter "the impenetrableness of the human heart" (*PJ*, 386). Godwin means this in two ways that showcase the proximity of reason to imaginative practice and his lifelong attack on the sentimental novel. The first emphasizes the cognitive aspects of fiction that make "romance writers" better suited than historians at predicting the future.[18] Variously termed by Godwin a "science of man," a probing of the "secrets of the heart," fiction writing makes human hearts less impenetrable by delineating the concatenation of cause and effect, motive and outcome in human activity and, in so doing, aids citizens in calculating the probability on which foresight into futurity generally, and the possibility of a offender "repeating his offence" specifically, depends (the likelihood of that eventuality being the only legitimate basis for punishment and, then, only by restraint [*PJ*, 387]). A second service concerns fiction's capacity to make people less hard-hearted, which in Godwin's rendition requires *altering*, not activating, "ineradicable sentiments" of the human heart in order to make the operations of sentimental probability more just.[19] Chief among the targeted sentiments are the domestic affections, long touted as the seedbed of one's humanity and of one's love for humanity but which New Philosophers like Godwin, Thomas Holcroft, Mary Hays, and, arguably, Mary Wollstonecraft view as the primary impediment to justice because of the ways that love for family sanctions self-absorption through the inculcation of love for one's own.

Beccaria too raises the issue of "family feeling" in chapter 26 of *On Crimes and Punishments*, one out of forty-seven chapters that otherwise treat more conventional aspects of judicial thinking such as "the obscurity of the laws," "the proportion between crimes and punishments," "of honour," "of duels," "of torture," "on setting a price on men's heads." The chapter specifies the habit of "regarding society as a union of families rather than as a union of persons" as authorizing "injustices" even in the "freest republics" and among the "most enlightened men," because through this habit the "spirit of monarchism" gradually "infiltrate[s] the republic itself" (*CP*, 60). For "the laws of the family" inspire "submissiveness and fear," teach individuals to "limit beneficence to a small number of people whom one has not oneself chosen," and demand "continual self-sacrifice to a false idol going by the name of the *good of the family*, which is frequently not the good of any of its members"—all of which laws "lead men to spurn the pursuit of virtue" (*CP*, 61). But whereas Beccaria's critique of family loyalty exists side by side with his appeal to sentimental humanism as the foundation for justice, Godwin views attainment of justice as requiring the eradication of the twin habits of viewing society as a union of families, not of individuals, and viewing love for family as the grounds of humanism of any kind.

Steven Bruhm has underscored the "curious mixture of rationality and sensitivity" on which Beccaria bases his argument for legal reform, by which the extreme rationalism of his claims that laws should be clear, simple, and consistent and that law should not consider the motives of the offender are undercut by his attempts to motivate legal reformers through appeals to their sympathy and outrage ("the groans of the weak, the barbarous torments . . . ought to have roused that breed of magistrates who direct the opinion of men").[20] He then traces this ongoing paradox in romantic-era fictional treatments of pain, whereby romantic authors including Godwin and Shelley find the community-building claims of sympathy undermined by the capacity of pain to shatter awareness of one's fellow in ways that make literal the felt "tyranny of pain" and thus reveal the body in pain to be "deeply untrustworthy" as a source of moral appeal. My interest is in how the presumed untrustworthiness highlighted by a "criminal" body in pain threatens apprehension of the legitimacy of the rule of law by those who are disenfranchised. After all, the legal history of torture shows that torture is viewed as necessary to establish the truth from categories of person deemed incapable of acknowledging truth and categories of body considered insensitive to pain. This legacy of abuse, what Colin Dayan outlines as the "history of cruel and unusual," is built into not only the law but also the sentimental probability that literature inculcates and that Godwin's fiction aims to undo.[21]

Caleb Williams (*CW*), as Jonathan Grossberg has argued, is Godwin's most thoroughgoing fictional critique of the criminal justice system, a novel that constitutes "an epoch in the history of law and literature."[22] It is useful for our purposes in linking its rejection of torture to a wholescale indictment of the criminal justice system and addressing both aspects of the impenetrability of heart that make the rendering of justice so difficult. For Caleb's case exposes the inhumanity of a legal system whose operations are so manifestly biased toward those in power that subordinated people lose all hope of having their truth affirmed or even heard. It finds even more objectionable the way that law itself nullifies every incentive to reform. As the noble outlaw Raymond explains to a fugitive, but fundamentally law-abiding, Caleb, "Those very laws, which by a perception of their iniquity drove me to what I am, now preclude my return. . . . They leave no room for amendment, and seem to have a brutal delight in confounding the demerits of offenders," for they condemn to death any person who commits a murder with no regard for "the character of the individual at the hour of trial. How changed, how spotless, and how useful avails him nothing" (*CW*, 203). Footnoting the historical case of Eugene Aram, who murdered a friend whom he suspected had committed adultery with his wife and, when the crime was discovered fourteen years later, was executed despite having subsequently led a blameless life, *Caleb Williams* indicts the legal system for actually undermining the incentives to perfectibility on which respect for law is ostensibly based. The persistence of Godwin's outrage over this situation is evident in his instancing the same case as forming the backdrop to his last novel, *Deloraine* (1833).[23]

In this regard, *Caleb Williams* enacts in a double sense Godwin's abandonment of courts of law for courts of literature by not only fictionalizing his political indictment of the legal system in *Political Justice* but also thematizing the transfer of venue in Caleb's rationale for writing and preserving his memoirs.[24] Caleb is clear that he is writing to a future jury of his peers who, through acquaintance with his story and others like it, will someday be in position to try his case without bias and through appeal to no code but the code of reason.[25] This is a significant rendition of Godwin's general defense of fiction, by which writing embodies the grounds for hope that things as they are will not always be as they are. But exactly this belief is tried through the final quasi-courtroom encounter between Caleb and Falkland that, in both the manuscript and published versions, places the grounds for this hope on trial. What is tried is whether the psychic structure of sympathy, in placing such asymmetric burdens on disenfranchised subjects, retains credibility as the route to justice. For disenfranchised subjects, the impartiality of that internalized spectator who represents the sentiments of the community is legitimately placed in doubt.

The manuscript version gives a chilling assessment of the dehumanizing consequences that occur to subordinates who attempt to speak truth to power. When Caleb pleads his case before the assembled gentlemen, "the consistency and probability of [Caleb's] narrative" prove no match for the consistency with which collective bodies deem the probability of veracity to reside in the privileged party (*CW*, 335). To the issue of trustworthiness ("Which of the two would they believe?"), Falkland adds the question of motive (*CW*, 336). What is the likelihood that an individual like Caleb has as his motive a truly disinterested concern for truth? To Caleb's assertion that he "stood there for justice. I observed that it was of consequence, in a degree beyond any thing they could suspect, that justice should be done," the assembled gentlemen reply that his motive is revenge, that he is clearly "out for blood," and that the "rapidity, perturbation, and vehemence" with which Caleb asserts his truth incriminates him (ibid.). "Do you believe you can overbear and intimidate us? . . . We have heard you too long" (*CW*, 337).

The swift silencing of a voice whose vehemence bespeaks the newness of its ability to make a claim is only one of the still-current strategies of power that this ending exposes. A second is its assessment of the effects it has on Caleb by which he comes to doubt not so much the truth of his story as the possibility that even the impartial spectator within himself would apprehend it as true. "Perhaps all men will reason upon my story as these men reasoned. Perhaps I am beguiling myself during all this time, merely for want of strength to put myself in the place of an unprepossessed auditor, and to conceive how the story will impress every one that hears it" (*CW*, 338). This recognition that even one part of himself would rule against himself if he could muster the strength to think from an entitled position is the "bitterest aggravation of all my sufferings" (ibid.). It results not only in bouts of insanity, which he suspects are drug-induced, but also in a total loss of hope. Indeed, the two are equated. A literal leave-taking of the senses, loss of hope results in a longing for insensibility and achievement of it. "True happiness lies in being like a stone. HERE LIES WHAT WAS ONCE A MAN!" (*CW*, 340).

The published ending, by contrast, deems "criminal" the yielding to this level of "despair," an indictment that the now externally exonerated Caleb levels at himself. "I am sure that, if I had opened my heart to Mr. Falkland, if I had told to him privately the tale that I have now been telling, he could not have resisted my reasonable demand. . . . I despaired, while it was yet time to have made the just experiment; but my despair was criminal, was treason against the sovereignty of truth" (*CW*, 274). Such reasoning, not to mention Falkland's response of throwing himself into Caleb's arms, has never felt very satisfying to readers who have just made their way through several hundred pages that depict the unlikelihood of such an encounter ever succeeding. And yet, this is the point, as well as serious challenge, of Godwin's advocacy of sincerity as the means to reform. Precisely *against all probability* the disenfranchised have to believe that those in power are at times capable of responding to appeals to their humanity. If they lose this faith, the transition to more democratic social arrangements will only intensify the thirst for blood that is the other side of the demand for justice. I take this to be the force of Caleb's self-accusation that, in despairing of the capacity of sincerity to access the basic humanity of the other, "I have been a murderer—a cool, deliberate, unfeeling murderer" (*CW*, 275). Conceding the improbability that Caleb will prevail is why he and we have been subjected to the preceding narrative and expresses the depth of the charge leveled against things as they are. Nonetheless, the trial scene is meant to demonstrate the necessity of still assaying the path of sincerity, even as it too, like the first version but differently, pinpoints various imped-iments to making such a trial. At first Falkland suspects that even Caleb's "expressions of liberality and sentiment" are merely a "pretence" to "give new edge" to his hostility. But ultimately Falkland "sees" Caleb's sincerity and, for the first time, is able to register the "greatness and elevation" of the mind of his until-then subordinate (ibid.).

Viewed in this light, what feels like the realism of the unpublished ver-sion's linkage of hopelessness to insanity is rejected as defeatist. One has to maintain hope in futurity or else it *is* better to be "a stone" or stoned (*CW*, 340). But realism regarding the unfair burdens placed on subordi-nated beings persists in two aspects of the published version's more senti-mental outcome, both of which acknowledge the partiality of the truth that such subjects are accorded. One pinpoints the rhetorical style most likely to convince those in power: not self-assurance, but humility; not vehemence and perturbation, but artlessness. The assembled gentlemen "could not resist the ardour with which I praised the great qualities of Falkland; they manifested their sympathy in the tokens of my penitence" (*CW*, 275). A second involves Caleb's loss of the conviction of his innocence once he succeeds at vindicating himself, which is connected to his feeling pity when he sees Falkland so "dreadfully reduced" (*CW*, 272). This unexpected change of heart causes him to doubt that, in pressing his case, he had in fact "determined impartially," "such as an impartial spectator would desire," with "a total neglect of the miserable suggestions of self-regard." Instead, Caleb comes to ascribe an "overweening regard" for himself as the "source" of his errors (*CW*, 271, 276).

Overweening self-regard is a particularly cruel indictment to level against a subject who has been systematically disregarded, and yet lack of self-regard, what Godwin elsewhere calls "self-postponement" or the capacity to consider oneself as a "rill of water . . . irrigat[ing] and fertiliz[ing] the intellectual soil," is essential to the attainment of benevolence, perfect-ibility, and decisions for the common good.[26] In vowing from then on to "think only of" Falkland and to place the memoirs intended to "vindicat[e] my own character" in the service of posterity's fuller comprehension of Falkland, Caleb's self-reform posits how to counteract the self-regard enjoined by the legal system's emphasis on self-defense. Nor does this effort require retracting his vehement condemnation of the "corrupt wilderness of human society" for the ways that its "rank and rotten soil" poisons the "growth" of every talent. Instead, it seeks to ensure that, by viewing the poisoning from the privileged perspective of a Falkland, Caleb keeps from imbibing the poison of despair or thirst for revenge that is more likely to accompany viewing it from a subordinate, and thus more structurally hopeless, position (*CW*, 276, 277, 276). By exercising *this* kind of sympathy, Caleb consecrates a truly "disinterested tear" to the memory of Falkland and is able to survive. Moreover, by understanding how Falkland too is conditioned by circumstances, chief among them how his having "imbibe[d] the poison of chivalry" and romance litera-ture in his youth eventually infiltrated his "most laudable intentions," Caleb comes to view Falkland as mortal rather than all-powerful and as limited by his situation. This is not an identification with power but with the fal-libility in all persons, which, in awakening sympathy for the circum-stances that distort virtue, puts the onus of judgment back on reason. At the same time, it sets the novelistic agenda to follow: making persons less hard-hearted by having ineradicable sentiments extend beyond love for one's own.

Shelley's Godwin: Changes of Heart

> Love is like understanding, that grows bright/Gazing on many truths.
> —Shelley, *Epipsychidion*

One of the darkest plays on record, Shelley's *The Cenci* pushes to extremes the legal issues raised in *Caleb Williams* regarding the corruption of (canon) law, the impartiality of truth, the criminality of despair, and the dehumanizing effects on subordinated subjects of knowing that every social institution, including the family and even language itself, is pitted against them. The play is Shelley's most searing indictment of the law of the father, and the collaboration it exposes among father, count, priest, pope, and God makes clear that, subject to such a chain of command, women have nowhere to turn when seeking redress for crimes against them. The sheer overkill of the Cenci story suggests that, in choosing to restage it, Shelley means to highlight the naivety and optimism that underlie Godwin's critique of things as they are in *Caleb Williams*, especially its portrayals of criminality. Crimes in *Caleb Williams* are truly no match for those in *The Cenci*, both in pitting a crime of passion (murder as a response to dishonor) against two fully premeditated crimes (rape/incest and parricide) and, within *The Cenci* (*C*), portraying the crime against Beatrice as triply unspeakable and thus by definition without any redress other than through the perpetrator's or victim's death.[27] The criminality of the perpetrators is also radically asymmetric. Whereas Falkland's and Beatrice's crime is portrayed as exceptional and wholly circumstantial, Cenci's crimes are multiple and the result of a hardheartedness that has become constitutional. As he asserts, a life of crime has "hardened" him and, as such, made him impervious to reform or the workings of sympathy (*C*, 245). Yet to view *The Cenci* as a critique of Godwinian optimism, or to find the antidote to its despair only in the extreme idealism embodied in its enveloping lyrical drama, is to misconstrue the Shelleyan refinements to sympathy that safeguard and deepen Godwin's recourse to fiction in his pursuit of justice. The retrial of sympathy pursued in and by *The Cenci* is fundamental to solidifying the hope for better days that underlies both men's philosophical approaches to reform, at the Shelleyan heart of which, too, is counteracting those "enemies of reform" whose "overweaning" self-love, in its tendency to confine "the human heart" within the "narrow circle of our kindred and friends," sanctions indifference to the sufferings of others.[28]

James Chandler gives the fullest elaboration in *England in 1819* of how this hope is secured through Shelley's historicist method in general and the

profundity of the threat to it embodied by the Cenci story and his dramatization of it. Central to perceiving a ray of hope is how *The Cenci* mobilizes
the "pastness of past cultures" (in this case late-sixteenth-century Italy)
through establishing two sets of parallel relations: past character to past
culture, in which Beatrice adopts the casuistic reasoning of her Jesuitical
culture in justifying her act of parricide; present audience to that past character-culture relationship, in which then-current audiences, by themselves
seeking the justification of Beatrice while feeling that she needs it, come to
recognize how casuistry produces "self-revelation."[29] In other words,
Shelley's play enlists the split consciousness of sympathy but expands the
split to encompass differences in temporal perspective occurring in the
audience. Evoking sympathy in contemporary audience members for a
flawed character in the past underscores how that identification entails
both recognizing the extent to which the motivations and actions of any
person are largely determined by their historical situation *and* apprehending the differences between their sets of historical circumstance as grounding hope in progress. Even more to the point, in recognizing that the
situation of a character like Beatrice is hopeless and her "efforts at self-
exculpation" are "a function of her helplessness," contemporary audiences
perceive what makes their cultural circumstances more propitious for eradicating still-existing forms of tyranny that *A Philosophical View of Reform*
outlines and that Shelley's recourse to theater is mobilizing them to alter.[30]
Those existing forms target with particular vengeance persons marked by
gender and race.

Chandler's second point is equally crucial: that we apprehend in this
characterization of Beatrice a "Godwinian account of her fate and her case"
and a striking resemblance in the "structure of action" and audience psychology between *Caleb Williams* and *The Cenci*. As he shows, Shelley explicates this psychology in his 1817 review of Godwin's *Mandeville* by way of
specifying the major difference between that novel and *Caleb Williams*,
which Shelley otherwise deems of equal, or *Mandeville* of superior, interest.
"Yet there is no character like Falkland, whom the author, with that sublime casuistry which is the parent of toleration and forbearance, persuades
us personally to love, whilst his actions must for ever remain the theme of
our astonishment and abhorrence."[31] This characterization of audience
reaction to Falkland applies even more fully to portrayals of Beatrice Cenci,
the "story" of whom has produced "national and universal interest" for
"two centuries and among all ranks of people" and the "tragedy" of whom
deserves "approbation and success" in its capacity of "awakening and sustaining the sympathy of men"—a degree of familiarity that makes more

probable Shelley's claim that restaging the Cenci story for British audiences provides a "light to make apparent some of the most dark and secret caverns of the human heart" (*C*, 239). Pursuing the recognized resemblance between Falkland and Beatrice Cenci uncovers Beatrice's less acknowledged resemblance to Henrietta in Godwin's *Mandeville* (1817), the novel that Bruhm highlights as delineating ongoing tensions between the rational and sentimental in depictions of pain. Bringing Henrietta into the picture deepens our apprehension of the indebtedness of Shelley's sympathy to Godwin's, still a weak spot in critical assessments of Godwin's influence on Shelley, which stems from entrenched perceptions of the former as rationalist and cold, the latter as imaginative and warm, even hot.

Two points regarding *A Philosophical View of Reform* foreground the impact of Godwin's sympathy on Shelley's. Its trial run of the concluding paragraph in *A Defence of Poetry*, which identifies poets as the unacknowledged legislators of the world in their capacity to apprehend the shadows of futurity within the present, is actually a rerun of Godwin's formulation in *Life of Chaucer* (1803) in which, by way of narrating and endorsing the shift in Chaucer's career plans from lawyer to poet, Godwin asserts that "the poet" is the "legislator of generations and the moral instructor of the world."[32] In this, Godwin portrays the canonical father of the English language and literature as modeling the shift in disciplines that contemporary justice now requires. Shelley's better-known version works from the opposite direction, by which poets offer as one of their services the capacity to produce an enlightened and reasonable judicature once a people's capacity to envision the future through the calculation of probability has been sharpened and expanded through analysis of literary character. Stressing this point is part of the force of the more Godwinian definition of poetry advanced in the 1819 *Philosophical View*—"meaning by poetry an intense and impassioned power of communicating intense and impassioned impressions respecting man and nature"—that is substantially altered in the 1821 *Defence*.[33]

Second, Shelley's promotion in *A Philosophical View of Reform* of a historically split consciousness is what Shelley claims in his review of *Mandeville* also to have learned from Godwin. There he states that Godwin's *Essay on Sepulchres*, which enjoins contemporaries not only to commune with the illustrious dead but also to perceive the dead as some of their best friends and most worthy interlocutors, reveals "*a mind that sympathizes, as one man with his friend*, in the interests of future ages, and in the concerns of the vanished generations of mankind."[34] Mandeville lacks this radically self-postponing capacity, and he ascribes the entire ensuing tragedy to his not having a friend in a passage that is a striking rewriting of the impartial spectator of Smithian sympathy.

> No man needs a friend, so much as he who is under the slavery of a domineering passion. A friend is like Time, the master of us all, or like boundless Space. He removes us to a due distance from the object . . . and makes us view it in the light, in which the generation yet unborn shall view it. . . . I can hardly describe to my friend the thing that torments me, in the wild and exaggerated way in which I view it within closed doors. What I deliver to him, is a compounded notion, made up partly of the impression I have myself entertained, and partly of the temper of his mind, and of my anticipation of the way in which he will regard the facts I have to relate.[35]

Recasting as friend the internalized spectator, whose impartiality toward nondominant subjects is legitimately in doubt, works to ensure that the character at risk is "assured of his love for me" and thus that the advice he proffers truly voices "the truth that my welfare require[s]."[36] To wit, bloodying one's hands in the name of justice is a "pernicious mistak[e]" that, however apparently necessitated by the array of circumstances stacked against one and the length of time that they have been so, violates the humanity of either party—meaning by humanity the noncontingent or immutable, but precisely not religious or transcendental, aspect of being: what Godwin calls sincerity and Shelley calls beauty.[37]

Here is where imagination as the faculty of approximation to the beautiful comes into play and achieves its ends, to the extent that its moral dimensions operate in concert with its aesthetic means of rendering less substantial, familiar, or fixed the features by which we recognize the human or its beauty. That is, fostering "an identification of ourselves with the beautiful which exists in thought, action, or person, not our own" means multiplying and depersonalizing the objects one loves along the lines specified in the short essay "On Love," which in turns entails keeping subject and object worlds mobile, fluctuating, shadowy, and disembodied—in a word, nonfixated (517). The markedly different stances toward love that Godwin and Shelley take (call it prosaic versus lyrical) should not occlude perception of their shared commitment to expanding the heart, an expansion that they facilitate largely through critiquing the types of relationship that reliance on sentimental probability favors. Each repudiates the ties of marriage, monogamy, and blood family, deeming them vitality-endangering constraints. Each evaluates living and the living from the point of view of the dead or unborn and from one's radical mortality.

Adopting the latter perspective is how they believe that oppressed subjects find some incentive to sympathize with their oppressor, the apparent invincibility of whose power is literally only a matter of time (the point of the pity aroused in Caleb at the sight of a Falkland so palpably reduced). Adopting the former requires an unbinding of love that is both cause and effect of justice.

Enjoining both perspectives is the essence of sister Henrietta's "pleadings" to Mandeville, which, Shelley writes, encapsulate "the genuine doctrine of 'Political Justice' presented in one perspicuous and impressive view" and embody "the most perfect and beautiful piece of writing of modern times." Stunning as praise, Shelley's account of Henrietta is equally noteworthy as a dress rehearsal for Beatrice.[38] The two female characters resemble each other in being initially "beautiful" beings, encircled by "a mist of dazzling loveliness which shuts out from the sight all that is mortal in [their] transcendent charms" until, through their succumbing to circumstance, they "'fade into the light of common day.'"[39] Moreover, Shelley's depiction of the nature of the circumstances that Henrietta should have resisted in order to remain exemplary suggests Shelley's highly distinctive approach to the moral virtue of fidelity particularly as it pertains to femininity. For Henrietta's flaw is a "divided affection" that keeps her "faithful there only where infidelity would have been self-sacrifice." That is, torn between love for brother and a fiancé who is that brother's archenemy, Henrietta suffers in a pronounced fashion the situation endemic to females in the family where, even in name, to move on is to betray. But by succumbing to the division, rather than affirming a higher unity through the multiplication of beloved objects, Henrietta "act[s] and feel[s] no otherwise than the least exalted of her sex."[40] Cause for "regret" in the (Shelleyan) reader, the outcome results in a work of fiction without "one gleam of light," useful insofar as it "enforces the moral, 'that all things are vanity'" and thereby better preparing readers for the "instability of our nature," but ultimately too despairing, perception of the gap between the ideal and reality of Henrietta's character "weigh[ing] like disappointment on the mind."[41]

Enter Beatrice Cenci to see if Shelley can better capture the "something" "vast" and "uncommon" "imagined" in "the original conception of the character of Henrietta" that embodies the essence of *Political Justice*.[42] The plot of *The Cenci* fuses the two most familiar strands of Godwin's inquiries, his attacks on the criminal justice system and on the domestic affections, issues kept separate in that text. As affecting the depiction of Beatrice, the issue is how ethically to respond to a father who not merely hates his progeny, but desires the total negation of their autonomy, figured most "successfully" not just in the act of raping his daughter, but the intention that motivates it: mastery of her will, "let her understand/Her coming is consent" (C, 276).[43] To imagine *this* portrayal of things as they are as more propitious for recovering the hope that Shelley finds wholly absent in *Mandeville* is a startling look into the imagination of Shelley. It invites Mary Shelley's question as voiced by Mathilda whether, in making a "tragedy" out of what is "dreary reality" for women, Shelley is "profiting" off of identification with suffering femininity that secures male power through rescue fantasies that screen from view one's actual indifference to others.[44] This remains a valid question, even if Mary Shelley's protracted answering of it ultimately exonerates Percy Shelley of the charge.[45] Worth defending in my view is the scrutiny that his embodiment of hope places on the aesthetic forms that imagination must deploy if it is to penetrate, not merely soften, hearts and avert the bloodying of hands.

Beatrice's own approach to hope is instructive, for she does not view the depth of her despair as reason to counsel abandonment of hope. Beatrice's parting advice to brother Bernardo, whose last-ditch petition to the Pope is rejected on grounds that aging patriarchs must be defended against the uprisings of youth, is "Err not in harsh despair,/But tears and patience" (C, 300). Nor does such counsel invalidate the wisdom or sincerity of her opposing conviction, "Worse than despair,/Worse than the bitterness of death, is hope," a sentiment often voiced in survivor memoirs that testify to the unbearable nature of dreams in making the reawakening to reality one of the greatest challenges to survival (C, 299).[46] What the formulation bespeaks is the necessity of rejecting false hopes (the "perhaps/It will be granted" [C, 299]) that thwart gaining clarity on the gravity of the current situation, the first step toward adequate reprisal. Better "plead/With famine, or wind-walking Pestilence" than with "[c]ruel, cold, formal man: righteous in words,/In deeds a Cain" (ibid). Despite their apparent passivity, what makes her final words neither empty nor casuistic consolation resides in the conjunction of the "tears and patience" that Beatrice advises. As the visible sign of sympathy and of the potential justice of its workings, the tears evoked from Cardinal Camillo, our first glimpse of whom in Scene One has him in league, if not cahoots, with Count Cenci, shows how far a patriarch can be moved under certain conditions. "Shame on these tears! I thought the heart was frozen/Which is their fountain," a melting that then releases him to "use my interest with the Holy Father" on Beatrice's behalf (C, 290, 293). Patience, the sign of hope that there will be a future, relies on the workings of poetry to penetrate more such hardened hearts.

In the precise way that *The Cenci* stages Camillo's emergent sympathy, we witness the placing of sentimental probability on trial. On the one hand, Camillo's capacity to perceive and mobilize himself on behalf of Beatrice's humanity speaks to the power of sympathy to prompt people, against all probability, to act against their self-interests. At the same time, the condition that triggers his sympathy has to be altered before arousal of sympathy is likely to serve those perceived as other: family resemblance. Camillo resists the Judge's order that "she must be tortured" because Beatrice resembles his dead nephew, who, if he still lived, "would be just her age; / His hair, too, was her colour, and his eyes / Like hers in shape, but blue and not so deep," and whom Camillo cannot fathom torturing (*C*, 290). Clearly a first step, the issue is how to keep this benevolent impulse from being the last, from remaining where perceived resemblance to one's own is the necessary condition of deeming the torturing of any body inhumane.

As a general rule, Shelley attempts to change the grounds of resemblance poetically by employing highly figural language and placing simile at the core of his poetry and conception of identity. This entails two interrelated epistemological moves: stipulating that what "thou art" is knowable only through what "is most like thee," and making what feels "most like" encompass radically dissimilar things.[47] His essay "On Love" defines love as a "bond" that "connects not only man with man, but with every thing which exists," including natural objects, concepts, and ideas, depicting it as a "powerful attraction towards all that we conceive, or fear, or hope beyond ourselves, when we find within our own thoughts the chasm of an insufficient void and *seek to awaken in all things that are, a community with what we experience within ourselves.*"[48] Forging such connections reprises that stage of infancy where "thirst" after "likeness" means making what is radically dissimilar part of one's own. It links individual and cultural infancy, where words are poetic because they are perceived as alive, magical, transformative. In more prosaic times, it explains the preeminence of poets as social reformers, since their arena is figures of speech, and thus they are the ones who refashion identity as and through the making of new connections. Their accompanying insight into the arbitrary and artful nature of connection-making is what makes poets ideal legislators. As William Keach demonstrates, Shelley's mastery at unmasking power by showing its arbitrary nature is intimately tied to his deployment of figurative language and language as figurative.[49] At the same time, what and how he writes avoids intensifying the despair that ensues when arguments regarding the arbitrary nature of power ignore or mystify its highly predictable targets and operations.

As Shelley's most avowedly popular work, *The Cenci* takes the opposite aesthetic approach, as Shelley scholars have long noted. Its form (theater), language (common, "careless," deliberately unpoetic), and protagonist (arousing universal interest) are expressly familiar, and *The Cenci* is the only work of Shelley's that is based on a well-known true story that is centrally about family. Shelley risks this popularizing for reasons that return us to Beccaria's contention that any law that differs from the ineradicable human sentiments on which public morality is founded "will always meet with a resistance that will overcome it in the end" (*CP*, 10). Shelley grants the interconnection between possibility of reform and state of public opinion, acknowledging that without adequate public sentiment, "reasoned principles of moral conduct" are as "seeds cast upon the highway of life which the unconscious passenger tramples into dust, although they would bear the harvest of his happiness."[50] Moreover, *A Philosophical View of Reform* stipulates that the time is ripe, in the senses that need for reform is urgent, near "universal consensus" exists regarding this fact, and the current state of poetic excellence suggests that nonviolent imaginative efforts will lead the charge.[51] I also believe that Shelley risks the popularizing of *The Cenci* to make a basic point about demands for familiarity: those rooted in love for one's blood family endorse as much as they counteract being out for blood.

Recognizing the resemblances between Shelley's Beatrice and Shelley's description of Godwin's Henrietta underscores the thematic endeavor to expose and reformulate the "great secret of morals which is love." Their shared resemblance to Godwin's Falkland showcases the "casuistry" that Shelleyan imagination works to activate in readers and audience members, which is the "parent of toleration and forbearance." Beatrice's difference from her peers suggests the aesthetic work still to be accomplished if we are to envision the achievement of more humanely habitable worlds. As the only dramatic character of the three, Beatrice is doubly embodied in being a fleshed-out character intended to be portrayed by actress Eliza O'Neil. Here the aesthetic challenge is mind-boggling: as audience member how to keep one's eyes on that "mist of dazzling loveliness which shuts out from the sight all that is mortal" in Beatrice's or Eliza O'Neil's "transcendent charms" while that woman is physically present. This question is related to the nature of her appeal. To what extent does sympathy for her depend on conventional rescue fantasies associated with beauty in distress? Or on defending the honor of daughters whose sexuality must be bound in order to keep their world or the world safe? Beatrice's difference from Falkland is discernible in the "restless" versus "sublime" casuistry that each is said to activate. Is this the residue of conventional disarticulations of women from sublimity, whose materiality is then doubled by the materials and materialism of theater? Shelley's recorded reactions to viewing Beatrice (actual and imagined) provide a lead into the divisions yet to be resolved by poets legislating in the cause of humanity. One route is highly conventional, whereby his viewing the (misidentified) "portrait of Beatrice at the Colonna Palace" evokes erotic tenderness for "one of the loveliest specimens of the workmanship of Nature," whose features are described in intimate, even voyeuristic detail—an approach to beauty that does little to expand the kinds of object that beauty allegedly encompasses (*C*, 242). Another is more disturbed, whereby the outcome of Shelley imagining himself viewing O'Neil's embodiment of Beatrice live on stage "tears his nerves to pieces." As it happens, Shelley is spared the actual vision because the arbiters of public opinion deem theater publics unprepared to tolerate such a dark view of what femininity suffers and refuse to stage his play. But Shelley's notion of poetic events keeps that vision alive until and so that audiences are formed to perceive it. Depicting as torture to a Shelley-like viewer the staging of torture of a woman is a step toward sensitizing audiences to the humanity of disenfranchised beings. By enlisting a then-outdated practice to remind audiences of their progress in humanitarianism, he mobilizes support for the further work to be done.

Coda: Torture Briefs

If recourse to torture in convicting Beatrice in late-sixteenth-century Italy is one of the circumstances that allow early-nineteenth-century British audiences to apprehend their progress on the score of humanity, what does the renewed applicability of such scenes say to us in the United States entertaining once again statements regarding the legitimacy or necessity of torture? Besides demonstrating the validity of Shelley's highly nonlinear view of progress, I wish to develop two interconnected thematic points made in *The Cenci* for what they suggest about how a Shelleyan notion of poetry strengthens compliance with international laws against torture— the right not to be tortured being the least derogable of all human rights. One takes off from the play's linkage of domestic violence, sexual violence, and church/state violence to questions of torture, especially its insight, not only that each type of violence resembles torture, but also that those categories of person most frequently victimized by sexual and state violence are the ones that the law initially found, and continues to find, legitimate to torture. A second explores the play's portrayal of the assault on truth and meaning-making systems that follows from the traumatic effects of torture. In Beatrice's words, "My brain is hurt; / My eyes are full of blood; . . . I see but indistinctly. . . . There creeps / A clinging, black, contaminating mist / About me . . . poisoning / The subtle, pure, and inmost spirit of life! . . . Oh, what am I? / What name, what place, what memory shall be mine? / What retrospects, outliving even despair?" (*C*, 261, 262, 263).

By connecting sexual domestic violence to state violence and portraying both as traumatic in their assaults on a person's memory, language, bodily and psychic integrity, *The Cenci* spotlights the inadequacy, not only of law, but also of language, to articulate the reality of subordinated subjects. It thus identifies two obstacles to maintaining faith in "the system" that legal positivists, in affirming the stakes for humanity of the rule of law, must ensure that their law addresses. The first relates to the fact that, from the perspective of nondominant parties, the law has been, and is, often out for their blood, and thus to respect it is to consent to one's subordination, if not dehumanization and annihilation.[52] In this regard, attempts to cordon off torture from other massive human rights violations can appear authoritarian-state-serving, even if its chief motive is the ability to litigate torture cases more effectively and to hold state authorities accountable for massive betrayals of trust.[53] The problem is not simply that the authority invested in men makes them the likelier carrier of the "spirit of monarchism," when not despotism, into the household, an authority that for centuries has kept rape, incest, and sexual abuse—what feminists now call intimate violence—a private, therefore nonlitigable, matter (*CP*, 60).[54] It is also that the history and ongoing legacies of slavery, lynching, and asymmetric rates of incarceration place men of color in a "feminized," sexually exploitable situation, a subject position with serious restrictions on the capacity to exert discernible agency, imagination, or revolt in the effort to claim their rights.[55]

This reality, which Darieck Scott explores through twentieth-century literary treatments of the sexual exploitation of black men, makes the interpenetration of torture, slavery, and sexual violence constitutive of the subordinate position.[56] The same set of interconnections prompts George Elliott Clarke to rewrite *The Cenci* as *Beatrice Chancy*, the drama of a sixteen-year old slave girl whose sexual violation by her master, who is also her father, impels her to commit parricide, for which she is hanged.[57] Put a different way, those on the receiving end of slavery, rape, incest, or torture are often linked through a linguistic and graphic vocabulary that feminizes and eroticizes them in the moment and in the representation of their abuse.

As the judge puts the question (in both senses) to one of Beatrice's hired assassins, "Dare you, with lips yet white from the rack's kiss/Speak False? Is it so soft a questioner,/That you would bandy lover's talk with it/Till it wind out your life and soul?" (*C*, 289). In light of these realities, liberal concepts of rights serve authoritarian purposes to the extent that their "masculinity" refuses or denies penetrability.

A second obstacle is the "false speak" elicited by torture that raises the larger question of the adequacy of language to truth, especially as experienced by marked subjects. Epitomized by the historical euphemism for torture (the question), which is literally unanswerable on several levels, *The Cenci* thematizes problems of language in emphasizing the "unspeakability" experienced by victims of rape/incest. This unspeakability is multiple: in addition to the severe reduction in speech ability that attends any body in pain are the facts that to name the crime is to render "one's name a byword" because of the then-premium on chastity as the site of any woman's integrity and, to the extent that the experience proves traumatic, the accuser is not "present" to the event to which she must testify.[58] Trauma studies are the domain in which literature makes the largest, and most acknowledged, contribution to universal human rights by providing witness to these abuses, both through narrative, fact-fictional testimonials and by devising new words to better bespeak the kind of truth that is adequate to courts of law *and* to survivors of torture and trauma. A case can be made for Godwin's and Shelley's pioneering efforts in both these arenas, especially in Godwin's clarity on the fact value of fiction and Shelley's insight into how figuration keeps language vital. I want to close, however, by delineating how their engagement with sentimental probability—with how literature affects a *culture's* ability to imagine difference differently—sets the agenda for contemporary poet-legislators against torture. What precisely do they contribute to Gayatri Spivak's recent brief for the humanities as training people in the "uncoercive rearrangements of desire" that are the only means through which to "remove the binary" that sustains a dehumanizing approach to anti-terrorism?[59]

One thing they contribute is a continual effort to defamiliarize the familiar. Affirming that the familiar *is* coercive to the extent that it does not open out into other possibilities, their work begins by critiquing the family and the familiar strategy by which authors attempt to showcase the humanity and singularity of the other (slave, woman, Muslim, terrorist) through emphasizing their identities as mother, father, wife, son—a strategy that Godwin and Shelley view as producing a sentimentalism that barely masks its thirst for blood. At the same time, their writings demonstrate that moving beyond the familiar is no easy matter, nor does it justify trampling on one's familiars in taking heroic leaps into the unknown. Here I find Caleb's concluding approach to Falkland, wherein he vows to devote his self-justifying memoir to exonerating the memory of Falkland, a useful model for how to rearrange desire uncoercively. What keeps this decision to think from the perspective of his former enemy from being an identification with his oppressor is that what Caleb identifies, and identifies with, is the fact of mortality as limit for all beings, even the most powerful, and thus a potential source of alliance and patience[60]—patience both with the current blind spots of the powerful, who have been formed on a literary-cultural tradition that, until recently, has portrayed only their values, mindsets, and perspectives as meaningful, and patience until literature, by depicting the dreams and realities of those not yet represented, effects their eventual political enfranchisement and sustains the long meanwhile through pleasure. To the counterclaims that recognizing the weakness of the powerful does nothing to alter their current power or that thinking in relation to them is all too familiar and difference-evacuating come Shelley's shape-shifting means of perpetuating hope by defamiliarizing it.

To see this, we need a quick look at Shelley's ballad-style poem *The Mask of Anarchy*, written also in the composition period of *The Cenci*. Composed in Italy in the wake of news of the Peterloo Massacre, in which Manchester militia charged into a peaceful crowd of workers attending a rally in support of Parliamentary reform in which at least six persons were killed and more than eighty were wounded, *The Mask of Anarchy* brings up to the moment the circumstances for despair delineated in Shelley's tragedy set in sixteenth-century Italy. Indeed, at the beginning of this poem, the "maniac maid" Hope is in such despair that she is preparing to let herself be trampled to death by the forces of Anarchy that are named as government officials ("I AM GOD, AND KING, AND LAW!") because her father, Time, is "tired of waiting for another day." As it turns out, "a mist, a light, an image" intervenes and the next thing we see is Hope alive, Anarchy dead, and we hear a voice speaking as if from Mother Earth about the conditions of the people's transformation.[61] Lest this sound merely like magical thinking, where cause and effect are inverted at the expense of the iron logic of history, we should recognize how the poem's deployment of one trope, simile, *effects* in two different ways the transformation that the narrative is delineating. On the basic level, the most rousing call for the solidarity of the oppressed—the only stanza that is repeated in the poem and as its concluding stanza—occurs through simile: the people are to "rise like lions after slumber" and "shake their chains to earth like dew/Which in sleep has fallen on you/Ye are many, they are few" (lines 151–56, 368–72). Though still apparently magical, especially in understating the problem, envisioning chains as dew places the "falling" of them outside human agency and of vindictively preferential treatment, thereby obviating a thirst for revenge, except against nature. At the same time, it suggests the people's potential for agency and responsibility (even that those chains fell when, and arguably because, they were sleeping), a rousing and arousing that the ensuing verses channel by encouraging "the many" to now congregate in open spaces, pronounce themselves free, keep their words sharp as targes and their hands free of weapons, and include within the ranks of the many all those receptive to the cries of suffering—in other words, criteria not of identity, but aural and moral sensitivity.

On a deeper level, solidarity with the many, whose ultimate goal is the oneness of all persons, occurs through a psycholinguistic process that simile enacts in theory and practice. By rendering perceptible "the before unap-prehended relations between things," simile approximates the beautiful by forging connections between all manner of persons and things.[62] Moreover, simile makes its connections through using what is familiar to make what is unfamiliar less incomprehensible and frightening. In this regard, know-ing what "thou art" through "what is most like thee" is a demand not for conformity or resemblance to the questioner (the "what is most like me"), but for imaginative ingenuity in finding what is common to the most appar-ently unlike, and unlikeable, things. And it is artful, even while being the most basic and familiar of the tropes, akin to childlike wonder, curiosity, delight in surprise and in stringing things together.

Both aspects of simile, its solidarity-building and solidarity-enhancing properties, are tied in *The Mask of Anarchy* to an explicit platform of non-violence. Even when "the few" come to mow down the many, the many must fold their arms and rely on the future that is *being created through* the persuasive power of their words, which will only remain "oracular" to the extent that they are free of blood. Here is where *The Mask of Anarchy* joins *The Cenci* (and *Prometheus Unbound*) in countering anti-torture legal real-ists whose promotion of law includes turning its capacity for violence back onto state officials who perpetrate torture. As Lisa Hajjar writes, "[t]he violence of law is a *good* that is underappreciated and under-theorized by progressive scholars" that should be mobilized to penalize, punish, disem-power, and terrorize rights violators, thereby "crushing the conditions in which impunity thrives."[63] While Shelley deeply sympathizes with the logic that motivates this position, stating in *A Philosophical View of Reform* that "so dear is power that the tyrants themselves neither then, nor now, nor ever, left or leave a path to freedom but through their own blood," he refuses to condone violence as an inherent part of a vision of law.[64] In his view, activating desires for revenge makes the power sought by those oppressed by power repeat the tyranny that they are asserting their power to resist.

The Cenci dramatizes this reality in the "contaminating mist" that envelops Beatrice once her violent act against Cenci causes a resemblance between them from which it is difficult, if not impossible, to break free (*C*, 262). The master's tools will never dismantle the master's house. Not that *The Cenci* equates Beatrice's crime with the crimes of her father, but it forges an unapprehended connection between convictions of purity and evil in justifying the taking of law into one's hands. This is hardly to cultivate sympathy *for* oppressors like Count Cenci, and thus by implication for the Cheneys of the world—instead, it arouses sympathy for those who resort to violence because circumstances are experienced as thwarting the perception and enactment of their essential benevolence, but also holds them accountable for it. One can question the usefulness of featuring such improbably ideal characters as a Falkland or Beatrice, but one should also see that through cultivating audience identification with them Shelley expresses sympathy with the character of his audience. For the question being pursued is how to mobilize a people's need, and right, to hold those in authority accountable for their acts without activating within individuals a thirst for blood. Being out for blood, even of the most bloodthirsty characters, damages one's humanity. The kind of world produced in succumbing to that thirst is part of the illumination still sought through the restless casuistry of Shelley's intertwining of torture and domestic tragedy. One should not have to imagine one's own mother or nephew being tortured for one to find oneself moved to take a position against such acts.[65]

CHAPTER 15

The Fine Details:
Torture and the Social Order

Darieck Scott

[N]ecessary limitations on the aesthetic presentation of what the body may undergo, either in pleasure or in suffering, immediately and *a priori* restrict what the mind is allowed to contemplate: For nothing encourages the practice of political torture and sabotages the pursuit of happiness more than blanket restrictions on speaking, in precise, articulate, and graphic terms about either.

—Samuel R. Delany, "Pornography and Censorship"

Samuel R. Delany makes the comment above in a discussion of how he—a prolific author whose work spans a number of genres, including literary fiction, science fiction, fantasy, memoir, literary and cultural criticism, and erotica—had immense difficulty trying to publish his novel *Hogg*, a pornographic work that depicts violence, sexual torture, and rape, including of children. *Hogg* was completed in 1973; it first saw print in 1995, though it was, for periods of time during that twenty-two-year span, under consideration (and repeatedly rejected) by various publishers. Delany's comment specifically concerns *Hogg*'s content, which I intend to examine below, but what interests me is his larger claim: that censorship of representations of the suffering (and pleasure) of human bodies—here, within the genre of pornography—is directly related to the practice of political torture. I cannot devise a good way to definitively test this proposition in an essay and suspect it might prove challenging to investigate even in a book-length sociological treatise; in lieu of such an investigation, my aim in this essay is to meditate on some of the ways Delany's claim may be true and to speculate about how the history of his novel's rejection and neglect illuminate aspects of recent public debates about US torture of detainees.

There is a link in recent public discourse between the tortures conducted against prisoners in so-called "black sites" under the aegis of the Bush administration and the secrecy around, and censored information about, those tortures. We might expect that link to be that prisoners were tortured under orders from high administration officials and that this fact was largely concealed by those responsible—and this is arguably to some extent the case: For example, Mark Danner notes that when former Vice President Dick Cheney took to the airwaves to defend the Bush record after the Obama administration announced its intention to close Guantánamo prison and vowed that it would not countenance torture as a response to terrorist threats, Cheney was able to draw from a depressingly deep well of mute public tolerance for invoking secrecy to justify national security policies. Torture, Cheney insisted, produced vital intelligence that prevented terrorist attacks. Says Danner, "Cheney's story is made not of facts but of the myths that replace them when facts remain secret: myths that are fueled by allusions to a dark world of secrets that cannot be revealed."[1] Further, "Barack Obama may well assert that 'the facts don't bear [Cheney] out,' but as long as the 'details of it' cannot be revealed 'without violating classification,' as long as secrecy can be wielded as the dark and potent weapon it remains, Cheney's politics of torture will remain a powerful if half-submerged counter-story, waiting for the next attack to spark it into vibrant life."[2]

But this familiar grid of relations between torture and public discourse, which would seem to buttress the simplest reading of Delany's claim with respect to torture and permissible art, itself conceals the fact that one of the more disturbing aspects among many regarding this matter is that public information about the Bush tortures has *not* been censored, at least not consistently, as Danner persuasively argues. The relation between censorship and the practice of torture is not nearly as transparent as a cause-and-effect or mutual-reinforcement mapping of it suggests. (It's also the case that the simplest reading of Delany's claim obfuscates *its* meaning—but more on that later.) Cheney's argument tries to throw a shroud of secrecy over the effectiveness of torture (whether it produces actionable intelligence), not the fact that torture happened or the methods by which it was conducted. If we view the torture of terror suspects and the public discussion of torture-as-policy over time, it's possible to see that, as Danner puts it, "The first paradox of the torture scandal is that it is not about things we didn't know but about things we did know and did nothing about."[3] Danner observes that the last known time American officials waterboarded a detainee was in 2003, and that the American public was first told that this had happened in a May 13, 2004, *New York Times* article. "[T]hough some of the details provided—and officially confirmed for the first time—in the ICRC [International Red Cross] report [on torture of detainees, confidentially prepared in 2007, publicly released in 2009] are new . . . one can't help observing that the broader discussion of torture is by [2009] . . . in its essential outlines nearly five years old, and has become, in its predictably reenacted outrage and defiant denials from various parties, something like a shadow play."[4]

As a riposte to the political appeal of Cheney's fear-mongering arguments, and as a move toward beginning to shoulder our collective responsibility as US citizens for the torture of detainees, Danner calls for not only a searching, credible inquiry into torture and the policy machinery that decreed it, but an empirical assessment of whether in fact the practice of torture interrogation leads to information that actually protects the public. Danner firmly suspects, or more than suspects, that torture does not provide such information, but thinks this inquiry is nonetheless a political necessity: "What is lacking is not information or revelation but political credibility. What is needed is not more disclosures but a broadly persuasive judgment . . . on whether or not torture made Americans safer." And: "The only way to defuse the political volatility of torture and to remove it from the center of the 'politics of fear' is to replace its lingering mystique, owed mostly to secrecy, with authoritative and convincing information about how it was really used and what it really achieved."[5] Again, the mystique and secrecy have to do with what torture does for the torturer, not what it does to the tortured or the simple, brutal fact of its being conducted.

A humanist inquiry about censorship's relation to torture is unlikely to provide much by way of an assessment of whether intelligence gleaned under torture is actionable or not, but the political jockeying that frames questions of torture's effectiveness and responsibility for it as a "scandal" does address in an oblique way other kinds of questions for which a humanist perspective can give us some guidance. Danner concludes that public discussion of the scandal, which has heretofore not been treated as a scandal, though its lineaments were well-known, "cuts to the basic question of *who we are as Americans*, and whether our laws and ideals truly guide us in our actions or serve, instead, as a kind of national decoration to be discarded in times of danger"[6] (emphasis added).

Who are we indeed? The content of Delany's *Hogg*, and the two-decade history of its publication woes, which were in effect, as Delany contends, an elongated act of commercial (and cultural) censorship, provide such a mirror of our ideals and "who we are" in relation to the "scandal" of torture, one that is as "precise, articulate, and graphic" as the novel's disturbing content. The image revealed therein, though adorned by the quirky beauties of Delany's prose, is ugly.

Hogg's unnamed narrator is an eleven-year-old boy who willingly becomes the sexual slave of a violent truck driver named Franklin Hargus (a.k.a. Hogg). The narrator delights in sucking on Hogg's penis and other appendages, and in drinking his urine and playing with or eating his feces—all more or less standard sexual fare in Delany's erotica. The plot in the early part of the narrative tracks Hogg doing his work as a "rape artist": men, and apparently some women, hire Hogg to rape and terrorize women (and their family members) against whom they have a grudge. Hogg leads a small group of helpers, and as a tag-along the narrator becomes an observer and facilitator of Hogg's work, seeking his own sexual satisfaction through fellating or otherwise assisting Hogg and his fellow hires as they rape and beat their victims. At one point one of the gang members who's been invited to join in the violence, Denny, a voraciously horny teenager, decides to relieve the discomfort of his perpetual erection by performing an impromptu Prince Albert on himself. Having failed to sterilize the nail he uses to do the piercing, Denny becomes increasingly maddened by the pain (and very likely by the infection), and goes on a murder spree. Meantime the narrator takes a detour with two of Hogg's comrades to Crawhole, a dock area, where the two men briefly sell him to a fisherman, a carelessly brutal character who also keeps his twelve-year-old daughter as a sex slave. Denny, wandering about the town causing mayhem, brings his murder spree to Crawhole, where he kills two of the narrator's new acquaintances and their young child, and is in imminent danger of being caught by the police. Hogg arrives and helps both him and the narrator escape Crawhole. Hogg releases Denny to continue his murders as he sees fit, and then proposes to the narrator that they spend some time together in a small community somewhere in the woods. The invitation sounds a romantic note of settling-down-into-coupledom, though what Hogg envisions is chaining the narrator up near the outhouse so that no one actually has to use the facilities. The narrator seems to assent to this plan, but at the novel's end actually is busy plotting his return to Crawhole, and to two randy boatmen he met there who seem a better sexual match for him than Hogg.[7]

Hogg tends to be categorized as a pornographic work. Pornographer Maurice Girodias, when deciding against publishing it, wrote an explanatory note to Delany in which he said, "'*Hogg* is the only novel in my career that I have declined to publish *solely* because of its sexual content.'"[8] The bare-bones summary I've given may suggest something of the sexual content Girodias found objectionable, which is, just as we'd expect in pornography, front-and-center and explicit. But *Hogg* is significantly unlike Delany's earlier pornographic work *Equinox* (originally published as *The Tides of Lust* in 1973), and unlike the porn novel that he published later, *The Mad Man* (1995). Though there are currents that flow through all three texts, what distinguishes *Hogg*—and what makes it useful, I think, for a humanist consideration of questions surrounding torture—is its nearly relentless depiction of violence: There is as much of characters doing physical harm to others (primarily women and children) in the book as there is of characters doing one another sexually—and the latter, too, is frequently written to emphasize the violent aspects of sexual acts, since apart from taking singular joy in the excretions of the male body (sweat, urine, feces, and even blood), the narrator is aroused by, and interested in, men dominating him or *using* his body (and the bodies of others, like the female rape victims) for their own pleasure without much attention being paid to his (or, of course, to their victims') pain.

One example: "She ran down the alley, screaming."[9] This is the first line of the novel's second chapter and the first time we see Hogg—fittingly, by the lights of the sentence, we do not yet see *him*, but behold instead the effect he has, like the camera-view of a woman's bobbing backside and the soundtrack of screams familiar to us in the opening of so many monster movies. Hogg's initial appearance finds him engaged in his hired work. He catches the fleeing woman; she pleads not to be hurt, desperately offers to "'give it . . . any way you want it'" (31), and tries to appeal to sympathies Hogg doesn't possess, telling him that she has two children she needs to support and if he hurts her she won't be able to work and she'll lose her job, which would harm the children. In answer Hogg rips her skirt, punches her and knocks her around, forces his penis into her, and afterwards, when she complains that she can't walk and that he "tore" something, he kicks her hard in the stomach, apparently for fun (34). The sexual content of this first act of rape artistry—Hogg's penetration of the woman—is related in at most four sentences, in one of the twenty-odd paragraphs of various sentence lengths that describe Hogg's actions and the woman's responses. The rest recounts punches, kicks, ripping, and screams. (My description of course leaves aside the question of whether or not rape should be characterized as "sexual" at all, as opposed to purely an act of violence, but since this is a work of pornography I think we can provisionally count the penetration as having some sexual resonance.) The narrator, to whom we've been introduced in the previous chapter, where it's clear that others like to sexually use him and he likes being sexually used, witnesses this rape and brutalization. Hogg spies him watching and, like nearly every other man who comes across the boy in the novel, recognizes the boy's sexual interest in him. Hogg threateningly demands a blowjob ("'You wanna come over here and get it? Or maybe I'm gonna come over there and fuck your head off . . .?'" [33]), then urinates in the boy's mouth and on his face and shirt, and proceeds to spit in the narrator's face (which gives them both pleasure): these elements comprise the most fully described *sex* in the scene, taking place over eleven paragraphs, as we become acquainted, through the narrator's eyes and nose, with Hogg's physical attributes (blond and large) and pungent impressiveness ("He smelled like a stopped toilet-stall, where somebody had left six months of dirty socks, in the back of a butcher shop with the refrigeration on the blink, on fire" [33]—one of the funnier lines in a novel where there are, perhaps surprisingly, more than a few). Afterward Hogg tells the narrator, "'I think I'm gonna keep you around awhile. . . . That bitch back there was work . . . but you and me are gonna have a little fun'" (35). The distinction between "work" and "fun" is by no means stark in this first encounter, and as Hogg's categories for, one, violence and rape in which he delights, and two, violent, often abusive sex in which both partners delight, the terms challenge the reader to pay attention to the ways the acts and their meanings converge and diverge. Hogg and the narrator are together by mutual choice, but Delany does not allow "choice" and "consent" to have simple and thereby soothing significance: the fact that Hogg is a violent adult rapist and the narrator a sexually curious eleven-year-old fascinated by violence, and that this is not a relationship of safety even though it appears in erotic fantasy, is evident when Hogg affably lets the narrator know that if he hadn't happily complied with Hogg's sexual demands, Hogg would have killed him. And this is one of the milder scenes involving Hogg.

This is not to say that the text is not properly categorized as pornographic, or that *Hogg* might be better described along the lines of what speculative fiction writer Sherri S. Tepper, in her novel *Beauty*, calls "horroporn," an evocative coinage that gets at how the torture, suffering, and dismemberment of bodies in conventional slasher movies comprise the thrill of such horror entertainment, and *is* sexual, in the sense that visceral human enjoyment is rarely experienced without some reference to sexuality. *Hogg* does not by and large position its violent scenes as thrilling (and appalling) or sexy (/revolting) or beautiful (/ugly), even in the way that a mainstream film like *Pulp Fiction* might, though the sex in the novel often happens in close contiguity with violence. (This difference, and the ease with which such examples provide contrast, we might put down to the distinctions between the visual and the textual, and the different appeals to erotic arousal for audiences of film and readers of novels.) Nor is it the case that, as James Baldwin once remarked in an assessment of Richard Wright's fiction after his death, that in *Hogg* "there is a great space where sex ought to be; and what usually fills this space is violence." Baldwin goes on to say of Wright (somewhat unfairly) that the violence in his work is "gratuitous and compulsive because the root of the violence is never examined."[10] It may be curious to find the "root" of violence examined in a pornographic novel rather than in a more conventionally literary text, but, as we shall see, *Hogg*'s violence is not compulsive, which is to say it is not symptomatic of the repression of some other discursive element or thematic concern. It is rather directly expressive of an insight produced by social analysis. This insight is given to us, is perhaps all the more likely to impinge on the reader's consciousness *because* it is given to us, alongside accounts of men who, say, enjoy thrusting their penises through feces packed into the narrator's mouth. Delany in *Hogg* is trying to enact on the page the structural *fit* between the violence that is usually rhetorically cordoned off in the realm of harm and the sexual that often (though, in our puritanical society, by no means always) is positioned as occupying the realm of pleasure: this is the fit between these two realms in conventions and codes governing our *speaking* or *writing* of the practices that comprise and illustrate them—and it is also the less acknowledged, more relentlessly suppressed fit between these in actual practice—that is, the practice of our everyday living in a society that depends for its operation on various kinds of violence that it does not acknowledge.

The violence of the everyday, the violence in the everyday, is the key formulation for reading the presence of violence and torture in *Hogg*.

Delany is not making a point either that all or most or even some sex between people is inherently debasing or an expression of the powerful dominating the powerless—his essay "Pornography and Censorship," from which the quotation that begins this piece is taken, argues explicitly against such a sweeping condemnatory view of sexuality. Nor is the point of his claim about the political torture–enabling effects of censoring representations of torture: that porn like *Hogg* "blows off steam" or serves as some sort of safety valve for the hydraulic system of a societal psyche that will do the awful deed if it is not permitted to fantasize openly about it. Instead *Hogg* reveals that in a culture's rules about the representation of the fantasies and activities that make up the realm of sexuality—which operate with and through the universal facts of our bodies' and psyches' reactions to basic sensations of pleasure and pain—we can possibly see "who we are": the novel's content suggests that who we are can *both* be described as an ego fleeing with such aversion from pain that one of its signal pleasures is to deal pain to some Other in order to be assured it is not itself in pain, *and* who we are can be described as a nonegotistical, receptive entelechy sufficiently defined by nonjudgmental (and suggestively empathetic) orientation that it embraces the pains and pleasures of all Others. *Hogg* insists upon the presence of both (or all) positions on this continuum. Moreover, reading the novel in conjunction with "Pornography and Censorship" demonstrates that the failure to acknowledge the presence of one or both extremes—a "failure" that can be decreed by rules of representation, rules about what can and cannot be said—will likely coincide with, enact, and/or make possible dealing out pain to Others, torture being one way this occurs.

To flesh out the contributions *Hogg* makes to a humanist consideration of torture, I want to pause to consider the relationship between the censored and the everyday—or, to put it differently, between the *unspeakable* and "who we are." Excerpts from Delany's essay, "On the Unspeakable," provide helpful guidelines for how we might think of this relationship in *Hogg*, and within the scope of our larger inquiry. Delany notes,

> The unspeakable is, of course, not a boundary dividing a positive area
> of allowability from a complete and totalized negativity. . . . Rather it is
> a set of positive conventions governing what can be spoken of (or
> written about) in general; in particular, it comprises the endlessly
> specialized tropes (of analysis, of apology, of aesthetic distance) required
> to speak or write about various topics at various anomalous places in
> our complex social geography—places where such topics are specifically
> not usually (or ever) spoken of.[11]

The unspeakable, then, "is an area, a topic, a trope impossible to speak of outside (it is at once evil and extralinguistic) that range, equally difficult to describe, to define: 'The Everyday.' (*It* is at once banal and representationally difficult.) Both are terribly localized. Both are wholly and socially bounded. The division between everyday and unspeakable, difficult and extralinguistic, banal and evil may just be the prototype for all social division."[12] Further,

> "Unspeakable," then, is always shorthand for "unspeakable unless accompanied by especially pressing rhetorical considerations" . . . :
> I don't know how to tell you this, but . . . (The unspeakable comprises the wounds on the bodies of abused children, their mutilations and outrageous shrieking or tight-lipped murders at the hands of parents); I have something I really have to explain to you . . . (It is certainly any pleasure at such abuses, even private, pornographic, onanistic); Allow me to make a special point here . . . (It is civil or political prisoners tortured or slowly slaughtered by ideologues or their hire); You mustn't take this personally, but . . . (It is the uncritical conjunction in the mind of certain social critics of pornography and such pleasure—a conjunction that dissolves with any real experiences of the range of current, commercial pornography or the real practices of practicing sadists and masochists— that makes the pornographic unspeakable, beyond any rhetorical redemption, impossible to *apologize* for); Now, this may sound very cruel, but I feel I just have to say . . .[13] (all but first ellipsis in the original).

Thus, says Delany, it is possible to see *euphemism* as "the figure of the unspeakable."[14] Euphemism is the socially agreed-upon way (and until relatively recently in the development of obscenity laws, and still to some extent today depending on the context, the legally enforced way—which is to say, enforced by means of the threat of the deprivation of physical freedom or money) that we at once turn *from*, or apologetically, offering brackets, turn *to*, the graphic and/or the pornographic. Euphemism is a mechanism by which censorship, indeed, everyday censorship, is effected. The everyday is composed by these turns, and the *management* of information (again, another way of speaking of censorship) is of course at least an attempted management of what we (the collective that lives this every day) know, of what we imagine, and thus in part what we do. It also attempts to manage what *can* be done, both by "us" and by those who help manage the social order—though of course what "we" can do and what can be done by the social order's managers sometimes slip into separate spheres. Euphemism then in its relation to the unspeakable is an attempt at managing, and, in the process of managing, *constituting* "who we are."

The notion that there is a "who" that "we are," in the case of Danner's use of that phrase, contains an assumption of a collective identity that can be given a name: Danner's particular call for an investigation and discussion about the efficacies of torture that would help give such a name to us is a recognition of the fact that identity is always a construct, a misrecognition, a concealment of what it does not name, and thus also a challenge, at least from the standpoint of an interest in becoming knowledgeable about "truth" or of an aspiration toward ethics, to dig ever deeper. Delany's novel and essays elaborate upon this fact.

> I think it is terribly important to have a genre—or a genre-set—in which it is possible to say *anything*: true, untrue, or at any level of fantasy, metaphor, violence, or simple outrageousness. And I would rather such a genre-set be the genre-set of art than that it be the associated texts of religion, say, . . . or those that comprise journalism. . . . But there are social forces aplenty—and often the same forces that would take away the freedom of speech we vouchsafe for the arts—that, as they would deny that freedom *to* the arts, would redistribute it to religion and reportage. . . . It is not only the freedom to suppress what others say that is wanted, but the freedom to lie as well when necessary—because such lies are assumed somehow to be for "everyone's good."
>
> Samuel R. Delany, "Pornography and Censorship"

The "freedom to lie . . . for 'everyone's good'" that Delany identifies as a privilege sought by those acting as official censors plays a significant part in the story of American torture of detainees in the so-called war on terror. An April 22, 2009, *New York Times* article, "In Adopting Harsh Tactics, No Inquiry Into Past Use," reported that the interrogation methods employed against detainees were borrowed wholesale from a government program called "Survival, Evasion, Resistance, and Escape" (SERE). SERE's brief is to train military officers how to respond to capture; since it was anticipated that officers might face torture by captors who do not abide by the Geneva Conventions, these techniques were developed so that the officers could learn, as the program name suggests, to resist and escape.[15] According to *The Times*, these borrowed techniques were proposed by George Tenet, then CIA director, and John McLaughlin, deputy director and a career intelligence analyst, to a top-level group: President Bush, Vice President Cheney, then-National Security Advisor Condoleeza Rice, and Attorney General John Ashcroft. Tenet's and McLaughlin's briefings were apparently very precise as to the proposed, and subsequently approved, methods (including waterboarding, prolonged nakedness, prolonged standing, sensory deprivation, beatings, confinement in a box, and sleep deprivation)[16]—"so clinical and specific," in fact, "that at one briefing Mr. Ashcroft objected, saying that Cabinet officials should approve broad outlines of important policies, not the fine details, according to someone present. The attorney general later complained that he thought Mr. Tenet was looking for cover in case controversy erupted, the person said."[17]

Recounting this conversation in a discussion that attempts to link censorship to the enabling of practices of political torture might well prompt observers of Mr. Ashcroft's checkered career to note that his preference for "broad outlines" rather than "fine details" also expressed itself in an instance of aesthetic censorship: under Ashcroft's tenure at the Justice Department—and perhaps according to his orders, though this has been denied—the semi-nude Art Deco statues of the female Spirit of Justice and the male Majesty of Law, which have been fixtures at the Great Hall of the Department since it was built as a WPA project, were hidden behind a blue curtain. Justice spokespersons claimed that the curtain was put in place because "TV blue" was more photogenic than the statues. A number of journalists, as well as late-night comedians who seized on the story, taking note of Ashcroft's association with right-wing anti-pornography and pro-"decency" crusades, opined that the curtain had gone up so as to conceal the evident offense of the Spirit's aluminum breast (and perhaps Majesty's bare chest, as well).[18]

There is a link between the effort to conceal nakedness (and here we might guess that if we could persuade Ashcroft to explain his objections to the statues for us, he would say public nudity, even the partial nudity of unliving statues, wrongly represents the sinning race of humans as still "innocent" in the manner of prelapsarian Adam and Eve, though surely the core transgression is that such nudity provides possibly inciting evidence that human bodies can be sexual), and the effort to "not know," i.e., to be able to deny, that captive "enemy combatants" are tortured in defiance of the Geneva Conventions. This is the link that Delany describes: it is not likely that Ashcroft sought to close his mind to the contemplation of the injuries the interrogation techniques would inflict on detainees; that is, moral revulsion to the methods being proposed was likely not what prompted his desire to retreat from specific knowledge of them. Rather, such arranged ignorance would enable those injuries to occur: Ashcroft's objection was preparing him for the eventuality of lying about the infliction of injury for the greater good—just as he would be prepared, one imagines even eager, to lie about the ubiquity and diversity of human sexual practices (which the mere appearance of even a fake breast and bare chest summons to the sin-hungry mind) by concealing the evidence of them and denying having done so, in the service of a greater good like "public morality" or "preservation of the family." Ashcroft's parallel impulses are toward the regulation of public discourse and public knowledge, in one case to better permit practices that produce bodily and psychic pain, and in the other to better proscribe (by refusing to acknowledge and limiting the opportunity to imagine) practices that *might* produce bodily and psychic pleasures.

In this case, then, the revelation—if indeed it counts as one—is of what sort of nation, what sort of world, Ashcroft aimed to create by manipulating the discursive end of the two-way relation between the discursive and the material (exactly what, after all, an attorney's work is): a world where the public good is served by giving pain (to some), and curtailing pleasure (for all). Pain given, pleasure limited (a pairing that immediately raises the question of whether and to what extent there is any ultimate difference between these two effects): these are core elements by which a political authority controls a populace. To the extent that we elect persons with such a vision, or persons who appoint people with such aspirations, to the highest offices of our government, to the extent that we ourselves support or enable or enact the preference to conceal or turn away from the "fine details" of human suffering and human pleasure, Ashcroft's vision is also of the sort of country that, without having talked about it, through scrupulously *not* allowing ourselves to say "anything," we in fact imagine ourselves to be, that we also *are*, to answer the challenge Danner puts before us. Not allowing ourselves to say we know the "fine details" even though we do, and not permitting ourselves to say "anything" by confining the unspeakable to euphemism, is not only part of what makes the practice of torture possible, but a key component of the practice itself: it is part and parcel of torture, the shadowy discursive twin of its (in this case, though not always) well-lit material sibling. As Hortense Spillers observes, "material values engender symbolic and discursive ones (and vice versa) in perfect synecdochic harmony."[19] Not to say a whole range of things—or, having said them, to effectively undo our taking cognizance of them, by attending only to "broad outlines"—prepares the ground for, sets in motion (choose your metaphor)—what operates as an effect of the thereby limited discourse that is avowed, that is a linked skein of disavowed or obfuscated practices. Instructive again here are Spillers's remarks about the connection between discursive articulations of "black" skin to subhuman status and the mutilation, dismemberment, and torture of black bodies and the extinguishing of black people's lives as components of an "everyday" system of social order that we call, euphemistically, slavery, lynching, Jim Crow, apartheid, racism: "The marking, the branding, the whipping—all instruments of a terrorist regime . . . to get in somebody's face in that way would have to be centuries in the making that would have had little to do, though it is difficult to believe, with the biochemistry of pigmentation, hair texture, lip thickness, and the indicial measure of the nostrils, but everything to do with those 'unacknowledged legislators' of a discursive and an economic discipline."[20]

What is perhaps centuries in the making in this context is "a *semiosis* of procedure" (emphasis in original),[21] a development of discursive regulations, in which not-saying = not-seeing = not-knowing, and these equations enable, and sometimes (most times?) demand, violent, torturous *doing*.

Danner asks, how was torture "really" used and what it did it "really" achieve? In one sense, it was used to actualize who we as a nation want to be (purveyors of pain, restrictors of pleasure: i.e., authoritative), and to some extent, I fear, it "really" achieved this.

This possibility is something that the history of the censorship of *Hogg*, and the novel's continued neglect, reveals.

According to Delany's account of *Hogg*'s history—and we must briefly take note of the fact, painfully well-known to thousands of authors and would-be authors of various stripes, that an unpublished work has an anomalous, even paradoxical status in relation to the notion of *history*, and that this novel would have no account nameable as history had it not been eventually published, or had the author not published the story of its nonpublication—Maurice Girodias at Olympia Press had the opportunity to reject the *Hogg* manuscript because the publishing house that had more or less commissioned the work had gone out of business. Essex House, inspired by Olympia's relative commercial success in selling literate pornography in the 1960s, set out to publish its own literary porn; its editor approached poets and aspiring literary writers with the proposal that they write works focused on sex, though there would be no formal parameters—the work did not have to read like (and likely shouldn't read like) standard pulp-fiction-style and hardcore/softcore magazine pornographic stories. A number of these works were published; then Essex House stopped publishing. Thus what we call the market—which is, at least, the confluence of factors including the resources available to materialize, distribute, and promote such works, and the receptivity of distributing apparati and customers to the sale of them at a volume that produces a viable profit for the sellers: and therefore that we might also call the economic operation of broad regulations of public discourse, or, as Delany calls it, commercial censorship—had already once weighed in, negatively, on the *speakability*, or the capacity to sustain the speakability, of *Hogg*'s "genre." Either readers of pornography interested in literary iterations of the genre (or readers of literary fiction interested in pornographic iterations of the form) didn't exist in sufficient numbers or established commercial flows provided insufficient avenues to reach them. Once Olympia, the more successful house publishing such works had—to utilize another glorious euphemism painfully familiar to authors—taken a pass on *Hogg*, Delany's agent sought publishers for the novel and did not find them. Following the success of Delany's science fiction novel *Dhalgren*, in 1975 Bantam Books purchased the rights to all his earlier books—including *Equinox*, his first erotic novel (which had been published, under a different title, despite Essex's collapse, and had since gone out of print), and *Hogg*. Bantam, rather predictably, chose not to publish either, despite the purchasing editor's assessment that both erotic novels were "extraordinary," according to Delany.[22] The manuscript was again shown to other publishers off and on for some fifteen years more, without takers. (During this period, Delany attempted to Xerox a copy of the manuscript at a copy shop in London, England, and was told by the office manager that, after reading a page or two of it, the shop declined to copy it.)

In 1991 a small publishing collective based in Seattle, affiliated with Serconia Press, which had published a nonfiction book of Delany's, asked to see and consider the manuscript. As part of its decision-making process, the collective convened a discussion group of one gay man, two straight men, two straight women, and two gay women. The discussion was audiotaped. Delany summarizes the taped conversation he listened to thus: "The women—gay and straight—felt that, distasteful as it was, the book ought to be published. One even thought its publication imperative. . . . The men— gay and straight—felt that the danger to unstable minds was simply too great a risk."[23] One of the straight male discussants was providing funding for the publishing venture; with many apologies, the collective took a pass. Fiction Collective 2/Black Ice finally published the novel in 1994 (though it appeared in 1995), and issued a second edition, with corrections of mistakes that had crept into the first edition, in 2004.[24]

The hesitation, rejection, and what appears from points far removed from the particulars of the process to be astonishment and *fear* that have attended *Hogg*'s long desultory path to publication seem puzzling. *Hogg* is after all a story in which various harrowing, perhaps horrifying events (including but not confined to torture) are written about, not of course an instance of such events, nor even a primer on how to, nor an exhortation to, make the events occur. Nevertheless the men of the Seattle discussion group were evidently convinced that without the fortunate resource of mental stability to gird them up, something untoward would have occurred (in their own minds, to them, or to others) once they'd finished reading the book (or perhaps, after reading only a few pages, like the London copy shop manager—the tipping point of dangerous texts, the slippery descent from "broad outlines" into the quicksand depths of "fine details," being as yet undetermined by science).

What danger might these readers have divined for other readers, whom they could imagine possessing adequate literacy to read and understand the text, but who would otherwise be prone to mental collapse should the text include sentences ordinarily not-said? And why might male readers, in particular, have been so sensitive to these dangers? The explanation lies in the connection Delany himself has provided between censorship as a process of discursive regulation and political torture as a material expression of a social order that that censorship helps make possible—particularly in the case of *Hogg*, a social order with organizing principles of depressing familiarity: men's domination of women, whites' domination of black people.

For the character Hogg's actions are monstrous—as are those of many another character in the novel—but he is not himself reducible to a monster. Delany explains that *Hogg* examines "violence against women, torture, murder, racism, filth, the exploitation of children, and other acts too perverse to name . . . not from the point of view of sociologists and psychologists with their ready-made categories of 'victims' and 'monsters,' but examines them as seriously—and relentlessly—as the *people caught up in such acts* are capable of. That it finds touches of humanity here and there even among murderers and criminal psychopaths is, of course, troubling"[25] (emphasis in original). Or better, troubling and revealing: critic Ray Davis, perhaps the most insightful reader of the novel to date, notes, "Hogg is the nightmarish Other who understands both the 'systems of the world' . . . and also how those systems depend upon the surreptitious assistance of those 'outside' the system. The status quo's assumption of control is unspoken; therefore, when endangered, it must be re-established via the unspeakable."[26]

Hogg's knowledge of his—our—society's systems of misogyny and white supremacy allows him to give an admirably clear account of how his seemingly extreme actions function within those systems (especially admirable for porn, where the two, though key components of the erotic charge delivered by porn representations, usually go unremarked in the works themselves). "'So you just seen how I make my living now, boy,'" Hogg says to the narrator. "'Stickin' pussy. Hogg's old shit sticker is pretty much half hard all the time anyway. . . . And there's this whole bunch of racketeers and bulldykes and bankers and big men in this county who'll give me a hundred bucks . . . to bust up cunt'" (37). Hogg's list of his employers reads like the dramatis personae of a latter-day Dickensian novel of social life, arrowing from the "lower" or "marginal" or "excluded" to the very powers that be, all of whom, it would appear, have at some point or another some stake in the degradation and torture of women (as well as the sexual exploitation and possible torture—like a salad on the side—of children, since this seems to be an activity that accompanies the various rape-and-torture-for-hire jobs Hogg and his crew embark upon). The implication is clear: as a part of the everyday functioning of society, women and children are (must be, if the organizing principles are to hold) the targets of physical and sexual abuse, of torture. Is this because everyone, including women, hates women and despises children? In part, says Hogg, yes. "'You know what I'd do if I was a bitch?'" Hogg rants. "'I'd get me a gun, go out on the street, and—bip! bip! bip!—I'd put a bullet in everything I even *suspected* had a pecker swingin' between its legs. Anything else a bitch is gonna do is just crazy. . . . Men hate bitches, man. *All* men hate *all* bitches. . . . Well, if I was a bitch and I knew what I know 'cause I *ain't* one, I'd get out there and start killin' first'" (103, emphasis in original). But active animus toward women bears something of a chicken-and-egg relation to the societal structure that, as Davis suggests, both fuels and expresses that animosity as a kind of social glue. The women whom Hogg rapes are, it seems, always women who wouldn't likely report to the police because they're already in trouble with the law: It appears that the "normal" operation of law and the normal structure of the social order deems these particular women rape-able and abuse-able—the law colludes with such an outcome, permits it, and would seem to encourage it by failing to offer them protection—and by extension, it follows that other women, perhaps all women, become available by mandate for *some kind* of abuse, some kind of violation, or at the very least might always be threatened with the possibility of falling into the abuse-able category.

There is an ongoing question in the novel about the young narrator's racial identity. Hogg, articulating the studiedly casual racism pervasive in the novel's universe, takes a look at the narrator and says, "'Hey, you got a good crank on you, too! You colored? You look like you might be'" (39). Other characters remark upon various aspects of the narrator's physicality in order to align him with one race or another. In one plot development, one of Hogg's fellow rape artists (named Nigg, but mostly simply referred to as "the nigger") and a biker named Hawk decide to make some extra money by prostituting the narrator in Crawhole, which is the part of the harbor particularly frequented by African American boatmen. "'I know some niggers down there, man, who'd love to fuck this little blond-headed cocksucker's face,'" Nigg explains. Hawk replies, "'Yeah? A white kid?' Then I heard Hawk frown. 'He's white, ain't he?'"—to which Nigg answers, "'Sure he is . . .'" Hawk continues, "'You wanna sell the little cocksucker down on the nigger boats? . . . They'd really buy him?' . . . 'Sure they would,' the nigger said. 'They like cocksuckers like him—white ones'" (155). (Interestingly, in this discussion the narrator's race takes secondary importance to his youth and willingness in the determination of where he's placed in the social hierarchy—insofar as the relations between him and the two men can be characterized as social, and insofar as they're *really* hierarchical given the narrator's willingness—even though the contemplated sale of the narrator clearly evokes the history of racialized chattel slavery in the United States.) The mystery of the narrator's racial status is resolved for the reader by the narrator's own statement, at the very end of the book: "I wondered how they'd feel when they finally noticed I was a nigger" (266).

The narrator's ambiguous racial position and the resolution of this ambiguity underlines the partly anomalous position of black men in the hierarchies that determine who feels the necessity or the desire to "bust up cunt" in the unspoken fashioning of everyday living. Nigg and other black male characters joyously rape women and children in the novel, but of course the appellation "nigger" by which they are all *invariably* named is also therefore always an interpellation in the Althusserian sense, and as much as they take no umbrage at the name by which they're hailed, "nigger" keeps uncomfortably in the forefront of any action in the novel involving them their racialized, and socially inferior or degraded, status. Lest we be unclear on this point, Hogg again provides clarity. Hogg gets into a brutal fight with Big Sambo—Delany using names to make his point again—the black boatman who has purchased the narrator's services, and who happens to catch Hogg raping his daughter (Big Sambo himself has done that deed earlier). Afterward Hogg gives his maybe-black-maybe-not sex slave the "broad outlines" of a view for which his fists had already provided the "fine details." "'Shit, cocksucker . . .'" he says, ". . . but I sure like to beat up a nigger. Can't beat on old Nigg too much 'cause we always on jobs together. . . . Beatin' on the bikey [who is white] was fun. But it ain't like a nigger'" (232). At another point Hogg draws the parallel between society's active responsibility for misogyny with its active white-supremacist attitudes:

"'Men hate bitches the way white men hate niggers.'" And then, clearly speaking of both women and black folks, "'Long as they do like we say they're suppose to do, everything always looks fine. But let one of them get even a little, teeny, weeny bit out of line, then you watch what happens—we wanna kill. We may *not* kill, but we *wanna* kill'" (103).

Hogg's statements seem on the one hand to be horrifyingly revelatory about the ubiquity and relentless murderousness of white racism and male misogyny. Reading them in 2009, I think immediately of the blood-chilling screams of "Traitor!" and "Kill him!" that greeted mentions of Barack Obama at John McCain rallies during the last weeks of the 2008 presidential campaign. Interestingly, though, despite the fact that Hogg's ability to find fairly steady work as a rape artist seems to show that his analysis is true within the universe of the novel, and thus potentially true of our own world insofar as the novel's imagined reality bears a reflective or refractive relationship to our own reality (itself imaginary as much as it is physical and material), the novel also undercuts Hogg's view, or at least complicates his assessment of white male murderousness: for one, Hogg explicitly says he can't find *enough* such work to pay him as well as an ordinary job would. More significantly, Hogg's statement naturalizes these murderous sentiments toward women and black folks and assigns them as definitional characteristics to men and to whites (or at least white men); but in the novel, the actual *murder* victims are mostly not women and black folks, but the white men who hire Hogg: one murder is deliberate, by Hogg himself; another is accidental, of Hogg's upper-class contact who operates as a kind of broker for Hogg's services, who is killed when the biker Hawk, for the sheer thrill of it, forces a traffic accident that makes the broker's limousine flip and explode on the highway. The other murders are of various people engaged in everyday activities—filling up at a gas station, at home with the family, going to a grocery store. Women and children are tortured and raped in the novel; murders, however, are committed against the "normal" people whom Hogg has identified as the source of his pay. The murderers are Hogg and Hawk, both white men, and Denny, a young white male, who, as I noted above, is an overly horny teenager transitioning to adulthood, and goes insane due to the infection brought on by his piercing his penis with a nail. Denny's adolescent position might indicate that the movement into becoming an adult member of society is an initiation into a system that is itself insane, murderous, violent, and perhaps even cannibalistic in that it is violent against its own. "Normal" people repress the expression of this violence and hire the Hoggs of the world to do it for them; Denny, however, due to the happenstance of his infection, enacts the violence himself. He is psychologically *tortured* by the biological, chemical, and cultural process of his initiation into society and visits this torture on virtually anyone he encounters. The fact that those he encounters are so frequently the everyday exemplars of the adult society into which he is transitioning suggests that the savage murderousness is, in fact, already present; already, in a sense, theirs.

This is true despite the spectacular way that the murders are narrated, both to characters in the novel and to us as readers, through the device of radio news reports. Delany makes an effort to demonstrate the constructed nature of the news by giving us scenes of the producer and the reporter shaping their broadcast, and in showing us how what interviewees actually say to the reporter get censored in the broadcast report. On this level, too, then, censorship is a tool in the shaping of official discourse that distorts or conceals causes and their effects, as well as concealing various kinds of social connections and social practices, all in the name of public service and the public good: the reporter asks one of the Crawhole fishermen to describe the neighborhood after Denny murders a family there; the interviewee says, "'This is a pretty peaceful place, like, mostly. After a little fightin' and a little fuckin', there ain't really—'"; whereupon the reporter chastises him for his foul language, and minutes later the narrator hears the interviewer say on the radio, "'People fight some. Sometimes they . . . you know, mess around. But usually it's pretty peaceful'" (218–19, ellipses in original). The censorship of "bad words" in journalists' interviews with witnesses to Denny's crimes has its parallel in, as well as its lock-and-key fit with, the journalistic erasure of elements of social reality in order to, predictably, produce a spectacle of "innocence" violated: in keeping with the observations Delany makes, this discursive operation is depicted for us in the pornographic genre-set of art, which, in saying "anything," can give us an imaginary "real" world where people say bad words and do bad deeds, alongside a depiction of the way those "real" events are represented by reportage to the characters in it.

Perhaps this, then—a revelation of the misogyny, racism, torturousness, and murderousness of a social world that conventional discourse presents in more palliating terms—is what the Seattle male discussants of the manuscript feared would unhinge the mentally fragile. Davis makes a very acute observation regarding the challenge such a revelation poses. "What . . . [Hogg's world] lacks," he writes, "is the illusion of shelter. In *Hogg*, home is where the violence is. There's no respite."[27] The textual effect of being able to say "anything" and strip away the distortions of euphemism may leave readers of the novel without easy recourse to the protections offered by fantasies of impregnable privacy and inviolability. *Home* is where the violence is, because the violence is everywhere, and because home is not distinct from the outside against which its ideal appearance is defined. Indeed the text in some ways suggests home may be the nucleus of the violence that is pervasive. This is evident in a series of what would now be called home invasions that set the stage for at least one of the rapes and for a series of offstage events that make up Denny's murder spree, in which he enters two households to murder the inhabitants. It is evident, too, in the fact that the narrator's first "friend," a thirteen-year-old named Pedro, prostitutes his sister to a gang of bikers and to his own father; and that a father on a fishing boat (Big Sambo) has chased away the mother of his child so that he'll have free rein to rape his twelve-year-old daughter. Davis's observation leads us to understand that in *Hogg* home is the site where violence and violation are routine, and indeed, within the porno-graphic realm of the novel, they are constitutive aspects of the human relations that make up the home. And often, even when violence arrives from the outside in the guise of Hogg's retinue, the intruders have been invited to do so by someone who knows the victim and is seeking to hurt or punish her for mostly unarticulated reasons that seem to arise out of the betrayals or frustrations of intimate—i.e., in-home, of home—relations. In the case of Denny's violence, the violence crosses the threshold of pri-vacy with such ease that the distinction between private and public, with their connotations of protected/secret and open/exposed, has no purchase.

In this vein, Hogg articulates a theory about the pervasiveness of violence and violation in society, and the broad responsibility we all bear for it. He says, "'[A]in't nothin' you can do in this world today—go to the pictures, buy some food, or even throw away the package it come in—that don't bring somebody closer to hurt. At least this way you know . . . when you're hurtin' someone, *you're* hurtin' 'em. You look 'em right in the eye and do it. . . . [Y]ou ain't droppin' no bombs on five hundred people you ain't never seen. You ain't signin' no papers that's gonna put a thousand people ain't never heard your name out of a house and a job'" (62, emphasis in original). This fact does not excuse Hogg's acts or relieve him of respon-sibility for them; it merely contextualizes what he does. For Hogg, if the rapes and tortures he commits are justified at all, the justification is the satisfaction of genuine appetite, and the only possible morality of the acts is to take personal responsibility for the commission of them. This even extends to the acceptance of responsibility in the public arena *if* the genesis of the public accusation is the victim, not the falsely outraged sensibilities of the public or the state operating in ours or the victim's name: at one point Hogg takes action to avoid being informed on to the police by Jimmy (he kills him), who on one occasion joins the rape artists; but Hogg speculates that he would not oppose an accusation from one of his victims, saying, "'[W]ell, if it was from her, somehow that would be okay'" (120). On the other hand, to try to *rationalize* torture without reference to appetite is insane. Hogg says disparagingly of Jimmy, who joins Hogg in beating and raping a woman because he is the one who's hired Hogg, "'The fucker is up there *with* us, beatin' on the bitch, and fuckin' on the bitch, and just gettin' into the whole thing. Then he's gonna turn around and tell us he's got *reasons* for actin' like he's doin'? Now you do somethin' like that, man, 'cause you *want* to. 'Cause you get your fuckin' jollies that way. . . . But can you think of a goddamn *reason* for doin' something like that, the way we done them women?—of somethin' they could of possibly done to someone else to make that all right . . .?'" (121, emphasis in original) Still, such rationalizations reveal even as they try to obfuscate that this kind of sadistic insanity (threatening violence and enjoying meting out violence and violation on those designated as permitted to be threatened) is bound up with, is, a fundamental structure of social reality: it is home. The novel— perilously for unstable minds—tries to show that in home we are not only strangers, as the experience of the Freudian uncanny not-so-gently nudges us to recognize: we are also prey, acted upon, objects—and/or those who prey upon, act upon, subject others. As such the rape artists are not invaders so much as enforcers of the regulations already in place (in home), or messengers continuing an exchange of messages already in progress.

The relative lack of shelter, of respite, of *defense* depicted in the novel finds its correlate in the basic orientation of the narrative itself. The narrator's perspective on what he sees and the sexual acts he participates in presents something of a conundrum to the reader, in that the narrative voice avoids, if not outright refuses, to make valuating judgments—even the judgment that would seem to be fairly basic in a pornographic text, the distinction between pain and pleasure. As Davis puts it, pain and pleasure are neither separable from one another nor mistakable for one another in the novel's universe. Delany's narrator is, as I've said, eleven years old, though in the manner fairly typical for such a conceit in fiction, the narrative is told from an "indeterminate future age," says Delany. "This signals to the reader that he's survived the story's events and . . . lived to tell them. . . . [But] he attempts to narrate Hogg's story as it struck him *at the time* . . . there's a fibrillating quality to his sophistication, that registers (to you) as a discontinuity, or set of discontinuities."[28] The narrative voice's "discontinuities" and their intimation of the narrator's survival of the harrowing events in the novel further *Hogg*'s project of militating against the reader's likely assumption that the narrator is a victim. As Delany argues, the women in the novel that Hogg rapes and abuses are victims; the narrator is not. Apart from the ultimately temporal discontinuity the narrative voice spins like a protective cocoon around what we might otherwise assume to be the narrator's under-pressure and at-risk psyche, the novel's style of storytelling, as Davis observes, eschews *psychology* as a mode of rendering character altogether. Says Davis, "*Hogg*'s first-person narrator is as suspicious of expression and as compulsive about accurate observation as any [Dashiell] Hammett hero . . . his all-purpose analysis of any more complex inner state is 'It made me feel funny.'"[29] In this we might say the novel is more like pornographic fiction than literary fiction, where presumably what the narrator would experience psychically—and what Hogg and almost all the men we encounter experience, according to their explicit statements—is pleasure. The narrator's pleasure, though, is not the pleasure of being stroked, aroused to ejaculation (though, *Hogg* being a porn novel, this does happen occasionally), spoken to affectionately, given candy to eat, or any other common indicator of pleasure—indicators that, in the course of the novel, become revealed to us as merely the conventional content we give to the term, not its definition. The expression-suspicious narrator doesn't expound upon his enthusiasm for the acts in which he participates—in one rarely articulate moment, he says simply, "He liked the way he was getting it. I liked the way he was giving it" (58). But he does tell us at somewhat greater length what he *doesn't* like. The narrator recounts being kidnapped and held for sex for three days by two young men, one of whom was a college student: apart from the two calling him "nigger"—"I kind of liked that part," he says—he did not find the experience enjoyable. "But the rest of it hadn't been fun at all," he recalls, and then explains, "There was no rough stuff in it, both of them were cut, and they were all into talking 'bout how they really loved me and only sucked on me and wouldn't let me suck them off or pee on me or fuck my ass or nothing. . . . It made me feel all dirty and helpless and really scared" (266). Feeling soiled, violated, frightened—these of course are the psychological responses that rape victims generally report, but in the narrator's case it is not being held captive for sex that makes the narrator feel victimized; indeed, the two boatmen he plans to escape to at the end of the novel have promised to hold him captive, too. It's that the particular sexual acts and affection he's held for were not to his liking. Thus the *acts* have no transparent meaning, and what we might presume to be abuse—grown men demanding fellatio and anal sex from a prepubescent boy and insisting he consume their urine and feces—isn't. Thus the orientation of the narrative voice is, from a conventional standpoint, disorienting, in that the clarity in what we can understand as pain or pleasure, liked or disliked—good or bad—proves to be as mistaken as the assumption that home is refuge.

Is torture as we understand it then torture in the novel? Yes. The women who don't *want* to feel physical pain or discomfort, or to be used for the rape artists' sexual pleasure, are tortured thereby. The distinction, though, has little to do with the acts themselves and lies largely in the willingness and desire of the body and psyche feeling pain and being abused. More importantly, pain and sexual violation become torture insofar as they are the expression of a social order that is *not telling*, not acknowledging the violence it sanctions (by hiding behind its hires). My overall point here, however, is that the text's resolute refusal to render the narrator as a victim or the victimizers of real victims in the story as monsters means that its narrative voice and narrative structure hold the position I described above as a nonegotistical, receptive entelechy, defined by its nonjudgmental, empathetic standpoint in such a way that it embraces the pains and pleasures of all Others: This means *Hogg's* presence as a work to be read, its being published—which, as I've noted, was a struggle to achieve—is aimed at breaking the fit between censorship and political torture; the narrative position the novel holds is very strongly and very *ethically* not one of fleeing in ego-like fashion from its pain or anyone else's.

In a set of historical circumstances considerably different from those in which we are all now enmeshed—yet with echoes and analogies to the present (and, in a way, this history is an earlier part of a global story that our present continues)—Frantz Fanon and Jean-Paul Sartre were very critical of what we might think of as the liberal critique of state-sanctioned torture. Writing of French opposition to the use of torture by French soldiers in the Algerian war of independence, Fanon puts it thus: "One cannot be both in favor of the maintenance of French domination in Algeria and opposed to the means that this maintenance requires. . . . Torture in Algeria is not an accident, or an error, or a fault. Colonialism cannot be understood without the possibility of torturing, of violating, or of massacring."[30] Moreover, "The . . . colonialist structure rests on the necessity of torturing, raping, and committing massacres."[31] Sartre's description is more acid: "The pacifists are a fine sight: neither victims nor torturers! Come now! If you are not a victim when the government you voted for and the army your young brothers served in, commits 'genocide,' without hesitation or remorse, then, you are undoubtedly a torturer."[32] And: "It is not right, my fellow countrymen, you who know all the crimes committed in our name, it is really not right not to breathe a word about them to anybody, not even to your own soul, for fear of having to pass judgment on yourselves. . . . Eight years of silence have a damaging effect. And in vain: the blinding glare of torture is high in the sky, flooding the entire country. . . . Today whenever two Frenchmen meet, there is a dead body between them."[33]

Yes, the context is different: but do the same words apply?

"At the end of the book," Delany says, "the reader should ask: What punishment should Hogg receive for what he's done . . .? . . . What punishment should Denny receive . . .? . . . And, of course, the final question must be: personally, how are *you* engaged by these questions?"[34] (first and third ellipsis in original). The first two questions seem to emanate from some radically opposed reality when I close the book—they don't even occur to me, actually. This is because the characters are *not* punished in the book, and moreover the likelihood of their receiving punishment *for their crimes* is mitigated by Hogg twice outwitting or evading police as he aids mass-murderer Denny's escape, and Hogg's own apparent skill at avoiding capture by authorities. The operation of authority in its assessment of what constitutes crime and its measures for assigning responsibility and accountability in the mode of punishment is textually belayed, if not abrogated and undercut. Readers are thus pointedly not given punishment that could serve as a "relief" in the text as it would in any Hollywood film or super-hero comic book, where the vicious villain is caught and reviled or meets a grisly end that enacts for us the operation of justice and provides the psychic satisfactions of both stoking and quelling whatever fears the representation of monstrous acts evokes: no such expected satisfaction of the familiar the-wages-of-sin-is-death narratorial credo can be found.[35]

Without the satisfactions of punishment I'm not led to contemplate how they could be provided, but rather how to name having to do without them, and what their absence means: am I to push through the disturbance and at times revulsion that the text refuses to quell in order to acquiesce, to surrender to the insistently *torturous* structure of the world that the text creates and that is not without numerous echoes, reflections, and insights vis-à-vis my world? This seems one possibility, perhaps what the men of the Seattle collective most feared—though I think the direction and consequences of this acquiescence to a narrative and its revelations have no necessary relation to acts in the world, whether or not the mind that receives the information is "unstable." The point is that a stance, a decision or series of decisions about one's relation to the part torture plays in the social order becomes either possible or even necessary (if I've been "disturbed" enough)—which is the import of Delany's last question in this series.

This seems not so much a decision whether to stand in favor of or in rejection of torture and violation, but rather a decision to *see* it.

Fanon and Sartre present a seemingly stark choice, complicity or rejection—but this starkness is not simple: Fanon in particular is focusing on how torture is an inextricable expression of the colonialist system, and that while to aim one's critique and opposition at the eradication of *it* may be of strategic use, such opposition is of little consequence if it is not one strategy among a host deployed against the system that demands the practice: in that vein, then, the rejection of torture may not be sufficient as moral or political stance, and of the two choices, complicity has the broadest writ, and it may not be possible to disentangle it from a variety of other, seemingly less morally opprobrious practices.

Another possibility is *not* to push through the revulsion the novel may provoke, but to continue to wrestle with it, which leads in the same direction as the above. Or to allow the revulsion to stop you and make you condemn the work in part (but only in part) as a way of condemning the acts and practices that it depicts: This is to enter into the realm of willful ignorance and to participate in precisely the complicitous way Fanon and Sartre decry, in the mystifications by which culture and society conceal their mechanisms of regulation and reproduction. No text can be proof against such reader refusals—but obviously acts of censorship have already made this decision and done this work for (and against) us.

Who are we?

I quote Gore Vidal here in (necessarily, always partial) answer. Vidal is sometimes portrayed—dismissed—in the mainstream press as hyperbolic and a polemicist. I rather tend to think of him as insightful and prescient: I am reminded, for instance, of the fact that in an interview conducted in 2002, he predicted that George W. Bush would leave office as the most unpopular president in history.[36] Here then Vidal on who we are, in 1999: "[A] country like the United States . . . is very savage in all its attitudes. Look at our legal system. You have to have lived in other worlds besides America to realize that everything in the United States is adversarial. Everybody is attacking everybody else. Trying to steal his money away. Trying to destroy his reputation. Putting him to death. Keeping him in prison for life three times caught with marijuana. *This is now one of earth's most evil societies*" (emphasis added).[37]

In order to have a national identity—to be "who we are"—we model what is in fact collective, discontinuous, and wildly diverse on the compact fantasy that is individual ego (though it too is in fact discontinuous, diverse, and incomplete, but will never admit it). Reading *Hogg* along with Delany's comments in his essays shows us that we ignore "who we are" in order to be (or to become) *what* we want to be: an armored being impervious to the discomfiting pressures brought to bear by others or by the natural and manmade environment, defended, fleeing pain, so suffused with fear of pain that the greatest pleasure is to deal pain to others. This is a "who we are" consonant with a social order in which torture is inherent, though in ways largely concealed. And to aspire toward such a being is to imagine ourselves, as we Americans so frequently seem to do, in the position of authority—this is after all a polity where majorities frequently favor the abolishment of the estate tax, despite the fact that the majority will never have to pay it—rather than recognizing that it is us over whom authority reigns. *Hogg* suggests that a more carefully mapped collective identity, one we are unlikely to find without humanist inquiry, could take cognizance of the fact that it *is* collective and acknowledge as many of its myriad fears, pains, and pleasures as it can; and if it, we, should choose to play out those fears, pains, and pleasures, we might do so with full knowledge of our actions and aim to do so not against an unwilling *outside* (whether this is the alien-within or the standard "foreign"), but in a collaborative play such as the narrative being presented to readers as a fantasy models, *with* willing insiders. This would mean finding ways to acknowledge the wish to be Hoggs or to have Hoggs do what we would not admit to wishing to do, and at the same time accepting our cravings to be *done to*. Humanist inquiry insists on illuminating the fantasies that give rise to the torturous social order and on recognizing that the nature of fantasy is that the fantasist (or in this case, the collective of fantasists) in truth inhabits all the components of his fantasy: I may imagine giving pain or pleasure to you, or you giving the same to me, but in my—in *our*—fantasy, there is no outside: I am every-one, and we are as much our "foreign" enemies as we are our friends, lovers, and fellow citizens.

CHAPTER 16

Reasonable Torture, or the Sanctities

Colin Dayan

Yet the bird that rose from the blood of Beirut and its promises started to
ask: "Am I in open space or in a cage?"
—Mahmoud Darwish, *Memory for Forgetfulness*

A cure for all kinds of threats, reasonableness has long been a presupposi-
tion for extending enslavement, disability, torture. But this rationality is
tied to figurative power; and at any moment, its metaphors can become
more insistent and literal, operating, as Robert Cover famously wrote, "on
a field of pain and death."[1] What constitutes the reasonable when the traffic between the real and the fantastic, the acceptable and the horrific,
becomes unfair to the dead and dangerous to the living? In our "secular"
and "progressive" times, comprehensive forms of intimidation and punishment function as the backdrop to civil community. Nowhere is oppressive
state magic more accomplished than in cases of policing and torture, where
infernal treatment thrives under cover of necessity.

In Israel there remain everywhere signs of the intent to create the
unbearable in the reasonable expectation that Palestinians—especially

since the first Intifada—suffer harm for its own sake. What remains of a neighborhood? Uprooted olive trees. Piled-up trunks of fruit trees. Slabs of concrete standing out of the ground like tombstones. During my first visit to Jerusalem three years ago, I looked out my car window at the tangled mesh of fences, mud pits, razor wire, and earth mounds left after the building of the wall—also called the "separation barrier" or "fence"—in East Jerusalem. As a result of the wall built in and around East Jerusalem, the government provides no vital services to the nine Palestinian villages located within the municipal boundaries but outside the wall. The Jerusalem municipality does not remove garbage. There are no streetlamps. No new hospitals are built. There is not a single playground. Thousands of children must pass through roadblocks to get to school. Bulldozers tear up the yards. The upturned earth, the shards of glass, stones, and concrete pile up in the streets.

Collective isolation, the dividing up and stringing together of serial spaces, this regime of discipline and force provides terror with its platform. Terror is regulatory, and its absoluteness lies in its power to stratify and exclude, even as it renders increasing numbers of Palestinians so much human material exposed to violence. The politics of "closure" and "separation" take to extremes the commonplace ideas of "incapacitation" and "deterrence." Demolition, land expropriation, bypass and road construction, as well as the daily strangulation of towns and villages, compel a new understanding of the state and a somber revelation of what it means to be *held*, not by construction of ever more prisons—and there are many incarcerated Palestinians—but by the conversion of one's own land, one's beloved landscape into the means of punishment.

In this logic of terror the very land becomes a prison, and resistance is construed as cause, not the effect, of terror. The soil of the ancestors turns into the earth mounds that block travel. The sand of the desert fills the sandbags by the checkpoints. When olive trees are bulldozed, their remains are left behind to form blockades. What Avery Gordon calls "the disposability of a permanently confined life" depends on the skilled manipulation of grim technologies of psychic extermination.[2]

The management of rubbish, what we might call fecal motives, draws distinctions between the free and the bound, the familiar and the strange, the privileged and the stigmatized. And this ongoing, blatantly displayed cultivation of human waste bears witness to the recasting of torture as legitimate practice. Under the mantle of civility and reasonableness the Israeli government continues its assault on those it calls "terrorists," although it knows that the siege of Gaza in particular is instead collective punishment of an entire population. It is perhaps the cohabitation of claims of decency and barbarism that makes the lethal magic of state power less open to criticism. The illusionists who engineer terror rely on the claims of culture to guarantee its malignancy and predation.

Inhuman Reason

Two days after Christmas, in 2008, the Israeli Defense Forces began the assault on Gaza. The delirium of slaughter, violence, and indifference is justified as a reasonable response to Hamas rockets fired into Sderot and the western Negev. Absolute power, once set in motion by a panic of imperial brutality, depends on what Hannah Arendt described as "the general validity of reason as a purely formal quality."[3] With this exemplary support, the truths of reason, I argue, become easily separable from not only justification for, but acceptance, of terror. What is most unsettling about the lethal spectacle of Israel's closure, isolation, and punishment of Gaza is its extremism, the exhilaration of force and subsequent exemption of Israel from blame. Wanton harm becomes appropriate defense, and exceptional brutality common practice.

In the open-air prison that is Gaza the bombs fall. In Gaza one and a half million people are contained in 129 square miles. The attacks began in broad daylight as police cadets were graduating, women were shopping at the outdoor market, and children were leaving school. Al Jazeera shows scenes of running, continuous running. Ehud Olmert warns: "This is only the beginning." The bombardments continue. Olmert makes an announcement to the people of Gaza on this first day of the three-week war. After the blockades that for years have cut off food, supplies, first aid, he says that he wants "to avoid any unnecessary inconveniences to the people of Gaza." When did the argument of necessity become so brutal? "The people of Gaza don't deserve to suffer," he says, as Palestinians, their schools, police stations, and mosques are bombarded by F-16s. Ambulances, hospitals, UN sanctuaries, Red Cross vehicles are targeted. These excesses are not punitive. Obedience will not make them cease. Instead, indifferent killing, collective massacre, and torment are intended to humiliate, to break the spirit, to obliterate the person.

A Fire on the Wall of Gaza

It is the third day of the campaign. I see tanks outside my window. They are on trucks heading to the Gaza border for a possible ground invasion.

The taxi driver, a Palestinian from East Jerusalem, explains: "They're on their way. It's going to happen." *The Jerusalem Post* had photos of IDF troops singing as they lit candles for the seventh night of Chanukah. "Greasing their Guns at the Border," the headline read. There was laughter and dancing. I saw a televised broadcast of the troops at the staging area in Kibbutz Nir Am. A very young orthodox Jew carried a menorah into the circle of soldiers as they celebrated the Festival of Lights. It was sunset on the next to last night of Chanukah, the holiday marking the rededication of the Holy Temple in Jerusalem. Judah and the Maccabees—"Judah the Hammer" and his four brothers—defeated the forces of Antiochus IV, the Seleucid king of Syria, in the second century before Christ. This festival of joy and purification commemorates the miracle of the light—when the holy lamp in the Temple burned for eight nights, though there was enough oil for only one.

I kept wondering about the name "Operation Cast Lead." I asked the taxi driver. He answered without hesitation. "Lead like bullets. Fire so hot that it melts the lead." I keep thinking about the meaning. Every Israeli offensive into Gaza bears a name that evokes images meant for those locked up there, as well as for the Israeli public and the rest of the world. "If the clouds be full of rain, they empty themselves upon the earth."[4] So saith Koheleth the preacher in Ecclesiastes. "Operation Summer Rain" on June 27, 2006. "Operation Autumn Clouds" on November 8, 2006. Almost lyrical, like tremulous bits of haiku, these names are used in contexts that portend nature gone wrong: rain that does not moisten but scorches the earth; clouds that promise terror so unrelenting that no season can survive it. No more autumn, no summer any longer.

These codenames are more troubling in their understatement than the heralding of war in Iraq by the United States with hollow euphemisms like "Operation Enduring Freedom" for the military buildup in September 2001 or "Operation Iraqi Freedom" for the military campaign that began on March 20, 2003. Like oracles, such codenames for the assaults on Gaza are prophetic in their irony, ominous in their ambiguity. But "Operation Cast Lead," like "Operation Hot Winter" that preceded it on February 29, 2008, is different. Now, winter is dewintered, too. The words "cast lead" flaunt a cruel wit. Their festive atrocity prompts a chain of associations: not only the ancient Israelites in their biblical battles against Canaanites and Philistines, but a slew of other transformations. I recall the song of Moses in Exodus after the Lord saved Israel from their enemies: "Thou didst blow with thy wind, the sea covered them: they sank as lead in the mighty waters."[5]

Bodies are turned into lead, buried deep below the sea or cast into new shapes, molded not in the image of God, but changed into base metals, things unnatural and ripe for ruin. Language rebounds on its user, turning on the militaristic boast and revealing it for what it is. Lead is a neurotoxin that accumulates in soft tissues and bone over time. The lead covers Gaza and penetrates the land. Or perhaps "cast lead" refers to the micro-shrapnel, thrown out by explosions, that enters the body, not only ripping it apart—slicing through flesh—but also causing cancer when embedded in those hit. After the bombing of the UNRWA school in the densely packed Jabaliya refugee camp, where hundreds of Palestinians had sought refuge, medics wondered about the number of victims whose legs had to be amputated, the shrapnel-scattered flesh and unusual wounds that could not be treated.

"Cast thy bread upon the waters: for thou shalt find it after many days."[6] Echoing Koheleth, but transforming his words from the fruits of possible benevolence to the sowing of terror, the code name for this operation finds meaning again, at least for English speakers. "Cast your lead upon the waters." Not reaping a reward for charitable giving, but reaping the whirl-wind in laying Gaza in ruins. Bounty becomes dearth. Israeli leaflets of warning fall with the rain of white phosphorous shells. Before each new stage of the offensive, the leaflets warn civilians to "get out of harm's way," warning that the IDF plans "to escalate the offensive." The polite warn-ings, addressed to "residents of the area," repeat words that fly in the face of reality and sense: "We are not attacking civilians." "For your own safety you are required to leave the area immediately." Like snow, thousands upon thousands of leaflets drift down, terrorizing the residents of Gaza, who have nowhere to go. Along with the deluge of leaflets, bursting white like fireworks, explosive tendrils of phosphorous spark and sear the skin.

The message of this campaign lies ultimately in the language chosen to describe it. Remember that this military campaign began during the festi-val of Chanukah. The candles are lit one by one, burning bright into the night, until they melt into the arms of the menorah. I hear again the words of a song I learned in Sunday school. "A Dreydl of Cast Lead I Will Make for You," adapted from a Chanukah poem by Haim Nachman Bialik.

My teacher gave me a dreydl
A dreydl of cast lead
Oh, do you know what it is for?
Do you know what it is for?
Do you know what it is for?
It's for Chanukah.

Cast-lead dreydls are made by heating lead in a steel ladle until it melts; then the molten lead is poured into a closed mold. When the lead cools, it sets, the mold is opened, and the dreydl is removed. This children's toy is a four-sided spinning top with a letter of the Hebrew alphabet on each side. They are the initials of the words for "a great miracle happened here." What is this miracle reenacted in Gaza? A dramatization of catastrophic violence as biblical fulfillment, a destiny made manifest, a prophecy fulfilled: "and I will make your heaven as iron, and your earth as brass."[7]

The miracle of light and the game of the spinning dreydl mark the endpoint of a decades-long campaign to purify the land of Israel: no longer the "quiet transfer" of Palestinians, but a brazen demolition job. Estimates of the Palestinian dead in Gaza range from 1,166 to 1,417—eighty to ninety percent of them civilians. An estimated 4,000 Palestinian homes were destroyed. This scorched-earth campaign ensures that nothing is left to rebuild. At the heart of the festival of Chanukah is the nightly menorah lighting, a single flame on the first night, two on the second, and so on until the eighth night of Chanukah, when all the lights are kindled. The scourge is so absolute that it checks once and for all the pride and resilience of the inhabitants. Their towns, homes, and bodies are filled with lead and enveloped by smoke, burning well past the eight days of Chanukah and into an indefinite future.

Pursuing Justice

The dismissal from public consideration of Judge Richard Goldstone's committee report must not be ignored. Commissioned by the UN Human Rights Council, the 574-page report of the Gaza Fact-Finding Mission was overseen by Goldstone, a widely respected South African jurist who served on his country's highest court and went on to prosecute war crimes in Rwanda and the former Yugoslavia. Immediately following his report, Ian Kelly, the US State Department spokesperson, acknowledged that the United States is "deeply concerned by some of the conclusions," which condemned Israel for "war crimes" in the Operation Cast Lead campaign against Hamas. He added: "We note in particular that Israel has the democratic institutions to investigate and prosecute abuses, and we encourage it to use those institutions."[8]

What is most significant about the report is its attention to the long-term human rights violations—recognizing them as "war crimes" and "possible crimes against humanity"—committed by Israel not only in the Gaza Strip during the massacres from December 27, 2008, to January 18, 2009, but in the West Bank and East Jerusalem. The committee found that the daily crimes of occupation imposed on the civilian population after the election of Hamas, in fair and open elections, were as serious as the blockade of Gaza. Of particular concern were the use of excessive force by Israeli security forces, the targeting of Hamas supporters, and restrictions on movement, freedom of expression, and assembly.

The report exposes the myth that the Gaza onslaught was a temporary act of war. Once put in the context of the official Israeli policy of degradation and abuse, the three-week spectacle of annihilation represents an intensification of routine behavior, what Jonathan Cook has described as "experiments to encourage Palestinian despair."[9] The same focus on whether or not what Israel calls "the offensive against Hamas in Gaza" was or was not proportionate haunts the UN report. Though it is highly critical of Hamas as well as Israel, the report has been either condemned or ignored in the West. This reaction hinges on the immunity of Israel. Richard Falk, the UN special rapporteur on the Palestinian territories, anticipated the taboo against criticizing the burgeoning repression and force in Gaza documented in the report. "A referral to the ICC [International Criminal Court] should be a possibility—its role is to be activated in a situation of this nature. . . . But politically I think it's highly unlikely because the US and probably some European governments will create effective impunity for Israel by preventing the referral."[10]

When we are called upon to adduce a "rational" basis for sustaining the dominion of torture, much depends on assumptions that most of us claim to find intolerable. But recent events in the United States and Israel continue to prove how much we can tolerate. How easy it is for fear, dogma, and terror to allow us to demonize others, to deny them a common humanity, to do unspeakable things to them. In a morally disenchanted world, daily cruelty and casual violence accompany the call for order, the need for security.

The UN mission examined "Indiscriminate attacks by Israeli forces resulting in the loss of life and injury to civilians"; "Deliberate attacks against the civilian population"; "Treatment of Palestinians by Israeli security forces in the West Bank, including use of excessive or lethal force during demonstrations"; and "Detention of Palestinians in Israeli prisons," among numerous other examples of disproportionate acts of brutality. In reading through the descriptions, grotesque as they are, I recognize that they can be sanctifying precisely because they are disproportionate.

In the very intensity of harm lies the consecration of punitive sanction, the symbolic importance of actual slaughter. And perhaps the righteous haze surrounding such figurative potential hovers over the publication of the UN report, blinding the so-called civilized world to the literal violence recorded in these pages.

The threats and acts of physical and psychic harm, the rationales of violence against the people of Palestine, though extreme, remain intrinsic to the making of Israeli culture and necessary to the certainty and sacredness of its frame of reference. The sanction of holy authority does not remain separate from secular culture, but rather signifies their indelible bond. The terror schemes of the state penetrate the enclaves of cultivation. Both the civil and the military spheres enhance the sense of threat to Israel's existence that allows continued privilege at the expense of those believed to be enemies. A mandate for sacred violence can only endure if citizens systematically stigmatize the subjugated as dangerous and superfluous.

In this context of popular justification and complicity, the Public Committee Against Torture in Israel (PCATI) bears witness to the torture of Palestinian detainees and other cruel, inhuman, or degrading treatments or punishments in Israel and the Palestinian Occupied Territories. PCATI was founded in 1990 "in response to the years-long government policy that enabled systematic use of torture and ill-treatment during GSS [General Security Service] interrogations."[11]

The affidavits of the tortured in the draft report *Human Rights Situation in Israel* are harrowing. The egregious torture or ill-treatment of Palestinians by IDF soldiers and "other detaining forces," including police officers, occurred during arrest, transportation, detention, or interrogation, "when they were helpless and bound." Descriptions of interrogation methods used by the GSS/ISA (General Security Service/Israel Security Authority) are familiar to us, whether we turn to the everyday treatment of prisoners in the United States, the debates about the torture of detainees in the war on terror, or the legal limits of coercive interrogation in Iraq, Guantánamo, and Abu Ghraib.[12] Let us name these methods now, for the Israeli authorities introduce other torture methods, applied indiscriminately and deliberately. Prolonged incommunicado detention. Sleep deprivation. Forcibly bending the detainee's back backwards. Slapping and blows. Coerced crouching in a frog-like position. Prolonged shackling. Threats of arrest and physical abuse of family members. Exposing a suspect to a parent or spouse being abusively interrogated or exposing a family member to a son or brother exhibiting signs of physical torture.[13]

Israel's Dogs of War

The use of unmuzzled military working dogs, sometimes called "war dogs" to intimidate prisoners, became familiar to the American public after the disclosure of photos taken in the corridors and cells of Abu Ghraib. Two army dog handlers in camouflage combat gear restrain two German shepherds. The dogs bark at a man. Another image shows the naked Iraqi prisoner. He leans against the cell door, hands clasped behind his neck, crouching in terror. The dogs bark just a few feet away. In another, taken a few minutes later, the prisoner lies on the floor, writhing in pain. The final shot in these photos of incremental degradation is a close-up of the naked prisoner, just his waist to his ankles in sight. There is a large wound on his left leg, covered in blood.

The use of assault and tracker dogs to control prisoners exploits this proximity between prisoners and animals to humiliate and bestialize. In this trade-off between dignity and degradation, terrifying an inmate into compliance undermines personal integrity. The military dogs of Israel are used in order to make the most of the humiliation felt by many Muslims, who consider the dog an unclean animal. In every stage of detention, especially during and after Gaza, the military has depended on Belgian German shepherds trained and operated by the Sting (Oketz) unit, founded originally in 1939 as part of the Haganah—the pre-state army of the Jews in Palestine. Their use in missions against Palestinians increased after the second Intifada in September 2002. Oketz, the independent K-9 special force, is one of the most highly regarded of the army's units. Any dog that loses his life in action is entitled to a full military funeral. "For a long time, we kept the unit's existence in the background so as not to offend the survivors of the Holocaust who will never forget the images of Nazi soldiers unleashing their attack dogs," explained the officer in charge of Oketz's dog-training unit.[14]

Though many of the dogs' missions are classified, the reports of numerous human rights organizations reveal that dogs are not only used in prisons and during interrogations of detainees, but they are also sent into houses in the occupied West Bank during army attempts to arrest "terror" suspects. In *No Defense: Soldier Violence against Palestinian Detainees* (2008), the PCATI inquired about the forced interactions between detainees and dogs. These are "assault dogs," trained "to seek humans using their scent." But how can dogs, no matter how capable, sniff out innocence or guilt? "What history of 'criminality' can the dogs be trained to distinguish?"[15]

The dogs, after being disciplined to violence, are often unleashed by soldiers who have not been trained as handlers. Assault dogs are also used against shackled detainees for the sole purpose of terrorizing them, especially when the detainees are handcuffed and blindfolded.

Here is the testimony of Mohammed Jalab from Tulkarem refugee camp, arrested at a checkpoint between Qalqilya and Tulkarem on March 21, 2007.

> They took me into a room where there were [male] soldiers and one
> female soldier and she had a dog she talked to as I sat on the chair,
> handcuffed and blindfolded. The dog would walk around me and when
> the soldier spoke to him he would attack me and bark. I didn't
> understand what the soldier said, but—I realized that she said to the
> dog, "Arab, Arab," and then it would attack me. . . . The dog didn't bite
> me; I guess they had muzzled it. . . . I asked to be allowed to pray. After
> refusing, the woman soldier said, "Well, then, go ahead and pray." . . .
> I asked them to unshackle me so that I could pray but they refused. As
> I began to pray the woman soldier talked to the dog again and it began
> to attack me from the front and back as I prayed.[16]

In both their treatment and their use, dogs reveal how torturous acts determine status, both that of the torturer and that of his victim. Viciousness, once unleashed in these dog bodies, betrays an Israeli soldier's deep commitment to certain kinds of discrimination, coercion, and threat.

Designing Torture

Torture takes on meaning as it directs us to the experience of its victims. Organized terror becomes unbearable when it not only annihilates entire villages and maims and buries families, but when things taken for granted in times of normality—water, chickens, fruit trees, olive trees, greenhouses, flour mills, farmlands—are wantonly destroyed. The Goldstone report used the term "persecution" in order to describe the systematic breakdown and erasure of sustenance: the things that give persons pride, that prove affiliation, care, and belonging.[17] Subjected to prejudice and alternately irregular and systematic retribution, Palestinians live always in sight of their dispossession.[18]

The disabling of families and communities through the bulldozing of trees, the razing of land is an old story. The city of Tulkarem existed as far back as the third century C.E. under the name "Berat Soreqa." In later centuries it became "Tur Karma," which means "mount of the vineyard" in Aramaic. "Tur Karma" became "Tul Karem." Located in the foothills of the Samarian mountains about fifteen kilometers west of Nablus and fifteen kilometers east of the Israeli coastal town of Netanya, Tulkarem was one of the first districts targeted by the plan to build an Israeli Separation Wall in 2002. Over 42,000 dunums of these fertile agricultural lands have been destroyed, confiscated, or segregated by the wall's construction.

The disfiguring of the past, the blight of such violence becomes part of the processes of terror that make it impossible to take anything for granted. In his description of the "absolute power" of the concentration camp, Wolfgang Sofsky writes:

> Absolute power is not bent on achieving blind obedience or discipline, but desires to generate a universe of total uncertainty, one in which submissiveness is no shield against even worse outcomes. . . . It uses various procedures for total control—not for the development of individual self-discipline, but as instruments of quotidian harassment, of daily cruelty. . . . Absolute power goes on a rampage whenever it so desires. It does not wish to limit freedom, but to destroy it.[19]

The inconspicuous rituals of daily life turn into sites of irreparable damage. There is no place left for life. No one is safe. Though surrounded by corpses and the rubble of homes, a group of Gazans were handcuffed, eyes covered, herded into a pit, and kept there for three days, exposed to the cold air, wind, and rain, without food, water, or access to a toilet.[20] To reflect on the Gaza Strip is to encounter persons assailed, transformed, disposed of in what Sara Roy, nearly two years before Operation Cast Lead, describes as "the national dismemberment of the Palestinians."[21]

What has happened in Palestine prompts us to rethink definitions of torture, even as we bear in mind Jeremy Waldron's warning against the clarification of torture after the disclosure of the Bush White House torture memos of August 2002 and March 2003. The more specific the legal analysis of what is obviously torture, the more arbitrary the definition becomes and the more equivocal the limits of torture. "There are some scales one really should not be on," Waldron writes, "and with respect to which one really does not have a legitimate interest in knowing precisely how far along the scale one is permitted to go."[22]

Common Article 3 of the Geneva Conventions provides: "Persons taking no active part in the hostilities, including members of armed forces who have laid down their arms . . . shall in all circumstances be treated humanely." Prohibited is "violence to life and person, in particular murder of all kinds, mutilation, cruel treatment and torture." The article also prohibits "outrages upon personal dignity" and provides for treatment (in conditions of detention as well as interrogation procedures) that is not "humiliating and degrading." The spectacle of the Gaza assault, resulting in the destruction of the very foundations of civil life, gives us insight into the vexations of personhood and the erosion of dignity that accompany cruelty and inhuman treatment.

Torture is not always tied to judicial forms, but implemented in such a way that it suffuses everything—nothing in daily life can be seen or touched that is not a reminder of degradation. Let us now reconsider the extremities of torture: not in the interrogation cells but on the streets, in the homes, in the waking hours when the basic necessities of human life are no longer available, or granted only after rituals of humiliation, at the checkpoint, at the roadblock, in the market, at the university. The recurrent presence of temporal and spatial constraints, invested with infinite possibilities of desecration, asks that we expand our definition of torture.

While recognizing the ancient meaning of judicial torture as "the torment and suffering of the body in order to elicit the truth," I encourage a move beyond the legal definition to what Edward Peters describes as "a moral definition of torture" or even "a sentimental definition." I appreciate his concern with the dangers of such expansive application—taking torture to be "a moral-sentimental term designating the infliction of suffering, however defined, upon anyone for any purpose—or for no purpose."[23] Yet the indignities and damages committed against persons in various contemporary sites of disabling demand that we become sentimental, even hyperbolic, in our stand against systems of terror. The call for and increased reliance on reason perpetuate terror: atrocities purveyed in a language that blinds, manipulates, and deadens.

What Aimé Césaire, in *Discourse on Colonialism*, condemns as "the gigantic rape of everything intimate" recovers torture's range of meanings.[24] State coercion, wreckage, and waste are displayed not only in the public sphere, but inflicted in the most private places. Subordinated to the vagaries of military control and formal detention, Palestinians also suffer random attacks on their personal and moral integrity. Just as the wall and the settlements remold the boundaries of the Palestinian homeland, the rituals of humiliation and violence accomplished by soldiers, bulldozers, tanks, Apache helicopters, curfews, land grabs, and surveillance threaten personal identity. Prejudicial practices are designed to engineer the collapse of personality. To be in constant danger, to experience the self as no longer certain, exposed to arbitrary schemes that penetrate personal and

social existence, is to undergo a debilitation usually confined to total institutions such as prisons. This order of confinement goes beyond the pre-
cincts of punishment. And with the extension of such closure, the design of
torture prompts us to bear witness both to the excessive violence of the
perpetrators and to the incredible resilience of the victims. But the state of
terror seems to be hidden from the eyes of the world, immune to the pre-
scriptive force of morality, beyond the judgment of society.

September 2009

CHAPTER 17

John Yoo, the Torture Memos, and Ward Churchill: Exploring the Outer Limits of Academic Freedom

Richard Falk

There seems to be something terribly wrong with a moral calculus that is currently operating within American universities and, more broadly, in American society. It so far insulates John Yoo from any process of formal accountability, while subjecting such notable and respected teacher/scholars as Ward Churchill, Norman Finkelstein, William Robinson, Joel Kovel, Nadia Abu El-Haj, and Joseph Massad to institutionally complicit harassment, sometimes culminating in a punitive outcome.[1] What is painfully apparent at this point is that the canons of "academic freedom" are vulnerable to encroachment, owing to political pressures mounted by politicians, media, influential alumni, ideologically driven administrators, and extremist NGOs. These pressures have intensified during the last decade, especially resulting from the activism of ultrapatriotic groups during the Bush years directly following the 9/11 attacks and by pro-Israeli zealots seeking to stifle a growing tide of criticism of Israel within academic settings.[2]

In the worst of these cases, a promising academic career was substantially disrupted, if not destroyed (Churchill, Finkelstein, Kovel). Even if in the end no punitive action was taken, the accused individual was seriously damaged in his/her career prospects simply by being forced to defend against highly publicized, irresponsible charges that enjoyed a measure of credibility through being pursued by lengthy university procedures of inquiry, assessment, and punishment (Robinson, El-Haj, Massad). Often what are left behind in collective memory are the initial allegations and investigative process, and not the exonerating outcome.

Additional encroachments on academic freedom of this nature are achieved behind closed doors, with no way of definitively ascertaining whether the alleged grounds for withholding of tenure or reappointment or opposing a new appointment were based on the controversial views and activities attributed to an individual or arising from a proper judgment as to academic achievement and promise. Whatever the *real* reason for negative results, the outcome is explained and rationalized as flowing from an impartial evaluation process. There is no obligation in many faculty and administrative settings to disclose the grounds for a decision or to give the individual whose work is being assessed an opportunity to challenge an adverse outcome. If those holding controversial views are consistently denied tenure or promotion despite possessing exceedingly strong academic credentials, an impression is unavoidably created that certain attitudes are not likely to fare well in university communities. Such impressions are now widespread, which is itself inimical to an atmosphere of free public debate, which is an essential ingredient of academic freedom. It fosters the belief, whether accurate or not, that job security and career opportunities are likely to be put at risk if a faculty member is critical of sensitive government policy or overtly supportive of the Palestinian struggle for human rights and self-determination, either in public discussion or through scholarly or journalistic efforts. The mix of issues that currently generates pressures on academic freedom tends to ebb and flow with the historical setting. Such factors as the political orientation of government and the preoccupations of societal groupings with strong policy agendas help explain this variance. Also relevant are the scholarly credentials and organizational skills on the part of those who are targeted and who resist such encroachments.

Beyond the damage done to an individual merely by being inappropriately or maliciously charged is the series of constraints placed on the university as a marketplace of ideas and a venue where critical and controversial thinking, teaching, and research are highly valued and protected. The cumulative effect of these distressing developments in recent years has produced a "new McCarthyism." Unlike the original McCarthy assault on academic freedom, the main animus for the new McCarthyism comes from civil society (NGOs and the media) rather than government, although government institutions and political officials have on occasion been allied with repressive campaigns.

This unfortunate pattern certainly underscores the current importance of protecting academic freedom against shifts in political mood, or ideological swings, a concern that should not be disregarded when our attention turns to the insulation of Bush operatives such as John Yoo from criminal and professional accountability. Defenders of academic freedom should be equally vigilant in protecting viewpoints and conduct with which they vigorously disagree on policy or ideological grounds. The question presented with respect to Yoo relates to whether his contribution to the perpetration of torture while on leave from the university crosses a red line that justifies formal action of censure, suspension, reassignment, or dismissal.

Yoo's supporters, of course, invoke academic freedom in his defense, claiming that he acted in good faith while engaged in public service and is now the victim of unwarranted attacks from people who hated the Bush presidency and do not share Yoo's views on executive power or on the narrowing of the torture prohibition under international law, which he steadfastly claims to have articulated and recommended with sincerity and on the basis of scholarly competence. There are two issues that need to be kept distinct when evaluating the allegations of wrongdoing made against Yoo. First, Yoo's ideological support of the torture policies of the Bush presidency in his academic writing and speaking, however distasteful and legally questionable in their scholarly merit, is not by itself an adequate basis for challenging his academic credentials as a law professor. Second, the relevant inquiry needs to focus on acts and activities undertaken by Yoo while *officially* serving the government as an adviser, and should not become sidetracked by what he said or wrote, except to note revealing discrepancies between his performance in government and elsewhere as bearing on his sincerity and good faith.

The central question is whether Yoo so undermined his moral, legal, and professional credibility as to potentially make him a liability as a faculty member entrusted with the training of future lawyers. Even here there should be a presumption in Yoo's favor, as the launching of an investigation itself does harm to his academic reputation, even if no further sanction or action results, as now seems to be the case. What needs to be determined on a preliminary basis is whether sufficient grounds exist for believing that Yoo manifestly disregarded relevant legal norms and manipulated legal advice, either to produce policies sought by his political superiors or to provide those who carried out controversial policies a legal shield. Reports and recommendations resulting from governmental inquiries or formal action are helpful in evaluating whether a basis exists for undertaking an investigation within the University of California, but such external assessment should not be treated as resolving the question one way or the other. The issues posed are almost certain to harm the *distinctive* teacher/student relation in the setting of professional training of students for legal careers. This particular faculty identity raises special issues as to how support for academic freedom should be balanced against other considerations, including the educational importance of imparting to students of the law a sense of ethical responsibility as intrinsic to their professional identity.[3] This aspect of the Yoo controversy is particularly significant because the nature of his role can be viewed as validating, if not contributing to, the widespread reliance on torture under the auspices of the United States government in the post-9/11 period, a pattern of behavior that flagrantly violates international humanitarian law, the Universal Declaration of Human Rights, and numerous other international law instruments.

There are academic freedom dimensions of the Yoo controversy, however the allegations are formulated. There is some merit to Yoo's claims that, if the allegations are investigated, it will make future academicians either more reluctant to engage in government service or more risk-averse when they do so. But if no investigation results, it will create a precedent that irresponsible or even potentially criminal behavior while serving in the government is irrelevant to a faculty member's qualifications to teach law students. This is a particularly disturbing conclusion in the context of an apparent endorsement of torture as a mode of prisoner interrogation. These issues should be determined in the last analysis purely by university procedures as a matter of institutional autonomy and integrity, which should be free to consider outside assessments without being bound to respect their conclusions.

There is an additional factor present here. Yoo's alleged behavior relates directly to an ongoing controversy over restoring respect for international law, especially in the context of torture, after the years of disregard during the presidency of George W. Bush.[4] It raises the novel question of whether a stronger policy justification for investigating the allegations against Yoo exists as a way of expressing within educational institutions the importance attached to the *international* rule of law, as well as the aptness of according an academic priority to restoring respect for the absolute prohibition on torture. That is, the substance of the alleged wrongdoing in government service makes a difference. For example, if a law faculty member on leave gave manifestly unprofessional advice on Pentagon contracts with defense companies or on the legality of an immigration fence on the Mexican border, the behavioral consequences might be serious, and intense feelings of outrage might arise, but absent any strong indication of fraud or international lawlessness, the presumption of propriety should be strong enough to insulate such an individual from investigation, much less disciplinary action. To do otherwise would unduly inhibit the independence of those who are allowed to leave the university to serve in the government or elsewhere (e.g., in international institutions or NGOs). What I am suggesting in this case, in contrast, is that the national and international damage done through the legal authorization of interrogation techniques widely believed by experts to constitute "torture" is of such gravity in this historical moment as to overcome the presumption of propriety that normally insulates a faculty member from accountability investigations.[5] Yoo's interpretative maneuvers in redefining torture have been subject to detailed critique elsewhere, and I will not review them.[6] My view is that such redefinitions by Yoo were unprofessional in the extreme, as well as being patently incorrect, although I accept provisionally Yoo's good faith. Their unprofessional character can be easily grasped by considering what our reaction would be to a foreign adversary of the United States relying on such techniques as waterboarding, mock executions, or threats in the course of interrogating captive US soldiers. There is every reason to suppose that such behavior would be treated without even discussion as torture by the entire spectrum of opinion in the United States, including the legal profession, and that dissent from such a conclusion would be as irrelevant as it became in relation to the criminality of the institution of apartheid in South Africa or the commission of genocide in Cambodia.

This essay attempts to examine the atmosphere current within many universities that is so threatening to the precious institution of academic freedom, as well as the importance of recognizing the existence of certain carefully monitored outer limits to that freedom. Consideration of the cases of Ward Churchill and John Yoo are illustrative of the two antagonistic poles: protecting freedom, discerning limits. Admittedly, one walks a delicate tightrope in trying to balance unfettered freedom of expression within university settings and in public spaces with standards of responsibility for actions and activities that are crucially relevant to sustaining appropriate teacher/student respect in a democratic society. This concern over responsibility takes on added weight when it bears directly upon the contested activities of those teachers who train students for professional careers. In this regard, law teachers should not provide strong negative models with respect to the rule of law, just as teachers in medical school should not offer negative models in relation to the practice of medicine.

There are issues analogous to this dispute about the limits of legal professionalism in the context of academic freedom that have arisen in relation to medical and psychological experts who took part in or gave guidance to interrogation sessions that involved torture.

Commentary on the New McCarthyism: The Churchill Case

The widely reported case of Ward Churchill serves as a menacing instance of this recent onslaught on academic freedom. Churchill was a tenured full professor and chair of ethnic studies at the University of Colorado at Boulder when the controversy erupted. He enjoyed prominence within the institution, where he had been a faculty member since 1990 and was known as a popular and effective teacher. He was also nationally known as an influential and productive, if controversial, scholar, an eloquent advocate/ activist on behalf of the rights of indigenous peoples. His sharp critiques of American imperialism were also a prominent feature of much of his published writings.

Churchill's troubles surfaced in relation to a lecture he had been invited to give at Hamilton College in upstate New York, scheduled for delivery in February 2005. In the community where Hamilton is located, a campaign was launched to discredit the group that had issued the invitation; at the same time, an opinion piece was unearthed that had been written by Churchill and published shortly after the 9/11 attacks in an obscure online publication, *Day Nights Field Notes*. In that piece Churchill described the attacks as "chickens coming home to roost" and the financial workers in the World Trade Center as "little Eichmanns."[7] There is no doubt that Churchill's text contained provocative imagery based on a radical critique of the American role in the world economy that regarded the 9/11 attacks as inevitable responses to the lethal impact of US policies on Third World peoples. Churchill has subsequently explained that his intention was to analogize the role of investors in facilitating a world economy responsible for the death and impoverishment of millions of Third World peoples to that of Eichmann in arranging for shipment of human beings to the Nazi death camps.[8] A storm of media outrage followed upon disclosure of this material, led by Bill O'Reilly and reinforced by a variety of angry denunciations of Churchill by politicians, including the governor of Colorado, Bill Owens, and of New York, George Pataki. This led the local sponsoring group to withdraw the invitation for Churchill to lecture at Hamilton and to many public demands for Churchill's dismissal from his faculty position at the University of Colorado. In response, university leadership did not invoke academic freedom in Churchill's defense. Quite the contrary: the highest university officials made public statements extremely hostile to Churchill's comments on 9/11, as did a variety of leading Colorado politicians. The local media joined the campaign to have Churchill dismissed on the basis of his supposedly unacceptable views on the 9/11 attacks.

In this inflamed atmosphere a university disciplinary procedure was established in a manner that seemed to reinforce the allegations of an administrative bias against Churchill. Nimbly skirting the obvious obstacle of Churchill's right to free speech as a faculty member in a public university, the investigating committee never considered the offending speech that produced the furor, but switched gears and proceeded to examine an array of completely unrelated charges of "academic misconduct" against Churchill. The university committee's action amounted to a flagrant instance of bait and switch, recommending that Churchill be suspended without pay for one year and then reinstated without prejudice.

His alleged academic misconduct consisted of a few instances of misleading footnote material and some unacknowledged ghostwriting of the publications of others, followed by Churchill's supposedly misleading citation of the material allegedly ghosted to bolster his own arguments in subsequent publications. These findings provide evidence of occasional carelessness on Churchill's part in the course of a long and successful academic career, and some examples of poor judgment in his professional dealings, but nothing worse than what many professors have been guilty of in the course of their careers without having their professional stature formally questioned or even casually criticized.[9] So understood, there is no credible basis for disciplinary action, especially considering that Churchill's academic credentials had been periodically reviewed while he was at Boulder, and given the context that strongly supports the contention that the academic misconduct charges were invoked as a proxy because his actual offending acts (having nothing to do with his academic performance) were remarks insulated from disciplinary review, being constitutionally protected free speech. Even this unjust and undeserved punishment recommended by university procedures turned out to be far too mild for the incensed board of regents and university president, who ordered Churchill's permanent dismissal for academic misconduct on all charges by a seven to one vote.

Churchill reacted by initiating legal action in the Denver District Court, seeking reinstatement and lost compensation, arguing that his dismissal was retaliation for his words. This claim proved persuasive to the jury. From various sources it became clear that the jury understood that the real (and only) reason for punishing Churchill was due to his comments about 9/11, and implicitly that these comments, however unpopular and imprudent, were protected as free speech. The university successfully appealed the trial verdict, an appellate judge taking the unusual step of overturning a jury verdict, and doing so on extremely tenuous grounds, accepting practically verbatim the flimsy arguments of the legal brief submitted by the university. Churchill is currently appealing this decision. Whatever the eventual outcome, Churchill has already been severely victimized for his utterances in an inflamed political atmosphere and his career and credentials permanently damaged.

There is no doubt that these efforts to punish those within universities who express unpopular views or commitments have unjustly targeted and harmed those individuals, and more consequentially, that these highly publicized cases have eroded the intellectual atmosphere within American universities, encouraging various degrees of self-censorship and inhibition with respect to certain types of controversial questions. This deteriorating atmosphere is mainly generated by right-wing pressures and does not have any inhibiting effects on the espousal of conservative controversial views opposing abortion and gay marriage or in support of Israeli settlement expansion and aggressive uses of force. In this sense, the defense of academic freedom is an ideologically tinged struggle in which reactionary views have clear sailing, while liberal/left opinions, especially on selected sensitive subjects, produce political campaigns hurtful and harmful to the faculty member who is made the target of the attack. It may be the case that ultraright faculty members, who are not numerous at leading universities, may be victims of disguised ideological prejudice in tenure review and promotion situations where the rationale for votes and decisions does not have to be disclosed. In my experience this is more a matter of polemics and anxiety than a reality, as the liberal mentality that is often in control, especially in the social sciences, is genuinely imbued with an Enlightenment ethos of reason and fairness that evaluates the work of peers mainly on the basis of objective criteria of merit. In my forty years on the faculty of Princeton University, I never witnessed a single instance of such hidden discrimination against conservative candidates for jobs, tenure, or promotion, but I definitely did perceive what appeared to be examples of unacknowledged discrimination from time to time against women and against scholars thought to be "Marxist" or otherwise positioned on the political left.

Professional Responsibility versus Academic Freedom: The Difficult Case of John Yoo

Such a backdrop makes it a delicate matter to propose limits to the job security of tenured faculty, precisely the dilemma in which advocates of John Yoo's dismissal from the University of California Berkeley law faculty find themselves.

It should be clear that the Yoo controversy is not about academic freedom in any strict or normal sense of objecting to opinions expressed on or off campus or due to a controversial engagement in nonviolent citizen advocacy. And there is no challenge being directed against his classroom demeanor or scholarly competence; he is from all accounts a skillful and dedicated teacher, receptive to diverse views, and a prolific scholar contributing to leading professional journals and published by important academic publishers. The case against Yoo relates exclusively to those of his activities as a high-ranking government official that appear to have encouraged the United States government to violate fundamental norms of international law, especially and most vividly with respect to the prohibition of torture. The issue posed, then, is whether there is a *principled* basis for *assessing* Yoo's conduct, which treats him fairly, and takes due account of the inappropriateness of imposing any sanction merely to express disapproval of or to discredit his legal opinions and neoconservative political orientation. Rather, the argument advanced here is that there exist limits beyond which even a tenured faculty member cannot venture without being properly subject to censure or other disciplinary measures for unacceptable behavior. Such a punitive response, although rarely appropriate, would be applicable to *activities*, whether they occur inside or outside the university setting, provided that they bear fundamentally on his/her *moral* qualifications as a teacher/scholar. With respect to Yoo, what is involved is whether the advice he gave as a government official was so misguided or deliberately misleading as to break the trust normally attributed to someone claiming professional competence as a legal expert. Also relevant in assessing the case against Yoo is whether his role as a law school professor should be taken into specific account, as well as whether the societal importance of ensuring future respect for the torture prohibition matters in deciding whether to inquire into the professional propriety of Yoo's government service. At stake is the particular importance of encouraging professional responsibility on the part of those entrusted with the education of future lawyers, while at the same time not unduly constraining academic specialists when they are invited to do public service on behalf of the government. In this sense, there is a sharp, and in some ways arbitrary, distinction being drawn between protecting a scholar's right to advocate irresponsible government policy in a classroom or in a publication and not protecting the utterance of the same views as advice or guidance in one's role as a government adviser. In the context of hate speech or the advocacy of policies amounting to torture, as commonly understood, controversial grounds already exist for taking action, even if the effect is to inhibit free speech. After all, the views of a credentialed professor at an important university might exert as much or more influence on the formulation of government policy as those of a government advisor. At the least, then, proponents of investigation or censure need to evaluate each case individually, with sensitivity to the complex set of considerations that often pull in contradictory directions, as well as with a strong presumption in favor of the propriety of the words and deeds of a faculty member. In fact this presumption needs to be overridden twice: to justify investigation and then to justify a punitive result, remembering that the investigation itself is inevitably punitive in its impact on the person's professional reputation. In some sense, the concern is about what sort of precedent is being set, either by overlooking the offending behavior or by taking punitive action.[10]

My central contention is that there seems to be something terribly wrong with an assessment template that has resulted in the dismissal of Churchill while insulating Yoo from having to undergo even an investigation as to whether his government service was incompatible with his role as a law school professor. Yoo has experienced no official institutional pressure to resign his faculty appointment, nor has he even been formally criticized for his widely publicized promotion of detention and interrogation tactics, widely believed to constitute torture.[11] On the contrary, Yoo has been consistently, if ambivalently, defended by his immediate academic superior, Christopher Edley, the dean of the School of Law at the University of California, Berkeley. Yoo was also invited to be a distinguished visiting professor at Chapman Law School during the spring semester of 2009 without encountering formal difficulty, and was staunchly supported by the Chapman Law School dean, John Eastman, with more substantive approval than offered by Dean Edley.[12] In addition, Yoo has enjoyed access to opinion columns in leading newspapers, in which he has restated his self-justifying and unrepentant arguments in defense of his governmental role, and has even been offered a spot as a regular columnist in a nationally prominent newspaper, the *Philadelphia Inquirer*. This is not to deny that Yoo has been subject to harsh public criticism from some professional colleagues and has been the target of a variety of student protests and disruptions wherever he ventures to speak or teach on a university campus.

Despite these manifest differences in treatment, the comparison of Churchill and Yoo does not lead to an inevitable conclusion. The abundantly clear indication that Churchill was the victim of an inflamed political witch hunt says nothing in itself as to whether the allegations against Yoo should be given credence. It could well be that, despite the fact that the Yoo case is more problematic from the perspective of academic freedom, it still fails to meet the burden of persuasion necessary to overcome the strong presumption of propriety. I would recommend against taking a dogmatic view on either side of the debate. The fact that Churchill was wrongfully treated does not at all lead to the conclusion that, because Yoo was associated with some severe governmental wrongdoing, his behavior should be addressed punitively, or possibly, administratively.

However, there does seem to be something fundamentally misguided about an academic code of conduct that subjects controversial opinions to such intimidating pressure but insulates *behavior* that appears criminally indictable from scrutiny, even though it clearly produces violations of the human rights of vulnerable individuals in ways that cause irreparable mental and physical harm, including death. Of course, it is a mistake to confuse Yoo's objectionable opinions and affiliations with any challenge to his academic tenure. His academic writing, in which he argues on behalf of virtually unlimited presidential war powers, although an extremist, idiosyncratic, and objectionable interpretation of the Constitution that could prove dangerous to the country and the world, to the extent that it is made operational, falls well within the domain of protected speech. There is no respectable constitutional means to disallow such speech, even if its adoption by the government would lead directly to unlawful, and likely criminal, foreign policy initiatives.[13] The only question worth pursuing—but it is an extremely serious one—is whether Yoo's links to torture policy *when serving in the government* were of such an incriminating character that they could be seen to damage severely his credibility as a teacher of future law students, in which case they call out for an institutional investigation by the university to assess whether his conduct justifies removing him from a teaching role, or even from a faculty position. Putting the question more concretely, does giving advice to political leaders to engage in policies that are broadly conceived to constitute "torture" itself constitute such a dereliction of professional responsibility that the university must consider taking disciplinary action, including possibly even the withdrawal of an entitlement to faculty membership? There is also the option of reassigning

Yoo to teaching roles that do not involve the offending subject matter or to an administrative position, reflecting the view that independent of Yoo's personal responsibility, the university assumes an institutional responsibility to avoid any impression that it views the endorsement of torture as professionally acceptable.

The most comprehensive and important defense of Yoo maintaining his position as a tenured professor has been made by Dean Edley in a statement that gains persuasive weight because it is coupled with an expression of disapproval of Yoo's government role.[14] Edley grounds his analysis on the acknowledgment that Yoo "offered bad ideas and even worse advice during his government service," but insists nonetheless that such acts "would not warrant dismissal or even a potentially chilling inquiry." He contends that "as a legal matter, the test here" is set forth in a provision on unacceptable faculty conduct found in the Academic Personnel Manual adopted by both the academic senate of the University of California and the board of regents. He refers to the test set forth in that provision as "very restrictive": "Commission of a criminal act which has led to conviction in a court of law and which clearly demonstrates unfitness to continue as a member of the faculty."[15]

Edley refers to this standard as "binding on me as dean" procedurally and, in any event, takes note of the fact that authority for disciplinary action is exclusively vested in the provost, chancellor, and academic senate. On this basis he arrives at the stark conclusion that, absent "very substantial evidence of criminality . . . no university worthy of distinction should even contemplate dismissing a faculty member. That standard has not been met." There is an obvious contradiction in Edley's reasoning. The standard he invokes from the manual bases taking disciplinary action on a criminal conviction, whereas Edley's more flexible formulation specifies "substantial evidence of criminality" as sufficient. This standard has arguably been met by virtue of a variety of executive and congressional reports and scholarly assessments of the manifest illegality of justifying conduct that falls well within the torture prohibition. Somewhat misleadingly, I think, Edley asserts that it is important to defer to the views of the attorney general, "[m]y friend," as to whether criminality can be attributed to those who gave legal advice on torture: in his words, "We need to know what happened, and not just from journalists." According to Edley, "it is up to the Department of Justice to determine whether the basis lies for criminal prosecution and up to the court to determine whether a crime has been committed."[16] Quite rightly, he concludes that "[u]niversity faculty and administrators are not competent to answer these questions. If we try to do so in the circumstances at hand, we imperil values at our very core." Of course this is so, but beside the point. The real issue that is obscured by such reasoning is whether "substantial evidence" of criminality exists to undermine a faculty member's entitlement, a matter that ought not to be conclusively decided by government assessments or even by a formal determination as to criminality. Suppose the McCain-Palin ticket had prevailed in the 2008 presidential elections and a new attorney general supportive of the Bush interrogation policies had been appointed. Would it then be at all credible to insist that deference to official pronouncements is protective of the university interest in determining "unacceptable faculty behavior"? Of course, the fact that an Obama appointee cleared Yoo is also not determinative in my judgment, although entitled to more weight than if the clearance had come during the Bush presidency.

There is another problem with the Edley approach. The Academic Personnel Manual is not nearly as rigid and restrictive as he makes it appear. This restrictive criterion requiring a criminal conviction is found in a short section pertaining to the relations of a faculty member to the "community," which addresses matters not remotely related to the kind of concerns raised by Yoo's alleged misconduct: the misapplication of international law during his period of government service. The restrictive criterion upon which Edley puts so much weight in reaching his conclusion supportive of Yoo's status as a law faculty member sheds little light on how to evaluate the links between behavior that might not produce conviction for a crime, but that would undermine the credibility of a teacher of law students. The inflammatory nature of torture as a governmental tactic also would seem to create a special challenge for a law school dean that cannot be evaded by abstract argument.

Actually, the Academic Personnel Manual seems to allow greater flexibility than Edley acknowledges. The premise underlying the entire approach to unacceptable faculty conduct in the manual is based on the idea that the standards enumerated are *illustrative* and not exhaustive. In this regard each inquiry should be guided by the broader mandate to view "as unacceptable" any conduct that "is inconsistent with the mission of the university." Here, considerations pertaining to Yoo's advice to the government to take actions that manifestly violated basic rules of international treaty law and international criminal law would and should come into play. Edley acknowledges that "the vast majority of legal academics with a view of the matter disagree with substantial portions of Professor's Yoo's analysis; this includes most though perhaps not all of his Berkeley Law colleagues." The word "disagrees" in this sentence is troublesome in that it disregards the extent to which concerned law specialists view Yoo's advice as opportunistically and blatantly encouraging the adoption of "unlawful" and "criminal" policies by government officials. These policies facilitated recourse to torture by interrogators and political leaders, and possibly encouraged the perpetration of crimes against humanity in detention centers, prisons, and in the setting of covert operations under CIA auspices. By providing a mantle of legality Yoo gave professionally inappropriate aid and comfort to these policies, policymakers, and perpetrators; even if he did so in good faith, that advice, if in flagrant violation of clear norms of international criminal law, is unlawful and should be subject to accountability procedures.

Edley seems to recognize this in raising the following crucial question: "Was there clear professional misconduct—that is, some breach of the professional ethics applicable to a government attorney—material to Professor Yoo's academic performance now?" He adds later in his memorandum that "[l]awyers . . . should not have a blanket immunity for all their advice and actions," but then adds, somewhat disconcertingly and misleadingly, that "it matters to me that Yoo was an adviser, while President Bush and his national security appointees were the deciders." And finally, Edley seems to grant credence to the argument that Yoo's advice "was so wrong on these sensitive issues . . . that it amounted to an ethical breach or even a war crime." He appropriately points out that "[f]ew professions require an oath at entry, but law does. Oaths must mean something." If they do, then certainly criteria related to probable cause have been satisfied, and Yoo's conduct as a government legal official should be investigated according to University of California procedures, with Yoo accorded the full protection of his rights, including a presumption of innocence that should be made difficult to overcome.

It is unclear whether, in Edley's formulations, he equates the notion of "war crime" with "ethical breach," thereby making it exempt from disciplinary action. If he does, as seems to be the case, he endorses a most unfortunate and academically dubious downgrading of international law and a failure to respect Article VI (2) of the US Constitution concerning the performance of governmental duties, which requires that duly ratified treaties be treated as the supreme law of the land on a par with Congressional legislation. Equally troubling is Edley's strange assertion that ethical considerations may not be relevant to determining Yoo's qualifications to serve as a law professor because of the specific nature of his teaching duties. As Edley phrases the distinction, "[n]on-clinical faculty need not be a member of a bar, and Professor Yoo does not teach our courses on

Professional Responsibility." This seems to suggest that considerations of professional responsibility are not uniformly relevant to all aspects of legal education. Such an amoral outlook is disturbingly likely to produce an atmosphere of professional irresponsibility and amorality on the part of lawyers.

I direct this degree of attention to Dean Edley's treatment of Yoo's case in order to give a full account of the reasons it might be inappropriate to proceed further with an investigation of whether Yoo should be subject to any disciplinary action. My analysis suggests that there are sufficient grounds to support an investigation, even without questioning the claim that Yoo acted in good faith when offering legal advice as a government official, although the outcome of such an investigation if properly conducted is difficult to prejudge. Perhaps an adviser should be held to a lower level of accountability than a decision-maker, as Edley argues, but not necessarily. After all, the decider is probably not competent to assess the quality of advice received, and should be able to rely confidently on advice regarding legal guidelines provided by an expert, although such reliance would not provide an adequate defense if, as here, the violations of treaty obligations are flagrant. What seems clear is that offering advice that endorses behavior amounting to a war crime on a matter as important as the treatment of criminal detainees accused of terrorist activity should be taken into account in assessing the professional fitness of a tenured faculty member. In my view, one of the most serious indications of Yoo's professional *irresponsibility* in his governmental role arose from his failure to acknowledge that his line of preferred interpretation of legal principles (with respect to war powers, the applicability of treaties, the scope of the torture prohibition) departed significantly from the weight of expert opinion and from some of his own scholarly writing, where he does admit that his views are at odds with the professional consensus on this subject matter.[17] Suppressing such legal controversy or ambiguity is itself a serious failure to act responsibly as an adviser. This is particularly true in a case such as this, where those being advised have no familiarity with the legal issues or the relevant range of disagreements. As Yoo should have realized, his advice, in addition to being legally dubious, coincided with the strong policy preferences of the political leadership at the time. Providing excessively clear advice under such circumstances is itself misleading for those seeking guidance, assuming they are not merely using advisers to rationalize policies that have already been decided upon, and that are understood to be of questionable legality. If the latter was the pattern, as it seems to have been in the Bush presidency, then the professional irresponsibility and possible legal culpability of Yoo are compounded.[18]

University investigation into Yoo's conduct, then, is partly a matter of confirming the relevance of international law in the affairs of government and in the education of citizens and students. Such confirmation should be unnecessary in the aftermath of the Nuremberg judgment criminalizing a broad range of behavior in the Nazi period, but obviously the response of the US government to the 9/11 attacks suggests otherwise. In fact, there is evidence of a far broader pattern of American evasion of international law. In this regard, to pass over Yoo's torture memos in institutional silence sends the wrong message to law students and to society at this time. But to rush to judgment, concluding that Yoo is an unconvicted war criminal who deserves to be deprived of his academic credentials, is also grossly unfair, and not a good model for addressing comparable instances in the future.

A Concluding Remark

As I have suggested, determining where to draw the line in regard to faculty discretion on and off campus is difficult. It relates here to questions of academic freedom broadly, not in the usual sense of judging the propriety of one's opinions as a teacher/scholar, but in a larger sense of adjudicating one's accountability for actions taken while engaged temporarily in public service. In general, this kind of public sector experience is a recognition of academic stature and is believed to add a valuable dimension to a professor's teaching and scholarship, and universities recognize this by granting faculty members extended leaves longer than normally allowed. Therefore, imposing any disciplinary action should be undertaken with the greatest caution and with due regard for the rights of the accused individual. But having said this, it is crucial that national political leaders be given professional legal advice that is responsive to the requirements of international law, especially in the areas of human rights and international criminal law. In my judgment, these considerations should have tipped the balance against Professor Yoo. This means that the only acceptable way forward would have been to initiate formal investigative proceedings conducted with full due-process rights, awaiting the outcome to determine how to handle the Yoo case. It is unacceptable to defer unconditionally to extra-university procedures of assessment, especially of a governmental character, because its results are unlikely to be acceptable to both critics and apologists, and are thus likely to be dismissed by partisans on the losing side as reflecting politically biased judgments. These external assessments should certainly be taken into consideration, but not conclusively.

For instance, controversy already exists over the attorney general having drawn a line circumscribing legal accountability that, on the one hand, appears to hold the CIA perpetrators of torture legally accountable, while on the other, exempting from legal scrutiny both those officials who served in the Department of Justice, such as Yoo, and those who authorized the torture policies in the White House.

As discussed in the case of Professor Churchill, it remains urgent to restore confidence in academic freedom for professors with controversial views who become threatened or victimized within the university owing to pressure largely emanating from the community at large. Here the judicial institutions of society, entrusted with governmental authority and responsibility to uphold the rule of law, should shore up the protection of academic freedom when universities cave in to pressures or fail to uphold the rights of a faculty member. It is doubly disappointing that an appellate court in Colorado failed to provide such a backstop, and even went further by overturning a sensible jury outcome that exposed the speciousness of Churchill's dismissal on grounds of academic misconduct. In the end, there are no guarantees that a legal system, even in a democratic society, will provide consistently just results. As the struggle against slavery and racial discrimination in this country abundantly demonstrates, a concerted civil rights movement was necessary to overcome a long history of legally certified injustices. Similarly, in the struggle against torture in constitutional democracies, success depends on vigilance and citizen pressure and struggle from "below" that is strong enough to induce leaders to back away from the status quo. It is highly unlikely that torture will be eliminated from "above," even by leaders who appear to repudiate such practices. Obama's regrettable backsliding on issues of accountability for Bush-era officials is indicative of the problem: without a revolutionary mandate the dynamic of governance favors continuity and consensus, which means that divisive rule-of-law considerations of the past are subordinated to the need to address the political demands of present and future, a practical stand taken—but at the expense of the rule of law. The precariousness of Professor Yoo's faculty status reflects this rising civic pressure in the United States to take steps in various settings to implement the international law prohibition. Without such pressures his return to Berkeley would have resulted in even less friction than has been the case.

At issue here are two conflicting principles that are each a vital pillar of constitutional democracy in the early twenty-first century: (1) upholding academic freedom, thereby recognizing its essential role in safeguarding the university as a marketplace of ideas and as a venue for nurturing critical thinking and engaged citizenship; and (2) extending the rule of law to the conduct of American foreign policy, which includes the application of international law and imposes on academic advisers a professional responsibility to provide guidance that falls within the domain of reasonable interpretation and that includes, when appropriate, the admission of uncertainty and controversy with respect to the legal limits of national discretion.

In the background also is the importance of imparting professional responsibility to the legal profession. Such a consideration takes on added societal relevance in light of recent disclosures of the way in which financial and credit markets extensively relied upon legal loopholes and dubious legal maneuvers that led to great personal and collective damage. What emerges is the importance of instilling an ethos of accountability in all professions, and certainly among lawyers and their teachers.

FOR THE HUMANITIES
Julie A. Carlson and Elisabeth Weber

1. Marc Falkoff, "Notes on Guantánamo," in *Poems from Guantánamo: The Detainees Speak*, ed. Marc Falkoff (Iowa City: University of Iowa Press, 2007), 5; previous quote on 4–5. On this poetry collection, see Judith Butler, *Frames of War: When Is Life Grievable?* (London and New York: Verso, 2009), 55–62.

2. J. Hagan, H. Schoenfeld, and A. Palloni, "The Science of Human Rights, War Crimes, and Humanitarian Emergencies," *Annual Review of Sociology* 32 (2006): 329–49.

3. Elaine Scarry, *The Body in Pain: The Making and Unmaking of the World* (New York and Oxford: Oxford University Press, 1985).

4. See, for example, Françoise Sironi, *Bourreaux et victimes: Psychologie de la torture* (Paris : Odile Jacob, 1999), 29–30, 46–49.

5. See, for example, Julia Kristeva, *Desire in Language: A Semiotic Approach to Literature and Art*, ed. Léon S. Roudiez, trans. Alice Jardine, Thomas A. Gora, and Léon S. Roudiez (Oxford: Blackwell; New York: Columbia, 1980).

6. Marc Falkoff, "Notes on Guantánamo," 4.

7. Lisa Hajjar, "Does Torture Work? A Socio-Legal Assessment of the Practice in Historical and Global Perspective," *Annual Review of Law and Social Science* 5 (2009): 311–45.

8. See Angela Y. Davis, *Abolition Democracy: Beyond Empire, Prisons, and Torture* (New York: Seven Stories Press, 2005).

9. See, for example, Alfred McCoy, *A Question of Torture: CIA Interrogation from the Cold War to the War on Terror* (New York: Metropolitan Books, 2006), 190–206; Darius Rejali, *Torture and Democracy* (Princeton: Princeton University Press, 2007), 23–24, 446–79, 518, 536; and Mark Danner, "The Logic of Torture," *New York Review of Books*, June 24, 2004, http://www.markdanner.com/articles/show/34?class=related_content_link; and Danner, "Tales from Torture's Dark World," *New York Times*, March 15, 2009, http://www.markdanner.com/articles/show/152.

10. Hajjar, "Does Torture Work?" 140; see also McCoy, *A Question of Torture*, 128, 195, 212–13; and Amy Goodman, "Professor McCoy Exposes

the History of CIA Interrogation, From the Cold War to the War on Terror" [interview with Alfred McCoy], *Democracy Now!*, February 17, 2006, http://www.democracynow.org/2006/2/17/professor_mccoy_exposes_the_history_ of. During this interview, McCoy states: "There is no such thing as a little bit of torture. The whole myth of scientific surgical torture, that torture advocates, academic advocates in this country came up with, that's impossible. That cannot operate. It will inevitably spread."

11. Jacques Derrida, "Différance," in *Margins of Philosophy*, trans. Alan Bass (Chicago: Chicago University Press, 1986), 7.

12. Derrida, *Specters of Marx*, trans. Peggy Kamuf (New York: Routledge, 1994), 10.

13. See, for example, Orlando Patterson, *Slavery and Social Death* (Cambridge, Mass.: Harvard University Press, 1982); and Abdul R. JanMohamed, *The Death-Bound-Subject: Richard Wright's Archaeology of Death* (Durham: Duke University Press, 2005).

14. Patricia Ticineto Clough, ed., *The Affective Turn: Theorizing the Social* (Durham: Duke University Press, 2007).

15. Jean Améry, *At the Mind's Limits: Contemplations by a Survivor on Auschwitz and Its Realities*, trans. Sidney Rosenfeld and Stella P. Rosenfeld (Bloomington: Indiana University Press, 1980), 34, 36.

16. The prisoners have no registration number, and don't have access to lawyers or visits from the International Red Cross; their families have no knowledge of their whereabouts. The very existence of these prisons was first revealed to a larger audience through an article by Dana Priest, and the location of currently existing black sites is, obviously, unknown; see Priest, "CIA Holds Terror Suspects in Secret Prisons," *Washington Post*, November 2, 2005, A01, http://www.washingtonpost.com/wp-dyn/content/article/2005/11/01/AR2005110101644.html. In 2006, Priest won the Pulitzer Prize for this article and others she had written on the CIA and the War on Terror.

17. Derrida, "Poetics and Politics of Witnessing," in *Sovereignties in Question: The Poetics of Paul Celan*, ed. Thomas Dutoit and Outi Pasanen (New York: Fordham University Press, 2005), 68.

18. Ibid.

19. "I can claim to offer reliable testimony only if I claim to be able to witness about it in front of myself, sincerely, without mask and without veil, only if I claim to know what I saw, heard, or touched, only if I claim to be the same as yesterday, if I claim to know what I know and mean what I mean"; ibid., 79.

20. Rejali, *Torture and Democracy*, 4–10.

21. Ibid., 31; and Veena Das, "Language and Suffering," in *Social Suffering*, edited by Veena Das, A. Kleinman, and M. Lock (Berkeley: University of California Press, 1997), 88.

22. Idelber Avelar, *The Letter of Violence* (New York: Palgrave Macmillan, 2004), 48. Avelar adopts here Dori Laub's description of the "world of the Holocaust": Laub, "Truth and Testimony: The Process and the Struggle," in *Trauma: Explorations in Memory*, ed. Cathy Caruth (Baltimore: The Johns Hopkins University Press, 1999), 66.

23. Derrida, "Poetics and Politics of Witnessing," 66.

24. See Laub, "Bearing Witness or the Vicissitudes of Listening," in *Testimony: Crises of Witnessing in Literature, Psychoanalysis, and History*, ed. Shoshana Felman and Dori Laub (New York: Routledge, 1992), 57.

25. Toni Morrison, *The Bluest Eye* (New York: Vintage, 2007), xiii.

26. Derrida, "Poetics and Politics of Witnessing," 67.

27. Falkoff, "Notes on Guantánamo," 2.

28. Jacques Lacan, *Écrits: A Selection*, trans. Bruce Fink (New York: Norton, 2002), 6, 4.

29. Wolf Kittler, *The Middle Voice: Steady and Discrete Manifolds in Walter Benjamin*, Working Paper 3.25, Center for German and European Studies (Berkeley: University of California, 1996), 4.

30. Aimee Carrillo Rowe, "Be Longing: Toward a Feminist Politics of Relation," *NWSA Journal* 17, no. 2 (Summer 2005): 15–46.

31. Jumah Al Dossari, "Death Poem," in *Poems from Guantánamo*, 32.

32. See Mark Danner, *Torture and Truth: America, Abu Ghraib, and the War on Terror* (New York: New York Review of Books, 2004); and Darius Rejali, "The Real Shame of Abu Ghraib," *Time*, May 20, 2004, http://www.time .com/time/nation/article/0,8599,640375,00.html.

33. McCoy, *A Question of Torture*, 178.

34. Exemplary in this regard is Paul Bové, *Poetry against Torture: Criticism, History, and the Human* (Hong Kong: Hong Kong University Press, 2008); see, for example, page xv for Bové's argument that "poesis is the counterpoint to torture."

35. Nava generously donated his painting "Signing Statement Law or An Alternate Set of Procedures: Approved 9.29.06" as the art work used on our outreach materials advertising our series of events in 2007.

36. Gayatri Chakravorty Spivak, "Terror: A Speech After 9–11," *boundary 2* 31, no. 2 (2004): 81–111, here 81.

37. McCoy relates the use of euphemism to the "difficulty" that "strong democracies, far more than post-authoritarian societies have" with "dealing with torture." McCoy, *A Question of Torture*, 152. See also most recently Fred Halliday, *Shocked and Awed: A Dictionary of the War on Terror* (Berkeley: University of California Press, 2011).

38. David Feige, "The Real Price of Trying KSM," *Slate*, November 19, 2009, http://www.slate.com/id/2236146/.

39. See, for example, Jason Ryan, "In Reversal, Obama Orders Guantánamo Military Trial for 9/11 Mastermind Khalid Sheikh Mohammed," *ABC News*, April 4, 2011, http://abcnews.go.com/Politics/911-mastermind-khalid-sheikh-mohammed-military-commission/story?id=13291750#. TwOv9FawUcE.

40. For Obama's signing statement, see http://www.whitehouse.gov/the-press-office/2011/12/31/statement-president-hr-1540. For Scott Horton's comment, see Scott Horton, "Obama Signs the NDAA, World Does Not End (Yet)," *Harper's Magazine*, January 3, 2012, http://harpers.org/subjects/NoComment; and David Cole, "Gitmo Forever? Congress's Dangerous New Bill," http://www.nybooks.com/blogs/nyrblog/2011/dec/08/gitmo-forever-dangerous-new-bill/.

1. AN ASSAULT ON TRUTH: A CHRONOLOGY OF TORTURE, DECEPTION, AND DENIAL
Lisa Hajjar

1. See Stanley Cohen, *States of Denial: Knowing about Atrocities and Suffering* (Cambridge: Polity, 2001).

2. See Jane Mayer, *The Dark Side: The Inside Story of How the War on Terror Turned into a War on American Ideals* (New York: Doubleday, 2008).

3. The phrase "new paradigm" appears in a memo dated January 25, 2002, from then–White House counsel Alberto Gonzales to President Bush, but it was written by Addington; see R. Jeffrey Smith and Dan Eggen, "Gonzales Helped Set the Course for Detainees; Justice Nominee's Likely to Focus on Interrogation Policies," *Washington Post*, January 5, 2005, A1.

4. See Knut Dörmann, "The Legal Situation of 'Unlawful/Unprivileged Combatants,'" *International Review of the Red Cross* 85 (2003): 45–73.

5. Contrary to official claims that all detainees sent to GTMO had been captured "on the battlefield," in fact, some of the people were picked up as far afield as The Gambia and Bosnia; see David Rose, *Guantánamo: America's War on Human Rights* (New York: The New Press, 2004).

6. See "How Osama bin Laden Escaped," *Foreign Policy*, December 11, 2009, which excerpts a Senate Foreign Relations Committee report titled "Tora Bora Revisited"; available at: http://www.foreignpolicy.com/articles/2009/12/11/how_osama_bin_laden_escaped.

7. Mayer, *The Dark Side*, 186.

8. For an excellent critique, see Kim Scheppele, "Hypothetical Torture in the 'War on Terrorism,'" *Journal of National Security Law and Policy* 1 (2005): 285–340.

9. Cohen, *States of Denial*.

10. On June 10, 2006, the Pentagon announced that three GTMO detainees had committed suicide, which prison commander Harry Harris

characterized as "an act of asymmetric warfare committed against us." In 2010, new allegations surfaced that the three may have been tortured to death and that the claims of suicide were part of a cover-up; see Scott Horton, "The Guantánamo 'Suicides': A Camp Delta Sergeant Blows the Whistle," No Comment, *Harper's Magazine online*, January 18, 2010; available at: http:// harpers.org/archive/2010/01/hbc-90006368.

11. Seymour Hersh, "Torture at Abu Ghraib," *The New Yorker*, May 10, 2004, http://www.newyorker.com/archive/2004/05/10/040510fa_fact.

12. Jay S. Bybee, "Memorandum for John Rizzo, Acting General Counsel of the Central Intelligence Agency," August 1, 2002, http://luxmedia.com .edgesuite.net/aclu/olc_08012002_bybee.pdf.

13. See Mark P. Denbeaux and Jonathan Hafetz, eds., *The Guantánamo Lawyers: Inside a Prison, Outside the Law* (New York: New York University Press, 2009).

14. Dana Priest, "CIA Holds Terror Suspects in Secret Prisons," *Washington Post*, November 2, 2005, http://www.washingtonpost.com/ wp-dyn/content/article/2005/11/01/AR2005110101644.html.

15. In June 2008, the Supreme Court ruled in *Boumediene v. Bush* that the MCA unlawfully deprived prisoners of a *constitutional* right to habeas corpus because the United States exercises "de facto" sovereignty over GTMO.

16. In contrast, approximately 150 people were convicted in federal courts on terrorism charges during this period; see Center for Law and Security, *Terrorist Trial Report Card: September 11, 2001–September 11, 2009* (New York: New York University Law School, 2010).

17. Considering only foreign prisoners held overseas, there is no publicly available total for Afghanistan, but approximately 500–600 have been in custody at the Bagram prison at any given time since the invasion in 2001, a number that does not include prisoners held "off the books" by Special Forces. In Iraq, the number rose at the end of 2007 as a result of the "surge" to 51,000, including hundreds of juveniles. The GTMO total was approximately 775. An estimated 100 were held in secret CIA detention facilities.

18. See Andy Worthington, *The Guantanamo Files: The Stories of the 759 Detainees in America's Illegal Prison* (London: Pluto Press, 2007).

19. Scott Horton, "'The American Public Has a Right To Know that They Do Not Have To Choose between Torture and Terror': Six Questions for Matthew Alexander, Author of *How To Break a Terrorist*," No Comment, *Harper's Magazine Online*, December 18, 2008; available at: http://harpers .org/archive/2008/12/hbc-90004036. Former Navy JAG Alberto Mora expressed a similarly scathing critique in his testimony on June 17, 2008, before the Senate Armed Services Committee.

20. David Rose, "Tortured Reasoning," *Vanity Fair*, web exclusive, December 16, 2008, http://www.vanityfair.com/magazine/2008/12/torture200812.

21. See *ICRC Report on the Treatment of Fourteen "High Value Detainees" in CIA Custody* (Geneva: ICRC, February 2007), http://www.nybooks.com/icrc-report.pdf; see also Mark Danner, "US Torture: Voices from the Black Sites," *New York Review of Books* 56, April 9, 2009, http://www.nybooks.com/articles/archives/2009/apr/09/us-torture-voices-from-the-black-sites; and Danner, "The Red Cross Report: What It Means," *New York Review of Books*, April 30, 2009, http://www.nybooks.com/articles/archives/2009/apr/30/the-red-cross-torture-report-what-it-means/.

22. On the same day Cheney gave a speech at the American Enterprise Institute in which he reiterated his criticism of the new administration and his claims that the use of "enhanced interrogation methods" had "prevented the violent death of thousands, if not hundreds of thousands, of innocent people."

23. See Jane Mayer, "The Trial: Eric Holder and the Battle over Khalid Sheikh Mohammed," *The New Yorker*, February 15, 2010, http://www.newyorker.com/reporting/2010/02/15/100215fa_fact_mayer; and Dan Froomkin, "With Greg Craig Out of the Way, Coast Is Clear for White House To Make Legal Calls on Political Grounds," *Huffington Post*, March 30, 2010, http://www.huffingtonpost.com/2010/03/30/with-greg-craig-out-of-th_n_517417.html.

24. See Lisa Hajjar, "Grave Injustice: Maher Arar and Unaccountable America," *Middle East Report Online*, June 24, 2010, http://merip.org/mero/mero062410.

25. See Hajjar, "Bagram, Obama's GTMO," *Middle East Report* 41, no. 260 (Fall 2011), http://www.merip.org/mer/mer260/bagram-obamas-gitmo.

2. IN THE MINOTAUR'S LABYRINTH: PSYCHOLOGICAL TORTURE,
PUBLIC FORGETTING, AND CONTESTED HISTORY
Alfred W. McCoy

1. Central Intelligence Agency, "Proposed Study on Special Interrogation Methods," February 14, 1952, CIA Behavior Control Experiments Collection (John Marks Donation), National Security Archive, Washington, D.C. (hereafter, NSA).

2. US Senate, 94th Congress, 2d Session, *Final Report of the Select Committee to Study Governmental Operations With Respect to Intelligence Activities: Book I* (Washington, D.C.: Government Printing Office [GPO], 1976), 387–88.

3. Woodburn Heron, "The Pathology of Boredom," *Scientific American* (January 1957): 52–56.

4. D. O. Hebb, "This Is How It Was," Canadian Psychological Association, ca. 1980 (copy provided by Mary Ellen Hebb).

5. Lawrence E. Hinkle, Jr., "A Consideration of the Circumstances Under Which Men May Be Interrogated, and the Effects That These May Have Upon the Function of the Brain" (n.d., ca. 1958), 1, 5, 6, 11–14, 18, File: Hinkle, Box 7, CIA Behavior Control Experiments Collection (John Marks Donation), NSA; Lawrence E. Hinkle, Jr., and Harold G. Wolff, "Communist Interrogation and Indoctrination of 'Enemies of the States': Analysis of Methods Used by the Communist State Police (A Special Report)," *Archives of Neurology and Psychiatry* 76 (1956): 115–74.

6. Joseph Marguilies, *Guantánamo and the Abuse of Presidential Power* (New York: Simon and Schuster, 2006), 120–25; *New York Times*, August 23, 1954, August 14, 18, 1955; Dwight D. Eisenhower, "Executive Order 10631—Code of Conduct for members of the Armed Forces of the United States," August 17, 1955, American Presidency Project, University of California at Santa Barbara, http://www.presidency.ucsb.edu/ws/index .php?pid=59249#axzz1b6pwMI4v.

7. "KUBARK Counterintelligence Interrogation" (July 1963), File: Kubark, Box 1: CIA Training Manuals, NSA, 87–90. The term KUBARK is a cryptonym for the CIA itself.

8. Alfred W. McCoy, *A Question of Torture: CIA Interrogation, From the Cold War to the War on Terror* (New York: Metropolitan Books, 2006).

9. Central Intelligence Agency, Inspector General, "Special Review: Counterterrorism Detention and Interrogation Activities (September 2001–October 2003)" (May 7, 2004), 10; Central Intelligence Agency, "Human Resources Exploitation Training Manual—1983," Box 1, CIA Training Manuals, NSA.

10. *The Times* (London), March 3, 1972; Lord Parker of Waddington, *Report of the Committee of Privy Counsellors Appointed to Consider Authorised Procedures for the Interrogation of Persons Suspected of Terrorism* (London: Stationery Office, Cmnd. 4901, 1972), 3–17.

11. US Department of Defense, "Army Regulation 15–6: Final Report: Investigation into FBI Allegation of Detainee Abuse at Guantanamo Bay, Cuba Detention Facility" (April 1, 2005; amended June 9, 2005), 1, 20, http://www.defenselink.mil/news/Jul2005/d20050714report.pdf; US Senate Armed Services Committee, Hearing on Guantanamo Bay Detainee Treatment (July 13, 2005), 19, 20, 35, 55, http://humanrights.ucdavis.edu/ projects/the-guantanamo-testimonials-project/testimonies/testimonies- of-the-defense-department/senate-armed-services-committee-hearing- on-guantanamo-bay-detainee-treatment.

12. *New York Times,* July 20 and August 2, 1971; Victor Marchetti and John D. Marks, *The CIA and the Cult of Intelligence* (New York: Alfred A. Knopf, 1974), 246.

13. US House of Representatives, 92d Congress, 1st Session, Subcommittee of the Committee on Government Operations, Hearings on August 2, 1971, *US Assistance Programs in Vietnam* (Washington, DC: Government Printing Office, 1971), 319–21, 327, 349; US Senate, 93rd Congress, 1st Session, Committee on Armed Services, Hearings on July 2, 20, and 25, 1973, *Nomination of William E. Colby to be Head of Central Intelligence* (Washington, D.C.: Government Printing Office, 1973), 101–17; Dale Andradé, "Pacification," in *Encyclopedia of the Vietnam War*, ed. Stanley Kutler (New York: Charles Scribner's Sons, 1996), 423.

14. For sources on the failure of Phoenix, see Orrin DeForest and David Chanoff, *Slow Burn: The Rise and Bitter Fall of American Intelligence in Vietnam* (New York: Simon and Schuster, 1990); Ralph W. McGehee, *Deadly Deceits: My 25 Years in the CIA* (New York: Sheridan Square Publications, 1983); and Douglas Valentine, *The Phoenix Program* (New York: William Morrow, 1990).

15. John Ranelagh, *The Agency: The Rise and Decline of the CIA* (New York: Simon and Schuster, 1986), 571–76, 584–99.

16. *New York Times,* June 11, 1979.

17. *New York Times,* August 2, 1977.

18. *New York Times,* August 16, 1970; A. J. Langguth, *Hidden Terrors* (New York: Pantheon, 1978), 252–54, 285–88.

19. Manuel Hevia Cosculluela, *Pasaporte 11333: Ocho Años con la CIA* (Havana: Editorial de Ciencias Sociales, 1978), 121–24, 279–87.

20. US Senate, 92nd Congress, 1st Session, Committee on Foreign Relations, Subcommittee on Western Hemisphere Affairs, *United States Policies and Programs in Brazil* (Washington, D.C.: Government Printing Office, 1971), 17–20, 39–40.

21. Langguth, *Hidden Terrors*, 299–301.

22. Ibid., 301; US Senate, 93rd Congress, 2d Session, Committee on Foreign Relations, *Foreign Assistance Act of 1974: Report of the Committee on Foreign Relations United States Senate on S. 3394 to Amend the Foreign Assistance Act of 1961, and For Other Purposes* (Washington, D.C.: Government Printing Office, 1974), 42.

23. Thomas David Lobe, "US Police Assistance for the Third World" (Ph.D. diss., University of Michigan, 1975), 415, 421.

24. US Senate, Select Committee on Intelligence, "Transcript of Proceedings before the Select Committee on Intelligence: Honduran Interrogation Manual Hearing," Box 1, CIA Training Manuals, Folder: Interrogation Manual Hearing, NSA, 3–5.

25. Congressional Fact Sheet, June 8, 1988, introduction to Central Intelligence Agency, "Human Resources Exploitation Training Manual—1983," Box 1, CIA Training Manuals, NSA.

26. US Senate, 102d Congress, 1st Session, Report 102–249, Committee on the Judiciary, *The Torture Victims Protection Act* (US Senate, Calendar No. 382, November 26, 1991), 6–7; United States, *Congressional Record, Proceedings and Debates of the 102d Congress, First Session, vol. 137—Part 23* (Washington, D.C.: Government Printing Office, 1991), November 25, 1991, 34785; United States, *Congressional Record, Proceedings and Debates of the 102d Congress, Second Session, vol. 138—Part 3* (Washington, D.C.: Government Printing Office, 1992), March 3, 1992, 4176–78.

27. *New York Times*, June 13, 1993.

28. Office of the United Nations High Commissioner for Human Rights, "Convention against Torture and Other Cruel, Inhuman or Degrading Treatment or Punishment," http://www2.ohchr.org/english/law/cat.htm.

29. US Senate, 101st Congress, 2d Session, Committee on Foreign Relations, *Convention Against Torture: Hearing Before the Committee on Foreign Relations* (Washington, D.C.: Government Printing Office, 1990), 1, 12–18, 34, 35, 40–43, 66–69, 70–71.

30. United States, *Congressional Record, Proceedings and Debates of the 103d Congress, Second Session, vol. 140—Part 1* (Washington, D.C.: Government Printing Office, 1994), February 2, 1994, 827; Foreign Relations Authorization Act, PL 103–236, Title V, Sec. 506, 108 Stat. 463 (1994), 18 USC§ 2340–2340A.

31. United States, *Weekly Compilation of Presidential Documents 32*, no. 34 (Washington, D.C.: Government Printing Office, 1996), 1482; US House of Representatives, 104th Congress, 2d Session, *Congressional Record vol. 142—Part 14* (Washington, D.C.: Government Printing Office, 1996), 19562–63.

32. Michael T. Klare, *War Without End: American Planning for the Next Vietnams* (New York: Alfred A. Knopf, 1972), 300–4; *New York Times*, June 24, 2001.

33. James Hodge and Linda Cooper, *Disturbing the Peace: The Story of Father Roy Bourgeois and the Movement to Close the School of the Americas* (Maryknoll: Orbis, 2004), 1–4, 148–208.

34. Ibid., 157–66.

35. *Baltimore Sun*, January 27, 1997; *Washington Post*, January 28, 1997; *New York Times*, January 29, 1997.

36. Richard A. Clarke, *Against All Enemies: Inside America's War on Terror* (New York: Free Press, 2004), 24.

37. US Senate, Committee on Armed Services, 110th Congress, 2d Session, *Inquiry into the Treatment of Detainees in US Custody* (Washington, D.C.: GPO, 2008), xiii, http://www.democrats.com/senate-armed-services-committee-report-on-torture; George W. Bush, The White House, Washington, For: The Vice President, "Subject: Humane Treatment of Taliban and al Qaeda Detainees," February 7, 2002, http://www.pegc.us/archive/White_House/bush_memo_20020207_ed.pdf.

38. Stephen Grey, *Ghost Plane: The True Story of the CIA Torture Program* (New York: St. Martin's Press, 2006), 87, 181, 227, 269–308; *New York Times*, May 31, 2005.

39. *New York Times*, November 9, 2005.

40. Jay S. Bybee, Office of the Assistant Attorney General, "Memorandum for Alberto R. Gonzales, Counsel to the President, Re: Standards of Conduct for Interrogation under 18 USC. §§ 2340–2340A," August 1, 2002, http://www.washingtonpost.com/wp-srv/nation/documents/dojinterrogationmemo20020801.pdf; US Senate, *Inquiry into the Treatment of Detainees in US Custody*, xv–xvi, xxi.

41. Jay S. Bybee, Office of the Assistant Attorney General, "Memorandum for John Rizzo, Acting General Counsel of the Central Intelligence Agency," August 1, 2002, 11, http://dspace.wrlc.org/doc/bitstream/2041/70967/00355_020801_004display.pdf.

42. Jane Mayer, "The Black Sites," *The New Yorker*, July 21, 2009, http://www.newyorker.com/reporting/2007/08/13/070813fa_fact_mayer; US Senate, *Inquiry into the Treatment of Detainees in US Custody*, xiii.

43. US Senate, *Inquiry into the Treatment of Detainees*, xix; William J. Haynes, II, General Counsel, Department of Defense, "For: Secretary of Defense, Subject: Counter-Resistance Techniques," Nov. 27, 2002, http://www.gwu.edu/~nsarchiv/NSAEBB/NSAEBB127/02.12.02.pdf; *New York Times*, June 18, 2008.

44. M. Gregg Bloche and Jonathan H. Marks, "Doctors and Interrogators at Guantanamo Bay," *New England Journal of Medicine* 353, no. 1 (July 7, 2005): 7; Jonathan H. Marks, "The Silence of the Doctors," *The Nation*, December 7, 2005, http://www.thenation.com/doc/20051226/marks.

45. *New York Times*, November 30, 2004.

46. Jonathan Alter, "Time to Think About Torture," *Newsweek*, November 5, 2001, 45.

47. "Harvard Law Professors Urge Congress to Review Interrogation Policy and Hold Executive Branch Accountable," http://www.iraq-letter.com, posted June 14, 2004.

48. *New York Times*, June 24, 27, July 6, 2005; American Psychological Association, "Report of the American Psychological Association Presidential

Task Force on Psychological Ethics and National Security" (June 2005):
1, 5, 8–9, http://www.apa.org/pubs/info/reports/pens.pdf.

49. *24* (TV Series), *Wikipedia*, http://en.wikipedia.org/wiki/24_
(TV_series); Colin Freeze, "What would Jack Bauer do?" *Globe and Mail*,
June 16, 2007, http://license.icopyright.net/user/viewFreeUse.
act?fuid=NzI2NDYxOA%3D%3D.

50. *New York Times*, May 1, 2004; Seymour M. Hersh, "Torture at Abu
Ghraib," *The New Yorker*, May 10, 2004, 42–47; *New York Times*, June 18, 2004;
"Abuse of Iraqi POWs by GIs Probed," *CBS NEWS.com*, April 28, 2004,
http://www.cbsnews.com/stories/2004/04/27/60II/main614063.shtml.

51. See US Congress, Senate and House Armed Services Committees,
Testimony of Secretary of Defense Donald H. Rumsfeld, May 7, 2004,
http://www.defenselink.mil/speeches/speech.aspx?speechid=118; *New York
Times*, May 8, 2004, May 12, 2004.

52. *Washington Post*, April 13, 2005; Leon Worden, "SCV Newsmaker of
the Week: Brig. Gen. Janis Karpinski," *Signal Newspaper* (Santa Clarita,
Calif.), July 4, 2004.

53. US Supreme Court, *Salim Ahmed Hamdan v. Donald H. Rumsfeld*,
No. 05–184, Opinion of Stevens, J., June 29, 2006, 6, 69–73; *New York Times*,
March 27, June 30, 2006.

54. *New York Times*, September 22, 23, 26, 27, 28, 29, and 30, 2006;
US House of Representatives, 109th Congress, 2d Session, *H.R. 6166: A Bill
to amend title 10, United States Code, to authorize trial by military commission
for violations of the law of war and for other purposes*, September 25, 2006,
http://www.gpo.gov/fdsys/pkg/BILLS-109hr6166rfs/pdf/BILLS-
109hr6166rfs.pdf.

55. Jay S. Bybee, Office of the Assistant Attorney General, "Memorandum
for Alberto R. Gonzales, Counsel to the President, Re: Standards of Conduct
for Interrogation under 18 USC. §§ 2340–2340A," August 1, 2002,
http://www.washingtonpost.com/wp-srv/nation/documents/
dojinterrogationmemo20020801.pdf; US House of Representatives, 109th
Congress, 2d Session, *H.R. 6166: A Bill to amend title 10, United States Code, to
authorize trial by military commission for violations of the law of war and for other
purposes*, 29, 35.

56. House Armed Services Committee, Press Release, "Chairman Hunter
Opening Statement, Hearing on Military Commissions and Standards
Utilized in Trying Detainees," September 7, 2006, http://www.globalsecurity
.org/security/library/congress/2006_h/060907-hunteropeningstatement.pdf;
David Welna, "Military Lawyers Balk at President's Tribunal Plan," *National
Public Radio*, September 7, 2006, http://www.npr.org/templates/story/story
.php?storyId=5783523; *Washington Post*, September 8, 2006.

57. *New York Times*, September 16, 2006; *Washington Post*, September 19, 2006.

58. *New York Times*, August 12, 2009; Senate, Committee on Armed Services, *Inquiry into the Treatment of Detainees in US Custody*, 6–11.

59. *Washington Post*, May 13, 2009.

60. *Los Angeles Times*, May 23, 2009.

61. The White House, Press Office, "Statement of President Barack Obama," April 16, 2009, http://www.whitehouse.gov/the_press_office/ Statement-of-President-Barack-Obama-on-Release-of-OLC-Memos/.

62. *New York Times*, April 21, 2009; *Washington Post*, April 24, 2009, http://voices.washingtonpost.com/44/2009/04/23/a_commission_on_ enhanced_inter.html.

63. *New York Times*, January 22, February 18, May 24, July 22, August 25, 2009.

64. Steve Benen, "Political Animal: Nepotism Reigns," *The Washington Monthly*, May 22, 2009, 11:05 a.m., http://www.washingtonmonthly.com/ archives/monthly/2009_05.php; Anderson Cooper, "360 Degrees," *CNN.com*, May 21, 2009, Transcript, http://transcripts.cnn.com/ TRANSCRIPTS/0905/21/acd.01.html.

65. Jake Tapper, Jon Karl, and Karen Travers, "President Obama, Dick Cheney Face Off on National Security Issues," *ABC News*, May 21, 2009, http://abcnews.go.com/Politics/story?id=7643032&page=1.

66. Statement by Liz Cheney in Response to President Obama's National Security Remarks, Keep America Safe, January 6, 2010, http://www.facebook .com/note.php?note_id=243193612065.

67. "Dick Cheney: Waterboarding Should Have Been Option with Underwear Bomber," *Good Morning America, ABC News*, February 14, 2010, http://blogs.abcnews.com/thenote/2010/02/cheney-waterboarding-should- have-been-option-with-underwear-bomber.html.

68. Haroon Siddique and Chris McGreal, "Waterboarding is torture, Downing Street confirms," *The Guardian*, November 9, 2010, http://www .guardian.co.uk/world/2010/nov/09/george-bush-memoirs-waterboarding.

69. Ibid.

70. "Bush Waterboarding Claim Challenged," *Express.co.uk*, November 11, 2010, http://www.dailyexpress.co.uk/posts/view/210911/Bush- waterboarding-claim-challenged/.

71. *New York Times*, February 17, September 22, 23, December 14, 2009, January 4, 21, 2010; Peter Baker, "Obama's War Over Terror," *The New York Times Magazine*, January 17, 2010, 36–37; "America's Secret Afghan Prisons," *Democracy Now*, February 2, 2010, http://www.democracynow.org/2010/2/2/ americas_secret_afghan_prisons_investigation_unearths.

72. *New York Times*, February 19, 2010.

73. *New York Times*, March 8, 9, 2011.

74. *New York Times*, December 14, 2009.

75. NRO Symposium, "Bin Laden, No More," *National Review Online*, May 2, 2011, http://www.nationalreview.com/articles/266271/bin-laden-no-more-nro-symposium?page=6.

76. *New York Times*, May 3, 2011.

77. John Yoo, "From Guantanamo to Abbottabad," *The Wall Street Journal*, May 4, 2011, http://online.wsj.com/article/SB10001424052748703834804576 301032595527372.html; *Washington Post*, May 4, 2011.

78. "Ex-CIA Counterterrorism Chief: 'Enhanced Interrogation' Led U.S. to bin Laden," *Time Swampland*, May 4, 2011, http://swampland.time .com/2011/05/04/did-torture-get-the-us-osama-bin-laden/.

79. "Rumsfeld Flip-Flops in Harsh Interrogation of Detainees," *YouTube*, May 4, 2011, transcribed by Brett Reilly, http://www.youtube.com/ watch?feature=player_embedded&v=t50atNXQBHk; no longer available.

80. Catherine Herridge, "Bush-Era Interrogations Provided Key Details on Bin Laden's Location," *FoxNews.com*, May 3, 2011, http://www.foxnews .com/politics/2011/05/02/bush-era-interrogations-provided-key-details-bin-ladens-location.

81. "Cheney: Justice Probe of CIA Interrogators an 'Outrage,'" *Fox News .com*, May 8, 2011, http://www.foxnews.com/politics/2011/05/08/cheney-justice-probe-cia-interrogators-outrage/.

82. Office of Public Affairs, Department of Justice, "Statement of the Attorney General Regarding Investigation into the Interrogation of Certain Detainees," June 30, 2011, http://www.justice.gov/opa/pr/2011/ June/11-ag-861.html.

83. *New York Times*, July 1, 2011.

84. Embtel 242, Embassy Berlin to State, February 6, 2007, Secret/ Noforn, Subject: Al-Masri Case-Chancellery Aware of USG Concerns, WikiLeaks Cablegate Archive, Reference ID: 07BERLIN242, http://wikileaks.org/cable/2007/02/07BERLIN242.html.

85. Embtel 392, Embassy Madrid to State, April 17, 2009, Confidential, Subject: Spain: Attorney General Recommends Court Not Pursue GTMO Criminal Case vs. Former USG Officials, WikiLeaks Cablegate Archive, Reference ID: 09MADRID392, http://wikileaks.org/ cable/2009/04/09MADRID392.html#.

86. Matthew Cole, "Convicted Spy Says 'We Broke the Law,'" *ABC News: The Blotter*, November 4, 2009, http://abcnews.go.com/Blotter/exclusive-convicted-cia-spy-broke-law/story?id=8995107.

87. Amnesty International, "European Governments Must Provide Justice for Victims of CIA Programmes," November 15, 2010, http://www.amnesty .org/en/news-and-updates/report/european-governments-must-provide-justice-victims-cia-programmes-2010–11-15; Amnesty International, *Open Secret: Mounting Evidence of Europe's Complicity in Rendition and Secret Detention*, Executive Summary (London: Amnesty International Publications, November 2010), http://www.amnesty.org/en/library/info/EUR01/024/2010/en.

3. TORTURE AND SOCIETY
Reinhold Görling

1. Emmanuel Lévinas, *Otherwise Than Being: Or, Beyond Essence* (The Hague and Boston: M. Nijhoff, 1981).
2. Daniel Stern, *The Interpersonal World of the Infant* (New York: Basic Books, 1985).
3. Vittorio Gallese, "The Manifold Nature of Interpersonal Relations: The Quest for a Common Mechanism," *Philosophical Transactions of the Royal Society*, no. 258 (2003): 517–28, here 525.
4. Judith Butler, *Undoing Gender* (New York: Routledge, 2004), 33.
5. Françoise Sironi, *Bourreaux et Victimes: Psychologie de la Torture* (Paris: Odile Jacob, 1999), 47.
6. Cathy Caruth, *Unclaimed Experience: Trauma, Narrative, and History* (Baltimore: The Johns Hopkins University Press, 1996), 18.
7. Sironi, *Psychopathologie des Violences Collectives: Essai de Psychologie Géopolitique Clinique* (Paris: Odile Jacob, 2007), 56.
8. Maurice Merleau-Ponty, *Humanisme et Terreur* (Paris: Gallimard, 1947).
9. Achille Mbembe, "Necropolitics," *Public Culture* 15, no 1 (2003): 11–40.
10. Arnold Gehlen, *Der Mensch: Seine Natur und seine Stellung in der Welt* (Berlin: Junker und Dünnhaupt, 1940; Wiebelsheim: Aula Verlag, 2004).
11. Stephan Trinkaus, *Blank Spaces: Gabe und Inzest als Figuren des Ursprungs von Kultur* (Bielefeld: Transcript, 2005).
12. Michel Foucault, "Technologies of the Self," in *Technologies of the Self,* ed. M. Foucault, L. H. Martin, H. Gutman, and P. H. Hutton (Amherst: University of Massachusetts Press, 1988), 16–49.
13. Werner Bohleber, "Zur Psychoanalyse von Schamerfahrungen," *Psyche* 62 (2008): 831–39.
14. Edward Peters, *Torture* (Philadelphia: University of Pennsylvania Press, 1996).

15. Theodor W. Adorno and Arnold Gehlen, "Ist die Soziologie eine Wissenschaft vom Menschen? Ein Streitgespräch," in *Adornos Philosophie in Grundbegriffen: Auflösung einiger Deutungsprobleme*, ed. F. Grenz (Frankfurt am Main: Suhrkamp, 1974), 225–51, here 249.

16. Giorgio Agamben, *Remnants of Auschwitz: The Witness and the Archive* (New York: Zone Books, 2002), 106.

17. Donald W. Winnicott, *Playing and Reality* (London: Tavistock, 1971).

18. Peter Fonagy and Mary Target, "Playing with Reality: IV," *International Journal of Psychoanalysis* 88 (2007): 917–37.

19. Christopher Bollas, *Cracking Up: The Work of Unconscious Experience* (New York: Hill and Wang, 1995), 180–220.

20. Jan Philipp Reemtsma, *Folter im Rechtsstaat?* (Hamburg: Hamburger Edition, 2005).

21. Susanne Krasmann, "Outsourcing Torture: Zur Performanz von Rechtsstaatlichkeit," in *Gouvernmentalität und Sicherheit: Zeitdiagnostische Beiträge im Anschluss an Foucault*, ed. P. Purtschert, K. Meyer, and Y. Winter (Bielefeld: Transcript, 2008), 19–48.

22. Foucault, "La torture, c'est la raison (Entretien)," *Dits et Écrits* (Paris: Gallimard, 1994), 3:390–98.

23. George Orwell, *1984* (Harmondsworth: Penguin, 1969), 211–12.

24. Diana Taylor, *Disappearing Acts: Spectacles of Gender and Nationalism in Argentina's "Dirty War"* (Durham and London: Duke University Press, 1997).

25. Elaine Scarry, *The Body in Pain: The Making and Unmaking of the World* (New York and Oxford: Oxford University Press, 1985), 56.

26. Aleksandar Tišma, *Die Schule der Gottlosigkeit* (Munich: Deutscher Taschenbuch Verlag, 1995), 33–71.

27. Philip Gourevitch, *We Wish to Inform You that Tomorrow We Will Be Killed with Our Families: Stories from Rwanda* (New York: Picador, 1998), 95.

28. Butler, *Frames of War: When Is Life Grievable?* (London and New York: Verso, 2009), 93.

29. Jean-Luc Nancy, *Au Fond des Images* (Paris: Galilée, 2003), 36–37.

30. Ilse Grubrich-Simitis, "Vom Konkretismus zur Metaphorik," in *Kinder der Opfer-Kinder der Täter: Psychoanalyse und Holocaust*, ed. M. S. Bergmann, M. E. Jucovy, and J. S. Kestenberg (Frankfurt am Main: S. Fischer, 1995), 357–79.

31. Elisabeth Weber, ". . . buchstabierend bis aufs Blut: Zur Subjektivtät nach Levinas," in *Das Vergessen(e): Anamnesen des Undarstellbaren*, ed. E. Weber and G. C. Tholen (Vienna: Turia and Kant, 1997), 272–85, here 285.

32. Nicolas Abraham and Maria Torok, *The Shell and the Kernel: Renewals of Psychoanalysis* (Chicago: University of Chicago Press, 1994).

33. Fonagy, "The Violence in Our Schools: What Can a Psychoanalytically Informed Approach Contribute?" *Journal of Applied Psychoanalytic Studies* 5, no. 2 (2003): 223–38.

4. WHAT NAZI CRIMES AGAINST HUMANITY CAN TELL US ABOUT TORTURE TODAY
Susan Derwin

1. Micheline R. Ishay, *The History of Human Rights: From Ancient Times to the Globalization Era* (Berkeley: University of California Press, 2004), 215.

2. Eleanor Roosevelt, "Address to the United Nations Assembly on the Adoption of the Universal Declaration of Human Rights," http://www.americanrhetoric.com/speeches/eleanorrooseveltdeclarationhumanrights.htm.

3. Primo Levi, *Survival in Auschwitz*, trans. Stuart Woolf (New York: Simon and Schuster, 1993), 9.

4. Levi, *Survival*, 9.

5. Andrew Sullivan, "Bush's Interrogation Techniques Worse than Hitler's," *The Atlantic Online*, http://andrewsullivan.theatlantic.com/the_daily_dish/2007/05/verschfte_verne.html.

6. Ibid.

7. Ibid.

8. Scott Horton, "Six Questions for Darius Rejali, Author of 'Torture and Democracy,'" February 13, 2008, http://www.harpers.org/archive/2008/02/hbc-90002387.

9. Myriam Anissimov, *Primo Levi: Tragedy of an Optimist*, trans. Steve Cox (New York: Overlook Press, 2000), 417.

10. Levi, *Survival*, 55.

11. Ibid., 11.

12. For a consideration of why these men and women were referred to by this name, see Gil Anijar, *The Jew, The Arab: A History of the Enemy* (Stanford: Stanford University Press, 2003), 119.

13. For a discussion of the deterioration of the *Muselmänner* and their significance in the eyes of the other prisoners, see Wolfgang Sofsky, *The Order of Terror*, trans. William Templer (Princeton: Princeton University Press, 1999), 119–206.

14. Levi, *Survival*, 90.

15. Jonathan Barnes, ed., *The Cambridge Companion to Aristotle* (Cambridge: Cambridge University Press, 1995), 238. I thank Elisabeth Weber for framing the question of the prisoners' humanness with reference to Aristotle.

16. Primo Levi, *The Drowned and the Saved*, trans. Raymond Rosenthal (New York: Vintage, 1989), 84.

17. Quoted in Levi, *Drowned*, 126.

18. For a discussion of the existence of the *Muselmänner* as calling into question the very possibility of ethics, see Giorgio Agamben, *Remnants of Auschwitz*, trans. Daniel Heller-Roazen (New York: Zone Books, 2002), 41–86.

19. Levi, *Drowned*, 87.

20. Elaine Scarry, *The Body in Pain: The Making and Unmaking of the World* (New York and Oxford: Oxford University Press, 1985), 47.

21. Levi, *Drowned*, 109.

22. Ibid., 111.

23. Ibid.

24. Ibid.

25. Ibid., 27.

26. Ibid., 114.

27. Ibid.

28. Levi refers to this biblical passage; see Levi, *Drowned*, 114.

29. Jean Améry, *At the Mind's Limit: Contemplations by a Survivor on Auschwitz and Its Realities*, trans. Sidney Rosenfeld and Stella P. Rosenfeld (Bloomington: Indiana University Press, 1980), 28.

30. Ibid., 28–29.

31. Ibid., 29.

32. Ibid., 33.

33. Ibid., 40.

34. Ibid., 34.

35. Ibid., 70.

36. Ibid., 39. Agamben also invokes the notion of abandonment, specifically in characterizing the operation of sovereignty. He writes, "He who has been banned is not, in fact, simply set outside the law and made indifferent to it but rather *abandoned* by it, that is, exposed and threatened on the threshold in which life and law, outside and inside, become indistinguishable"; Agamben, *Homo Sacer: Sovereign Power and Bare Life*, trans. Daniel Heller-Roazen (Stanford: Stanford University Press, 1998), 28. And in a note: "The ban is a form of relation. But precisely what kind of relation is at issue here, when the ban has no positive content and the terms of the relation seem to exclude (and, at the same time, to include) each other? What is the form of law that expresses itself in the ban? The ban is the pure form of reference to something in general, which is to say, the simple positing of relation with the nonrelational"; ibid., 29. The notion of the ban as creating a (non)relation is consistent with Améry's assertion that torture is an experience of radical abandonment. But Améry and Agamben differ in the emphasis of their respective discussion of the individual banned from society. Agamben

traces this sacred man or *homo sacer* to a Germanic and Anglo-Saxon presocial history of the bandit as wolf-man: "What had to remain in the collective unconscious as a monstrous hybrid of human and animal, divided between the forest and the city—the werewolf—is, therefore, in its origin the figure of the man who has been banned from the city. That such a man is defined as a wolf-man and not simply as a wolf (the expression *caput lupinum* has the form of a juridical statute) is decisive here. The life of the bandit, like that of the sacred man, is not a piece of animal nature without any relation to law and the city. It is, rather, a threshold of indistinction and of passage between animal and man, *physis* and *nomos*, exclusion and inclusion: the life of the bandit is the life of the *loup garou*, the werewolf, who is precisely *neither man nor beast*, and who dwells paradoxically within both while belonging to neither"; ibid., 105. In his discussion of the torture victim, Améry also has recourse to a liminal space in order to conceptualize not the political meaning, but rather the experiential dimension, of existence outside of the law. For Améry the torture victim is the abandoned one, who, stripped of relationality, exists as pure corporeality: "The fellow man [of the torturer] is transformed into flesh and in this transformation he is already brought to the edge of death; if worst comes to worst, he is driven beyond the border of death into Nothingness"; Améry, *At the Mind's Limit*, 35. Existence "beyond the border of death" is only conceivable because, for Améry, relationality does not describe something forged between already constituted human beings, but is rather the very intersubjective precondition of human identity. Torture annihilates the human being by undermining this precondition.

37. Levi, *Drowned*, 25.

38. Scarry, *The Body in Pain*, 38.

39. Levi, *Survival*, 60.

40. Ibid., 85.

41. Ibid., 71.

42. Cynthia Ozick, *Metaphor and Memory* (New York: Vintage Books, 1991), 37.

43. Robert Krell, "Psychological Reverbations of the Holocaust in the Lives of Child Survivors," Monna and Otto Weinmann Lecture Series, June 5, 1997, United States Holocaust Memorial Museum, Center for Advanced Holocaust Studies.

44. Ibid. 15.

45. Ibid.

46. Ibid.

47. Ozick, *Metaphor and Memory*, 47.

48. Levi, *Drowned*, 168.

49. Deuteronomy 6:5 (New Jewish Publication Society).

50. Deuteronomy 6:6–7 (New Jewish Publication Society).

51. Levi, *Survival*, 11.

52. Ibid.

53. Ibid.

54. Ibid., 9.

55. Krell's work focuses primarily on child survivors; in referring to his comments about rage in relation to Levi, I do not mean to discount the significance of the specific social and political circumstances, individual ages, or personal histories of survivors before, during, and after their persecution. My intention, rather, is to recognize how, even with these differences among survivors, persecution triggers psychological responses that can be understood in relation to the universal dependency of human beings upon one another.

56. Levi, *Drowned*, 84.

57. For a discussion of the Knauer case in the context of the systematic killing of handicapped children during the Third Reich, see chapter 3 of Henry Friedlander, *The Origins of the Nazi Genocide from Euthanasia to the Final Solution* (Chapel Hill: The North Carolina University Press, 1995), 39–61. On the basis of legal transcripts, Friedlander states that the sex of the Knauer baby is unknown and that the precise nature of its handicaps is also not certain, although according to testimony, it was born without one leg and part of one arm. It may also have been blind. I also discuss the case in Susan Derwin, "The Psychic Life of Denial," *Cardozo Journal of Conflict Resolution* 9, no. 2 (2008): 456–57.

58. See Robert Jay Lifton, *The Nazi Doctors: Medical Killing and the Psychology of Genocide* (New York: Basic Books, 1986), 50.

59. Friedlander, *Origins of the Nazi Genocide*, 39, and Lifton, *The Nazi Doctors*, 51.

60. Lifton, *The Nazi Doctors*, 51.

61. Friedlander, *Origins of the Nazi Genocide*, 61.

62. Ibid., 45, 48.

63. Ibid., 54.

65. Seymour Hersh, "Torture at Abu Ghraib," *The New Yorker*, May 10, 2004, http://www.newyorker.com/archive/2004/05/10/040510fa_fact.

66. Ibid.

67. Mark Danner, "Torture and Truth," http://www.markdanner.com/articles/show/torture_and_truth.

68. Ibid.

69. Ibid.

70. Améry, *At the Mind's Limit*, 40.

5. "TORTURE WAS THE ESSENCE OF NATIONAL SOCIALISM":
READING JEAN AMÉRY TODAY
Elisabeth Weber

1. Jean Améry, "Jenseits von Schuld und Sühne," in *Werke*, vol. 2, ed.
G. Scheit (Stuttgart: Klett-Cotta, 2002), 57–58; Améry, *At the Mind's Limits:
Contemplations by a Survivor on Auschwitz and its Realities*, trans. Sidney
Rosenfeld and Stella P. Rosenfeld (Bloomington: Indiana University Press
1980), 22–23.

2. Alfred McCoy, *A Question of Torture* (New York: Holt, 2006), 190–96.

3. This group included the dean of the United States Military Academy at
West Point, General Patrick Finnegan, and three of the country's most
experienced military and FBI interrogators.

4. Jane Mayer, "Whatever it Takes," *New Yorker*, February 12, 2007,
http://www.newyorker.com/reporting/2007/02/19/070219fa_fact_mayer.
The typical "dilemma" with which the viewer of *24* is presented is
well-known: "a resistant suspect can either be accorded due process—
allowing a terrorist plot to proceed—or be tortured in pursuit of a lead. . . .
With unnerving efficiency, suspects are beaten, suffocated, electrocuted,
drugged, assaulted with knives, or more exotically abused: almost without fail,
these suspects divulge critical secrets."

5. Rosa Brooks, "America tortures (yawn)," http://www.latimes.com/news/
opinion/commentary/la-oe-brooks23feb23,0,1261650.column?coll=la-home-
commentary.

6. Giorgio Agamben, *State of Exception*, trans. Kevin Attell (Chicago:
Chicago University Press 2005), 3. "Of the 779 people who have been
detained at the United States military prison at Guantánamo Bay, Cuba,
600 have been transferred [i.e., released without charge] and 171 remain,
according to an ongoing analysis by the *New York Times*. In addition, seven
detainees died while in custody"; "The Guantanamo Docket," http://projects
.nytimes.com/guantanamo. In stark contrast to the executive order President
Obama issued one day after taking office, on January 22, 2009, to close the
facility within one year, he signed, on March 7, 2011, a new executive order to
"create a formal system of indefinite detention for those held at the US
military prison at Guantanamo Bay, Cuba, who continue to pose a significant
threat to national security"; Peter Finn and Anne E. Kornblut,
Washington Post, March 8, 2011). On June 12, 2008, the New York–based
Center for Constitutional Rights won a Supreme Court victory in *Boumediene
vs. Bush*, and secured the right for Guantánamo prisoners and other
non-citizens "to challenge the legality of their detention through habeas
proceedings in federal courts." Nonetheless, the current administration "still
seeks the power to hold men indefinitely without charge or trial";
http://ccrjustice.org/illegal-detentions-and-guantanamo.

7. Ulrich Rauff, "Interview with Giorgio Agamben—Life, A Work of Art Without an Author: The State of Exception, the Administration of Disorder and Private Life," *German Law Journal* 5 (May 2004): http://www .germanlawjournal.com/article.php?id=437.

8. Alfred McCoy, *A Question of Torture*, 195. McCoy continues: "The ideal solution to this conundrum, from a CIA perspective, is extrajudicial execution. . . . In effect, the logical corollary to state-sanctioned torture is state-sponsored murder," 195–96.

9. Giorgio Agamben, *Remnants of Auschwitz: The Witness and the Archive*, trans. Daniel Heller-Roazen (New York: Zone Books, 2002).

10. Primo Levi, *Survival in Auschwitz*, trans. Stuart Woolf (New York: Simon and Schuster, 1993), 90.

11. See note 14 of the Introduction. In one of his first executive orders, given on January 22, 2009, President Obama ordered all US personnel, including the CIA, to conduct interrogations in compliance with the Army Field Manual. The same day, the president also ordered the secret CIA-run prisons closed; see http://www.whitehouse.gov/the_press_office/ EnsuringLawfulInterrogations/.

12. Levi, *Survival in Auschwitz*, 90: "Their life is short, but their number is endless: they, the *Muselmänner*, the drowned, form the backbone of the camp, an anonymous mass, continually renewed and always identical, of non-men [*non-uomini*] who march and labour in silence, the divine spark dead within them, already too empty to really suffer. One hesitates to call them living: one hesitates to call their death death, in the face of which they have no fear, as they are too tired to understand."

13. Giorgio Agamben, quoting Eugen Kogon in *Remnants of Auschwitz*, 45. Agamben mentions the controversy surrounding the term; see *Remnants*, 44ff. "There is little agreement on the origin of the term *Muselmann*" (44). Through a study of the history of the word in Occidental thought and literature, Gil Anidjar proposes what he calls a "genealogy of a figure of absolute subjection"; Anidjar, *The Jew, the Arab: A History of the Enemy* (Stanford: Stanford University Press 2003), 119.

14. The term was coined by early twentieth-century German biologist Richard Semon.

15. Geoffrey Hartman, *Scars of the Spirit: The Struggle Against Inauthenticity* (New York: Palgrave Macmillan, 2002), 88.

16. William G. Niederland, *Folgen der Verfolgung: Das Überlebenden-Syndrom Seelenmord* [Consequence of persecution: the survivor-syndrome soul-murder] (Frankfurt am Main, 1980), 232; see also Agamben, *Remnants*, 47–48 passim.

17. "Ghost Detainee," *Wikipedia*, http://en.wikipedia.org/wiki/Ghost_ detainee; see also Alfred McCoy, *A Question of Torture*, 115.

18. Cf. Lisa Hajjar, "Our Heart of Darkness," *Amnesty Now* 30, no. 4 (Summer 2004): 5.

19. Josh White, "Army, CIA Agreed on 'Ghost' Prisoners," *Washington Post*, March 11, 2005, A 16, http://www.washingtonpost.com/ac2/wp-dyn/A25239-2005Mar10?language=printer.

20. In the following, Améry's text will be quoted by first indicating the pagination of the German edition (*Werke*, vol. 2), followed by the pagination of the English translation, here 65/28. The lost "trust in the world" (*Weltvertrauen*) has been commented on by a number of scholars. For example Siegbert Wolf, *Von der Verwundbarkeit des Humanismus: Über Jean Améry* (Frankfurt; Dipa Verlag 1995), 67; Thomas Mavridis, "'Wer der Folter erlag, kann nicht mehr heimisch werden in der Welt': Vom verlorenen Weltvertrauen Jean Amérys," *Fussnoten zur Literatur* 38 (1996): 73.

21. It is noteworthy that Darius Rejali starts his monumental *Torture and Democracy* with the account of police brutality, the Rodney King beating; see Rejali, *Torture and Democracy* (Princeton: Princeton University Press, 2007), 1.

22. Translation slightly changed.

23. Améry might be alluding here to Walter Benjamin's "Zur Kritik der Gewalt," in *Gesammelte Schriften*, by Walter Benjamin, vol. 2.1, ed. R. Tiedemann (Frankfurt: Suhrkamp), 203.

24. Jacques Derrida, "Poetics and Politics of Witnessing," in *Sovereignties in Question: The Poetics of Paul Celan*, ed. Thomas Dutoit and Outi Pasanen (New York: Fordham University Press, 2005), 66.

25. Shoshana Felman and Dori Laub, ed., *Testimony: Crises of Witnessing in Literature, Psychoanalysis, and History* (New York: Routledge, 1992), 57.

26. Darius Rejali, *Torture and Democracy*, 101.

27. The frequency of the word *Staunen*, astonishment or amazement, in this passage may indicate how philosophy, which is said to have had its beginning in astonishment (Plato, Aristotle, Heidegger) is here unfounded, if not demolished, in a very different "astonishment" or "amazement."

28. See also Siegbert Wolf's commentary: *Von der Verwundbarkeit des Humanismus*, 68.

29. G. W. Sebald, "Mit den Augen des Nachtvogels," *Études Germaniques* (July–September 1988): 314. For Sebald, such "content-heaviest insight" is possible "not in the willingness for reconciliation, but only in the unceasing denunciation of injustice [*Unrecht*]" (320). In a similar vein, Améry asserts, for example: "The piles of corpses that lie between them [my torturers] and me cannot be removed in the process of internalization, so it seems to me, but, on the contrary, through actualization, or, more sharply stated, by carrying-out the unresolved conflict in the field of influence [*Wirkungsfeld*] of historical practice" (129/69; translation modified).

30. "[N]eben der bedeutung des zu ende führens entwickelt sich der begriff 'über das ziel hinaus': verschlafen, versalzen"; Jacob und Wilhelm Grimm, *Deutsches Wörterbuch* 25 (Munich: DTV, 1984), s.v. "*ver.*" In the latter sense, it is an intensification of the action, but with the result of turning the intended goal into something negative.

31. Grimm, *Deutsches Wörterbuch*, s.v. "Verfleischung."

32. 74/33; translation modified.

33. See for example, Améry's reflections on the etymology of the word "torture" (73/32), the emphasis on the prefix *mit-* (74/33), the reflections on the hostility of the persecuted person's mother tongue (103–106/51–54); see also Petra S. Fiero, *Schreiben gegen Schweigen: Grenzerfahrungen in Jean Améry's autobiographischem Werk* (Hildesheim: Olms, 1997), 62–63.

34. While many commentators quote this "transformation into flesh" (most recently, for example, Marianne Hirsch, "Editor's Column: The First Blow—Torture and Close Reading," *PMLA* 121, no. 2 (March 2006), I have not yet found a commentary that listens to Améry's specific use of the word "Verfleischlichung." Two books in German on Améry are no exceptions: Petra Fiero, *Schreiben gegen Schweigen*, especially 48–54, and Siegbert Wolf, *Von der Verwundbarkeit des Humanismus*, especially 69–70.

35. See Jean Améry, *Unmeisterliche Wanderjahre*; Jean Améry, *Werke*, 2:324, 329; Améry, *Aufsätze zur Philosophie*, in *Werke*, vol. 6, ed. G. Scheit (Stuttgart: Klett Cotta, 2004), passim. Against Foucault, see especially in volume 6 of the *Werke* the essays "Michel Foucault's Vision des Kerker-Universums," 205–18, and "Michel Foucault und sein 'Diskurs' der Gegen-Aufklärung," 219–31. The criticism against French thinkers of the 1970s as the "new irrationalists" (6:163) characterizes most of the essays collected in vol. 6; against Deleuze, specifically 6:148–51, 165, 190, 197, 206; against Roland Barthes, ibid., 141–42; see also Hans-Martin Gauger, "Er fehlt uns, er ist da: Über Jean Améry," *Merkur: Deutsche Zeitschrift für Europäisches Denken* 59, no. 3 (March 2005): 254.

36. "[L]'homme qui souffre est une bête, la bête qui souffre est un homme" ("The man who suffers is a beast, the beast that suffers is a man"); Gilles Deleuze, *Francis Bacon: The Logic of Sensation*, trans. Daniel W. Smith (Minneapolis: University of Minnesota Press, 2002), 22; Deleuze, *Francis Bacon, Logique de la sensation* (Paris: Éditions de la Différence, 1981), 1:20–21. Roberto Esposito writes on Bacon's images in the context of the above-quoted commentary by Deleuze: "I don't know if flesh is to be related to the Nazi violence, as Deleuze would have it in his admirable comment (though the horror of that violence always remained with Bacon). The fact is that in no one more than Bacon is the biopolitical practice of the animalization of man carried out to its lethal conclusion, finding a reversed

correspondence perfectly in the disfigured figure of butchered flesh. . . . That the painter always saw in animal carcasses hanging in butcher shops the shape of man (but also of himself) signifies that that bloody mount is the condition today of a large section of humanity," Roberto Esposito, *Bíos: Biopolitics and Philosophy*, trans. Timothy Campbell (Minneapolis: University of Minnesota Press, 2008), 169.

37. 59/23–24, translation modified.

38. J. M. Coetzee, *Waiting for the Barbarians* (New York: Penguin, 1982), 118–19.

39. Roberto Esposito, *Bíos*, 159. A close reading of Améry informed by Esposito's path-breaking analyses of Nazi "biopolitics" and "thanatopolitics" cannot be undertaken in this context. I hope to do it elsewhere.

40. Esposito, *Bíos*, 159.

41. 75/33–34, translation slightly changed; see also 49/18.

42. *Bahnung* (facilitation) is also the concept used by Freud to describe the functioning of the psychic apparatus.

43. Page 34. "Wer gefoltert wurde, bleibt gefoltert. Unauslöschlich ist die Folter in ihn eingebrannt, auch dann, wenn keine klinisch objektiven Spuren nachzuweisen sind" (75). In the passage about the specific torture method he was subjected to, Améry describes "a crackling and splintering in my shoulders that my body has not forgotten until this hour" (73/32).

44. The English translation reads: "It is fear that henceforth reigns over him."

45. Elaine Scarry, *The Body in Pain: The Making and Unmaking of the World* (New York and Oxford: Oxford University Press, 1985), 40–41. Fiero dedicates several pages on the proximity between Scarry's and Améry's text in *Schreiben gegen Schweigen*, 55–56, as well as in her essay "The Body in Pain: Jean Améry's Reflections on Torture," *Publications of the Missouri Philological Association* 18 (1993): 26–32.

46. Idelber Avelar, *The Letter of Violence: Essays on Narrative, Ethics, and Politics* (New York: Palgrave MacMillan, 2004), 32.

47. In the sense Heidegger gives these notions; see, for example, *Being and Time*, trans. Joan Stambaugh (Albany: State University of New York Press, 1996), 12, 15, passim. We have seen above that it is this trust that, for Améry, is the first irretrievable victim of state violence.

48. Scarry, *The Body in Pain*, 37.

49. See Fiero, *Schreiben gegen Schweigen*, 55–56.

50. Scarry, *The Body in Pain*, 27, 29.

51. Améry, "Die Tortur"/"Torture," 85/40, translation modified (see above, 87).

52. Martin Heidegger, "Letter on Humanism," in *Basic Writings*, ed. David Farrell Krell, trans. Frank Capuzzi, 2nd ed. (New York: Harper and Collins 1993), 213.

53. Améry, *Werke*, 70/30. The quote continues: "He had to be capable of handling torture instruments, so that Himmler would assure him his Certificate of Maturity in History; later generations would admire him for having obliterated his feelings of mercy [*um seiner Austilgung der eigenen Barmherzigkeit willen*]," literally, "for his obliteration [or: extermination] of his own mercy."

54. Wolfgang Sofsky, quoted in Agamben, *Remnants of Auschwitz*, 47–48.

55. Ariel Dorfman, *Death and the Maiden* (New York: Penguin, 1992, 1994), 59–60; Coetzee, *Waiting for the Barbarians*, 113–19. In S. Yizhar's story "The Prisoner," the witness of the prisoner's entirely unjustified mistreatment, who accompanies the prisoner in a jeep to what most likely is an interrogation center and who could "stop the jeep" and "let the poor devil go," is described as having the powers of a "lesser demigod": "The fellow here at your feet, his life, his well-being, his home, three souls, the whole thread of his existence with all that was involved, were in your grip somehow or other as though you were some lesser demigod here in the Jeep. The man carried along, the collective flock of sheep and several souls in the mountain village, these variegated threads of life were twined together to be cut or grow inextricably involved, all because you were suddenly their master"; S. Yizhar, "The Prisoner," trans. I. M. Lask, in *Midnight Convoy and Other Stories* (New Milford: Toby Press 2007), 82–83.

56. Jean Améry, *Werke*, 2:506–7.

57. Georges Bataille, *L'érotisme, Oeuvres complètes* (Paris: Gallimard, 1987), 10:172; Bataille, *Eroticism: Death and Sensuality*, trans. Mary Dalwood (San Francisco: City Lights Books, 1986), 173 (translation modified). This is perhaps how the torturers in Améry can have breakfast after the torture session (78/35). Compare the questions the Magistrate asks the torturer in Coetzee's *Waiting for the Barbarians*: "'Forgive me if the question seems impudent, but I would like to ask: How do you find it possible to eat afterwards, after you have been . . . working with people? That is a question I have always asked myself about executioners and other such people. Wait! Listen to me a moment longer, I am sincere, it has cost me a great deal to come out with this, since I am terrified of you, I need not tell you that, I am sure you are aware of it. Do you find it easy to take food afterwards? I have imagined that one would want to wash one's hands. But no ordinary washing would be enough, one would require priestly intervention, a ceremonial of cleansing, don't you think? Some kind of purging of one's soul too–that is how I have imagined it. Otherwise how would it be possible to return to

everyday life–to sit down at table, for instance, and break bread with one's family or one's comrades?' . . . He [the torturer] wrenches himself free and hits me so hard in the chest that I gasp and stumble backwards. 'You bastard!' he shouts. 'You fucking old lunatic! Get out! Go and die somewhere!'" (*Waiting for the Barbarians*, 123–24).

58. Jean Améry, "Unmeisterliche Wanderjahre," *Werke*, 2:324; see also Améry, "Ein neuer Verrat der Intellektuellen" (1977), and Améry, "Neue Philosophie oder alter Nihilismus" (1978), *Werke*, 6:164, 240.

59. Jacques Lacan, *Le Séminaire Livre VII, L'Éthique de la psychanalyse 1959–1960*, ed. J.-A. Miller (Paris: Éditions du Seuil, 1986), 245; Lacan, *The Seminar of Jacques Lacan, Book VII, The Ethics of Psychoanalysis 1959–1960*, ed. J.-A. Miller, trans. Dennis Porter (New York: Norton, 1992), 207.

60. Bataille, *L'érotisme*, 66; Bataille, *Eroticism*, 63 (translation modified).

61. Bataille, *L'érotisme*, 68; Bataille, *Eroticism*, 65 (translation modified).

62. Dorfman, *Death and the Maiden*, 23.

63. Ibid., 59.

64. Ibid., 59–60. The reference to the mother is telling, since it insinuates that it is the mother who is at the origin of the fantasies and their transgression. It would invite an analysis based on the Lacanian definition of "desire" and what Lacan calls "La chose," but this would go beyond the scope of this essay.

65. Lacan, *Éthique*, 205; Lacan, *Ethics*, 174.

66. Lacan, *Éthique*, 84, Lacan, *Ethics*, 68–69; English translation slightly modified.

67. Carol Jacobs, *Skirting the Ethical* (Stanford: Stanford University Press, 2008), xvi.

68. Lacan, *Écrits* (Paris: Éditions du Seuil, 1966), 291; Lacan, *Écrits: A Selection*, trans. Bruce Fink (New York: Norton, 2002), 77.

69. For Lacan, it is beyond the space of contracts, beyond the space of utility, the surplus of desire.

70. Dorfman, "Foreword: The Tyranny of Terror," in *Torture: A Collection*, ed. Sanford Levinson (Oxford: Oxford University Press, 2004), 9.

71. Britta Jenkins, "There, Where Words Fail, Tears Are the Bridge," in *At the Side of Torture Survivors*, ed. S. Graessner, N. Gurris, and C. Pross, trans. J. M. Riemer (Baltimore: The Johns Hopkins University Press, 2001), 143.

72. Améry's categorical assertion may be problematic insofar as it is itself a totalization, a totalization that made it impossible for him to engage, for example, with Hannah Arendt (62/25). This totalization may be read as a testimony to the all-encompassing destructivity Améry experienced in flesh and spirit, and as a symptom of a repetition compulsion. In his book *The Belated Witness*, Michael Levine proposes a highly original reinterpretation of

"repetition" and "compulsion," revealing a new, rich potential of these concepts that can be made productive for Améry. Levine seeks "to view repetition as a movement that is never one with itself, as a *com*pulsion that is not only internally divided but doubly driven, impelled by *competing impulses* at work within it. Indeed, what comes together and insists in the mode of repetition . . . are both a drive to return obsessively to the same place and a driving, desperate search for some place different–for an uncanny difference that might emerge in the place of the same"; Levine, *The Belated Witness: Literature, Testimony, and the Question of Holocaust Survival* (Stanford: Stanford University Press, 2006), 12. In this context, one may add that Améry's insistence on "astonishment" (see note 27, above) may indicate moments where the overwhelming totality of the trauma is broken. I thank Rainer Nägele, Rüdiger Campe, Dori Laub, and Michael Levine for the insights they shared with me.

73. "Torture is universally condemned, and whatever its actual practice, no country publicly supports torture or opposes its eradication. The prohibition against torture is well-established under customary international law as *jus cogens*; that is, it has the highest standing in customary law and is so fundamental as to supersede all other treaties and customary laws (except laws that are also *jus cogens*). Criminal acts that are *jus cogens* are subject to universal jurisdiction, meaning that any state can exercise its jurisdiction, regardless of where the crime took place, the nationality of the perpetrator or the nationality of the victim"; Human Rights Watch News, "The Legal Prohibition Against Torture," June 1, 2004, http://www.hrw.org/legacy/press/2001/11/TortureQandA.htm.

74. Améry, *Werke*, 77/35, translation modified.

6. "what did the corpse want?": torture in poetry
Sinan Antoon

1. For a discussion of the status of poetry in terms of readership and cultural visibility, see Dana Gioia, *Can Poetry Matter? Essays on Poetry and American Culture* (Minneapolis: Graywolf Press, 2002).

2. For more, see Sinan Antoon, "Singing for the Revolution," *Jadaliyya* (an online e-zine on the Arab world), http://www.jadaliyya.com/pages/index/508/singing-for-the-revolution.

3. Ibid.

4. Elaine Scarry, *The Body in Pain: The Making and Unmaking of the World* (New York and London: Oxford University Press, 1985), 11.

5. See Nicholas Mirzoeff, "Invisible Empire: Embodied Spectacle and Abu Ghraib," *Radical History Review* 95 (Spring 2006): 21–44. "Abu Ghraib's imperial regime of sodomy can be understood as a means of disciplining the

body into a hierarchy in which the sodomitical—the anal, the oral, the animal—is subjugated to vision as the noblest sense, a disembodied intellectual force. . . . Empire renders this divide spatially, so that America becomes 'mind' and the rest of the world, especially the Muslim world, becomes 'body'" (36).

6. Scarry, *The Body in Pain*, 4.

7. Saadi Youssef, "al-A'mal al-kamila: al-juz'al-sadis," *Complete Works* (Beirut: Dar al-Jamal, 2009), 6:84–85. All translations are mine.

8. Frantz Fanon, *The Wretched of the Earth* (New York: Grove Press, 2005).

9. See Leor Halevi, *Muhammad's Grave: Death Rites and the Making of Islamic Society* (New York: Columbia University Press, 2007), particularly chap. 7, "The Torture of Spirit and Corpse in the Grave," 197–233.

10. Isaiah 26:8 (New American Bible).

11. *The Qur'an: A New Translation*, trans. Tarif Khalidi (London: Penguin Books, 2009), verses 4:43 and 5:6.

12. Youssef, *Complete Works*, 6:203–355.

13. See Youssef, "An Early Letter to General Tommy Franks," *Al-Ahram Weekly*, March 6, 2003.

14. "The Internationale," http://en.wikipedia.org/wiki/The_Internationale.

15. Scarry, *The Body in Pain*, 47.

16. Sargon Bulus, *Azma Ukhra li-kalb al-Qabila* [Another Bone for the Tribe's Dog] (Beirut: Dar al-Jamal, 2008), 123.

17. Scarry, *The Body in Pain*, 35.

18. Ibid., 4.

19. One is reminded of José Padilla, who was too damaged by torture to testify.

20. Scarry, *The Body in Pain*, 47.

21. Ibid., 11.

7. PAINTING AGAINST TORTURE
John Nava

1. "Bush on Waterboarding: 'Damn right,'" CNN, November 5, 2010, http://www.cnn.com/2010/POLITICS/11/05/bush.book/index.html.

8. TORTURE AND REPRESENTATION: THE ART OF *DÉTOURNEMENT*
Abigail Solomon-Godeau

1. I am considering the act of torture as a range of practices that may end in execution or cause death in and of themselves, but unlike other forms of violence, are utilized quite specifically to cause extreme bodily pain.

2. Oona A. Hathaway argues, however, that being a signatory to conventions that condemn or criminalize torture has little to do with actual practices "on the ground"; see Hathaway, "The Promise and Limits of the International Law of Torture," in *Torture: A Collection*, ed. Sanford Levinson (London: Oxford University Press, 2004).

3. Stephen F. Eisenman, *The Abu Ghraib Effect* (London: Reaktion Books, 2007).

4. The extended discussion of Laokoon and his suffering is found in J.-J. Winckelmann's *The History of Ancient Art Among the Greeks* (London: J. Chapman, 1850).

5. Eisenman, *The Abu Ghraib Effect*, 45–46, 51–52, and 69–70.

6. This shift, as Michel Foucault argued, was also based on an altered concept of punishment itself, from one inflicted directly on the corporal body to one based on incarceration; Foucault, *Discipline and Punish* (New York: Vintage Books, 1977).

7. Elaine Scarry, *The Body in Pain: The Making and Unmaking of the World* (New York and Oxford: Oxford University Press, 1985), 4.

8. The report can be found in *The Torture Papers: The Road to Abu Ghraib*, ed. Karen J. Greenberg and Anthony Lewis, trans. Joshua L. Dratel (New York: Cambridge University Press, 2005).

9. Roberta Smith, "Botero Restores the Dignity of Prisoners at Abu Ghraib," *New York Times*, November 15, 2006, http://www.nytimes.com/2006/11/15/arts/design/15chan.html.

10. Ibid.

11. First shown in conjunction with Artists Call Against U.S. Intervention in Central America in the public mall (facing W. 42nd Street) at the Graduate School and University Center of New York (1984); see Yves-Alain Bois, Douglas Crimp, and Rosalind Krauss, "A Conversation with Hans Haacke," *October* 30 (1984): 23–48.

12. Haacke's use of the medium of oil paint, referring to its status within "conventional" art making, was, of course, one of the critical elements, as is evident from the title of one such installation, the 1982 "Oil Painting: Homage to Marcel Broodthaers," as well as his 1983–84 "Taking Stock (Unfinished)," which included an oil portrait of Margaret Thatcher. Insofar as this work was also a consideration of Charles Saatchi's role as collector, patron, and art world power broker, the painting referred also to Saatchi's support of the so-called painting revival of the 1980s.

13. Born in South Africa, Fein directs a website, *Annoy.com*. In 1997, he was victorious in a Supreme Court case against Janet Reno, the US attorney general, regarding the constitutionality of the Communications Decency Act, invoked to block sale and distribution of Fein's CD-ROM entitled *Conduct Unbecoming: Gays and Lesbians in the US Military*. Fein now presides over the

board of First Amendment Project, a nonprofit organization that protects and promotes freedom of information, expression, and petition.

14. See, however, the link http://eclefusion.wordpress.com/tag/ abu-ghraib-prison-tortures/, which consists of a discussion with Fein (Basel Art Fair Miami).

15. In this respect, it is worth mentioning that prior to its purchase by New York's MoMA, Gerhardt Richter's *October 18* series, which deals with the Baader/Meinhof Red Army Brigade and their imprisonment and death in Stanheim Prison, was accompanied in its various exhibitions by massive documentation organized into a number of loose-leaf binders.

16. James Glisson, "Bringing to Light," *Afterimage* 34, no. 3 (November/ December 2006): 76.

17. See Leander Kahney, *The Cult of iPod* (San Francisco: No Starch Press, 2005), 140.

18. W. J. T. Mitchell has discussed the symbolic resonance of the hooded Iraqi tricked out with wires and the reasons for its iconic status; see Mitchell, "Sacred Gestures: Images from our Holy War," *Afterimage* 34, no. 3 (November/December 2006): 18–23.

19. See Douglas Crimp, *AIDS Demo Graphics* (Seattle: Bay Press, 1990); Crimp, *On the Museum's Ruins* (Cambridge, Mass.: MIT Press, 1993).

9. WATERBOARDING: POLITICAL AND SACRED TORTURE
Stephen F. Eisenman

1. Poll results originally reported at http://www.publicagenda.org/ specials/terrorism/terror.htm. That site is no longer live; see instead Cathy Young, "Interrogation Debate: Let's Have Some Humility," *Real Clear Politics*, http://www.realclearpolitics.com/articles/2009/04/30/interrogation_debate_ lets_have_some_humility_96251.html.

2. George W. Bush, *Decision Points* (New York: Random House, 2010), 28.

3. KUBARK Counterintelligence Interrogation, July 1963, http://www .scribd.com/doc/487663/CIAKubarkTorture-Manual, 8.

4. Giorgio Agamben, *State of Exception*, trans. Kevin Attell (Chicago: University of Chicago Press, 2005), 4.

5. Evan Wallach, "Drop by Drop: Forgetting the history of Water Torture in U.S. Courts," *The Columbia Journal of Transnational Law*, http://www.pegc .us/archive/Articles/wallach_drop_by_drop_draft_20061016.pdf.

6. Henri Alleg, *The Question*, trans. John Calder (New York: John Braziller, 1958), 60–61.

7. *A Memento for Holland, or a True and Exact History of the Cruelties Used on the English Merchants Residing in Amboyna* (London: 1653), 17–18.

8. David Levi Strauss, "Inconvenient Evidence: The Effects of Abu Ghraib," *The Brooklyn Rail*, January 2005, http://www.brooklynrail .org/2005/01/express/inconvenient-evidence.

10. *DAMNATIO MEMORIAE*
Hamid Dabashi

1. The original letter was published on *Saham News*, the official website of Mehdi Karrubi's Etemad Melli Party on August 8, 2009, at http://www .etemademelli.ir/published/0/00/65/6571/.

2. For a *New York Times* report of this letter, see "Iran Tries to Suppress Rape Allegations," http://www.nytimes.com/2009/08/15/world/ middleeast/15iran.html. For a *New York Times* editorial on this rape charges, see "Shame On Iran," at http://www.nytimes.com/2009/08/28/opinion/28fri2 .html?_r=1&adxnnl=1&ref=global-home&adxnnlx=1251454080– 9+nzy+AIqjK2uhSxa6+UUw. For my initial reflections on this letter, see my CNN commentary, "Iran Confronts Rape, Torture Allegations" August 22, 2009, http://www.cnn.com/2009/WORLD/meast/08/22/dabashi.iran .morality/index.html.

3. From the English translation of Karrubi's letter, see http:// enduringamerica.com/2009/08/10/iran-the-karroubi-letter-to-rafsanjani-on- abuse-of-detainees/.

4. For details of this testimony, see http://www.rahesabz.net/story/681/ (in Farsi).

5. In his subsequent public statements, Karrubi has accused the judiciary official of intimidating the victim and creating public embarrassment for him. The victim subsequently disappeared, after testifying in front of a camera for Karrubi to produce as evidence. For more details, see Karrubi's statement on his website available at http://tagheer.ir/fa/archives/1388,06,15/89. Soon after the victim disappeared, a prominent Iranian documentary filmmaker who lives in exile in Europe revealed his identity and reported that he has been in contact with the filmmaker, asking him to document his plight. For more details see the testimony of Allamehzadeh and the victim, Ebrahim Sharifi, on Allamehzadeh's website: http://reza.malakut.org/ (in Farsi).

6. For the complete text of Khamenei's remarks acknowledging the atrocities at Kahrizak and Tehran University dormitories, see his speech to a group of students on 4 Shahrivar 1388 (August 26, 2009), http://www.leader .ir/langs/fa/?p=bayanat&id=5793(in Farsi).

7. See Mahmoud Ahmadinejad's comments in this regard in "Majera-ye Kahrizak kar-e Barandazan bud" (the Kahrizak Incident was the work of the Enemies of the State), 7 Shahrivar 1388 (August 29, 2009), http://www .donya-e-eqtesad.com/Default_view.asp?@=171937 (in Farsi). Even the

state-run national television, Seda va Sima-ye Jomhuri-ye Islami, implicitly acknowledged that there had been abuses when it launched a massive propaganda campaign claiming these were by a few "rogue elements," and that the security apparatus was the real victim of the post-election violence.

8. See *Inconvenient Evidence: Iraqi Prison Photographs from Abu Ghraib* (New York: International Center of Photography and the Andy Warhol Museum, 2004).

9. See Seymour Hersh, *Chain of Command: The Road from 9/11 to Abu Ghraib* (New York: HarperCollins, 2004).

10. For some of the paintings, see http://www.flickr.com/photos/markart/sets/72157603015927074/.

11. Andrea K. Scott, "Susan Crile—Abu Ghraib: Abuse of Power," *The New York Times*, October 13, 2006, http://query.nytimes.com/gst/fullpage.htm l?res=9E0DE5DD1130F930A25753C1A9609C8B63.

12. Arthur C. Danto, "The Body in Pain," *The Nation*, November 9, 2006, http://www.thenation.com/article/body-pain.

13. See Susan Sontag, "Regarding the Torture of Others," *The New York Times*, May 3, 2004, http://www.nytimes.com/2004/05/23/magazine/regarding-the-torture-of-others.html.

14. For details of President Obama's decision not to release the Abu Ghraib related photos, see Mark Thompson, "The Next Detainee Photo Scandal: Get Ready for Abu Ghraib, Act II," *Time*, May 11, 2009, http://www.time.com/time/nation/article/0,8599,1897203,00.html.

15. See Martin Fletcher and a special correspondent in Tehran, "Raped and beaten for daring to question President Ahmadinejad's election," *The Times*, September 11, 2009, http://www.irancrimewatch.com/Campaign/Shocking%20Reports/English/Raped_and_beaten.pdf. The distinguished Iranian documentary filmmaker Reza Allamehzadeh (who for years has lived in exile in Europe) has also produced a number of videos in which he has interviewed the victims of torture and rape, and they are readily available on *YouTube*; see http://www.youtube.com/watch?v=GhKs4lZBkyE&eurl=http%3 A%2F%2Freza%2Emalakut%2Eorg%2F2009%2F09%2Fpost%5F469%2E html&feature=player_embedded.

16. See Nicholas Mirzoeff, *Watching Babylon: The War in Iraq and Global Visual Culture* (London: Routledge, 2004), 117–71; see also Giorgio Agamben, "The Camp as the 'Nomos' of the Modern," *Homo Sacer: Sovereign Power and Bare Life*, trans. Daniel Heller-Roazen (Stanford: Stanford University Press, 1998), 166–80; Agamben, "What Is a Camp?" *Means without End: Notes on Politics*, trans. Vincenzo Binetti and Cesare Casarino (Minneapolis, Minn.: University of Minnesota Press, 2000), 37–44.

17. Mirzoeff, *Watching Babylon*, 67.

18. Mirzoeff, *Watching Babylon*, 70–73.

19. Jean Baudrillard, *The Perfect Crime* (London: Verso: 1996), 4.

20. Mirzoeff, *Watching Babylon*, 68.

21. See Michael Fischer, *Mute Dreams, Blind Owls, and Dispersed Knowledges: Persian Poesis in the Transnational Circuitry* (Durham: Duke University Press, 2004).

22. See Talal Asad's *Anthropology and the Colonial Encounter* (New York: Prometheus Books, 1995) for the earliest critic of anthropology in this respect; see also Edward Said, "Representing the Colonized: Anthropology's Interlocutors," *Critical Inquiry* 15, no. 2 (Winter 1989): 205–25. For further elaborations, see Nicholas De Genova, "The Stakes of an Anthropology of the United States," *CR: The New Centennial Review* 7, no. 2 (Fall 2007): 231–77.

23. See Edward Said's preface to *Dream of a Nation: On Palestinian Cinema*, ed. Hamid Dabashi (London: Verso, 2006).

24. Agamben adopts two Greek terms to distinguish between "the simple fact of living common to all beings (animals, men, or gods)" –*zoë*, and "the form or way of living proper to an individual or a group"–*bios*; Agamben, *Homo Sacer*, 1.

25. Mirzoeff, *Watching Babylon*, 145.

26. Mirzoeff, *Watching Babylon*, 146.

27. Carl Schmitt, *The Concept of the Political*, trans. George Schwab (Chicago: Chicago University Press, 1996), 26.

28. Since Ghassan Kanafani's "Return to Haifa" (1968), in *Palestine's Children: Returning to Haifa and Other Stories*, by Ghassan Kanafani, translated by Barbara Harlow and Karen Riley (Boulder, Co: Lynne Rienner Publisher, 2000), made into a film in 1982, we have had no major film about Nakba until Elia Suleiman's *The Time That Remains* (2009).

29. For an excellent example of such modes of narrative distancing from the memories of being tortured, see Haifa Zangana, *Dreaming of Baghdad* (New York: Feminist Press, 2009). A young revolutionary activist, Haifa Zangana was tortured by Saddam Hussein's security forces in the infamous Abu Ghraib prison, and her *Dreaming of Baghdad* is a simultaneous act of remembering and distancing herself from having been tortured. The M.A. thesis of Shahla Talebi, another victim of torture under both the Pahlavi regime and the Islamic Republic, a former student and now a friend and colleague, works through a similar paradox. Her thesis is being revised and will soon be published.

30. For an examination of this Roman practice, see Harriet I. Flower, *The Art of Forgetting: Disgrace and Oblivion in Roman Political Culture* (Chapel Hill: The University of North Carolina Press, 2006).

31. For a compilation of secret memos describing in detail the torturing techniques used by the CIA under the Bush administration's "War on Terror," see David Cole, *Torture Memos: Rationalizing the Unthinkable* (New York: The New Press, 2009).

32. For a BBC report on the US Army's recruitment of anthropologists in its "War on Terror," see Kambiz Fattahi, "US army enlists anthropologists," *BBC News*, October 16, 2007, http://news.bbc.co.uk/2/hi/americas/7042090.stm.

33. Baudrillard, *The Perfect Crime*, 4.

34. See Agamben, *Homo Sacer*, 136–43, 154–59.

35. As does Ismael Hossein-zadeh, "Reflecting on Iran's Presidential Election," http://www.middle-east-online.com/english/?id=33816.

36. As does Rostam Pourzal, "Would MLK back Iran's Protestors?" http://www.fpif.org/fpiftxt/6270.

37. See Silvia Aloisi, "Iranian Street Protests Hit Big Screen in Venice," *ABC News*, September 11, 2009, now available at http://www.reuters.com/article/2009/09/11/us-iran-idUSTRE58A4F120090911.

38. See "A sneak peek at Iranian artist Shirin Neshat's award-winning movie," *Los Angeles Times*, September 16, 2009, http://latimesblogs.latimes.com/culturemonster/2009/09/a-sneak-peek-at-iranian-artist-shirin-neshats-awardwinning-movie.html.

11. RITUALS OF HEGEMONIC MASCULINITY: CINEMA, TORTURE, AND THE MIDDLE EAST
Viola Shafik

1. Stuart Hall, "Notes on Deconstructing 'The Popular,'" in *People's History and Socialist Theory*, ed. R. Samuel (London: Routledge, 1981), 227–40.

2. Patrick Fuery, as quoted in Marcus Stiglegger, "Einblicke: Neugier auf das Innere des Anderen," in *Splatter Movies: Essays zum modernen Horrorfilm*, ed. Julia Köhne, Ralph Kuschke, and Arno Meteling (Berlin: Bertz and Fischer, 2005), 127–38, here 127; see also Patrick Fuery, *New Developments in Film Theory* (New York: Palgrave, 2000).

3. Yvonne Tasker, *Spectacular Bodies: Gender Genre and the Action Cinema* (London: Routledge, 1993), 117.

4. Julia Hallam and Margaret Marshment, *Realism and Popular Cinema* (Manchester, UK: Manchester University Press, 2000), 70.

5. Stiglegger, "Einblicke," 127.

6. Ibid., 130.

7. Richard Dyer, *Only Entertainment* (London: Routledge, 2002), 66.

8. Ibid., 69.

9. Linda Williams, as quoted in *The New Brutality Film*, by Paul Gormley (Bristol: Intellect Books, 2005), 8.

10. Amy Taubin, as quoted in Gormley, *The New Brutality Film*, 12.

11. Gormley, *The New Brutality Film*, 22.

12. Ibid., 13.

13. See Jack Shaheen, *Reel Bad Arabs: How Hollywood Vilifies a People* (New York: Olive Branch Press, 2001).

14. Hall, "Notes on Deconstructing 'The Popular.'"

15. Edward Said, *Covering Islam: How the Media and the Experts Determine How We See the Rest of the World* (New York: Vintage, 1997), xxii.

16. Susan Jeffords, *Hard Bodies: Hollywood Masculinity in the Reagan Era* (New Brunswick: Rutgers University Press, 1994), 25.

17. Ibid., 192.

18. Ibid., 48ff.

19. Tasker, *Spectacular Bodies*, 11.

20. Ibid., 12.

21. Raewyn Connell, *Gender* (Cambridge: Polity Press, 2002), 141.

22. Michael Taussig, *Mimesis and Alterity* (London: Routledge, 1993), xiii.

23. Giorgio Agamben, *Homo Sacer: Sovereign Power and Bare Life*, trans. Daniel Heller-Roazen (Stanford: Stanford University Press, 1998).

24. Dora Apel, "Torture Culture: Lynching Photographs and the Images of Abu Ghraib," *Art Journal* 64, no. 2 (Summer 2005): 88–100, here 98–99.

25. Apel, "Torture Culture," 89.

26. Connell, *Gender*, 103.

27. Ibid., 105.

28. Viola Shafik, *Popular Egyptian Cinema: Gender, Class and Nation* (Cairo: American University of Cairo Press, 2007), 312ff.

29. Ella Shohat and Robert Stam, *Unthinking Eurocentrism: Multiculturalism and the Media* (London: Routledge, 1994), 302ff.

30. Dyer, *Only Entertainment*, 128.

31. See Apel, "Torture Culture," 93.

32. Georg Klauda, *Die Vertreibung aus dem Serail: Europa und die Heteronormalisierung der islamischen Welt* (Hamburg: Männerschwarm Verlag, 2008).

33. Slavoj Žižek, as quoted in Apel, "Torture Culture," 94.

34. See Beth Baron, *Egypt as a Woman: Nationalism, Gender, and Politics* (Cairo: American University of Cairo Press, 2005).

35. See Shohat and Stam's analysis of this scene; Shohat and Stam, *Unthinking Eurocentrism*, 255.

36. Intisar Dardir, "Nadia al-Gindi . . . wa i'tirafat khasa" (Nadia al-Gindi: Special Confessions), *Akhbar al-nujum*, Nov. 8, 1997.

12. MUSIC AND TORTURE: THE STIGMATA OF SOUND AND SENSE
Peter Szendy

1. These pages were largely written before the election of Barack Obama. Despite his renewed promise to dismantle the prison at Guantánamo, I leave the present indicative, for the time of torture is far from meriting the use of the past tense.

2. We have translated the author's own translation from the Italian and included in footnotes the references to the Cambridge translation of Beccaria's text: Cesare Beccaria, *Beccaria: "On Crimes and Punishments" and Other Writings* (New York: Cambridge University Press, 1995), here 39 (translators' note).

3. Ibid.

4. Ibid.

5. Ibid, 43 (translators' note).

6. Ibid., 40 (translators' note).

7. In the original the term is "se voit," which literally translates as "sees itself" (translators' note).

8. These last two sentences are translated from Szendy's quotation of the French translation. The English edition of Laks' text differs here from the French edition : Szymon Laks, *Mélodies d'Auschwitz* (Paris: Editions du Cerf, 2004), 112; Laks, *Music of Another World*, trans. Chester A. Kisiel (Evanston, Ill.: Northwestern University Press, 1989), 98–99 (translator's note).

9. Laks, *Music of Another World*, 98–99.

10. Cited by Robert Alford and Andras Szanto in their remarkable study, "Orpheus Wounded: The Experience of Pain in the Professional Worlds of the Piano," *Theory and Society* 25, no. 1 (February 1996): 4–5. The authors also recall similar comments from pianist Ruth Slenczynska, a virtuoso who made her debut in Berlin in 1931, at the age of six. In *Music at Your Fingertips*, she writes: "You will suffer physical pain and learn to endure it; pain is like a tunnel of fire that forges muscles of steel. You will emerge at the other end invigorated, with a tremendous margin of reserve, and with the knowledge of complete mastery, which is well worth the effort" (New York: Da Capo Press, 1976), 39.

11. Cf. Peter Szendy, *Hits: Philosophy in the Jukebox*, trans. William Bishop (New York: Fordham University Press, 2011).

12. Joshua 6:20; see the analysis of this passage I propose in Szendy, *Sur écoute: Esthétique de l'espionnage* (Paris: Éditions de Minuit, 2007).

13. A definition that was already included in the list given by Beccaria of motives for torture: "The torture of a criminal while his trial is being put together is a cruelty accepted by most nations (*la tortura del reo mentre si*

forma il processo) whether to compel him to confess a crime, to exploit the contradictions he runs into, to uncover his accomplices . . . (or, lastly, to expose other crimes of which he is guilty but with which he has not been charged)"; Beccaria, *"On Crimes and Punishments,"* (Cambridge translation), 39.

14. Suzanne G. Cusick, "Music as Torture/Music as Weapon," *Transcultural Music Review*, no. 10 (2006), http://www.sibetrans.com/trans/trans10/cusick_eng.htm.

15. In English in the original (translators' note).

16. Cited by Cusick, "Music as Torture."

17. Ibid.

18. "Sesame Street breaks Iraqi POWs," May 20, 2003, http://news.bbc.co.uk/2/hi/3042907.stm.

19. Moustafa Bayoumi, "Disco Inferno," *The Nation*, December 26, 2005, http://www.thenation.com/article/disco-inferno.

20. Mark Steyn, "Facing the Music," *The New York Sun*, June 20, 2005, http://www.nysun.com/opinion/facing-the-music/15711/, cited in Bayoumi, "Disco Inferno."

21. Emphasis mine.

22. In English in the original (translators' note).

23. Theodor W. Adorno, *Mahler: A Musical Physiognomy*, trans. Edmund Jephcott (Chicago: University of Chicago Press 1992), 5 (translators' note).

24. Walter Carlos was the author of the first big hit entirely carried out on a Moog synthesizer: "Switched-on Bach," to which Glenn Gould had paid tribute in an article published by the weekly magazine *Saturday Night*.

25. Anthony Burgess, *A Clockwork Orange* (London: Heinemann, 1962 [original publication]). The book offers a glossary for Alex's argot, nicknamed Nadsat.

26. Irony from Kubrick? This motif (i.e., the musical motif of Beethoven's *Fifth Symphony*), which corresponds to the letter V as in Victory in Morse code, preceded the radio speeches of General De Gaulle from London during the Second World War. It thus becomes, precisely in London itself and its surroundings, the beginning of a nightmare.

27. The beating of the bum seems to be triggered by the fact that he sings old, unbearable refrains: "One thing I could never stand," says Alex's voiceover, "is to see a filthy, dirty old drunkie, howling away at the filthy songs of his fathers . . . as it might be a filthy old orchestra in his stinking rotten guts."

28. *Malenky*, a Russian word, means "little" in Nadsat; *plott* means "body."

29. *Sloosh*, from the Russian *slushat*: "to listen" in Nadsat.

30. See Michel Foucault, *Discipline and Punish: The Birth of the Prison*, trans. Alan Sheridan (New York: Random House, 1977).

31. "... our dear old friend," he says, "the red, red vino on tap. The same in all places like it's put out by the same big firm, began to flow."

32. Let us remember, among other examples, this speech, which chills the spine, pronounced by Georgia governor Zell Miller, on January 13, 1998, in his budget presentation. Here the politician echoes a whole series of American scientific works of the 1990s: "And while I'm on children, I want to tell you about another initiative I'm proposing and am very excited about. We know that a baby's brain continues to form after birth, not just growing bigger as toes and fingers do, but developing microscopic connections responsible for learning and remembering. At birth, a baby has 100 billion or more neurons forming more than 50 trillion connections, or synapses as they are called, which sounds like a lot. But during the first months of life, the number of synapses increases 20 times to more than 1,000 trillion. This amazing growth allows a baby to do all kinds of miraculous things, from focusing its eyes on an object to shaping the word 'Da-da.' The new research on brain development in babies is unbelievable. *Time* devoted a special issue to it, and I recommend its reading. I have a lot of research I'd be glad to share with you. Enrichment clearly makes a difference in brain development. In October we had an early childhood development seminar for teachers, medical professionals, staff of our state agencies that work with children, and businesses with products and services for tiny customers. It was fascinating. Why am I telling you all this in a speech that is already far too long? Because I want to propose something extraordinary that I don't think any other state does. And it is this. Research shows that reading to an infant, talking with an infant and especially having that infant listen to soothing music helps those trillions of brain connections to develop, especially the ones related to math. There is research that links the study of music to better school performance and higher scores on college entrance exams. There's even a study called the 'Mozart effect' that showed after college students listened to a Mozart piano sonata for 10 minutes, their IQ scores increased by nine points. Some argue that it didn't last, but no one doubts that listening to music, especially at a very early age, affects the spatial-temporal reasoning that underlies math, engineering and chess. So I propose that the parents of every baby born in Georgia—over 100,000 a year—be given a cassette or CD of music to be played often in the baby's presence. It's not a big ticket item in the budget— only $105,000—but I believe it can help Georgia's children to excel. I have asked Yoel Levi, the world-famous conductor of the Atlanta Symphony, to help me with the musical selections for the tape, although I already have some ideas. For instance, here's one that a Georgia baby might hear. That, of course, is Beethoven's 'Ode to Joy.' Now don't you feel smarter already? Smart enough to vote for this budget item, I hope"; "Remarks by Governor Zell Miller: FY 99 Budget Address 1/13/98," http://bit.ly/mozart_effect.

It would be necessary to show, though I lack the space, how such a concept of music was already at work in the project of the Muzak society. On the latter, see David Toop, "Environmental Music" at Grove Music Online, Oxford University Press: "In 1922 George Owen Squier, a . . . military officer who had conducted research into wireless systems, launched a company that would attempt to pipe music, advertising and public service announcements into homes and businesses. As well as foreseeing the late-twentieth-century home entertainment reality of cable communications, Squier coined the name *Muzak*, a fusion of the words 'music' and 'Kodak.' During the 1930s the Muzak company, based in New York City, began systematic broadcasting to hotels, clubs, restaurants and shops. This programme of centralized transmission came to be rationalized into a system of stimulus codes, supported by scientific studies that demonstrated links between music, productivity and safety in factories.

Even silence wouldn't escape this logic, as John Cage's words suggest when he talks about what will become his famous silent piece, *4'33"*: "I have [. . .] several new desires [. . .]: first, to compose a piece of uninterrupted silence and sell it to Muzak Co. It will be 3 or 4½ minutes long—those being the standard lengths of 'canned' music—and its title will be Silent Prayer." Cf. John Cage, "A Composer's Confessions" (1948), in *John Cage, Writer: Previously Uncollected Pieces*, ed. Richard Kostelanetz (New York: Limelight Editions, 1993), 43.

33. As Alex's voiceover recounts: "I woke up. The pain and sickness all over me like an animal. Then I realized what it was. The music coming up from the floor was our old friend, Ludwig van and the dreaded *Ninth Symphony*. . . . Suddenly I viddied what I had to do, and what I had wanted to do—and that was to do myself in, to snuff it, to blast off forever out of this wicked cruel world. One moment of pain perhaps and then sleep–forever and ever and ever." On the term "biopolitic" and its use, see Michel Foucault, "Crise de la médecine ou crise de l'antimédecine," *Dits et écrits* (Paris: Gallimard, 2001), 2:40ff. The generalization without limits of medical intervention is described there in terms of "bio-history" ("a new dimension of the medical possibilities which I will call the question of the bio-history," 48). Allow me to state here that, vis-a-vis a certain expansion of the term biopolitic, in Foucault himself (starting with his course at the College of France in 1976: *Il faut défendre la société* [Paris: Seuil/Gallimard, 1997, 216ff]), then in Giorgio Agamben and others, it is not without a certain hesitation that I mobilize it. And if I do, it is not in the sense in which the biopolitic would mark a new scansion, unheard of in the history of politics, which would all of a sudden have to do with "life itself" (*Dits et écrits*, 2:48). It is rather, in a more circumscribed way, in the sense in which Foucault speaks of an "indefinite medicalization" (ibid), for example, when he writes: "When we

want to resort to a domain believed to be external to medicine, we realize that it has been medicalized. And when we want to object to medicine on the basis of its weaknesses, its drawbacks, and its harmful effects, it is done in the name of a more complete medical knowledge, more refined and more diffuse" (51).

34. In fact, as Esteban Buch showed in a remarkable essay, *La Neuvième de Beethoven: Une histoire politique* (Paris: Gallimard, 1999), "Ode to Joy" could serve the most opposing political causes: it became the European anthem as well as the anthem of the racist regime of ex-Rhodesia.

35. Jacques Lacan describes "incessant sliding of the signified under the signifier" as "a twofold flood" in "The Instance of the Letter in the Unconscious," in *Écrits: A Selection*, trans. Bruce Fink (New York: Norton, 2002), 145. The perpetual slippage of images above or below the musical flow was what Nietzsche already described in *The Birth of Tragedy*, when he spoke of the "fiery showers of images" (*Bilderfunken*) that the popular strophic song projects: "Melody gives birth to poetry from itself, over and over again. That is what the strophic form of the folk song indicates to us. I always observed this phenomenon with astonishment, until I finally came up with this explanation. Whoever looks at a collection of folk songs, for example, *Des Knaben Wunderhorn* [The Boy's Magic Horn] with this theory in mind will find countless examples of how the continually fecund melody emits fiery showers of images around itself"; Friedrich Nietzsche, *The Birth of Tragedy*, trans. Ian Johnston (Arlington: Richer Resources Publications, 2009), 43.

36. Lacan, "The Subversion of the Subject and the Dialectic of Desire in the Freudian Unconscious," *Écrits*, 291: "what I have called the 'button tie' (*point de capiton*), by which the signifier stops the otherwise indefinite sliding of signification."

13. THE LANGUAGE OF FEELING MADE INTO A WEAPON: MUSIC AS AN INSTRUMENT OF TORTURE
Christian Grüny

1. Illias Chrissochoidis, "Composed in Hypocrisy: Music, Torture, and the Drama of American Musicology," *The Chronicle Review*, May 8, 2009, http://chronicle.com/free/v55/i35/35b01001.htm. It should be noted that the author is not arguing against condemning music torture, but denouncing the Association's public attitude, which he finds hypocritical.

2. Jonathan Pieslak includes a discussion of all this in his very instructive book *Sound Targets: American Soldiers and Music in the Iraq War* (Bloomington: Indiana University Press, 2009). However, his extensive discussion of whether the utilization of music on detainees in Iraq may really be called torture seems to be marred by his identification with the soldiers he interviewed. Still, his descriptions and analyses of the practices involved are detailed

and useful. There is now (March 16, 2011) even a Wikipedia entry on music in psychological operations: http://en.wikipedia.org/wiki/Music_in_ psychological_operations.

3. See Alfred W. McCoy, *A Question of Torture: CIA Interrogation, from the Cold War to the War on Terror* (New York: Metropolitan, 2006).

4. Amnesty International, *Für eine Welt frei von Folter* (Bonn: 2000), 155.

5. Gustav Keller/Amnesty International, *Psychologie der Folter* (Frankfurt am Main: Fischer, 1981).

6. Cf. the 2008 report of the Armed Services Committees of the US Senate about the treatment of detainees: http://armed-services.senate. gov/Publications/Detainee%20Report%20Final_April%2022%202009.pdf.

7. See Plenary Court Judgment of the European Court of Human Rights, Case of Ireland vs. The United Kingdom (Application no. 5310/71), Strasbourg, January 18, 1978.

8. See Alfred W. McCoy, *A Question of Torture*, 134–35. Surprisingly, Suzanne G. Cusick draws the opposite conclusion from McCoy's book, namely that music as an instrument of torture has been part of "a standard set of practices" by the CIA for decades (cf. Susanne G. Cusick, "Music as Torture/Music as Weapon," *Transcultural Music Review* 10 (2006), www.sibetrans.com/trans/trans10/cusick_eng.htm.) Indeed, the use of music comes as no surprise and fits well with the practices of "no-touch torture," but McCoy's book shows precisely that until recently it was not a standard practice at all.

9. Pieslak shows how technical possibilities have changed the role of music in wars in recent years: for example, *Sound Targets*, 3, 46–49.

10. Hans Jonas, "The Nobility of Sight," in *The Phenomenon of Life: Toward a Philosophical Biology* (Evanston: Northwestern University Press, 2001), 139.

11. Ruhal Ahmed, quoted in Andy Worthington, "A History of Music Torture in the 'War on Terror,'" December 15, 2008, http://www .andyworthington.co.uk/2008/12/15/a-history-of-music-torture- in-the-war-on-terror/.

12. The sound of babies crying was used in Iraq, as well: one of the soldiers Pieslak interviews "also said that he made a tape of babies crying; detainees usually answered questions after a half hour"; Pieslak, *Sound Targets*, 88. Significantly, the use of this method seems to be a result of the soldiers' own imagination and initiative, not of detailed orders or training.

13. Richard Wagner, "Beethoven," *Richard Wagner's Prose Works*, trans. William Ashton Ellis (New York: Broude Brothers, 1966), 5:71. "Das Objekt des vernommenen Tones fällt unmittelbar mit dem Subjekt des ausgegebenen Tones zusammen: wir verstehen ohne jede Begriffsvermittlung, was uns der

vernommene Hilfe-, Klage- oder Freudenruf sagt, und antworten ihm sofort in dem entsprechenden Sinne"; Richard Wagner, *Gesammelte Schriften und Dichtungen* (Hildesheim: Olms, 1976), 9:71. What is translated as "reasoning go-between," is *Begriffsvermittlung* in German, literally the mediation by the concept.

14. Eduard Hanslick, *On the Musically Beautiful: A Contribution towards the Revision of the Aesthetics of Music*, trans. and ed. Geoffrey Payzant (Indianapolis: Hackett, 1986). The English translation is of the 8th edition of Hanslick's book, which no longer includes the "Foreword to the first edition," from which this quote stems. However, the "Foreword to the first edition" is included in the "Translator's Preface," where Hanslick's formulation is translated as "decaying walls of the 'feeling-theory,'" even though in chapter 1 the translator chooses "aesthetics of feeling" for *Gefühlsästhetik* (p. xiii).

15. Ibid., 9–11.

16. Pieslak, *Sound Targets*, 137.

17. Cusick, "Music as Torture/Music as Weapon."

18. Pieslak, *Sound Targets*, 169.

19. Ibid., for example 149–53. Pieslak speaks of a "battlefield psychology of timbre" (167).

20. Ibid., 46–57.

21. Ibid., 163. This immediately perceptible analogy is the basis of a more elaborate cultural coding, which the US army itself has started to rely on: since 2003, Metal is used as a soundtrack for army, navy, and air force commercials (42).

22. Of course this seemingly unproblematic account doesn't do justice to the complex problems concerning music and meaning. Still, the way a core of musical meaning or expressiveness is determined in two different, but related ways seems to me to be a prime example of how musical meaning is determined by an interaction between the music itself and the context it is perceived in, a point Cook discusses in detail; see Nicholas Cook, "Theorizing Musical Meaning," *Music, Performance, Meaning: Selected Essays* (Aldershot: Ashgate, 2007), 213–40.

23. Hanslick, *On the Musically Beautiful*, 29.

24. Ibid., 30, translation modified. The English translation reads "mind giving shape to itself from within." Elsewhere in the chapter "Geist" is translated with "spirit" (29), and "full share of ideality" (30), among others.

25. Daniel Stern, *The Interpersonal World of the Infant: A View from Psychoanalysis and Development Psychology* (New York: Basic Books, 1985).

26. Stern, "One Way to Build a Clinically Relevant Baby," *Infant Mental Health Journal* 15, no. 1 (1994): 9–25.

27. Philosophically, Susanne K. Langer's theory of art may be drawn on. Langer considers music the paradigmatic form of the "symbol of feeling" that

characterizes all art. What she calls "feeling" far exceeds mere emotionality and encompasses all levels of consciousness that are implied in Stern's theory, including reason as "any appreciation of form, any awareness of pattern"; Langer, *Feeling and Form: A Theory of Art Developed from Philosophy in a New Key* (New York: Scribners, 1953), 29.

28. For a musicologically accurate account of these structures, see Ernst Kurth, *Musikpsychologie* (Hildesheim and New York: Olms, 1969).

29. Bob Singleton, "Barney the Purple Torturer?" *Los Angeles Times*, July 2, 2008.

30. Binyam Mohamed, quoted in Andy Worthington, "A History of Music Torture in the 'War on Terror,'" December 15, 2008, http://www.andyworthington.co.uk/2008/12/15/a-history-of-music-torture-in-the-war-on-terror/.

31. Amnesty International, *Bericht über die Folter* (Frankfurt am Main: 1975), 48.

32. Moustafa Bayoumi, "Disco Inferno," *The Nation*, December 26, 2005, http://www.thenation.com/doc/20051226/bayoumi.

33. Ibid.

34. Elaine Scarry, *The Body in Pain: The Making and Unmaking of the World* (New York and Oxford: Oxford University Press, 1985), 41. Scarry mentions ways of using all these objects in torture.

35. *zero dB (Against Music Torture)*, http://www.zerodb.org.

14. ROMANTIC POET LEGISLATORS: AN END OF TORTURE
Julie A. Carlson

1. Percy Bysshe Shelley, *A Defence of Poetry* (1821) in *Shelley's Poetry and Prose*, ed. Donald Reiman and Sharon Powers (New York: Norton Critical Edition, 2002), 535.

2. Shelley, *A Defence of Poetry*, 512–13.

3. Lynn Hunt, *Inventing Human Rights: A History* (New York: W. W. Norton, 2007), 30–34.

4. James K. Chandler, "Moving Accidents: The Emergence of Sentimental Probability," in *The Age of Cultural Revolutions: Britain and France, 1750–1820*, ed. Colin Jones and Dror Wahrman (Berkeley: University of California Press, 2002), 138; see also Chandler, *England in 1819: The Politics of Literary Culture and the Case of Romantic Historicism* (Chicago: University of Chicago Press, 1998), 229–30, 312–20.

5. Hunt, *Inventing Human Rights*, 19.

6. Among others, see Markman Ellis, *The Politics of Sensibility: Race, Gender, and Commerce* (Cambridge: Cambridge University Press, 1996); Jeffrey N. Cox, introduction to *Drama*, ed. Peter J. Kitson and Debbie Lee, vol. 5,

Slavery, Abolition, and Emancipation: Writings in the British Romantic Period
(London: Pickering and Chatto, 1999), vii–xxvii; Felicity Nussbaum, *The
Limits of the Human* (Oxford: Oxford University Press, 2003).

7. Lisa Hajjar, "Rights at Risk: Why the Right Not to Be Tortured Is
Important to You," *Studies in Law, Politics and Society* 48 (2009): 102. Hajjar's
position is based on a "very clear definition" of "what rights *are*," namely,
"practices that are required, prohibited or otherwise regulated within the
context of relationships governed by law" (102). That is, as a "legal positivist,"
she contends that rights only "exist" if they are "enshrined in law" and that
so-called "natural" or "divine rights are alchemical unless they have been
enshrined in laws made, interpreted, and used by people" (103). This is
because rights are created "when laws are promulgated to regulate certain
types of practices," and that this occurs "when there is a perceived need for
them *and* conditions exist in which such laws can be passed to create a new
right or to extend a right to new subjects" (103).

8. See, for example, Jerome McGann, *The Romantic Ideology: A Critical
Investigation* (Chicago: University of Chicago Press, 1981); Forest Pyle, *The
Ideology of Imagination: Subject and Society in the Discourse of Romanticism* (Palo
Alto: Stanford University Press, 1995); Oona A. Hathaway, "The Promise and
Limits of the International Law of Torture," in *Torture: A Collection*, ed.
Sanford Levinson (Oxford: Oxford University Press, 2004), 199–212.

9. See Frederick A. Pottle, "The Case of Shelley," in *English Romantic
Poets: Modern Essays in Criticism*, ed. M. H. Abrams (New York: Oxford
University Press, 1960), 289–306.

10. Edward Peters, *Torture: Expanded Edition* (Philadelphia: University of
Pennsylvania Press, 1985), 76. See Hunt on Beccaria and torture in *Inventing
Human Rights*, 76–82.

11. On the question of Britain and torture, see Brian Innes, *The History of
Torture* (New York: St. Martin's Press, 1998), 85–94; Edwards, *Torture*,
91–104. Bentham credited Beccaria with being "the father of Censorial
Jurisprudence," [editor's] introduction to Cesare Beccaria, *On Crimes and
Punishments and Other Writings*, ed. Richard Bellamy (Cambridge: Cambridge
University Press, 1995), xvi. All subsequent references to this work are from
this edition, abbreviated *CP*, and included with page numbers in parentheses
in the text.

12. Godwin notes in his diary that he is reading Beccaria's text on
October 30, November 3, and November 5, 1792 (when he finishes it),
the same period that he is writing book 7 (http://godwindiary.bodleian
.ox.ac.uk).

13. William Godwin, *An Enquiry Concerning Political Justice* (1793), in
Political and Philosophical Writings of William Godwin, ed. Mark Philp (London:
William Pickering, 1993), 3: 380. All subsequent references are from this

edition, abbreviated *PJ*, and included with page numbers in parentheses in the text.

14. Godwin's views on intention are part of a complex discussion regarding the nature of his necessarianism, utilitarianism, and understanding of human psychology; see especially Mark Philp, *Godwin's Political Justice* (London: Duckworth, 1986), and John P. Clark, *The Philosophical Anarchism of William Godwin* (Princeton: Princeton University Press, 1977).

15. Victoria Myers spells out why matters of jury competence and the mitigation of punishment are of general concern in her account of innovations in judicial thinking at the end of the eighteenth century in "Joanna Baillie: Speculations on Legal Cruelty," *The Wordsworth Circle* 35, no. 3 (2004): 123–27.

16. George Lipsitz, *The Possessive Investment in Whiteness: How White People Profit from Identity Politics*, rev. and expanded edition (Philadelphia: Temple University Press, 2006).

17. See Julie A. Carlson, *England's First Family of Writers: Mary Wollstonecraft, William Godwin, Mary Shelley* (Baltimore: The Johns Hopkins University Press, 2007), esp. 66–92.

18. William Godwin, "Essay of History and Romance" (1797), in *Educational and Literary Writings*, ed. Pamela Clemit, 290–302, vol. 5 of *Political and Philosophical Writings of William Godwin*, ed. Mark Philp; see Jon Klancher, "Godwin and the Genre Reformers: On Necessity and Contingency in Romantic Narrative Theory," in *Romanticism, History, and the Possibilities of Genre: Reforming Literature, 1789–1837*, ed. Tilottama Rajan and Julia M. Wright (Cambridge: Cambridge University Press, 1998), 21–38.

19. On fiction by these New Philosophers, see Gary Kelly, *The English Jacobin Novel, 1780–1805* (Oxford: Oxford University Press, 1976).

20. Steven Bruhm, *Gothic Bodies: The Politics of Pain in Romantic Fiction* (Pittsburgh: University of Pennsylvania Press, 1994), 96, 98.

21. Colin Dayan, *The Story of Cruel and Unusual* (Cambridge, Mass.: MIT Press, 2007).

22. Jonathan H. Grossberg, *The Art of Alibi: English Law Courts and the Novel* (Baltimore: The Johns Hopkins University Press, 2002), 38, 37. Godwin's next novel, *St Leon* (1799), explores the specific issue of torture in prison.

23. The "Introductory Note" specifies as well that around 1829 or 1830, Godwin projected writing a novel that argues for "an Act of Parliament that would absolve a man of a crime such as Aram's if, after a lapse of ten years, he had been found to have 'spent that period blamelessly, and in labours conducive to the welfare of mankind'"; *Deloraine*, ed. Maurice Hindle, v, vol. 8 of *Collected Novels and Memoirs of William Godwin*, ed. Mark Philp (London: William Pickering, 1993).

24. On the relation between legal and literary argument in romantic writers, besides Grossberg, see Victoria Myers, "William Godwin and the *Ars Rhetorica*," *Studies in Romanticism* 41 (2002): 415–44, and Myers, "Joanna Baillie: Speculations on Legal Cruelty," *The Wordsworth Circle* 35, no. 3 (2004): 123–27; Michael Scrivener, "Trials in Romantic-Era Writing: Modernity, Guilt, and the Scene of Justice," *The Wordsworth Circle* 35, no. 3 (2004): 128–33.

25. "His fame shall not be as immortal as he thinks. These papers shall preserve the truth: they shall one day be published, and then the world shall do justice to us both. Recollecting that, I shall not die wholly without consolation"; *CW*, 267.

26. "Godwin/Shelley Correspondence," ed. Mark Philp, 75, vol. 1 in *Collected Novels and Memoirs of William Godwin*.

27. P. B. Shelley, *The Cenci* (1819), in *Shelley's Poetry and Prose*, 265. All subsequent citations are from this edition, abbreviated as *C* and included with page numbers in parentheses in the text.

28. Shelley's footnote to this passage then contends that there "are individuals who can be just judges even against themselves," who, through "study and self-examination have established a severe tribunal within themselves to which these principles which demand the advantages of the greater number are admitted to appeal"; *A Philosophical View of Reform*, 21, 336, vol. 7 in *The Complete Works of Percy Bysshe Shelley*, ed. Roger Ingpen and Walter E. Peck (New York: Gordian Press, 1965).

29. Chandler, *England in 1819*, 508. See also, on the centrality of hope in Shelley, William Keach, *Arbitrary Power: Romanticism, Language, Politics* (Princeton: Princeton University Press, 2004), 128–30, 144–58.

30. Chandler, *England in 1819*, 513.

31. Ibid., 509.

32. William Godwin, *Life of Geoffrey Chaucer, the Early English Poet: Including Memoirs of His Near Friend and Kinsman, John of Gaunt, Duke of Lancaster: With Sketches of the Manners, Opinions, Arts, and Literature of England of the Fourteenth Century* (London: Richard Phillips, 1803), 1:370.

33. Shelley, *A Philosophical View of Reform*, 7:19. I am also intrigued by the congruence between claims regarding imagination in Godwin's Preface to *Bible Stories* and the first paragraph of *A Defence of Poetry*.

34. "On Godwin's 'Mandeville,'" *The Complete Works of Percy Bysshe Shelley*, 6:219; my emphasis. On this in Shelley, see Chandler, *England in 1819*, 513.

35. *Mandeville*, ed. Pamela Clemit, *Collected Novels and Memoirs of William Godwin*, 6:145.

36. *Mandeville*, 145.

37. These terms and this maxim appear in Preface to *The Cenci* (*Shelley's Poetry and Prose*, 240), Preface to *Prometheus Unbound* (*Shelley's Poetry and*

Prose, 133), and *A Philosophical View of Reform* (*The Complete Works of Percy Bysshe Shelley*, 7:13).

38. Shelley, "On Godwin's 'Mandeville,'" *The Complete Works of Percy Bysshe Shelley*, 6:221.

39. Ibid.

40. Ibid. Here Shelley is anticipating his infamous revision of love in *Epipsychidion*—the claim that "True love in this differs from gold and clay,/That to divide is not to take away." The next lines, "Love is like understanding, that grows bright/Gazing on many truths" are a Godwinian version of sympathy, directed toward different ends.

41. "On Godwin's 'Mandeville,'" 6:222.

42. Ibid.

43. In this context it is intriguing that Godwin dramatizes the divided nature of the woman's position in the family in three of his four plays (*Antonio, Abbas,* and *Faulkener*), but none of his novels; See Carlson, "Godwin's Heavy Drama," *Godwinian Moments: From the Enlightenment to Romanticism*, ed. Victoria Myers and Robert Manniquis (Toronto: University of Toronto Press, 2011), 217–38.

44. This is Mathilda's famous indictment of Woodville in *Mathilda*; on it, see Mary Jacobus, "Guilt that Wants a Name: Mary Shelley's Unreadability," in *Psychoanalysis and the Scene of Reading* (Oxford: Oxford University Press, 1999), 165–201.

45. I explore Mary's reconciliation with the poetic spirit of Percy in Carlson, *England's First Family of Writers*, 193–221.

46. Primo Levi gives a poignant account of this betrayal by dreams in *Survival in Auschwitz* (New York: Touchstone, 1958), 56–64.

47. "To a Sky-Lark," *Shelley's Poetry and Prose*, 305. On the thirst after resemblance, see Mark J. Bruhn, "Shelley's Theory of Mind: From Radical Empiricism to Cognitive Romanticism," *Poetics Today* 30, no. 3 (Fall 2009): 373–422.

48. "On Love," *Shelley's Poetry and Prose*, 503, my emphasis; see Thomas Pfau, "Figuring the 'Insufficient Void' of Self-Consciousness in Shelley's 'Epipsychidion,'" *Keats-Shelley Journal* 40 (1991); 99–126.

49. Keach, *Arbitrary Power*, 155–58.

50. Preface to *Prometheus Unbound, Shelley's Poetry and Prose*, 135.

51. Shelley, *A Philosophical View of Reform, Complete Works of Percy Bysshe Shelley*, 7:21.

52. See, for example, Avery Gordon, "The US Military Prison: The Normalcy of Exceptional Brutality," in *The Violence of Incarceration*, ed. Phil Scraton and Jude McCullogh (London: Routledge, 2007).

53. See Peters, *Torture*, 1–6.

54. See, for example, Carin Benninger-Budel and Lucinda O'Hanlon, "Expanding the Definition of Torture," *Human Rights Dialogue* 2, no. 10 (Fall 2003): 14–15; Rhonda Copelon, "Gendered War Crimes: Reconceptualizing Rape in Times of War," in *Women's Rights Human Rights: International Feminist Perspectives*, ed. Julie Peters and Andrea Wolper (New York: Routledge, 1995), 197–214.

55. See, for example, Jerome H. Skolnick, "American Interrogation: From Torture to Trickery," in *Torture: A Collection*, ed. Sanford Levinson (Oxford: Oxford University Press, 2004), 105–28. More generally, see Hortense J. Spillers, "Mama's Baby, Papa's Maybe: An American Grammar Book," *Black, White, and in Color: Essays on American Literature and Culture* (Chicago: University of Chicago Press, 2003), 203–29; Philip Brian Harper, *Are We Not Men?: Masculine Anxiety and the Problem of African American Identity* (New York: Oxford University Press, 1996); and Abdul R. JanMohamed, *The Death-Bound-Subject: Richard Wright's Archaeology of Death* (Durham: Duke University Press, 2005).

56. Darieck B. Scott, *Extraordinary Abject: Abjection, Power, and Masculinity in the African American Literary Imagination* (New York: New York University Press, 2010).

57. George Elliott Clarke, *Beatrice Chancy* (Polestar Press, 2001).

58. Elaine Scarry, *The Body in Pain: The Making and Unmaking of the World* (New York and Oxford: Oxford University Press, 1985); Jacques Derrida, "Poetics and Politics of Witnessing," in *Sovereignties in Question: The Poetics of Paul Celan*, ed. Thomas Dutoit and Outi Pasanen (New York: Fordham University Press, 2005), 65–96.

59. Gayatri Chakravorty Spivak, "Terror: A Speech After 9–11," *boundary 2* 31, no. 2 (2004): 81, 94 ("I am suggesting that if in the imagination we do not make the attempt to figure the other as imaginative actant, political [and military] solutions will not remove the binary which led to the problem in the first place. Hence cultural instruction in the exercise of the imagination"); see also Marc Redfield, *Rhetoric of Terror: Reflections on 9/11 and the War on Terror* (New York: Fordham University Press, 2009), esp. 86–91.

60. Godwin's suggestion is akin to Judith Butler's conception of "precarious life."

61. *The Mask of Anarchy* (1819), *Shelley's Poetry and Prose*, 319, 317, 319.

62. *A Defence of Poetry* (1821), *Shelley's Poetry and Prose*, 512.

63. Lisa Hajjar, "Rights at Risk," 104; see also Hajjar, "Chaos as Utopia: International Criminal Prosecutions as a Challenge to State Power," *Studies in Law, Politics, and Society* 21 (2004): 3–23.

64. Shelley, *A Philosophical View of Reform*, in *Complete Works of Percy Bysshe Shelley*, 7:106.

65. Here is Ariel Dorfman's response to a reporter inquiring whether the chance of General Pinochet being extradited to Spain to face charges of torture had been radically diminished, given that the House of Lords had only been able to try him for one instance of death by torture (the case of Marcos Quezada Yáñez heard on March 24, 1999): "When I answered, I was surprised by my own vehemence. 'What if it were your mother who had died under torture?' I demanded of the reporter. 'If it were your own mother, wouldn't you want justice to be done?'" ("The Tyranny of Terror: Is Torture Inevitable in Our Century and Beyond?" in *Torture: A Collection*, ed. Levinson, 8).

15. THE FINE DETAILS: TORTURE AND THE SOCIAL ORDER
Darieck Scott

1. Mark Danner, "Review of *ICRC Report on the Treatment of Fourteen 'High Value Detainees' in CIA Custody*," by the International Committee of the Red Cross, *New York Review of Books* (April 30, 2009), 48–56, here 48.

2. Ibid., 49.

3. Mark Danner, "If Everyone Knew, Who's to Blame?" *Washington Post*, April 26, 2009, http://www.markdanner.com/articles/show/154.

4. Danner, "Review of *ICRC Report*," 52.

5. Ibid., 5.

6. Ibid., 56.

7. The summary of *Hogg*'s plot in this paragraph paraphrases and follows the structure of a summary that appears in Samuel R. Delany, "The Making of *Hogg*," *Shorter Views: Queer Thoughts and The Politics of the Paraliterary* (Hanover and London: Wesleyan University Press, 1999), 298–310, here 298.

8. Delany, "The Making of *Hogg*," 301.

9. Delany, *Hogg*, 2nd ed. (Normal/Tallahassee: Fiction Collective 2, 2004), 31. All subsequent references to this work are cited parenthetically by page number.

10. James Baldwin, "Alas, Poor Richard," *James Baldwin: Collected Essays*, ed. Toni Morrison (New York: Literary Classics of the United States, 1998) 247–68, here 251.

11. Delany, "On the Unspeakable," *Shorter Views: Queer Thoughts and the Politics of the Paraliterary*, 58–66, here 61–62.

12. Ibid., 58.

13. Ibid., 62–63.

14. Ibid., 58.

15. This information had been earlier reported by Mark Danner in the article appearing in the *The New York Review of Books* from which I've quoted above; the *Review* issue is dated April 30, but was available to subscribers earlier; see Danner, "Review of *ICRC Report*," 50.

16. The particulars I've listed are drawn from Danner's account rather than the more muted account in *The New York Times* article; see Danner, "Review of *ICRC Report*," 51.

17. Scott Shane and Mark Mazzetti, "In Adopting Harsh Tactics, No Inquiry Into Past Use," *New York Times*, April 22, 2009, A1.

18. See Maureen Dowd, "A Blue Burka for Justice," *New York Times*, January 30, 2002; Eric Lichtblau, "At Ashcroft's Farewell, Much Reverence," *New York Times*, January 25, 2005.

19. Hortense Spillers, Preface, *Black, White, and in Color: Essays on American Literature and Culture*, ed. Hortense Spillers (Chicago: University of Chicago Press, 2003), ix–xvi, here xiii.

20. Spillers, "Introduction: Peter's Pans: Eating in the Diaspora," *Black, White, and in Color*, 1–64, here 21.

21. Ibid., 21.

22. Delany, "The Making of *Hogg*," 303.

23. Ibid., 305.

24. This account appears in detail in "The Making of *Hogg*."

25. Delany, "The Making of *Hogg*," 307.

26. Ray Davis, "Delany's Dirt," in *Ash of Stars: On the Writing of Samuel R. Delany*, ed. James Sallis (Jackson: University Press of Mississippi, 1996), 162–188, here 174.

27. Davis, "Delany's Dirt," 176.

28. Delany, "The Making of *Hogg*," 308.

29. Davis, "Delany's Dirt," 173.

30. Frantz Fanon, "Algeria Face to Face With the French Torturers" (1957), trans. Haakon Chevalier, in *Toward the African Revolution: Political Essays*, 2nd ed. (New York: Grove, 1988), 64–72, here 66.

31. Ibid., 72.

32. Jean-Paul Sartre, Preface, *The Wretched of the Earth*, trans. Richard Philcox (New York: Grove, 2004), xliii–lxii, here lviii.

33. Ibid., lx–lxii.

34. Delany, "The Making of *Hogg*," 307.

35. With one exception: Hogg's murder of Jimmy, the man of reason, who both for readers and in the world of the novel is killed in a way that meets the conventional standards for a "just" death in fiction. Delany calls Jimmy "morally loathsome" ("The Making of *Hogg*," 309), and Davis finds Jimmy's demise "very satisfying" (Davis, "Delany's Dirt," 175.

36. Marc Cooper, "The Last Defender of the American Republic: An Interview with Gore Vidal," *Dreaming War: Blood for Oil and the Cheney-Bush Junta* (New York: Thunder's Mouth/Nation Books, 2002), 183–97, here 192.

37. Gore Vidal, "The Best Man," unpublished interview by Donald Weise, January 26, 1999, 9; excerpted with permission of the interviewer.

16. REASONABLE TORTURE, OR THE SANCTITIES
Colin Dayan

1. Robert Cover, "Violence and the Word," *Yale Law Journal* 95 (1985): 1601–29.

2. Avery Gordon, "The Prisoner's Curse," in *Traces in Social Worlds*, ed. Macarena Gómez-Barris and Herman Gray, forthcoming.

3. Hannah Arendt, "The Enlightenment and the Jewish Question," in *The Jewish Writings*, ed. Jerome Kohn and Ron H. Feldman (New York: Schocken Books, 2007), 3.

4. Ecclesiastes 11:3 (New Revised Standard Version).

5. Exodus 15:10 (Authorized [King James] Version).

6. Ecclesiastes 11:1 (Authorized [King James] Version).

7. Leviticus 26:19 (Authorized [King James] Version).

8. Ian Kelly, quoted in Marian Houck, "US State Department wants to limit reaction to Goldstone report on Gaza war," *Un-Truth*, September 18, 2009, http://un-truth.com/israel/u-s-state-department-wants-to-limit-reaction-to-goldstone-report-on-gaza-war.

9. Jonathan Cook, *Disappearing Palestine: Israel's Experiments in Human Despair* (London and New York: Zed Books, 2008).

10. "UN report that will be difficult for Israeli government to ignore," *Guardian*, September 16, 2009, http://www.guardian.co.uk/world/2009/sep/16/un-report-goldstone-israel-gaza/print. Human rights organizations in Israel, including Adalah, B'Tselem, HaMoked, Physicians for Human Rights—Israel, and The Public Committee Against Torture in Israel, among others, called upon the Israeli government to take the report seriously and to "conduct an independent and impartial investigation into these suspicions and to cooperate with an international monitoring mechanism that would guarantee both the independence of that investigation and the implementation of its conclusions (press release, September 15, 2009). After completion of this essay, on February 4, 2011, thirteen Palestinian and Israeli Human Rights Organizations wrote an Open Letter to the UN High Commissioner for Human Rights: "Is the Goldstone Report Dead, High Commissioner?" http://australiansforpalestine.com/38233; see Goldstone's "retraction" of his report, published after this essay was completed: "Reconsidering the Goldstone Report on Israel and War Crimes,"

April 1, 2011: http://www.washingtonpost.com/opinions/reconsidering-the-goldstone-report-on-israel-and-war-crimes/2011/04/01/AFg111JC_story.html. While disavowing his previous condemnation of Israel for intentionally killing Palestinian civilians during its invasion of Gaza, Goldstone reminds his readers about the Israel's government's "lack of cooperation" and further condemns continued attacks by Hamas. For an incisive analysis of Israel's indiscriminate warfare in Gaza, which Goldstone's disavowal in no way negates, see the Guardian editorial: http://www.guardian.co.uk/world/2011/apr/06/goldstone-report-unanswered-questions-editorial.

　　11. I thank Louis Frankenthaler, Development and International Outreach Director of PCATI, for his ongoing work and his generosity in making available these reports: *Back to a Routine of Torture: Torture and Ill-treatment of Palestinian Detainees during Arrest Detention and Interrogation* (September 2001–April 2003), http://www.stoptorture.org.il/en/node/762; *No Defense: Soldier Violence against Palestinian Detainees* (Periodic Report: June 2008), http://www.stoptorture.org.il/ar/node/1136 (in English, Hebrew, and Arabic); and now the draft document *Human Rights Situation in Israel: The Implementation of the Convention against Torture and Other Cruel, Inhuman or Degrading Treatment or Punishment*, an alternative report with the World Organisation Against Torture submitted to the UN Committee Against Torture (June 2009).

　　12. The best edition of the famous torture memos, as well as of the full texts of the legal memoranda that sought to redefine what constituted torture, is *The Torture Papers: The Road to Abu Ghraib*, ed. Karen J. Greenberg and Joshua L. Dratel (Cambridge: Cambridge University Press, 2005; see also Mark Danner, *Torture and Truth: America, Abu Ghraib, and the War on Terror* (New York: *The New York Review of Books*, 2004); *Torture: The Debate*, ed. Sanford Levinson (New York: Oxford University Press, 2004), and *The Torture Debate in America*, ed. Karen J. Greenberg (Cambridge: Cambridge University Press, 2006).

　　13. *Human Rights Situation in Israel*, 28–34.

　　14. "Israel's Dogs of War," Agence France Presse, December 12, 2005, http://www.sawf.org/newedit/edit12122005/worldwatch.asp.

　　15. *No Defense: Soldier Violence against Palestinian Detainees*, June 2008, PCATI, 11.

　　16. Ibid., 13.

　　17. *Human Rights in Palestine and Other Occupied Arab Territories: Report of the United Nations Fact Finding Mission on the Gaza Conflict*, September 15, 2009, http://www2.ohchr.org/english/bodies/hrcouncil/specialsession/9/factfindingmission.htm.

18. The harrowing of the Palestinian people from the Nakba to the present is powerfully described by Ilan Pappe in *The Ethnic Cleansing of Palestine* (Oxford: Oneworld Publications, 2006). In order to entrench the occupation, Palestinian lands were destroyed, turned into parks, turned into ancient biblical sites, or simply resettled by Israelis. See his description of the "reinvention of Palestine" by the Jewish National Fund, 225–34.

19. Wolfgang Sofsky, *The Order of Terror: The Concentration Camp* (1993), trans. William Templer (Princeton: Princeton University Press, 1997), 17.

20. Amira Hass, "Gazans detained in 'giant pit' during Cast Lead," *Haaretz*, August 15, 2009. According to *No Defense*, 42, adults and minors were held in ditches six to ten feet deep, "handcuffed for hours and days, and at times with their eyes covered. . . . About 70 people were reportedly held in each ditch, and it appears that scores, possibly hundreds, were detained in these appalling conditions."

21. Sara Roy, *Failing Peace: Gaza and the Palestinian-Israeli Conflict* (London and Ann Arbor, Mich.: Pluto Press, 2007), 315.

22. Jeremy Waldron, "Torture and Positive Law: Jurisprudence for the White House," *Columbia Law Review* 105 (October 2005): 1701; see also Dayan, *The Story of Cruel and Unusual* (Cambridge, Mass.: MIT Press, 2007).

23. Edward Peters, *Torture* (Philadelphia: University of Pennsylvania Press, 1985), 2.

24. Aimé Césaire, *Discourse on Colonialism* (1955), trans. Joan Pinkham (New York: Monthly Review Press, 1972), 77.

17. JOHN YOO, THE TORTURE MEMOS, AND WARD CHURCHILL:
EXPLORING THE OUTER LIMITS OF ACADEMIC FREEDOM
Richard Falk

1. For an excellent overview, see Edward J. Carvalho, ed., "Academic Freedom and Intellectual Activism in the Post-9/11 University," *Works and Days* 26 and 27 (2008–09): 7–27.

2. Such efforts were spearheaded by several organizations, perhaps most notably by Campus Watch, a project of the Middle East Forum directed by Daniel Pipes and dedicated to launching attacks upon professors and academic programs viewed as critical of Israel. For a vigorous and irresponsible right-wing attack on academic freedom that especially targets prominent critics of Israel; see David Horowitz, *The Professors: The 101 Most Dangerous Academics in America* (Chicago: Henry Regnery, 2006).

3. There exists a special need to overcome the vocational tendency of lawyers in their professional roles to stretch the truth and even the facts to gain their goals on behalf of a client. Consider, in this regard, the following assertion: "'Lawyers can be at particular risk of pushing the boundaries of

acceptable spinning,' said Stephen Gillers, a law professor and an expert on legal ethics. 'Their legal training and experience in practice,' he said, reinforce the notion that 'a fact becomes true if a jury or opponent can be persuaded to think that it is true—even if it is false.' 'Lawyers and politicians alike,' he said, 'work this alchemy through performance'"; John Schwartz, "Résumés Made for Fibbing," *New York Times*, Week in Review, May 23, 2010. I believe this strengthens the argument for doing something to exhibit institutional disapproval of Yoo's behavior while serving in government.

4. For representative works by legal scholars critical of the Bush administration's response to 9/11, see Phillippe Sands, *Lawless World* (New York: Viking, 2005); Marjorie Cohn, *Cowboy Republic: Six Ways the Bush Gang Has Defied the Law* (Sausalito, Calif.: PoliPoint Press, 2007).

5. Incidentally, the contention that "torture works" is irrelevant to the professional responsibility to give accurate advice and guidance as to applicable legal obligations. For opposing views on the pragmatics of torture see Jane Mayer, *The Dark Side* (New York: Doubleday, 2008); Benjamin Wittes, *Law and the Long War* (New York: Penguin Press, 2008); in general, on the political relevance of respecting international law, see David Cole and Jules Lobel, *Less Safe, Less Free: Why America Is Losing the War on Terror* (New York: New Press, 2007).

6. A persuasive legal assessment of the torture debate can be found in David Cole, ed., *The Torture Memos* (New York: New Press, 2009); even a generally conservative legal official during the post-9/11 period criticizes Yoo sharply for his unprofessional pro-torture zeal; see Jack Goldsmith, *The Terror Presidency* (New York: Norton, 2007).

7. For Churchill's account see Ward Churchill, "'The Myth of Academic Freedom': Experiencing the Application of the Liberal Principle in a Neoconservative Era," *Works and Days*, 26 and 27, nos. 51, 52, 53, and 54 (2008–2009): 139–230, esp. 140–46.

8. For a more detailed account of Churchill's position, see ibid.; see also Churchill, "What Did I Really Say? And Why Did I Say It?" Z-Net, February 22, 2005, available now at http://www.counterpunch .org/2005/02/21/what-did-i-really-say-and-why-did-i-say-it/; for commentary on the original offending text, see Churchill, *On the Justice of Roosting Chickens: Consequences of U.S. Imperial Arrogance and Criminality* (Oakland: AK Press, 2003).

9. For argument along these lines, see Stanley Fish, "Ward Churchill Redux," *New York Times*, April 6, 2009, Opinion Pages, http://opinionator .blogs.nytimes.com/2009/04/05/ward-churchill-redux/.

10. A related approach would rely on administrative discretion to reassign Yoo either to a nonteaching role or to courses outside the area in which his professionalism has been questioned. Such an approach would be based on

educational and professional responsibility of the law school to provide future lawyers with unambiguous models of professional ethics and responsibility. Of course, Yoo could contest such treatment as disguised punitive action, and such objection should be fairly considered by some sort of university procedure. The advantage of the administrative approach is that it would make the judgment on the basis of institutional integrity and commitments rather than by assessing the legality or propriety of the behavior of a member of the academic community.

11. It is relevant to note that the prohibition of torture is a fundamental norm of international human rights law that cannot be abridged, even in times of war or national emergency. In sharp contrast, the wrongs attributed to Churchill (and to other victims of right-wing attacks on academic freedom) are treated as matters of national discretion from the perspective of international law, but are generally viewed as protected instances of free expression in secular democracies.

12. See John C. Eastman, "Yes: His views spark important debate," *Los Angeles Times*, April 9, 2009, http://www.latimes.com/news/opinion/commentary/la-oe-eastman9-2009apr09,0,1890401.story. There exists a contrast between the relative mobility of a scholar like Yoo and the immobility of Churchill or Norman Finkelstein, suggesting an absence of ideological symmetry in current US universities that consistently favors the right, despite the frequent allegation of a liberal faculty bias. This pattern undoubtedly reflects institutional considerations that are mainly outside of faculty control, ranging from community attitudes and donor pressures to board of trustee conservatism. These factors vary in their relevance from institution to institution and over time.

13. For exposure to John Yoo's academic writings, see Yoo, *The Powers of War and Peace: The Constitution and Foreign Affairs after 9/11* (Chicago: University of Chicago Press, 2005); Yoo, *War by Other Means: An Insider's Account of the War on Terror* (New York: Atlantic Monthly Press, 2006).

14. See Dean Christopher Edley, Jr., "The Torture Memos and Academic Freedom," April 10, 2008, http://www.law.berkeley.edu/news/2008/edley041008.html.

15. Manual, Section 015, part 2.

16. The final outcome of the Department of Justice investigation of Yoo's role as government adviser, as announced by the Assistant Deputy Attorney General David Margolis, concluded that Yoo had used "poor judgment" but was not guilty of "professional misconduct" because there was no indication that a specific rule had been violated; Debra J. Saunders, "Yoo case about politics, not ethics," *SF Gate.com*, February 23, 2010, http://www.sfgate.com/cgi-bin/article.cgi?f=/c/a/2010/02/23/EDVU1C5CBO.DTL.

17. Compare the recognition of the diversity of views bearing on Yoo's views in his scholarly writing with the dogmatic presentation of advice in his governmental role; see Yoo, *War by Other Means*, vii–viii. See also seemingly inconsistent criticism of the extensive use of presidential authority in the course of carrying out foreign policy during the Clinton presidency; see Yoo, "The Imperial President Abroad," in *The Rule of Law in the Wake of Clinton*, ed. Roger Pilon (Washington, D.C.: Cato Institute, 2000), 159–79.

18. Such a conclusion as to the atmosphere with the government after 9/11 is strongly reinforced by the accounts of several insiders—for instance Jack Goldsmith, *The Terror Presidency* (New York: Norton, 2007).

Sinan Antoon studied English literature at Baghdad University and Arabic literature at Georgetown and Harvard, where he obtained his doctorate in 2006. His poems and essays have appeared in numerous publications in the Arab world and in the *Journal of Palestine Studies*, *Middle East Report*, *Banipal*, *Ploughshares*, *The Nation*, and *World Literature Today*, among others. He has published two collections of poetry in Arabic and one collection in English: *The Baghdad Blues* (Harbor Mountain Press, 2007). His novels include *I'jaam: An Iraqi Rhapsody* (City Lights Publishers, 2007) and *The Pomegranate Alone*. His poetry was anthologized in *Iraqi Poetry Today* (Modern Poetry in Translation, 2002) and *Inclined to Speak: An Anthology of Arab-American Poetry* (University of Arkansas Press, 2008). He has also contributed numerous translations of Arabic poetry into English. His translation of Darwish's last prose book, *In the Presence of Absence*, was published by Archipelago Books in November 2011. Antoon returned to Iraq in 2003 to codirect a documentary, "About Baghdad" (2004), about the lives of Iraqis in a post-Saddam occupied Iraq. He is a contributing editor to *Banipal*, a member of the editorial committee of *Middle East Report*, and on the advisory board of the *Arab Studies Journal*. He is an associate professor of Arabic literature at the Gallatin School, New York University.

Julie A. Carlson is professor of English and Comparative Literature at the University of California, Santa Barbara. She is the author of *In the Theatre of Romanticism: Coleridge, Nationalism, Women* (Cambridge, 1994), guest-editor of *Domestic/Tragedy* (*SAQ*, 1997), and *England's First Family of Writers: Mary Wollstonecraft, William Godwin, Mary Shelley* (Johns Hopkins, 2004) and of articles on Romantic theatre, literature and radical culture, and literary modes of attachment.

Hamid Dabashi is Hagop Kevorkian Professor of Iranian Studies and Comparative Literature at Columbia University, New York. His most recent books include *Dreams of a Nation: On Palestinian Cinema* (Verso, 2006), *Masters & Masterpieces of Iranian Cinema* (Mage Publishers, 2007),

Islamic Liberation Theology: Resisting the Empire (Routledge, 2008), *Post-Orientalism: Knowledge and Power in Time of Terror* (Transaction, 2008), *Iran, The Green Movement and the USA: The Fox and the Paradox* (Zed Books, 2010), and *Shi'ism: A Religion of Protest* (Harvard University Press, 2011).

COLIN DAYAN is the Robert Penn Warren Professor of the Humanities at Vanderbilt University. She is the author of *Haiti, History, and the Gods* (University of California Press, 1995), *The Story of Cruel and Unusual* (MIT Press, 2007), and *The Law is a White Dog: How Legal Rituals Make and Unmake Persons* (Princeton University Press, 2011).

SUSAN DERWIN received her Ph.D. in Comparative Literature from the Johns Hopkins University. She is chair of the Comparative Literature Program at UCSB and a faculty member of Germanic, Slavic, and Semitic Studies. Her fields of teaching and her research areas include Holocaust Studies, humanities in times of torture, contemporary literature, memoir, and psychoanalytic theory. She is the author of *The Ambivalence of Form: Lukács, Freud, and the Novel* (Johns Hopkins University Press, 1992), and essays on Holocaust denial, the Simon Wiesenthal Museum of Tolerance, *Huckleberry Finn, Blue Velvet*, and the writings of M. F. K. Fisher. Her recently completed *Rage Is the Subtext: Readings in Holocaust Literature and Film* (Ohio State University Press, 2012) treats the relationship between testimonial narrative and healing in texts by Jean Améry, Primo Levi, Saul Friedlaender, Imre Kertész, Binjamin Wilkomirski and in Liliana Cavani's film *The Night Porter*.

STEPHEN F. EISENMAN is professor of Art History at Northwestern University. He is the author of seven books, including *Gauguin's Skirt* (Thames and Hudson,1997), *The Abu Ghraib Effect* (Reaktion Books, 2007), and *From Corot to Monet: The Ecology of Impressionism* (Skira, 2011). He is also the editor and principal author of *Nineteenth-Century Art: A Critical History* (Thames and Hudson), the most widely adopted textbook in its field. The fourth, revised edition of the book was published in January 2011. Dr. Eisenman has in addition curated major international exhibitions devoted to Gauguin, Impressionism, and William Morris. He is currently completing a book titled *Meat Modernism*.

RICHARD FALK is the UN Human Rights Council's Special Rapporteur for the Occupied Palestinian Territories. He is Albert G. Milbank Professor of International Law Emeritus at Princeton University, and since 2002, research professor of Global and International Studies, University of California, Santa Barbara. He also directs a project on "Global Climate

Change, Human Security, and Democracy" under the auspices of the Orfaela Center at UCSB. He is chair of the Board of the Nuclear Age Peace Foundation. Among his recent books are *The Great Terror War* (Olive Branch Press, 2003), *The Declining World Order: America's Imperial Geopolitics* (Routledge, 2004), and *Achieving Human Rights* (Routledge, 2008).

REINHOLD GÖRLING is a professor of Media and Cultural Studies at the Heinrich-Heine-University Düsseldorf. He works at the intersection between media philosophy, psychoanalysis, and visual studies. His publications include *Heterotopia: Lektüren einer interkulturen Literaturwissenschaft* (Fink, 1997), *Kulturelle Topografien* (editor, Metzler, 2004), *Geste: Bewegungen zwischen Film und Tanz* (editor, Transcript, 2008), and *Die Verletzbarkeit des Menschen: Folter und die Politik der Affekte* (editor, Fink, 2011). Currently he is preparing a book on torture and film.

CHRISTIAN GRÜNY, assistant professor of Philosophy at Witten/Herdecke University, studied philosophy and linguistics in Bochum, Prague, and Berlin and received his Ph.D. from the Ruhr-Universität Bochum. His areas of research are aesthetics, the philosophy of music, image theory, phenomenology, pain, and violence. Publications include "Zur Logik der Folter," in *Gewalt Verstehen*, edited by Burkhard Liebsch and Jürgen Straub (Oldenbourg Akademie Verlag, 2003); *Zerstörte Erfahrung: Eine Phänomenologie des Schmerzes* (Königshausen and Neumann, 2004); "What About the Materiality of the Body, Judy?" in *Formfelder*, edited by Dirk Rustemeyer (Königshausen and Neumann, 2006); "Figuren von Differenz: Philosophie zur Musik," in *Deutsche Zeitschrift für Philosophie* 57, no. 6 (2009).

LISA HAJJAR is associate professor of Sociology at the University of California, Santa Barbara. She is the author of *Courting Conflict: The Israeli Military Court System in the West Bank and Gaza* (University of California Press, 2005); her current work focuses on American torture and anti-torture lawyering.

ALFRED W. MCCOY is the J. R. W. Smail Professor of History at the University of Wisconsin-Madison. He is the author of *The Politics of Heroin: CIA Complicity in the Global Drug Trade* (Lawrence Hill Books, 2003), *A Question of Torture: CIA Interrogation from the Cold War to the War on Terror* (Metropolitan Books, 2006), and, most recently, *Policing America's Empire: The United States, the Philippines, and the Rise of the Surveillance State* (University of Wisconsin Press, 2009).

JOHN NAVA studied art at the University of California, Santa Barbara, and did his graduate work in Florence, Italy. His work is found in numerous private, corporate, and public collections throughout the United States, Europe, and Japan, including the National Museum of American Art in Washington, D.C., and is represented in such publications as *Post-Modernism: The New Classicism in Art and Architecture* (Rizzoli, 1987), by Charles Jencks, who coined the term "post-modernism," and Edward Lucie Smith's *American Realism* (Abrams, 1994). Nava has done large-scale public works, including a 45-foot-wide mural for the Tokyo Grain Exchange in Tokyo, Japan. In 1998 he was commissioned by the Seattle Symphony to paint a life-size double portrait of Jack and Rebecca Benaroya for Benaroya Hall in downtown Seattle. In 1999 the Archdiocese of Los Angeles commissioned him to create three major cycles of tapestries for the new Cathedral of Our Lady of the Angels, the largest Catholic cathedral in the United States. Nava's tapestries won the 2003 National Interfaith Forum on Religion, Art, and Architecture (IFRAA) Design Honor Award for Visual Art. From 2006 to 2008 an ensemble of paintings and large-scale tapestries entitled "Neo-Icons" critical of the Bush-era war and torture policies was exhibited at galleries and museums in Santa Barbara and Fresno, California, Santa Fe, New Mexico, and New York City. In 2010 Nava completed work on a large-scale tapestry (22 by 22 feet) for the entryway of the newly built Ronald Tutor Campus Center complex at the University of Southern California, Los Angeles.

DARIECK SCOTT is associate professor of African American Studies at the University of California, Berkeley. He is the author of *Extravagant Abjection: Blackness, Power and Sexuality in the African American Literary Imagination* (NYU Press, 2010), and of the novels *Hex* (Carroll and Graf, 2006) and *Traitor to the Race* (Plume, 1995). He is the editor of *Best Black Gay Erotica* (Cleis Press, 2004).

ABIGAIL SOLOMON-GODEAU is a professor of Art History at the University of California, Santa Barbara. She is the author of *Photography at the Dock: Essays on Photographic History, Institutions and Practices* (University of Minnesota Press, 1992); *Male Trouble: A Crisis in Representation* (Thames and Hudson, 1997), and, with Gabriele Schor, *Birgit Jurgenssen* (Hatje Cantz, 2010). She writes frequently on contemporary art, nineteenth-century visual culture, and photography.

VIOLA SHAFIK is a freelance filmmaker, film curator, and film scholar. She is the author of *Arab Cinema: History and Cultural Identity* (American University of Cairo Press, 1998 and 2007) and *Popular Egyptian Cinema: Gender, Class and Nation* (American University of Cairo Press, 2007). She has published numerous articles and studies, primarily on Arab cinema and culture, as well as on transnational film. She has lectured at the American University in Cairo, has cooperated with national and international film festivals, and is a consultant to the al-Rawi Screenwriters Lab and a member of the selection committees of the World Cinema Fund (Berlinale) and the Dubai Film Connection. She has directed experimental short films and documentaries: *Shajarat al-laymun/The Lemon Tree* (1993), *Musim zar 'al-banat/Planting of Girls* (UNICEF/Ford Foundation, 1999), *Die Reise der Königin Teje/Journey of a Queen* (ZDF/Arte, 2003–2004), and *Jannat 'Ali/My Name Is Not Ali* (2011), among others.

Peter Szendy is professor of Philosophy at the University of Paris Ouest Nanterre La Défense and musicological adviser for the concert programs at the Cité de la musique. He is the author of *Kant chez les extraterrestres: Philosofictions cosmopolitiques* (Éditions de Minuit, 2011), *Hits: Philosophy in the Jukebox*, trans. William Bishop (Fordham University Press, 2011), *Sur écoute: Esthétique de l'espionnage* (Éditions de Minuit, 2007), *Prophecies of Leviathan: Reading Past Melville*, trans. Gil Anidjar (Fordham University Press, 2009), *Membres fantômes: Des corps musiciens* (Éditions de Minuit, 2002), and *Listen: A History of Our Ears*, trans. Charlotte Mandell, foreword by Jean-Luc Nancy (Fordham University Press, 2007).

Elisabeth Weber is a professor of German and Comparative Literature at the University of California, Santa Barbara. Her books include *Verfolgung und Trauma: Zu Emmanuel Levinas' Autrement qu'être ou au-delà de l'essence* (Passagen Verlag, 1990), *Das Vergessen(e): Anamnesen des Undarstellbaren*, coeditor (Turia and Kant, 1997), and *Questioning Judaism* (Stanford, 2004), a collection of interviews with Jacques Derrida, Jean-François Lyotard, Emmanuel Levinas, Pierre Vidal-Naquet, and others. She has also edited several works by Jacques Derrida. Her edited volume *Living Together: Jacques Derrida's Communities of Violence and Peace* is forthcoming from Fordham University Press.